Letters, Kinship, and Social Mobility in Nigeria

Africa and the Diaspora: History, Politics, Culture

Edited by Neil Kodesh and James H. Sweet

Letters, Kinship, and Social Mobility in Nigeria

Olufemi Vaughan

THE UNIVERSITY OF WISCONSIN PRESS

Publication of this book has been made possible in part through the support of the Office of the Provost, Amherst College.

The University of Wisconsin Press
728 State Street, Suite 443
Madison, Wisconsin 53706
uwpress.wisc.edu

Printed in the United States of America
This book may be available in a digital edition.

Library of Congress Cataloging-in-Publication Data

Names: Vaughan, Olufemi, author.
Title: Letters, kinship, and social mobility in Nigeria / Olufemi Vaughan.
Other titles: Africa and the diaspora.
Description: Madison, Wisconsin : The University of Wisconsin Press, [2023] |
Series: Africa and the diaspora: history, politics, culture |
Includes bibliographical references and index.
Identifiers: LCCN 2022049587 | ISBN 9780299344504 (hardcover)
Subjects: LCSH: Vaughan, Olufemi—Family. |
Ibadan (Nigeria)—Biography—Sources. |
Ibadan (Nigeria)—History—20th century—Biography.
Classification: LCC DT515.9.I2 V38 2023 |
DDC 966.9/25092 [B]—dc23/eng/20230307
LC record available at https://lccn.loc.gov/2022049587

ISBN 9780299344542 (pbk.)

For Rosemary, Moni, Ayo, Olu

Contents

Illustrations

Foreword

ADESOJI ADELAJA

It is my pleasure to write this foreword to *Letters, Kinship, and Social Mobility in Nigeria*, a unique and iconic book based on a critical analysis of over three thousand family letters compiled from 1926 to 1994 by Abiọdun Alfred Vaughan, father of the book's author, Olufemi "Femi" Vaughan. In his analysis of the letters, Femi Vaughan constructs real-life stories of Abiọdun Vaughan's family members, in-laws, close friends, and compatriots in Ibadan, the cosmopolitan Yorùbá city in western Nigeria. Before I offer my perspective on the importance and unique qualities of this book, I should mention that Femi and I have been close friends for forty-two years, starting in 1980 while I was pursuing a PhD in economics and Femi was completing his undergraduate studies in political science. Incidentally, our lives intersect in many other important ways: our mothers are related by marriage and were pioneer women educators at the dawn of Nigerian independence in the early 1960s; we both have deep Yorùbá Church Missionary Society (CMS) roots, in my case, Lagos and Ijebu-Ode (my late father, Venerable Archdeacon B. A. Adelaja, a renowned Nigerian educationist, was principal of Nigeria's first secondary school, the CMS Boys Grammar School, an Anglican school for boys in Lagos that was founded in 1859) and in Femi's case, Ibadan; and we have collaborated on landmark research projects as scholars working in American universities. Femi was also the best man at my wedding, and somehow we managed to marry two sisters, thereby having the privilege to be godfathers to each other's children. All of these are to say that writing the foreword to a book steeped in deep Yorùbá kinship values provides for me a personal affirmation of the friendship and comradeship consistently reflected in the words of the letter writers in this book.

I have read all of Femi Vaughan's books to date. Given their depth and quality, I would conclude that this one is particularly intriguing not only because of the subject matter but also because of its analytical rigor, intellectual sophistication, and methodological innovation. I thought that his last book, *Religion and the Making of Nigeria*, published in 2016 by Duke University Press, was the brilliant masterpiece that Femi could not surpass. That rigorously researched book wove historical, religious, and political studies together to analyze how religious and ethnic structures combined to play a central role in the processes of state-society formation in colonial and postcolonial Nigeria. After reading *Letters, Kinship, and Social Mobility in Nigeria*, I feel this could very well be Femi's best work yet—certainly an exemplar across the African humanities.

As far as I am aware, *Letters, Kinship, and Social Mobility* is the first scholarly book that critically engages the medium of letter writing to explore the everyday experiences of Africans in the modern world. Focusing on the experiences of Abiọdun Alfred Vaughan, his immediate relatives, in-laws, close friends, and compatriots, this book provides a compelling analysis of substantive social, cultural, economic, and political issues that defined the world of the major letter writers in an Ibadan CMS community in colonial and postcolonial Nigeria. The book's central objective is not simply to engage the historiography of literacy in modern Africa, nor is the book a contribution to the scholarship on African family history per se; rather, in this book, Femi Vaughan is primarily concerned with the wide range of everyday social and economic issues that motivated and sustained the actions of these Ibadan CMS letter writers. As the author contends, this is what animates the "intersecting, multilayered, and overlapping story lines" that shaped the many contours of the book. In this context, *Letters, Kinship, and Social Mobility* focuses on the human agency of Femi Vaughan's forebears and their compatriots against the backdrop of a dynamic modern Nigerian state and society from the late nineteenth century to the late twentieth century. On this central objective, Femi Vaughan draws on his breathtaking scholarship across the African humanities and social sciences, as well as a wealth of extensive archival research, interviews, and fieldwork—a methodological and analytical perspective that has shaped his outstanding scholarship for three decades.

In this book, Femi Vaughan, through the comprehensive correspondence of the major letter writers, has given us a new perspective on how to critically explore the evolution of modern Yorùbá society within the context of the formation of the Nigerian state and society. The many stories constructed from these letters are narratives about how modern African experiences evolved out of indigenous local structures, values, and ideas at a transformative moment in history. Thousands of men and women like Mariam Vaughan (1866–1972), Samuel Ariyibi Vaughan (1887–1985), Dorcas Olayinka Brainerd (1894–1973),

S. A. Ọlọkọ (1894–1984), Rachel Ayodele Akinloye (1898–1993), Jadesola Juliana Odebunmi (1902–96), Abiọdun Alfred Vaughan (1907–2004), Bamidele Theo Brainerd (1916–2004), Adisa Meredith Augustus Akinloye (1918–2007), and Gladys Adukẹ Vaughan (1920–2014), the principal letter writers in this book, as clerks, administrators, health officers, teachers, nurses, writers, and students laid the foundation of modern Yorùbá society in colonial Nigeria's southern and northern provinces in the first half of the twentieth century. With the intriguing stories woven out of the vivid issues discussed by these men and women in their letters, Femi Vaughan articulates the remarkable human agency of a Yorùbá family—along with their wider kinship network—in Nigerian history.

It is particularly fascinating to me that Femi Vaughan has imaginatively constructed the stories in this book largely from letters written by his parents, older relatives, and their close friends. As a younger relative of many men and women who had social experiences similar to those of the main characters in this book, I agree with the author that many men and women of his father's social background as educated people in Yorùbá communities compiled primary documents over many decades that could shed much light on the lived experiences of Yorùbá people in the nineteenth and twentieth centuries. Indeed, in several conversations with Femi, we discussed the thousands of primary documents that I know that my father meticulously compiled over many years. Alas, unfortunately, in my family's particular case, like several other examples that Femi references in the conclusion, these invaluable primary documents were lost after the death of my father—primary documents that I can safely presume would have shed much light on the wide range of family, civic, and professional issues that engaged the lives of my parents and other family members, especially in Lagos and Ijebu communities.

In conclusion, I am glad that Abiọdun Alfred Vaughan meticulously compiled these letters, which span eighty years. I am glad that these letters were preserved after his death. I am glad that his son, Femi Vaughan, skillfully created this exceptional book out of these family documents. In essence, after reading the book and reflecting on the background story Femi shared with me about the serendipity that brought the book to fruition, I am confounded by the slim chances that resulted in this imaginative work. Through this remarkable book, Femi Vaughan has not only creatively translated the everyday lives and human agency of his forebears and their compatriots but also profoundly transformed how we think of the Yorùbá past in the present—and how we explore innovative research materials and methodologies to interrogate Nigerian and Atlantic West African histories with the expansive and deep voice of the people themselves.

Acknowledgments

As a scholar in the lettered social sciences, I have found the process of writing this unconventional book quite intriguing. It is, after all, based on a critical analysis of over three thousand letters compiled by Abiọdun Alfred Vaughan, my late father, from 1926 to 1994 and has thus engaged, quite naturally, my awareness of the concepts of "subjectivity" and "objectivity." The many letters, which are understandably of deep personal value to me, are, in their own right, historical artifacts. These letters were written by and exchanged between and among not only my father, older members of his natal family, and several of his in-laws but also my father's close friends and various compatriots, all at a moment of significant social, political, and economic change in colonial and postcolonial Nigeria.

During the initial stages of this book project, eight of my students at Amherst College (and one earlier student at Bowdoin College) assiduously labored alongside me to make sense of the piles of letters on which this book would ultimately be based. Simply witnessing how thoughtfully and enthusiastically these amazing young scholars engaged the wide range of issues discussed by the letter writers proved to be a true source of inspiration and encouragement for me. At the initial moment of exploration, these students threw caution to the wind. Their infectious enthusiasm and intelligent engagement with what initially seemed like random collections of letters provided the critical impetus for me to explore, with added zeal, the complicated ideas, concepts, and contexts in which my forebears and their compatriots engaged multilayered dialogues through the medium of letter writing. My heartfelt gratitude goes to these remarkable students: Joelle Crichlow, Diego Gomez, Mariah Hill, Max Huckaby, Misky Jimba, Madison Matthews, Sebastian Stiles-Sierackie, and Aniah Washington—all of whom have gone on to exciting ventures after completing their rigorous liberal arts education.

In various ways, several friends and good colleagues with disparate foci as well as academic and intellectual training weighed in incisively at different stages of the book's intellectual gestation. Their keen and supportive interventions aided the project greatly. In retrospect, many of the methodological, conceptual, and theoretical perspectives that I engaged encouraged me to cobble together a distinctive interdisciplinary perspective—an essential intellectual approach that ultimately centered, I believe rightfully, the agency of the letter writers in Nigeria's rapidly changing society. Many of these scholars read the draft copy of the introduction, which explores critical conceptual and contextual issues during the early stages of the book project, and provided insightful ideas that consolidated the intellectual foundation of the book. Special thanks to Rowland Abiodun, Wale Adebanwi, Susan Bell, Bunmi Bernard, Sara Berry, Stefan Bradley, Rhonda Cohbam-Sander, Jallicia Jolly, Carlton Long, Paul Lubeck, Moses Ochonu, Ayodeji Ogunnaike, Funke Okome, Jacob Olupona, Tom Spear, and Nimi Wariboko. I offer a special thanks also to Adesoji Adelaja, who graciously accepted my invitation to write the foreword to this book. I hasten to add that Toyin Falola and Ebenezer Obadare read the finished manuscript. The brilliant interventions and affirming words of these two renowned Africanists were and have remained a tremendous source of inspiration. I am profoundly grateful for their kindness and generosity of spirit. My special thanks extend also to Katherine Duke, a conscientious and thoughtful editor, for her excellent editorial assistance. To Andy Anderson, I express much gratitude for the excellent maps contained in this book. Nathan MacBrien, editor in chief of the University of Wisconsin Press, believed in this book project from the onset. Along with the editorial staff of the press, Holly McArthur, Jessica Smith, and Mary Hill—and Neil Kodesh and Jim Sweet, the editors of University of Wisconsin Press's Africa and the Diaspora series—Nathan guided the book manuscript diligently through the publication process with remarkable professionalism. I am grateful to all of them for believing in this work.

To clarify questions that arose from my analysis of the letters included in this book, I conducted interviews with older relatives who, as children and young adults, knew the letter writers at the prime of their lives from the 1940s to the 1990s. With much love and deep affection, I express my gratitude to these relatives for their abiding faith and integrity and their inspirational leadership over the years: Ronke Adefope, Bolanle Awe, Lamide Bakare, Lawunmi Idowu, Bimpe Lawson, Kunle Odumosu, Abiodun Pomary, Folake Thomas, and Olaolu Thomas. I end these acknowledgments where I began. I thank my father and the late Mojisola Oladeji for their support and love. I also express heartfelt gratitude to Funso Adegbola, Bode Akindeji-Oladeji, and Gbemi

Brainerd. I am grateful for the love and unflinching support over the years of many relatives and friends, especially Adebayo and Akua Adefope, Bola Atta, Ife Ijewere, Data and Dawari Longjohn, Fidelis and Priscilla Oditah, Ladunni Okwudinka, Shubu Vaughan, and Wole Vaughan. For his hospitality when I visited the Cathedral Church of St. Peter's, Aremọ, Ibadan, an important socioreligious nucleus for the letter writers in this book, I thank the provost of the cathedral, Venerable Archdeacon Adewale Adebiyi. Last and certainly not least, my loving gratitude to Rosemary, my wife, and Moni, Ayo, and Olu, our children, for their love and steadfast support. In the spirit of my forebears and their compatriots whose social world graces the pages of this book, I dedicate this book to them. Drawing on the deep kinship values that shaped the stories teased out of the letters compiled by Abiọdun Vaughan, I say to you all—and the extended family in Ibadan and beyond—Alâjọbí àti alâjọgbé á gbè wá o.

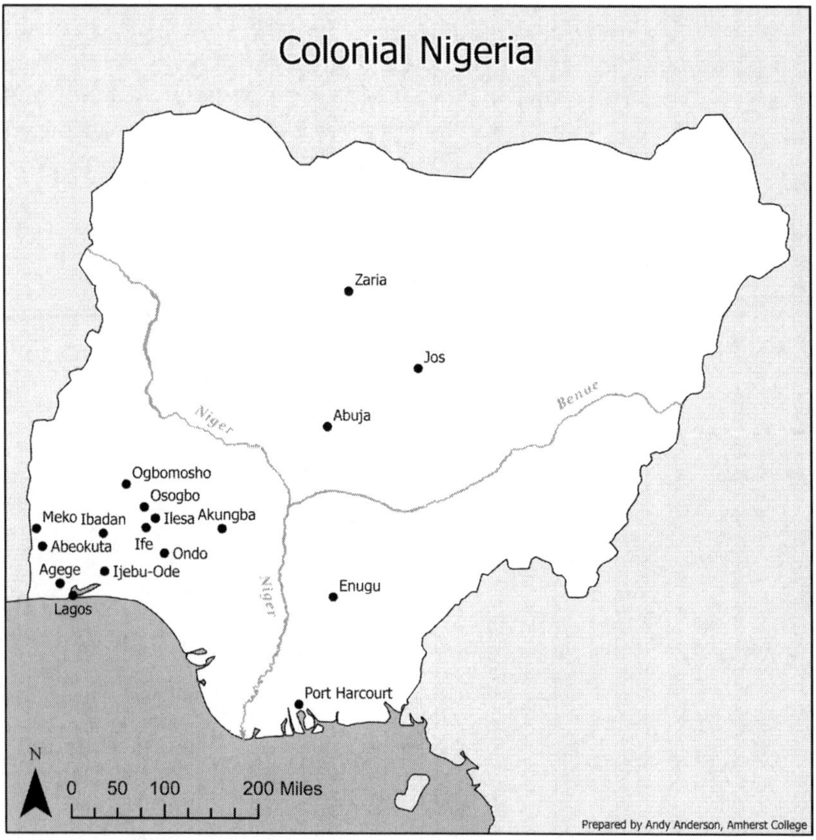

Map 1. Colonial Nigeria (Locations of the Letter Writers)

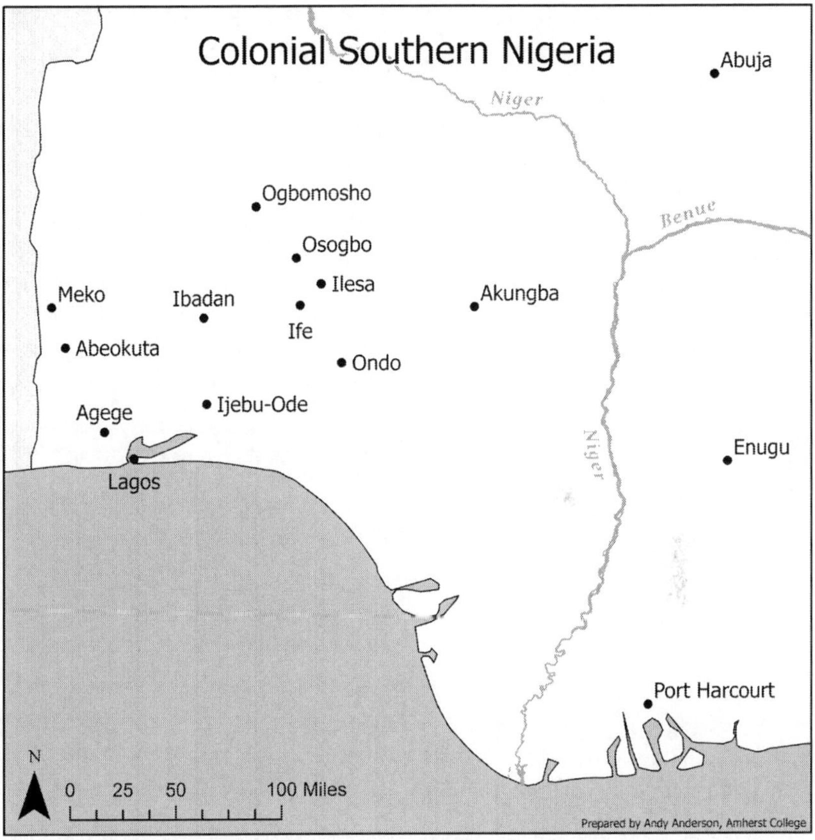

Map 2. Colonial Southern Nigeria (Locations of the Letter Writers)

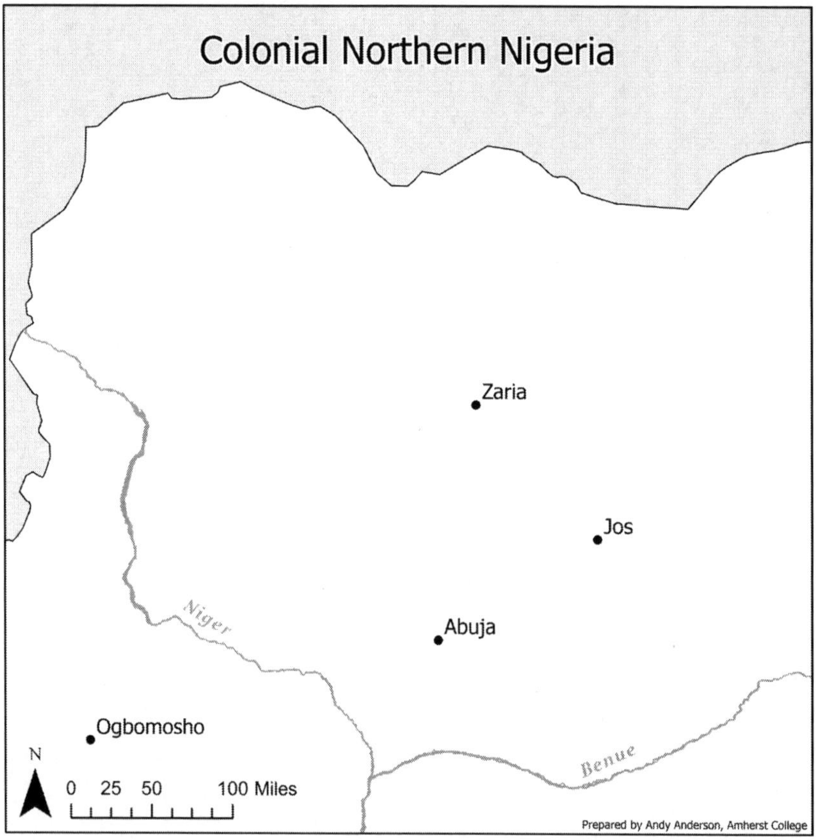

Map 3. Colonial Northern Nigeria (Locations of the Letter Writers)

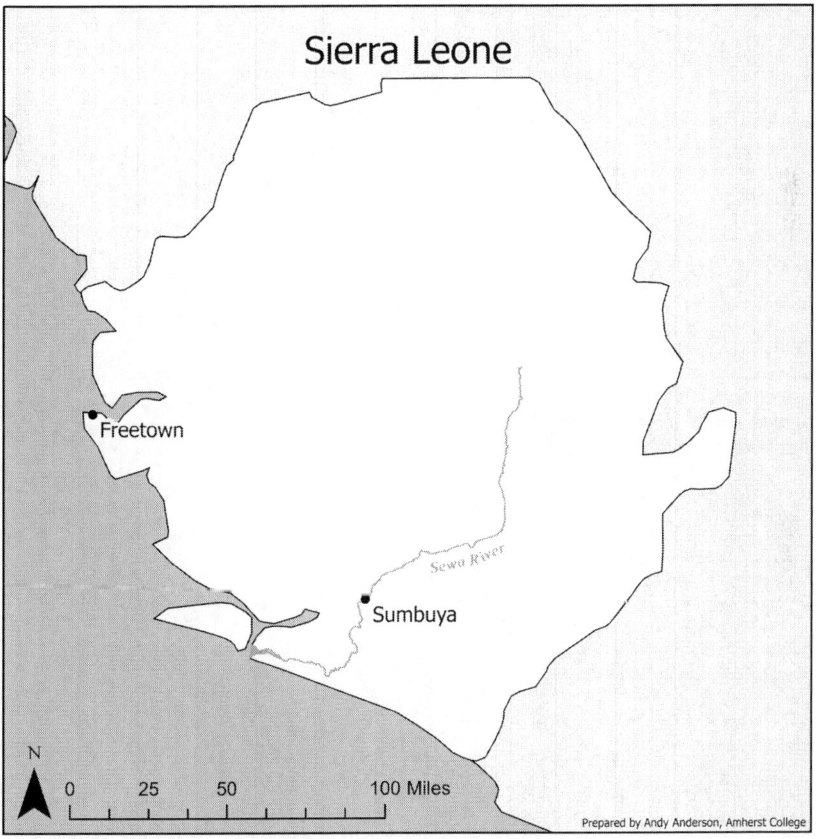

Map 4. Sierra Leone: Freetown and Sumbuya (Locations of the Letter Writers)

Map 5. England: London, Oxford, Durham, and Bournemouth
(Locations of the Letter Writers)

Letters, Kinship, and Social Mobility in Nigeria

Introduction

IN THE SUMMER OF 2003, while visiting my ninety-five-year-old father, Abiọdun Alfred Vaughan, in Ibadan, Nigeria, I posed the same question that I had asked him over several summers: "Dad, what are you planning to do with the documents in your bedroom cabinet?" In the past, he had politely dismissed my question. But this time, to my surprise, he replied, "You can take them all with you."

Although I could not have known it at the time, that simple reply established the pathway to this book. Over the years, my father probably assumed that, as a scholar whose work focuses on analyzing primary documents, I was interested in preserving what was in the cabinet for future generations. While I expected the files to contain important family records, I did not simply feel obligated to preserve them. I was more concerned about what might happen to them when my father was no longer with us. What if they fell into the wrong hands? Or what if family members discarded them, failing to see their value? Just seven months after I took the files home to New York, my father passed on peacefully at the age of ninety-six.

As their custodian, Abiọdun Vaughan had been the only person who knew what was in these files. I assumed—correctly, as I later found out—that the files contained extensive information on major characters and issues that had shaped his adult life. Most intriguing, at least to me, was what the documents might reveal about my parents' relationship. But, far beyond the assorted family papers I expected, the extensive collection consisted of some five thousand documents, including about three thousand letters, sequentially and thematically organized, from Abiọdun's family members, in-laws, close friends, and compatriots.

It was not until eleven years after my father's death that I had the time, energy, and courage to explore the files. Following the restlessness that accompanied the submission of the manuscript that became my previous book, *Religion and the Making of Nigeria*, to my editor in April 2015, I started my review of the documents. I began, not surprisingly, with the files my father had labeled with my mother's name, Gladys Adukẹ Vaughan. In these letters, I noticed a pattern of story lines that, I realize in retrospect, defined the essence and shaped the contours of this book.

As I reviewed the other files—notably, those labeled S. A. Vaughan, Vaughan Family, S. A. Ọlọkọ, and Freetown—over months and years, I saw similar story lines sustained in multilayered epistolary dialogues. I also discovered a simple idea that united the eclectic issues discussed in the letters: the familiarity and intimacy with which the letter writers engaged Abiọdun, revealing strong kinship ties predicated on shared values, even as their relationships changed over time.

Abiọdun Vaughan's compilation of these letters began in 1926 and ended in 1994. The letters were written by men and women who had emerged from the religious, social, and educational institutions established by the Church Missionary Society (CMS) in Ibadan starting in the second half of the nineteenth century. The CMS was the preeminent Anglican mission in the Atlantic Nigerian region following the decline of the Yorùbá Wars and the imposition of British colonial rule at the turn of the twentieth century.[1] And so this book is *not* merely a history of my family written for its own sake. Through close reading and textual analysis of this collection of letters, this book constructs the dominant story lines that shaped the lived experiences of a Yorùbá Christian-educated family and their close friends in colonial and postcolonial Nigerian society. This book seeks to recover major themes in the everyday lives of these men and women through the medium of letter writing in a transformative moment in modern African history.

Context of and Rationale for the Book

The CMS contributed enormously to the foundation, emergence, and consolidation of a modern elite in southwestern Nigeria—the region of the Yorùbá people—from the mid-nineteenth century to the end of the twentieth century.[2] This well-established perspective in Nigerian historical studies is reflected in the extensive information gathered from the letters exchanged between Abiọdun Vaughan (1907–2004) and ten of his immediate relatives and close friends. All of the major letter writers were products of several CMS primary, secondary, vocational, and postsecondary schools in Atlantic Yorùbá cities—notably, Ibadan, Lagos, Abẹokuta, and Ijẹbu-Ode—and universities in Sierra Leone and England. These people were educated between the late nineteenth century, when much of the Yorùbá region was incorporated into the

British Empire, and the middle of the twentieth century, when Nigeria attained independence from Britain. Abiọdun's correspondence with these letter writers provides an important lens to explore the critical intersection between Yorùbá kinship ties and a Western-educated Christian elite in an emergent southern Nigerian colonial society in the first half of the twentieth century.

Abiọdun Vaughan grew up as an active member of St. Peter's Church on Aremọ Hill (Òkè Aremọ), one of the three missions established by the CMS in Ibadan in the mid-nineteenth century. Founded in 1865, St. Peter's Church, Aremọ, by the beginning of the twenty-first century, had served as the nucleus for seven generations of Ibadan Anglicans.[3] Abiọdun attended one of a handful of primary schools in the city—a CMS elementary school in Kudeti—and then, in the 1920s, Ibadan Grammar School, established in 1913 as the first secondary school in the city. He then became part of a small group of educated Christian men who were recruited to junior civil service positions in the headquarters of the colonial Department of Agriculture, which had been established in a modern layout on the outskirts of Ibadan in 1899.[4] He worked as a civil servant in this colonial bureaucracy for twenty-six years, from 1930 to 1956.

The stories in this book were driven largely by the interplay among a tight-knit group of CMS-educated Yorùbá men recruited into the colonial civil service and their social-familial kinship networks during the consolidation of British colonial rule from the late 1920s to the early 1950s. With established careers in the Department of Agriculture, other colonial departments, and European trading companies, some of these letter writers had risen to senior clerical and administrative positions by the time Nigeria gained independence in 1960. In the specific case of the Department of Agriculture, these young men were posted to various regional branches of the department in colonial Nigeria's northern and southern provinces. (Along with service in the headquarters in Ibadan, Abiọdun Vaughan had service tours in Zaria in the Northern Provinces in the early 1930s, in Abẹokuta in the Southern Provinces in the late 1930s and early 1940s, in Lagos in the mid-1940s, and in Enugu in the Southern Provinces in the late 1940s and early 1950s.) The British imperial project, shaped profoundly by the impact of mission Christianity and the priorities of a colonial "developmental" state, in convergence with the human agency of the letter writers, thus provides the social, religious, economic, and political framework in which these men and their relatives exchanged the letters compiled by Abiọdun Vaughan. As far as I am aware, this analysis of the fascinating correspondence between Abiọdun Vaughan and the other letter writers is the first book in the African humanities that explores the lived experience of a Western-educated Nigerian family and their close friends and compatriots in a rapidly changing colonial and postcolonial Nigerian society. Rather than shoehorn the dominant themes in the dialogue between Abiọdun Vaughan and other letter writers into the evolution of modern Nigerian history, my analysis of these epistolary discourses animates the eclectic social world of the letter writers against the backdrop of Nigeria's complicated colonial and postcolonial history.

Sources and Methods

To provide the essential analytical perspectives to critically explore the main issues discussed by the letter writers, I conducted archival research on Western-educated Yorùbá Christians and civil servants in colonial Nigeria at the Nigerian National Archives (Ibadan); at the Hoover Institution Library & Archives, Stanford University (George D. Jenkins Papers on colonial Ibadan Division); at the Church Missionary Society Archives (Birmingham, England); and at the Bodleian Library, University of Oxford. To answer questions and clarify issues that arose from my analysis of the letters, I also conducted extensive interviews with relatives in Nigeria, England, and the United States who, as children and young adults in the 1940s, 1950s, 1960s, and 1970s, knew many of the letter writers at the prime of their lives.

Drawing on textual and contextual analysis, careful review of the epistolary scholarship in African studies,[5] and distinctive interdisciplinary humanistic social science research, especially historical studies—with reflections on relevant scholarship in sociology and politics—this book focuses on the longtime correspondence of Abiọdun Vaughan with the following close relatives and compatriots:

his mother, Mariam O. Vaughan (1866–1972)

his older brother Samuel Ariyibi Vaughan (1887–1985)

his older sister Dorcas Ọlayinka Brainerd, née Vaughan (1894–1973)

his older sister Jadesọla Juliana Ọdẹbunmi, née Vaughan (1902–96)

his second wife, Gladys Adukẹ Vaughan, née Akinloye (1920–2014)

his second wife's mother, Rachel Ayọdele Akinloye, née Ọkẹowo, also Oke (1898–1993)

his second wife's brother Adisa Meredith Augustus Akinloye (1918–2007)

his "cousin" and mentor, S. A. Ọlọkọ (1894–1984)

his nephew Bamidele Theo Brainerd (1916–2005)

Six of these major letter writers wrote about 120 letters each, sustained over a period of at least fourteen years, while the others wrote a minimum of about 70 letters each, over at least eight years, to Abiọdun. Indeed, Bamidele Theo Brainerd, one of Abiọdun's nephews, wrote him uninterrupted from Freetown, Sierra Leone, for thirty-eight years, from 1956 to 1994.

In addition, the book analyzes the letters of relatives who featured less prominently in the files compiled by Abiọdun Vaughan:

his first wife, Dorcas Bọlaji Ajibose-Vaughan, married to him from 1937 to 1943 (1916–76)

his older brother David Oladunjoye Vaughan (1899–1941)

his brother-in-law, Ọlayinka Odumosu (1918–2009)

his eldest child, Lamide Bakare, née Vaughan (1938–),

the wife and children of his nephew Bamidele Theo Brainerd, from Freetown, Sierra Leone: Viola, Fọlakẹ, Rotimi, and Ọlaolu

several other nieces and nephews, notably, Tunde Ọdẹbunmi, Bisi Alalade, née Ọdẹbunmi, and Agboọla Vaughan

many close friends and compatriots—notably, G. O. Ogunṣọla, J. A. Ayorinde, and E. O. Alayande—in the Department of Agriculture and in three mutual aid and civic organizations: the Ibadan Brotherhood Fund Association, the Ibadan Cooperative Savings Society, and the Ibadan Progressive Union, in which Abiọdun Vaughan was an active member (discussed below)

These secondary letter writers provide ancillary evidence that reinforces the major issues, questions, and values sustained in the correspondence of the major letter writers listed above.

After a close reading of the letters in the files, I summarize the dialogues between Abiọdun Vaughan and the other letter writers in comprehensive narrations and discussions that are contained in five extensive chapters (minus this comprehensive introduction and a conclusion). To construct coherent story lines from the perspective of the letter writers, these chapters follow Abiọdun's organization of the files and the evolution of his correspondence with the letter writers both thematically and chronologically. The analysis of the narratives is reinforced with assertive quotations from the letters to underscore the agency of the letter writers and capture the real-life experiences and contexts in which they carried out their correspondence. Where relevant, the story lines teased out of the letters are put into dialogue with essential scholarship on kinship, Western education, elite formation, modernity, and social mobility in colonial and postcolonial Africa—all central issues that I discovered in close reading of the letters. Following a second set of interviews with relatives to clarify the ethnobiography of the letter writers during the period of their correspondence with Abiọdun Vaughan, I provide deeper articulation of the historical contexts in which they expressed their ideas and perspectives, revealing the personal aspirations, priorities, and values that shaped the story lines in the various chapters in the book.

Consequently, this book not only critically interrogates the historiography on Yorùbá modernity within the context of Nigerian, African, and Atlantic studies but also explores new methodological opportunities to excavate the past of an emergent West African–educated elite through the medium of letter writing. The exploration of this methodological approach advances a new archival realm of interpersonal sources to uncover the everyday lives of these letter writers during these transformative decades in modern African history. The book thus underscores how these people integrated Yorùbá and Western values, revealing a unique microhistory in colonial and postcolonial Nigerian society.

Conceptual Perspective and Historical Context

The central themes in the story lines of this book lie at the intersections of the roles of mission Christianity, Western education, kinship, and civic values in the processes of elite formation in colonial Yorùbá society in the first half of the twentieth century. To provide the essential historical context in which the letter writers conceived of their world, I analyze the familial, social, and political structures that were prevalent when many of the parents of the letter writers and even some of the writers themselves migrated to the garrison city of Ibadan from various Yorùbá subregions—principally, Ẹgba, Ijẹṣa, Ijẹbu, Ọyọ, Ondo, and Ekiti—during the decline of the Yorùbá Wars in the late nineteenth century to sustain the nucleus of Christian converts in Ibadan's small but vibrant CMS mission under British colonial rule at the turn of the twentieth century.[6]

With this evolving historical context, common threads in the content of the letters open up a conceptual space to interrogate endogenous and exogenous forces as dialectical interactions through which the letter writers made their world anew.[7] This conceptualization critically engages the human agency of the letter writers, revealing how they integrated Yorùbá values with the new Western training they acquired from CMS institutions in the earlier decades of colonial rule (Ìgbà Òyìnbó, "the era of the white man"). This transformative moment was sustained by an enduring Yorùbá kinship system in Ibadan's dynamic CMS community under British colonial rule.

Akinṣọla Akiwọwọ, I. A. Akinjogbin, and John Peel have all produced groundbreaking works on the moral order on which Yorùbá society was traditionally structured, even as these communities experienced dramatic transformation from the consequences of the Yorùbá Wars, the impact of mission Christianity, and the imposition of British colonial rule. Their works provide important conceptual ideas to articulate the dramatic social, political, and economic conditions that shaped the everyday issues discussed in the letters analyzed in this book.

To conceptualize and contextualize the moral order in which the letter writers expressed their aspirations, values, and ideas, I interrogate Akiwọwọ's concept of the Yorùbá kinship system as the fundamental basis of the letter writers' social action. Akiwọwọ contends that "groundedness" in Yorùbá culture shapes the social action of everyday life. He argues that in the "grounding" of dynamic Yorùbá social relations there is always continuity in past and present consciousness. These social relations, Akiwọwọ denotes, are everchanging interactions between the Yorùbá kinship system of *àjọbí* (consanguinity—the lineal and collateral relationships based on bloodline, birth, and connection to shared ancestry) and *àjọgbé* (coresidence—sharing the same or contiguous shelter whether or not the people concerned are related by blood). *Àjọgbé* is distinctive because of its malleability, incorporating and connecting blood relatives, friends, compatriots, and associates in a dynamic fictive kinship structure consonant with changing conditions. For Akiwọwọ, "the purpose of such knitting together is social . . . according to this view, that which is called human society is what we call *aṣùwà ènìyàn*. Human society, *aṣùwàdà ènìyàn*, provides for each member who makes it up, five categories of inalienable social values which constitute the purpose and goal of human collectivities." Five interconnected social values sustain these relationships:

1. *ire ikú* (the value of good health to an old age)
2. *ire owó* (the value of financial security)
3. *ire ọkọ-ya* (the value of intimate companionship and love)
4. *ire ọmọ* (the value of parenthood)
5. *ire aborí ọ̀tá* (the value of assured self-actualization)

Akiwọwọ continues: "A human society therefore has meaning for its members if and only if these values are consciously sought as common goals. These five are internalized as *ire gbogbo*, values belonging to all members of the collectivity;

or simply we may call them social values common to all."[8] To conclude the conceptualization of this Yorùbá kinship system, Akiwọwọ notes:

> Both *àjọbí* and *àjọgbé* possess different fractions of sociation. In *àjọbí* the magnitude of concord and consensus is ideally very high because each member is able to link his or her identity to a common source such as the same mother or the same father, or the same father and mother. In this form of sociation, it is probable for the individuals who compose it to grow up together and realize their common interest within it. However, discord and disharmony may emerge to separate them as a result of sibling rivalry which every *aláj ọbí* eventually suffers from. . . . Out of the disharmony in one or more aspects of the relationship and separations of the members of an *àjọbí*, comes new forms of sociations of the members of an *àjọbí* such as *ọ̀ré* (friendship), *ará* (neighbors) and *ìletò* (settlements).[9]

These human values resonate in the actions and aspirations of the principal letter writers in this book in the context of a rapidly shifting modern Yorùbá society under the shadows of colonial and postcolonial Nigerian state-society formation. My analysis of the letters underscores the moral authority of *àjọbí-àjọgbé* relations, discerning their significance in a transformative social context. The challenge of this system is to firmly anchor *àjọbí*, with its emphasis on consanguinity, or blood relations, to the fictive kinship ties that resonate in *àjọgbé*. This nexus between *àjọbí* and *àjọgbé* is predicated on the concept of *ọmọlúàbí*, the essential values of a person dedicated to the service of a just community and self-actualization. This moral order, I show in the analysis of the letters, shaped the values of the principal letter writers.

As I analyzed the letters, I observed repeatedly how the natal family of Abiọdun Vaughan—as the foundational element of what Akiwọwọ posits as *àjọbí*—sustained formidable ties to in-laws, distant relatives, family friends, old CMS schoolmates, members of local civic groups, and coworkers that embody the fictive kinship of *àjọgbé* in modern Yorùbá society. As I witnessed the formation, consolidation, and contestations of relationships in the correspondence between Abiọdun and members of his natal family as well as members of his fictive kinship network—whether in-laws, close family friends, coworkers in the colonial Department of Agriculture, comembers of several civic groups, or old boys of the CMS Ibadan Grammar School—I observed a moral order that approximated Akiwọwọ's concept of *àjọbí* and *àjọgbé* as mutually reinforcing, self-perpetuating, and self-sustaining in Nigeria's evolving colonial and postcolonial society.

Consequently, it stands to reason that the CMS in Ibadan emerged as the nucleus around which the letter writers articulated the moral values and codes of *àjọbí* and *àjọgbé* in time and space. For members of the Vaughan natal family as *alájọbí* (members of the kinship structure based on consanguinity, *àjọbí*) in juxtaposition to *alájọgbé* (members of the fictive kin, *àjọgbé*), the relationships had their original focal point at the mission station at Oke Aremọ and extended to the two other mission stations in Kudẹti and Ogunpa. Over time, these CMS mission stations were loosely connected to other CMS and CMS-oriented educational, social, and cultural institutions:

- CMS Boys Grammar School, Lagos: Nigeria's first secondary school, founded in 1859, where Samuel Ariyibi, Abiọdun Vaughan's older brother, was a student in the early 1900s and where his uncle J. A. Vaughan was a teacher in the late 1800s
- CMS Girls Seminary School (later CMS Girls Grammar School), Lagos: Nigeria's first secondary school for girls, founded in 1869, where Dorcas Ọlayinka Brainerd, Abiọdun's older sister, and Rachel Ayọdele Akinloye, née Ọkẹowo, Abiọdun's mother-in-law, were students in the 1910s and where Gladys Adukẹ Vaughan, née Akinloye, Abiọdun's wife, was a student in the 1930s
- Ibadan Grammar School, founded in 1913, where Abiọdun and various members of his social network in civic groups and the Department of Agriculture—such as S. A. Ọlọkọ, G. O. Ogunṣọla, and J. A. Ayọrinde—as well as his brothers-in-law Adisa Akinloye, Ṣupọ Akinloye, and Olayinka Odumosu were students in the 1910s, 1920s, and 1930s
- CMS Kudẹti Girls Secondary School, founded as a primary school in 1896, where Gladys Adukẹ Vaughan, née Akinloye, Abiọdun's wife, was a secondary school student in the 1930s
- St. Andrew's College, Ọyọ, a teacher training college founded in 1896 (initially the CMS Training Institution, Abẹokuta, founded in 1853), where E. O. Alayande, Abiọdun's compatriot, was a student in the 1920s and Ọlayinka Odumosu, Abiọdun's brother-in-law, was a student in the 1930s

In addition to those attending these CMS institutions, many other Vaughan relatives and their compatriots attended other CMS secondary and postsecondary institutions, including Abẹokuta Grammar School (a secondary school for boys founded in 1909); Ijẹbu-Ode Grammar School (a secondary school for boys founded in 1913); Igbobi College, Lagos (an Anglican-Methodist secondary school for boys founded in 1932); and Fourah Bay College (founded in 1827 and later part of the University of Sierra Leone). In short, this emergent Christian-educated elite, alongside their ideas and practices, whether religious or secular, traveled through multiple CMS religious, social, and educational institutions and networks over four generations, from the late nineteenth century, when Britain imposed its colonial rule on Yorùbá communities, to the initial decades of Nigerian independence from the 1960s to the 1990s.

Whether kinship was sustained by blood relations or through fictive connections, the aspirations, claims, and demands made in the letters analyzed in this book were founded on and expressed through two recurring and overlapping CMS socioreligious identities that I recall my forebears—especially my mother, Gladys Adukẹ Vaughan, and maternal grandmother Rachel Ayọdele Akinloye—consistently referencing during my preteen and teenage years in Ibadan in the late 1960s and 1970s: Àwọn Ọmọ Aremọ, referring to the children of the Aremọ CMS community, and Àwọn Ọmọ Kudẹti, the children of the Kudẹti CMS community. These two socioreligious identities took their origins from two of the three CMS mission stations (the third being Ogunpa, later Oke Bọla) founded in Ibadan in the 1850s and the 1860s.[10] The CMS mission station at Aremọ was thus critical to the formulation of the *àjọgbé* kinship network that sustained many of the exchanges over several generations. But why? The analysis of the letters in this book reveals a small but formidable Ibadan Anglican community forged in the crucible of a broader Atlantic Yorùbá CMS community at the turn of the twentieth century—a fecund environment for the blossoming of networks of kinship, solidarity, and interpersonal relationships following the imposition of British colonial rule in Ibadan in 1893.[11]

This "sociation in everyday life" as a conceptual device opens up the semiotic lives of the letters—a type of shared *àjọbí* and *àjọgbé* esoteric tradition—that shaped intimate dialogues among the members of this tightknit network. In other words, the analysis of the letters reveals the inner layers of meaning and possible hidden semiotics that underpin the discourse of the letter writers. This critical reading provides insight into biographies of the letter writers in specific social and historical contexts, revealing the dynamism of the structures, norms, and practices encoded in Akiwọwọ's concepts of *alájọbí* and *alájọgbé*.[12] C. Wright Mills, in *The Sociological Imagination*, notes, "We have come to know that every individual . . . from one generation to the next . . . lives out a biography, and that he [or she] lives it out within some historical sequence. By the fact of his living he contributes, however minutely, to the shaping of society and to the course of history, even as he is made by society and by its historical push and shove."[13] This perspective underscores the social agency of these letter writers—through the discourse of their letter writing—in a dynamic Nigerian colonial and postcolonial society.

The familial and kinship ties of the letter writers reflect the corporate unit of *ẹbí*, the extended family structure, which has sustained Yorùbá communities for generations. Akinjọgbin argues that despite the social disruptions of the nineteenth century, this system remained dominant because the relationship "was not forced, but natural." In Yorùbá communities, "the bond of society was blood relationship. . . . Nobody could assume citizenship without being born into it, and once born into it, no one could opt out. The smallest unit within the state was not the individual, but the family, which included dead and unborn generations, and to which belong such things as state office, agricultural lands, industries, priesthood and the like."[14]

The connection between mission Christianity and indigenous Yorùbá worldview was equally critical to the messages conveyed in the letters analyzed in this book. Peel contends that the conversion of the Yorùbá people to Christianity starting in the second half of the nineteenth century took place in the framework of a complicated and contradictory dialogue between traditional Yorùbá belief system and mission Christianity. The method by which the messages of Christian missionaries were received—whether the missionaries were Yorùbá returnees from Sierra Leone or Europeans—brought together religious and social forces that were firmly anchored in the indigenous Yorùbá belief system. Although Christian evangelical perspectives drew a distinction between the secular and religious, Yorùbá converts to Christianity, such as the letter writers analyzed in this book, reconciled temporal and transcendental forces, connecting the power of their new faith to changing social conditions within a Yorùbá frame of reference.[15] Consequently, in their socioreligious expressions, these Ibadan CMS letter writers consistently engaged in "a process of intercultural translation, moving back and forth between indigenous religious knowledge and the terms of Christian doctrine, practice, and authority."[16]

While my analysis of the letters reflects on the scholarship on literacy in modern Africa, the focus of this book is primarily on a critical discussion of substantive social, cultural, economic, and political issues that motivated the actions of the letter writers.[17] In this context, I explore the following questions:

1. Why was letter writing so pivotal to the everyday existence of these men and women in Nigerian society during much of the twentieth century? Put simply, why were these men and women such judicious letter writers at a transformative moment in Nigerian colonial and postcolonial history?

2. What dynamic personal and interpersonal conditions and priorities sustained the correspondence of these letter writers over long durations of letter writing?
3. What do these letters tell us about the production of knowledge and ideas in the construction of familial, kinship, and civic relations in twentieth-century Nigerian history?
4. What does the new medium of letter writing reveal about the changing modes of communication from a dominant Yorùbá oral tradition to a literary culture in modern Nigerian society?

In short, through a detailed and critical analysis of the correspondence between Abiọdun Vaughan and these other letter writers, I engage the voices and imaginations of Yorùbá social actors by revising, extending, and deepening the pioneering scholarship on kinship, associational life, elite formation, modernization, and social action in African studies.[18] In this context, the human agency and social dynamism expressed through letter writing cannot be understated. Liz Stanley notes:

> First, letters are *dialogical.* They are not one person writing or speaking about their life, but a communication or exchange between one person and another or other. Thus, conceptual ideas about the dialogical are especially pertinent in thinking about the structural properties that develop around the unfolding communication between letter writers and readers, for an important feature of correspondence, rather than one-off letters, is their turn-taking and reciprocity. Secondly, letters are *perspectival.* Their "point" is not that they contain fixed material from one viewpoint, nor that their content is directly referential, but that their structure and content changes according to the particular recipient and passing of time.[19]

This book critically analyzes major themes that have resonated in African historical and social studies since their inception as academic fields during the decolonization process after World War II—kinship and family ties; the impact of world religions on African societies; elite formation and consolidation; economic activities and development; marriage, family, and society; civic and associational life; gender and generation; migration and social change; human striving and agency—all against the backdrop of the rapid modernization under colonial and postcolonial conditions in much of the twentieth century.

Based on my analysis of 264 letters exchanged between Abiọdun Vaughan and his much older brother Samuel Ariyibi Vaughan, chapter 1 captures the essence of dialogues at the intersection of brotherhood, kinship, generation, and social mobility in colonial Yorùbá society from 1926 to 1941. The correspondence between Abiọdun and Samuel Ariyibi took place while both men were working in colonial bureaucracies in southern and northern Nigerian provinces. The letters reveal the deferential nature of the relationship between Samuel Ariyibi, initially a clerk in the Department of Railways at the onset of colonial rule, and Abiọdun. With his older brother's mentorship, Abiọdun secured a position as a career junior civil servant in the Department of Agriculture, with its headquarters in Moor Plantation, established by the colonial authorities in 1899. The correspondence reveals persistent mentoring of the young Abiọdun by his older brother on critical matters pertaining to personal and professional development.

A common thread in the letters between the brothers, as Western-educated CMS professionals starting in the earlier decades of colonial rule, is their moral obligations to their natal family (*alájọbí/àjọbí*), located in Gbenla in the Agodi section of Ibadan, where the colonial authorities were beginning to connect an emerging estate to the core of the city. Abiọdun and Samuel Ariyibi were regularly earning salaries in colonial bureaucracies and then providing financial remittances to members of their natal family to meet the cost of food, education, professional training, health care, and the reconstruction of their natal family house in Gbenla.

Chapter 1 also follows a fascinating dialogue between the brothers in a protracted correspondence about Abiọdun's unsuccessful attempt to secure the hand of a young woman from his CMS Arẹmọ community in marriage. This sustained dialogue (also discussed in the letters of Abiọdun's mother, his sisters, and S. A. Ọlọkọ in chapters 2 and 3) provides extensive insight into Yorùbá marriage practices, evolving ideas on Christian elite marriage, kinship ties, and family life in colonial Yorùbá communities.[20]

Consisting of about 297 letters spanning more than two decades (1931–53), the letters analyzed in chapter 2 focuses on family, kinship, remittances, marriage, gender, and generational matters (in the context of *alájọbí/àjọbí*). Written mostly in the Yorùbá language in the Latin alphabet, the letters are from Abiọdun's mother, Mariam O. Vaughan, and his older sisters Dorcas Ọlayinka Brainerd and Jadesọla Juliana Ọdẹbunmi. The first sister, Dorcas Olayinka Brainerd, a nurse, married a Sierra Leonean immigrant, John Brainerd, who came to Nigeria to work as a clerk in the colonial Railway Department at the beginning of the twentieth century. (Abiọdun's correspondence with Dorcas Olayinka's only son, Bamidele Theo Brainerd, and his family in Freetown, Sierra Leone, is the subject of chapter 5 of this book.) The other sister, Jadesọla Juliana Ọdẹbunmi, was married to a member of CMS St. Peter's Church, Aremọ, Samuel Ọdẹbunmi, who worked as a clerk for a European trading company, Paterson and Zochonis, in the 1930s and 1940s.

The letters in this chapter reflect other perspectives on many of the same issues that sustained the correspondence of the brothers, especially matters pertaining to the provision of financial remittances for family support and the reconstruction of the Vaughan natal house in Gbenla. The financial resources provided by Abiọdun and Samuel Ariyibi helped to support three generations, namely, Mariam, her children, and her grandchildren. The remittances from the two brothers supplemented Vaughan family members' income for food, housing, education, vocational training, and health care. However, the letters also reveal that the pressure on these limited financial resources might have led to tensions among family members. The analysis of this recurring issue in the letters of the older Vaughan women provides an illustration of changing economic and social systems in Yorùbá society, when social mobility and accumulation required parents to invest significant financial resources in their children, mitigating against the prevailing traditional system in which children provided material resources for their parents through regular provision of labor.[21] The chapter also analyzes the unique perspectives of the matriarchs on Abiọdun's unsuccessful attempt to secure the hand of an Ọmọ Aremọ (child of the Aremọ CMS community) in marriage in the mid-1930s, discussed in the previous chapter.

By critically engaging the significant human agency of these women letter writers as they appealed to various salient variables encoded in Yorùbá tradition, norms, and customary ways—such as seniority through age, financial responsibility of successful male figures to natal family members, and control over familial affairs—as well as their own status as working women, this chapter complicates the scholarship on gender in Africa. The crucial issues raised by these women as matriarchs of the Vaughan family put gender issues into dialogue with other pertinent social, cultural, and economic variables, especially kinship, generation, familial obligations, social mobility, and socioeconomic status, to provide a more nuanced perspective on the place of gender in African studies.[22]

The issues analyzed in chapter 3 are drawn from correspondence between Abiọdun Vaughan and his mentor and "cousin," S. A. Ọlọkọ, a fellow Ọmọ Aremọ and senior official of the colonial Department of Agriculture who provided leadership for a group of Ibadan CMS men through the auspices of several mutual aid and civic groups, notably, the Ibadan Brotherhood Fund Association, the Ibadan Cooperative Savings Society, and the Ibadan Progressive Union, from the 1930s to the 1950s. The missives between Abiọdun and Ọlọkọ are interspersed with letters from members of their wider social network. The letters analyzed in this chapter, unlike those in other chapters, were not written by Abiọdun's direct blood relatives or in-laws. Nevertheless, these dialogues reveal strong kinship bonds and dogged aspirations for social mobility, professional advancement, and self-improvement that animate the letters of Abiọdun Vaughan's relatives in other chapters.

Similar to the correspondence between Abiọdun Vaughan and older members of the Vaughan natal family discussed in chapters 1 and 2, the issues and ideas analyzed in this chapter were articulated against the backdrop of the rapid social, economic, and political transformations occurring in colonial Ibadan from the early 1930s, when colonial rule was being consolidated in Ibadan Division, to the late 1950s, when Nigeria embarked on a process of decolonization. This correspondence, in essence, provides a panoramic view of colonial Nigeria from the perspective of two Yorùbá Christian-educated men and their compatriots from shortly after the consolidation of Northern and Southern Nigerian Protectorates up until the attainment of independence in 1960. The analysis of these letters also underscores the tireless commitment of these men to the mission of two of the three mutual aid groups, Ibadan Brotherhood Fund Association and Ibadan Cooperative Savings Society, revealing the men's status as Christian educated men in the city.

This chapter also focuses on the correspondence between Abiọdun Vaughan (promoted senior clerk in the Department of Agriculture in 1952), Ọlọkọ (promoted acting accountant in the Department of Agriculture in 1950), and their compatriots in the Ibadan Brotherhood Fund Association and the Ibadan Cooperative Savings Society.[23] Revealing strong bonds of friendship with deep roots in Ibadan CMS institutions, these letters exhibit the vibrant associational life of the men through their deep commitment to these civic groups in the three decades in which Abiọdun assiduously filed their letters (1931–62).

Most of the men in these civic and mutual aid groups were products of the handful of CMS secondary schools in southwestern Nigeria early in the twentieth century, notably, Ibadan Grammar School; CMS Grammar School, Lagos; Abẹokuta Grammar School; Ijẹbu-Ode Grammar School; and St. Andrew's College in Ọyọ. With a strong foundation in the CMS communities in Aremọ, Kudẹti, and Ogunpa, many of these men later developed a strong commitment to the progress of Ibadan under colonial rule. The analysis of the correspondence among Vaughan, Ọlọkọ, and their compatriots as civic actors in Ibadan also reveals the interpersonal relations among these men as they explored Yorùbá enlightenment ideas in colonial Yorùbá society. For example, discussed within the institutional framework of their civic and mutual aid groups, many of the letters of these men reflected on the idea of *ọ̀làjú* (enlightenment), *ìlọsíwájú* (progress), and *ìdàgbàsókè* (uplift) that were common in the associational life of an emergent educated Christian elite in many Yorùbá cities by the late colonial period.[24]

Based on about 285 letters and documents, chapter 4 provides a comprehensive analysis of the correspondence between my father and mother, Abiọdun Vaughan and his second wife, Gladys Adukẹ Vaughan, née Akinloye.[25] Gladys Adukẹ was a schoolteacher whose maternal family had deep roots in Aremọ's CMS mission station going back to the 1870s with the arrival of her grandfather Samson Ọkẹowo as a young man from Ijẹbu-Ode and her grandmother Hannah Ọkẹowo from Ileṣa as a "ward" in a prominent family in Aremọ's CMS community at the tail end of the Yorùbá Wars. In correspondence sustained through two decades, from 1943 to 1961, many of the issues analyzed in this chapter reflect those discussed in previous chapters, notably, family health challenges, family tragedies, family obligations, financial remittances for family support, family wellbeing, married life, social mobility, professional advancement, socioreligious life, and personal development, including an extensive correspondence between Adukẹ and Abiọdun while the former was a mature student in London living thousands of miles away from her husband and five children from 1958 to 1961.[26]

The chapter also analyzes the extensive letters from Adukẹ's mother, Rachel Ayodele Akinloye, a nurse who worked in a CMS missionary hospital in Abẹokuta and colonial welfare center in Abuja, Northern Provinces, in the 1930s and 1940s, and Adukẹ's brother Adisa Akinloye while he was a law student at the London School of Economics and Inns of Court from 1946 to 1950, as well as another brother, Ọlayinka Odumosu, while he was a law student in London in the late 1940s and early 1950s. Discussed against the backdrop of shared social values derived from Aremọ's St. Peter's Church community (Àwọn Ọmọ Aremọ), these letters articulate Yorùbá notions of modernity during a moment of heightened social change in colonial Ibadan.

Drawing on about 195 letters and family documents (Freetown files), chapter 5 analyzes the correspondence between Abiọdun Vaughan (based in Ibadan) and his nephew Bamidele Theo Brainerd (based in Freetown, Sierra Leone)—and Bamidele's wife and children—on matters pertaining to family obligations and general issues of family wellbeing spanning thirty-eight years, from 1956 to 1994. Focusing on the resilience of Yorùbá kinship ties (as expressed through *alájọbí*), the chapter underscores the significance of family obligations and support through intergenerational and transnational correspondence among three generations of Abiọdun Vaughan's family in Ibadan and Freetown.

Specifically, this chapter analyzes the following major issues in the letters contained in the Freetown files: the care for Bamidele's aging mother, Dorcas Ọlayinka Brainerd (Abiọdun's older sister); the celebration of the life and the maintenance of the estate of Dorcas Ọlayinka Brainerd after her death in 1973;

the educational and professional progress of a new generation of the Vaughan family in the context of dramatic social, economic, and political transformations in Nigeria and Sierra Leone following the attainment of independence by these two West African countries in the early 1960s; and a sustained discourse on politics and society in postcolonial Nigeria and Sierra Leone in the letters of Bamidele to his uncle Abiọdun from the 1960s to the 1990s.

The book's conclusion underscores the significance of the major themes analyzed in the letters, revealing their implications for modern Yorùbá society in colonial and postcolonial Nigerian contexts. Additionally, it assesses the conceptual and analytical importance of the medium of letter writing to further explore the methods of African historical studies and interrogate everyday African experiences, especially in a moment of profound social, economic, and political transformation.

CHAPTER ONE

The Brothers' Letters

In the files that Abiọdun Vaughan labeled S. A. Vaughan were about 264 letters exchanged between Abiọdun and his older brother Samuel Ariyibi Vaughan. These letters revolve extensively around the obligations of the brothers to one another and to other members of their natal family in Gbenla, notably, their widowed mother, Mariam O. Vaughan; two married sisters, Dorcas Olayinka Brainerd and Jadesọla Juliana Ọdẹbunmi; a brother, Oladunjoye (Ladun) Vaughan, who had severe health challenges and died in his early forties; and their children, nieces, and nephews.

Mariam Vaughan, Abiọdun and Samuel Ariyibi's mother, was born in about 1866 in Akunu, Akoko-Yorùbá region, about 130 miles east of Ibadan, in the thick of the Yorùbá Wars. Her husband, Akintọla Solomon Vaughan, born in the early 1860s, was a migrant from Abẹokuta and a trader with connection to the CMS, having received some formal elementary school education in Freetown, Sierra Leone, in about the late 1870s.[1] Mariam, who as an adult had limited exposure to Western education through Ibadan CMS, became an active member of St. Peter's Church, Aremọ, when she and her husband settled in Ibadan in the early 1880s.[2]

The arrival of Mariam and Akintọla Vaughan, along with many new Christian converts, in the Aremọ CMS mission station and its parish church, St. Peter's, converged with the decline of the Yorùbá Wars and the consolidation of CMS missions in the Atlantic Yorùbá region in the last quarter of the nineteenth century. By the standards of the early twentieth century—especially the 1920s and early 1930s, when colonial rule was being consolidated in southern Nigeria—the couple's sons (Samuel Ariyibi and Abiọdun) were well educated, having graduated from two of Nigeria's relatively few secondary schools of their day.[3] Samuel Ariyibi Vaughan attended Nigeria's first secondary grammar school, CMS Grammar School, Lagos (founded in 1859), at the turn of the twentieth century, and Abiọdun graduated from the CMS secondary school for boys, Ibadan Grammar School (established in 1913 as the first secondary school in the city), in the 1920s.[4]

From both the tone and the content of the brothers' correspondence, it was apparent that Samuel Ariyibi had assumed tacit leadership of their natal family by the time of their father's death in 1930. In my interviews with elderly family informants who interacted with the two men in the 1940s and 1950s—notably, Lamide Bakare, née Vaughan, the eldest child of Abiọdun, who was born in 1938, and Mojisọla Ọladeji, née Ọdẹbunmi, daughter of Abiọdun's older sister Jadesọla Juliana, born in 1930—I was informed that Samuel Ariyibi worked as a clerk in the Railway Department during the earlier decades of British colonial rule in southern Nigeria. From his letters to Abiọdun in the late 1920s and the 1930s, I observed that Samuel Ariyibi worked briefly as a schoolmaster in the technical training school for the Railway Department in Port Harcourt (T.T. School), in the eastern region of the Southern Nigerian Provinces, about 400 miles southeast of Ibadan; as stationmaster at the Railway Department in Ọṣogbo, in the Ọṣun-Yorùbá area about 85 miles northeast of Ibadan; and as a senior clerk at the Railway Department in Jos, northern Nigerian provinces, about 385 miles from Ibadan, and Aba, in the Igbo region of the southern Nigerian provinces, about 290 miles from Ibadan.[5]

From these and other business activities he undertook over the years, Samuel Ariyibi accumulated enough wealth to construct two modern brick houses in Ibadan and to construct one other house and purchase another in new estates in Yaba and Ebute-Mẹta on the Lagos mainland by the late 1930s. The construction of modern houses drew on the sophisticated artisanship of Afro-Brazilian returnees (Yorùbá returnees and their children) who started to arrive in the Atlantic Yorùbá region during the decline of Atlantic slavery in the second half of the nineteenth century. The construction of brick houses typified modern Nigerian architecture, as opposed to the traditional Yorùbá mud building, and reflected the social status of a small Yorùbá elite such as Samuel Ariyibi in the early decades of colonial rule.[6]

Samuel Ariyibi's letters indicate that he had lent financial support to his younger brother when Abiọdun was a student at Ibadan Grammar School in the mid- to late 1920s.[7] Samuel Ariyibi also funded the primary, secondary, and vocational education of his own children, especially that of one of his sons, Agboọla, at Abẹokuta Grammar School (founded in 1909) in the late 1930s and early 1940s. Samuel Ariyibi, along with Abiọdun, provided modest financial support for nieces and nephews attending secondary schools, notably, Queens College, Lagos; CMS Kudẹti Girls School, Ibadan; CMS Girls Grammar School, Lagos; Igbobi College, Lagos; and Ibadan Grammar School in the late 1930s and the early 1940s.[8] Additionally, evidence from the brothers' letters suggests that remittances they provided also supported the vocational training of other young members of the Vaughan natal family.[9] It is thus apparent that, because of his position as the eldest man in the family and his professional success in the colonial Railway Department, Samuel Ariyibi, in the short term, assumed a position akin to a surrogate father to Abiọdun and became somewhat of a provider to ensure the wellbeing of the next generation.

With familial obligations linking three generations of the Vaughan natal family, the bonds of *alájọbí* established the framework on which I analyze the core issues and values that shaped the correspondence between Abiọdun and Samuel Ariyibi. These strong kinship bonds, personal interest, and temperament, as well as other traits, also shaped the outcome of the brothers' correspondence. The issues that dominate the brother's correspondence—like other correspondence analyzed in this book—reveal the everyday social world of the letter writers.

Managing the Home Front

The brotherly correspondence I analyze below began in the late 1920s, when Abiọdun graduated from Ibadan Grammar School and secured a clerical position in the newly established colonial agricultural complex at Moor Plantation, Ibadan, in the Department of Agriculture. The exchange of letters continued into the late 1930s, when Abiọdun consolidated his position as a steadily employed provider in his natal family.

Throughout this same period, Samuel Ariyibi was sending financial remittances to the dependents he left behind in Ibadan while he was away at work in Port Harcourt in the eastern region of the Southern Provinces and Òṣogbo in Òyọ́ Province, with travel assignments in Jos in the southern region of the Northern Provinces and Aba in the eastern region of the Southern Provinces. From 1928 to 1934 his younger brother and protégé, Abiọdun, back at home in Ibadan, was charged with disbursing these remittances to family members. Samuel Ariyibi provided Abiọdun with specific instructions on what the remittances were for and orders on how to ensure the wellbeing of his children.

During the initial stages of the compilation of the S. A. Vaughan files in the late 1920s, it was evident that Abiọdun was arriving at a watershed moment in his life. The first set of letters in the S. A. Vaughan files established the foundation for the correspondence between the two brothers: Samuel Ariyibi instructed his younger brother Abiọdun on how to manage the important issues Samuel Ariyibi had left behind at home while he was on service tours for the Railway Department. Samuel Ariyibi specifically instructed Abiọdun on how to manage Samuel Ariyibi's estates in Ibadan, coordinate the affairs of his family, and distribute essential remittances to meet the pressing needs of family members. To provide moral authority to the implementation of these important assignments, Samuel Ariyibi's letters suggest that he had established himself as the dominant figure in Abiọdun's life in the late 1920s, when Abiọdun graduated from Ibadan Grammar School, and in 1930, when he secured a position as a clerk in the Department of Agriculture. Referencing a graduation "certificate" noted in a letter from Abiọdun dated June 17, 1929, Samuel Ariyibi wrote back, "I am pleased to note your success" and asked his younger brother to "accept my heartfelt congratulations" while indicating that the "success" and the "congratulations" were extended by "us all at home."[10]

While working at the T.T. School in Port Harcourt from the late 1920s to the early 1930s, Samuel Ariyibi depended on Abiọdun to carry out essential repairs and collect rents from tenants in Samuel Ariyibi's house in Ekotẹdo, a new development in Ibadan that had been established by colonial authorities in the early 1900s and populated by migrants from various Yorùbá towns and from the eastern region of the Southern Provinces. Samuel Ariyibi provided specific instructions for the care of his house, insisting that Abiọdun attend to all aspects of the house that "require immediate attention." In a 1929 letter, he acknowledged the effort of his younger brother: "[I] . . . highly praise you for regular correspondence that you have been keeping since my departure from home. This is a very reliable adherence to my orders and I wish [for] you to continue doing the same thing."[11]

Samuel Ariyibi continued with instructions for the upkeep of his house in a letter in August 1930: "Happy to hear that you will be living in Ekotẹdo now. This will give you the opportunity to take care of the house very well." He went on to provide some advice to his younger brother to resist temptations from young women and focus attention on his new clerical work at the Department of Agriculture in Moor Plantation: "Be careful because women may be coming to you now more than before. . . . Things are not easy now, so face your work squarely and be punctual. Collect the house rent from Mr. Jones. Go around whenever it is raining so that you can know where we need to repair in the house. I hope Mama [their mother, Mariam Vaughan] got the £1: 1: 10, I sent to her."[12]

In May 1929 Samuel Ariyibi not only gave instructions on the maintenance of his house but also expressed concern about a delinquent tenant. He ordered Abiọdun to take swift action: "Inspect the house at Ekotẹdo regularly. You know we are in the raining season. If the carpenter did not pay his rent let him pack and lock up the room."[13] Several months later, Samuel Ariyibi outlined sage advice for his younger brother: "Face your studies [for examination for colonial clerical positions] squarely because time waits for no one." He then provided clear instructions:

> Please go to Ekotẹdo quickly to collect the house rent. Have these people paid their house rent? Ìyá ["Mama" or "Mother"] Cole 5. 10, Ìyá Comfort 16 for two room, 8-n-½, Ìyá Peters. Keep the key I gave you properly and collect the one from Ìyá Samuel. Tie the two keys together. I told you and Jones to buy some planks to repair the shelf in the room. Collect the receipt of the keys you bought. I also want you to call a bricklayer to repair the shop of the shoemaker. All the rooms upstairs should be repaired including the room from where the carpenter packed out. Guide them to use enough cement please.[14]

With regard to another tenant, Mr. Jones, who had repeatedly failed to pay his rent, Samuel Ariyibi wrote: "I have written you several times that Mr. Jones should vacate the house all this while. You have been silent about the issue. What is really going on. I will be around by the end of this month and it is his room that I will use when I am around so ask him to quit and let me know the amount of months he is owing."[15]

In January 1931 Samuel Ariyibi instructed Abiọdun to address an unspecified municipal requirement: "I want you to measure the distance between the house at Ekotẹdo and the house that Baba has just built. Do not write any letter to the D.O. [British district officer] until my arrival, God willing. Let me know if he used his house to block our own at the back. My land starts from the wall by the right. There is a pillar at the back. It is 50 feet in breadth and 150 feet in length. Show the pillars to Mr. Okoya and mark the place properly so that they will not change it."[16] In July 1931 Samuel Ariyibi provided a breakdown of the financial remittance to family members as follows: "Mama [their mother, Mariam Vaughan] £2 (money I borrowed), Mama 15 shillings (food allowance), Adeoti 2 pounds, 5 shillings (food allowance), Agboọla 5 shillings (for his clothes). Tell them to be prudent in spending their allowance. Things are a little difficult now. Each person should write to show that they received the money."[17]

From the tone of his letters, Samuel Ariyibi appears to have been a dedicated father, great provider, and disciplinarian. He set high standards for his dependents, especially his children, but also members of the Vaughan natal family who depended on him for financial assistance. Many of his letters revealed that he was particularly concerned about his young son, Agboọla. Samuel Ariyibi wrote to Abiọdun: "I have written two letters to you now without any reply. Please let me know about Agboọla now so that I will know what to do. Don't allow anybody to send Agboọla on an errand on the street. He is fond of looking at unnecessary things. Write back to inform me if the boarding room will be better."[18]

In addition to the regular remittances that Samuel Ariyibi sent back home and his concern for the proper care of his children, matters pertaining to the maintenance of his house in Ekotẹdo and the collection of rent from tenants continued to dominate his correspondence with Abiọdun in 1931. In reference to another house that he was building, he wrote, "I am in darkness concerning the house at Ekotẹdo. Has it been roofed? Has it been cemented? When you are writing me, let me know every little thing that is going on in the construction of the house. Your name is on all the postal order. I sent £7 to Mr. Craig [the contractor] for the building project. I will write Baba Adeoti on his care for the children."[19]

Samuel Ariyibi constantly instructed Abiọdun on how to manage his house in Ekotẹdo, writing in August 1931, "Please collect Ekotẹdo home rents and use them in the usual way. Take ten shillings yourself." In the same letter, Samuel Ariyibi promised support for his younger brother's professional advancement: "Yes, I had approached 3 white men who promised you work by the end of this month."[20] He also recounted a terrifying incident in which his "dear child" swallowed a two-inch nail, noting the difficulty of obtaining proper medical care. Eventually, an Xray located the nail in her stomach and showed that the nail was not doing much harm. He wrote: "Do not make Mama and the others to worry their minds too much as they need not tell many persons, just keep quiet and pray." Eventually, Samuel Ariyibi informed Abiọdun that his daughter successfully passed the nail. It is clear from these sets of letters that Samuel Ariyibi balanced the business of the Vaughan natal family with that of his own, with Abiọdun performing the critical role of connecting the two families.

Of the fourteen letters from Samuel Ariyibi from mid-1929 to early 1931 contained in the S. A. Vaughan files, most referenced conditions of Samuel Ariyibi's houses, requesting their renovation and the collection of rent. In one notable case in July 1929, a letter boldly titled "INSTRUCTIONS" contained keywords such as "cement" and "fencing." It gave Abiọdun instructions on the renovation of a house, regarding a bathroom, the backyard, and other structures, and more instructions on the collection of rent from tenants. In addition, though, this letter included instructions on Abiọdun's professional training: "I do not want you to leave the school yet until you reach the highest standards of your school. This is the best way. Do not be too hasty in doing things."[21] In a topically diverse letter written the following month, Samuel Ariyibi moved seamlessly between expressing concern for a loss, giving instruction for business, and giving Abiọdun advice on professional training. He stated that he wanted his younger brother to stay in school. He signed off and then added a postscript that called attention to the care of his son, Agboọla: "I do not like Agboọla to stay at home."[22]

The management of the house continued to dominate Samuel Ariyibi's attention. In a matter concerning the delinquent tenant, Mr. Jones, Samuel Ariyibi again requested swift action: "Press Mr. Jones to pay the house rent and keep them [the rent] well. Move carefully with them and do not follow bad company."[23] Several months later, Samuel Ariyibi instructed Abiọdun to deliver this strongly worded letter to Mr. Jones: "I have to inform you to pay and settle all the rents you have been owing me. . . . You are my friend and we should do good to each other. Therefore, buck up to make good of this account. I wish to make use of the house myself, as I'll be shortly coming home on leave and you are hereby requested to pack up and vacate the house."[24]

Samuel Ariyibi reacted to news back home and reported on the delicate status of his work in Port Harcourt: "I am happy when I heard that Adeoti [a female relative] has put to bed [given birth to a baby] and that you have done the naming ceremony too. . . . I name the baby Babatunde [meaning "the father has returned"]. Take care of the house at Ekotẹdo. My school was closed on 5/9/31 temporarily. I am in Divisional Office managing now. I should have been retrenched, but thanks to God that he takes care of those who are hardworking."[25] In another set of letters, Samuel Ariyibi expressed displeasure at the condition of his children: "I am not happy at all with what I heard and this is why I sent a telegram to you. I am not happy at all with the way the children I left behind are doing. Please if you cannot take care of them, I can come and take them to where I am living? Adeoti was at home primarily to monitor the children to do their work and to face their studies. Please tell her to supervise them very well."[26] A week later, Samuel Ariyibi provided the breakdown of remittances to meet the essential needs of his children and Vaughan natal family members, instructing Abiọdun to give "Mama £2. 0, Abiọdun, 5 shillings, Adeoti, 2 pounds and 10 shillings." He concluded by advising him to "be at peace with everybody."[27] The following month, Samuel Ariyibi sent further instructions on house maintenance: "Please check the house at Ekotẹdo often. I don't want rain to spoil it. I don't want people to spoil it because of the little money they are paying. I will send something [money] to Ọladunjoye [Ladunjoye, a brother with serious health challenges] at the end of the month."[28]

Less than a week later, another letter from Samuel Ariyibi instructed Abiọdun to give "Mama £1, Adeoti 2 pounds, 10 shillings, Jadesọla [a sister], 10 shillings, Ọladunjoye [brother], 5 shillings. Please inform all other members of the family to avoid misunderstanding among yourselves. The last letter I wrote before this is to tell you that you should name the boy [Adeoti's baby] Babatunde. . . . Let me know how things are going please."[29] More instructions on financial transactions followed in the next month: "[Give] £2. 8 shillings to Jadesọla for the Àdìrẹ [tie-dye cloth that she sells] she sent to me. Ìyàwó [a woman married to a member of the Vaughan natal family] will send money to Adeoti when she finishes selling the Àdìrẹ. It pains me when I heard the telegram of the death of my brother Dan Vaughan [a first cousin]. Please be at peace with everyone at home and keep reminding Adeoti to take care of the children."[30] Around Christmas of 1931, Samuel Ariyibi's instructions on the management of affairs back home in Ibadan, the maintenance of his estate, and financial assistance to meet the essential needs of family members continued with even greater intensity because of the special celebration that came with the festive season. He meticulously outlined the specific amount and purpose of the remittances: "Mama, 1 pound, 10 shillings, for Christmas, Adeoti 2 pounds, 6 shillings for food, Adeoti 8 shillings for Christmas, 6 shillings—from her Ìyálé [senior wife in the natal family], Agboọla 10 shillings for Christmas, Ìbejì [the twins], Ìdòwú [a child born after the twins] & boy 12 shillings for Christmas, Abiọdun 5 shillings, for Christmas."[31] In the same letter, Samuel Ariyibi again provided instructions for the care of his children: "Take good care of the children and do not allow them to take taxis during this festive period because of the reckless driving of the drivers. Be indoors and continue to praise God. The cloth I sent are for the children. Give extra care to Agboọla. I am sad about the death of Dan."[32]

Not surprisingly, the following year, 1932, opened with Samuel Ariyibi explaining the division of remittances to family members, again with specific instructions for the purpose of the money: "I enclose 4 pounds in this letter and it should be shared in this way: Mama, 1 pound, Adeoti: 2 pounds, 10 shillings, children's school fees. I don't know the amount Adeoti spent on the books of the children, but I sent 10 shillings to her which I feel should be enough. Please tell Adeoti to take care of the children very well especially, Agboọla. He should be well fed, get him a cap because of the cold weather."[33] Several months later, while on assignment in Aba in the eastern region of the Southern Provinces, Samuel Ariyibi wrote: "Thanks to God for the quick recovery of Jadesọla [from illness]. Keep reminding Adeoti to give the children extra care. . . . Adeoti & the children 2 pounds, 5 shillings, Abeo, 15 shillings, Madandola. 7 shillings, Children's clothing 2 pounds."[34]

Two months after that, Samuel Ariyibi continued with the disbursement of financial allowances to meet the needs of close relatives, again providing stringent instructions for the proper care of his children while calling his brother's attention to his own physical and mental health: "The purpose of the letter is to inform you of two things. First, I am having skin disease. Second, I am dreaming of masquerades." As will become clear below, Ibadan's masquerade tradition was a source of anxiety for Samuel Ariyibi, presumably for religious reasons. He continued:

> I have discussed this issue [the skin disease] with Mama's younger sister's husband and he promised to be of help. . . . [S]o go to him and collect it [the medicine]. Wrap it very well with clothes and twine and send it as soon as possible. Listen carefully to his instruction so that you can explain it to me effectively. Don't forget that I will be traveling to Jos [in the Northern Provinces] on 4/26/32. I enclosed 8 pounds 6 shillings in this letter. Share as follows: Adeoti food allowance for May & June, 4 pounds, Mama May & June, 2 pounds, Jadesọla's 'Àdìrẹ,' 1 pound, 1 shilling, medicine. Keep the two monthly allowances very well. Give it to them every month until I return from Jos. Tell mama and Adeoti to take care of the children. The children must not play rough. If the money is not enough, please let me know the amount you add to it. . . . The primary assignment of Adeoti is to take care of the children.[35]

In another letter written later in the month, Samuel Ariyibi divided the remittance as follows: "Mama 1 pound, Baba [an uncle] 9 shillings, Adeoti 1 pound 10: Total 3 pounds. Save the remaining in the book." Now the tacit leader of his natal family, Samuel Ariyibi gave specific instructions not only for younger members of the family but also for the older relatives now under his care: "Baba should be at home now. Age is not on his side again. I don't want mama to stress herself by saying she wants to go to Baba's place. She is of age too. She needs to be resting now. Layinka [a cousin] is in position to be taking care of the home now. Tell him to do so. I will write him as well."[36] In another letter, Samuel Ariyibi provided the breakdown of remittances: "Mama 1 pound, 5, Baba, 10 shillings; 1 pound 15."[37]

Still engaging the usual mix of managing his house in Ekotẹdo and responding to the material needs of his natal and nuclear families, Samuel Ariyibi instructed Abiọdun: "Tell Mr. Jones [the delinquent tenant] to quit the house immediately. Mama should not bother herself economically. On Layinka's issue: I have written to him not to repair the house until my arrival." On an apparent matter of discord among some members of the Vaughan family back home in Ibadan, Samuel Ariyibi noted, "How many are we that we should not allow peace to reign."[38] He informed his younger brother about developments in the nightmares he experienced a few months earlier, posed the usual queries about the welfare of his children and other close relatives, and provided unsolicited edits on Abiọdun's letter: "I stopped dreaming of masquerades. I will continue to give you the situation of things. I sent back your letter. I want you to go through all the area where I marked with red pen. I got to this place on 28/4/32 and I started work on 30/4/32. Take care of the children and Adeoti. They must not lack any thing please. May Mama live long with good health."[39]

Writing from Jos, in the southern region of the Northern Provinces, where he was on assignment in May 1932, Samuel Ariyibi expressed frustration over the condition of the new house he was building: "I am fed up with this house at Ekotẹdo. Despite all the amount I have spent, termites are still eating all the roof. I have written to thank Mr. Craig. Inform the carpenter to change the roof and ceiling. I want a neat carpentry work. After this, the carpenter should paint it with Solignum [a wood preservative against termite and fungal damage]. Mr. Craig should also supervise the work as well." He concluded his letter with an expression of anxiety over his children's wellbeing during the annual Ibadan masquerade festival, insisting on a clear distance between traditional Yorùbá beliefs and his Christian faith: "This is masquerade season. The children should not come out to watch them. They can observe the masquerades from the window in the house. I don't want masquerade to enter the house. The house belongs to Jehovah. The children should not go to school when Ololu [the fierce Ibadan masquerade] is out. Please don't forget the issue of the termite (white ants)."[40] A few months later, Samuel Ariyibi sent four pounds back home to Ibadan with instructions on how it should be distributed: "Mama, 1 pound, Adeoti and Children, 2 pounds, 10 shillings, Abiọdun, 5 shillings, Agboọla 2 shillings, 6 pence, Kehinde & Taiwo, 2 shillings, 6 pence. We shall be going to Port Harcourt tomorrow 2/7/32. Reply as soon as possible so that I can know how things are going."[41]

As the year 1932 progressed, Samuel Ariyibi's letters continued with the same concerns regarding the status of his house in Ibadan and the condition of close relatives that had dominated his correspondence with his brother. After complaining about Abiọdun's tardiness in replying his letter ("It is over three weeks that I heard from you") and admonishing him to "be careful as you ride your bicycle when you are commuting to work," Samuel Ariyibi gave the normal instructions for the maintenance of his house and the wellbeing of his children: "Tell those who cannot pay the house rent at Ekotẹdo to quit and check all the rooms downstairs because rain can be entering the rooms through the windows. Hope someone is taking the children to school. The distance of the school is far to let the children go there by themselves. Please help me to warn Adeoti not to put rubber beads round the neck of the children."[42]

A subject that dominated many of Samuel Ariyibi's letters in the early 1930s was a consistent inquiry about the condition of his children, especially his son, Agboọla. Though the initial correspondence does not provide enough information to explain Samuel Ariyibi's anxiety over Agboọla, some minor discussion between the brothers reveals that while Agboọla exhibited academic promise, he may have had some chronic health challenges that required extra attention. For example, in one letter from July 1931, Samuel Ariyibi wrote, "[I] hope you will take care of him properly. Do not allow anybody to illtreat him."[43] In another letter written a week later, Samuel Ariyibi asked Abiọdun to inquire from the headmaster of a boarding school about tuition and boarding fees for Agboọla's possible enrollment in the school.[44]

In many letters to his older brother (carbon copies of which are stored in the S. A. Vaughan files), Abiọdun provided vital information about the well-being of Samuel Ariyibi's children, the condition of the houses in Ekotẹdo, Vaughan natal family affairs, and general financial conditions back home in Ibadan. For example, following Samuel Ariyibi's inquiry about the academic performance of his son, Agboọla, Abiọdun replied with specific information: "Yes, with regard to Agboọla's progress, I found that the boy is trying and has got the brain to learn. He goes to school every day. It was detected by his teacher that he is very backward in arithmetic. Even Agboọla cannot successfully work out addition sum. In English, he is the champion in his class and there is no one among his classmates to oppose him." Abiọdun went on to write that he had been tutoring Agboọla in arithmetic and concluded that failing arithmetic or English would result in Agboọla "being detained in his class for one year." Importantly, while Samuel Ariyibi was away from home, Abiọdun assumed the role of a surrogate father to his nephew Agboọla.[45]

The following month, Abiọdun reported that Agboọla was promoted to the next class, commenting that he was sure Agboọla would do well in his new class and had "advised him strongly to fight against arithmetic heart and soul." Abiọdun then proceeded to provide a list of school materials that Agboọla would need in his new class. A few years later, in the late 1930s, Agboọla attended Abẹokuta Grammar School, a leading CMS secondary school for boys.

Finally, as always, Abiọdun updated Samuel Ariyibi on the status of his houses in Ekotẹdo and informed him that their brother, Oladunjoye, and brother-in-law Samuel Ọdẹbunmi had secured employment at Òkè Màpó (Mapo Hill), the headquarters of the colonial divisional administration.[46] The following year, Abiọdun explained to his older brother why he could not visit him in Ọṣogbo as promised: "I really promised to come to you but I have no money to travel with. January is always the woeful month for poor clerical man as far as money matters are concerned. I am not tendering any promise again, but one day, you shall find me there with you."[47]

Samuel Ariyibi's integration of his business mandate with the family's welfare would continue apace even as the Great Depression persisted in colonial Nigeria in the early 1930s. In one instance during this period, he wrote to

Abiọdun: "I am now advising you to pay attention to the house and collect rents regularly; and should you come across a tenant insolvent to pay, tell him to vacate the place."[48] Later in 1932, as the Great Depression intensified, Samuel Ariyibi focused even more attention on the wellbeing of his natal and nuclear families. Before their brother Ọladunjoye secured employment at Òkè Màpó in January 1932, Samuel Ariyibi had noted that he was having trouble finding work for him: "I have tried all possible means to get Ọladunjoye something here to do, all my efforts are unavailing knowing very well that times are very hard (with axe of retrenchment). . . . Please inform him to keep on praying and keep his feeling away from those woeful ways of thoughtlessness." After thanking Abiọdun for informing him about Agboọla's progress, Samuel Ariyibi inquired about his children's school fees: "What is the balance of the school fee . . . ? Help me know this so that I may arrange without further delay."[49]

Emotionally speaking, the conveyance of personal sentiments by Samuel Ariyibi when addressing Abiọdun did not always reflect that of a father—or father figure—to a son. Regarding personal matters, the two bothers appeared passionate in their endeavors. Samuel Ariyibi did not hide his feelings from Abiọdun, nor did he expect Abiọdun to conceal his from him. This came across mostly in how Samuel Ariyibi freely exchanged information on a variety of important matters, such as the delinquent payment of rents by his tenants, the maintenance of his houses in Ekotẹdo, and his struggles over the wellbeing of his children, while he was away from home.

In August 1932 Samuel Ariyibi informed Abiọdun of a long-awaited transfer from Port Harcourt to Ọṣogbo but asked his brother to "keep this news strictly confidential."[50] This was welcome news, since Samuel Ariyibi would now be closer to Ibadan. In his reply several weeks later, Abiọdun expressed pleasure at the good news ("Glory be to God in the Highest") and advised Samuel Ariyibi to take his leave at home in Ibadan before reporting for duty in Ọṣogbo.[51]

The first letter Samuel Ariyibi wrote from his new location in Ọṣogbo contained more than the regular topics of discussion. "I am not pleased with your carelessness. All the keys should be labeled and kept in a box after the doors have been locked," he told Abiọdun. "If you play any carelessness with my likings, know that I will not be friendly or brotherly with you, but will ask you to pay for any damage done. BE CAREFUL." In an authoritative tone, Samuel Ariyibi seemed to be saying, What did I tell you to do with the keys? How many times have I told you to be more careful? How could you be so careless? And what are you going to do to fix it? Most often, this line of questioning takes place between a parent and child, the questions intended to force the child to consider what they have done wrong and correct their actions. Unfortunately, this line of questioning also occurs when adults address other adults, often as an attempt to reassert control in a fragile relationship.

After several years of working in the Department of Agriculture, Abiọdun, in collaboration with his older brother, had assumed greater financial responsibility for their natal family. For example, starting in the early 1930s, their correspondence indicates that the brothers were largely responsible for the rebuilding of the Vaughan natal family house in Gbenla, Agodi, after the colonial government demolished the three houses built by their father in Gbenla at the turn of the century to make way for a major road that would connect Agodi, an evolving commercial area, to the core section of the "old" city.[52] In a reply to his older brother's letter on the laying of the foundation of their natal family house, Abiọdun wrote: "I cannot but agree entirely with your decision to try to contribute the sum of 30 pounds. But I shall crave for your indulgence to allow me to contribute 25 pounds at the commencement of the building and the remaining 5 pounds [later]."[53]

After several years of consistent correspondence between Samuel Ariyibi and Abiọdun, the tone of their dialogue had begun to shift somewhat by 1933. This paragraph from Abiọdun's letter is worth quoting in full: "I thank you very sincerely for the fraternal way you have received me and discussed matters with me. . . . As a true brother, I cannot help but disclose my mind to you, and I hope and trust you will renovate your father's house and put aside the ill treatment and disappointment you have encountered in our family circle. If this is done it will stand as a credit and honour in your part and we the followers shall have shares out of it and your children in addition."[54] At this point, it is clear that Samuel Ariyibi's relationship with his younger brother had been evolving into a transactional relationship that was different from what I observed in their earlier letters. Despite the twenty-year gap between the brothers, the tone of their correspondence by 1933 was gradually growing into a collaborative one in which Abiọdun, who had been a salaried junior civil servant in the Department of Agriculture for several years, was emerging as Samuel Ariyibi's junior partner in the financial affairs of the Vaughan natal family. Consequently, with the resources that come with three years as a clerk in the Department of Agriculture, along with his older brother's mentorship, Abiọdun's letters reflect growth, confidence, and assertiveness by 1933.

In February 1934 Abiọdun's life made a major turn when he was transferred to the Zaria branch of the Department of Agriculture in the Northern Provinces. In his letter to inform his brother of the transfer, Abiọdun expressed ambivalence about moving to faraway Muslim Northern Nigeria. He stated that major changes were likely to take place at home while he was away in Zaria and hoped that Samuel Ariyibi, now back in Ibadan, could serve as a vital connection to developments at home.[55] As Abiọdun prepared for Zaria, he wrote an impassioned letter about an unspecified marital problem between Samuel Ariyibi and his wife. This letter, which defines Abiọdun's first major departure from Ibadan, is instructive because it sheds light on a critical attitude that is often openly expressed in Yorùbá society—and wider Nigerian communities—regarding the supposed natural attributes of women. On such an important interpersonal matter, with its far-reaching implications for the Vaughan natal family, Abiọdun appealed to his older brother to be considerate in his assessment of what he deemed a serious marital "infraction" by his wife. In his plea, Abiọdun argued that as a woman, Samuel Ariyibi's wife has an inherent shortcoming that he (Samuel Ariyibi) should carefully consider before arriving at the desirable decision of understanding and forgiveness. Abiọdun wrote, referring to his sister-in-law:

> The latter part of your letter betrayed your recent mode of living with my sister, and I meditated on what might have brought the quarrel about. In any case, I remind you that however a lady may be honest to her husband, and however with good quality she may be endowed, there must be some defects in her character. In short, all human beings are not created without natural defect but proportionately that of women exceed. Now I would not say that my sister is not offending you in some respects but I would ask you to consider her ways and the tender and amiable love she has for you. So far as I can judge of her, she seeks for your interest daily. May God spare the lives of the two of you and your children. Amen. Above all, I beg you very immensely to deal with my sister very leniently; remember she is a woman. . . . Before you act, remember my mother and your children. I would have communicated to you immediately after the receipt of your letter but through imagination I wish you to view my present position with regard to my proceeding to Zaria shortly. I do not like to leave my people and at the same time I must labour to get my earthly requirements. What can I do, I must answer the call of duty in the Northern Provinces.[56]

Tension in the Vaughan Family

As family members develop divergent personal interests on pressing issues, perspectives among them are unlikely to follow the patterns that had defined prevailing family dynamics in previous years. Such shifting interests and perspectives were evident in the correspondence between the Vaughan brothers while Abiọdun was away in Zaria in 1934 and 1935. As Abiọdun grew more secure in his civil service career in the Department of Agriculture, his letters became more assertive in tone. During this period, Samuel Ariyibi and Abiọdun's correspondence revealed considerable tensions, which were also reflected in the letters of other senior members of their natal family, notably, their mother, Mariam, and sister Dorcas Olayinka, analyzed in the next chapter. These tensions revolved around the provision of financial remittances for family support, disagreement over the management of the Vaughan natal house in Gbenla, and Abiọdun's unsuccessful marriage proposal to an Ọmọ Aremọ. These issues are discussed in detail later in this chapter and in the next chapter.

The first hint of tension in the Vaughan natal family was revealed in a reply from Abiọdun to Samuel Ariyibi in which he commended his older brother for reinstating their mother's allowance after having halted these payments earlier in 1934. "First and foremost, I have to thank you for reconsideration of your decision against your mother," Abiọdun wrote upon arriving in Zaria in September. "I shall be very thankful for your entire forgiveness of my shortcomings, if there is any, during these few days especially when writing in connection with the recent quarrel. I am too junior to advise or even write you on such a very delicate subject, and whatever might have been my mistake I crave forgiveness."[57]

With financial issues dominating the brothers' correspondence, Abiọdun, in a notable letter the following year, inquired about the status of the construction of his brother's house in a new estate in Ebute Mẹta on the Lagos mainland: "To what stage you have brought your building now? . . . I advise you to complete this glorious job before embarking upon another worldly thing. A step and then another. It is advisable you furnish the building with good painting and bring it up to the admiration of the people." The circumstantial boldness of this statement is fairly obvious: Abiọdun was beginning to address his older brother with renewed confidence. He continued with a request for a loan from his brother: "I shall be very glad to receive that money by August or September ending if convenient to you. It will well serve my purpose if I get it in August or September." This was a reminder of a request he had made for the purchase of an organ a few months before. (Abiọdun was a gifted pianist who played at the daily assembly while a student at Ibadan Grammar School in the 1920s.)[58] At this point, it appears that Abiọdun was abandoning his initial status as a "son" and protégé to Samuel Ariyibi that we saw in earlier correspondence between the brothers.[59]

At the end of 1935, Samuel Ariyibi completed the construction of his house in Lagos, and Abiọdun congratulated him on this landmark accomplishment, which was a source of pride not only for Samuel Ariyibi but also for Vaughan family members: "Indeed this is a great achievement—the honor and pleasure of which are not for you alone but also your kindred. It is natural that when a member of a body is affected the whole body is injured and evident too that when a mention of a part is made the whole part has its automatic reflection, so in conclusion I am very glad and thank God for assisting and giving you the power to do such eminent things."[60] Abiọdun's appreciation of this notable achievement is a reflection of a deep Yorùbá concept in which success as a manifestation of individual accomplishment is a positive reflection on one's natal kinship unit, further reinforcing the pride inherent in *alájọbí*.

Two months earlier, financial matters had remained an important aspect of the correspondence between the two brothers. Writing in his usual formal style, Abiọdun explained that he had "cleared one order which exhausted my pocket" and politely requested: "Will you kindly let me know your opinion so that I can further my arrangement."[61] The following week he stated that his main concern was not his financial challenges but how his older brother saw him: "It is the condition of my saving that has brought this and I believe that you know I am not so useless."[62]

The growing tension between the brothers over financial matters was more obvious in Abiọdun's letter the following month. "I suspect that you have formed a certain opinion of me on the following grounds: Failure to receive your letter advising me of the payment of the money to my mother which she has acknowledged," he wrote. "I have put before you in very a fraternal manner my present condition and it is surprising to note of this treatment. At any rate, I take it that you may not know of this. If in reality you feel I offend you, I ask for pardon."[63] On this matter, Samuel Ariyibi had little to say: "We all thank God that there is nothing slowing us down and my work is going on nicely." Given Samuel Ariyibi's detailed discussion of financial issues earlier in their correspondence, this lack of response to Abiọdun's queries spoke volumes.[64]

With news of the challenging economic conditions faced by close relatives in Ibadan, Abiọdun appealed to his brother to lend support to members of their family:

> Now my dear brother I come to the important part of my letter. I have received a request from my mother indirectly to raise a helping hand towards my senior sister, because of her present condition, which really is pitiable . . . And again, I received letters from Brother Ladun [Oladunjoye] to the effect that he has no penny in hand. I looked for a job for her, but oh! Pity the effort is in vain. Really speaking my mother's womb was blessed and God mercifully blessed all the children of her womb but alas.[65]

In the first sets of letters, from the late 1920s to the early 1930s, Samuel Ariyibi did most of the writing, instructing his younger brother on a course of action to take, while Abiọdun's letters reflected a passive role, especially on matters relating to their family. In these letters from the mid- to late 1930s, by contrast, Abiọdun actively made requests of Samuel Ariyibi, especially on Vaughan family matters. However, unlike his older brother, who gave instructions and commands in the earlier years, Abiọdun's appeal to Samuel Ariyibi called on his sense of kinship, generosity, and kindness. Abiọdun included the following assertion in a letter from 1934: "I really sympathise with Sister. She has love for all and emotional feeling to help her brethren despite her character." He follows this by stating the exact amount of money he would regularly contribute for the upkeep of their family, acknowledging the apparent strain from such familial obligation. Ultimately, Abiọdun pleaded with Samuel Ariyibi to match his contribution so that the amount received by their mother, sister, and brother would be sufficient to help them. He concluded with this curious statement: "At the close of this letter I humbly beg you to do away with palm wine drinking. If not, let the rate be averagely minimized. Know that our fall originally depended on drinking," probably referring to the biblical fall of mankind. "As you are now shouldering a great responsibility with regard to your work, you need to be very careful, especially in your own town. If there is any mishap, son of man will say 'Ẹmu ti poju' (too much alcohol). The success of your present appointments is for the glory of your people, your race, and your country."[66]

Abiọdun's next letter continued to underscore the need for the brothers to lend support to their siblings and for Samuel Ariyibi to moderate his drinking:

> Finally, I will address what is important—the financial situations of my sister and our brother Ladunjoye. They are both in need of our help, and I plan to help them in hope that you will do the same. We owe it to them, and they are deserving of our help. While we are discussing family who are not doing well, please allow me to address your drinking problem. What you are doing currently is not wise, and I advise against it. I know you have a lot riding on you right now, but I trust you to be strong.[67]

With these strong words from Abiọdun, who had merely carried out the instructions of his much older and successful brother only four years earlier, the table seems to have turned in the relationship between Abiọdun and Samuel Ariyibi.

Abiọdun's next letter a few weeks later revealed the extent of Samuel Ariyibi's alienation from their family. Rebuking his older brother, he wrote:

> It is a pity to still learn that you have entirely stopped your mother's monthly allowance in order to starve her and to bring her end up prematurely. I have to point out in this connection that it is not only the stoppage of this monthly

> allowance [that] will give her cause to think but there are a lot for her to think of, especially when she remembers your origin and come to mind that you are her fruit—the forerunner. I am an inexperienced boy—the youngest of all—and I am not in a position to say a word on this matter, I therefore beg you to think very deeply on this subject.[68]

Abiọdun continued with a staunch defense of their widowed mother:

> I take it that there can be no offence or cause from our *mother* that can justify any of us illtreating her. She had done what a father can do, and no one is perfect. She stands with us as father when father was away. She stands with us and with her grandchildren after the death of her husband. She stands with us from the beginning enduring various hardship. . . . I have written 15 pages on the subject, but I thought it wise to keep them because I am too junior to address you. But I know that God liveth and He will speak to you directly.[69]

In this important letter, Abiọdun was pushing the envelope: scolding his older brother perhaps outside the confines of what was acceptable in the norms of Yorùbá society of his day. Though many years younger than Samuel Ariyibi, Abiọdun was walking a delicate line by reminding his brother of his responsibility not only as the eldest child but also as the most successful person in their family. These sets of letters written while Abiọdun was in Zaria reveal, for reasons that are not entirely apparent in the letters contained in the S. A. Vaughan files, that Samuel Ariyibi had ceased providing financial support for his mother and other members of the Vaughan natal family, a responsibility that he carried out judiciously in the late 1920s and early 1930s, even as the Great Depression ravaged the economy of colonial Nigeria. Given the importance of remittances to meet the essential needs of close relatives, Samuel Ariyibi's decision to withhold financial support for his mother—for a second time—was rather drastic. Indeed, Abiọdun, in several of his letters on the subject, felt the need to underline the word *mother*—and it is not difficult to comprehend this point of emphasis, given the centrality of the mother in Yorùbá families. Is a mother not the most important part of a family, especially this family after the death of their father? Was the Vaughan natal family becoming less of a priority to Samuel Ariyibi? The answers to these important questions were not revealed in the content of the brothers' letters.

Marriage Proposals

In keeping with what would be expected of a young Christian-educated man of his social standing in colonial Yorùbá society—particularly a gentleman with an increasingly secure career as a junior civil servant in the Department of Agriculture—Abiọdun began in the early 1930s to explore having his own family, starting with a desire to marry a woman of appropriate Yorùbá social standing.[70] Based on the letters contained in the S. A. Vaughan files and the Vaughan Family files, analyzed in the next chapter, Abiọdun, starting at the age of twenty-six, made attempts to marry four women from 1933 to 1937 (three of these attempts did not come to fruition). Of the four, three were barely mentioned in the S. A. Vaughan files, but the proposal to Miss Ibironkẹ Alalade, a young woman with deep roots in the Aremọ CMS community, provides more insight not only into the relationship between the two brothers but also into marriage practices, at least for Yorùbá-educated Christians of Abiọdun's social background in the era of British colonial consolidation.

A carbon-copied letter in the S. A. Vaughan files from Abiọdun to his older brother reveals that Abiọdun's first unsuccessful attempt at a marriage proposal took place in 1932, two years before his posting to Zaria. After thanking Samuel Ariyibi for the gifts of used suits, at the time the required attire for Nigerian civil servants in the Department of Agriculture, and claiming that the suits fitted him perfectly, Abiọdun mentioned a young woman he was considering as a possible wife and sought his brother's support in discussions required with the woman's family. Abiọdun went to great lengths to explain to Samuel Ariyibi that he had not yet made a commitment to the woman. Abiọdun talked around his actions toward her, instead filling Samuel Ariyibi in on her living and family situation, demeanor, character, and physical appearance, as well as the current status of their relations. He hoped his older brother would return to Ibadan in time to meet her, adding finally that she was not "thoroughly lettered but has training that will help her manage domestic affairs." The letter shows the extent to which Abiọdun needed his older brother's approval. Abiọdun was essentially pitching the idea of this woman to Samuel Ariyibi, making sure to include favorable details for his older brother's consideration. Abiọdun wrote:

> She came to Ibadan from Ilesha and lives at Agodi—Ọlọkọ's House—She is under the junior wife of Mr. S. A. Ọlọkọ as sewing mate. She moves to me and I know her actions. As far as her general character is concerned, she is qualified. She is beautiful and of a ruddy complexion and energetic. I have entered into talk with her and she told me that she had no intended [fiancé] at present; and she will be finishing up her course of training—sewing—during December and she is going back to Ilesha. I do not know if you will be here before or by that time. Let me know of this.[71]

With no other entries on this informal marriage proposal in the S. A. Vaughan files or other files compiled by Abiọdun Vaughan, it is reasonable to conclude that not much came of this attempt at marriage.

It would take another eleven months for the subject of a marriage proposal to resurface in the S. A. Vaughan files. In August 1933, slightly over a year before traveling to Zaria, Abiọdun presented the idea of another marriage proposal to his older brother: this time he wished to propose to Ibironkẹ Alalade.[72] Abiọdun's brother replied the following month, "I am not prepared to undertake any extra expenses at this time," and admonished his younger brother to focus on his work and save his money "so other things will then be easy."[73] In his next letter, Abiọdun was more direct in his request: "Sir, I know that you shall do your duty as a father [figure to me] re the matter of my girl. I shall not be very pleased to visit her before you write to the [girl's] father as you promised. So long as there is no objection to the doing, I beg that you try to write the letter [to her father] this week. If the father is informed by you, my position with his daughter will get light [favorable attention]."[74] Samuel Ariyibi's reply was lukewarm, if not a rebuttal to Abiọdun's request: "It is not time yet to go to the parents of your girl. The matter should for the time being remain between the two of you. We have to watch how you love each other first. Remember that love is blind, but sincere love will never fade away. There is no necessity to be too anxious."

In the interaction between the brothers, two opposing views on this important issue were emerging: Abiọdun wanted Samuel Ariyibi to contact Ibironkẹ's father so that he could secure her hand in marriage, while Samuel Ariyibi was in no hurry to assume the role typically reserved for a father to formally approach a prospective father-in-law on behalf of the groom's family for reasons that are not entirely clear in the letters.[75] The divergent objectives of the brothers on Abiọdun's plans for a marriage proposal, especially the need to reconcile Samuel Ariyibi's position as the leader of the Vaughan family with Abiọdun's prospective father-in-law's demands, exacerbated the growing divide between the brothers.

With so much at stake, Abiọdun took a more assertive posture in his next letter:

> I deem it necessary for me to write to you on your proposal with regard to the invitation you intended sending to Mr. Alalade [the father of the prospective bride]. This will not sound well my dear brother, as I thought seriously over the subject and arrived at one certain conclusion that I would not like it myself if I am in his position as a father. . . . Sir, I know you will handle this matter with

> interest and to success, for if on the contrary it shall stand against me as a shame mainly because I have boasted about you. . . . I know you are the father and I must communicate with you first. The end of this year shall bring Miss Alalade's course of teaching to 2 years, when I shall become a man of 28. Is that not reasonable enough, Sir? What is worth doing is still worth doing well, Sir.[76]

Samuel Ariyibi's response to Abiọdun was swift and harsh:

> I do not see my way clear as yet to anybody concerning Miss Alalade. . . . You had better keep quiet and take off your mind from her. So long you had been written to, stop writing and visiting her. Note that you are still young and there is no reason for you to worry much about a burden of this kind at present. It is up to you if you allow a blind love to push you too hard. My advice to you is to take care of your work and keep your money and leave other things in the hands of God to arrange and decide.[77]

With such a stern response to Abiọdun's direct request, Samuel Ariyibi threw down the gauntlet.

But if Abiọdun was disappointed with his brother's reaction, he did not show it in his reply. Rather than assert his desire forcefully, Abiọdun took a more conciliatory tone in his next letter:

> Again Sir, I know my father is dead and I shall know that he is still living in this connection and in any matter pertaining to me in particular. Mr. Alalade took indirect action to show that he will not yield to the request mainly on the strain of your letter. He prefers you address him "my dear brother" and the contents of the letter to ask for his favor of giving up his daughter to your brother then he will believe you will receive *his daughter as your own daughter*. Well, I have nothing to add and I know you will take a fatherly action. . . . I really have love for this lady because of her manner, condition of her parents, and her training.[78]

To persuade his older brother, Abiọdun abased himself by conceding moral authority to Samuel Ariyibi, hoping the latter would temper his position to meet the demands of Ibironkẹ Alalade's father.

After what appears to be a long silence on the matter, at least in the S. A. Vaughan files, a letter from Abiọdun, writing from his new post in Zaria six months later, in June 1934, brought an end to the saga over his marriage proposal to Ibironkẹ. First, he expressed concern over the limits that distance imposed on his engagement with his family in Ibadan, noting, "Naturally, I shall never be satisfied with a welfare report of my people from an outsider for they can see and know of you but little." Abiọdun then launched into a discussion of the marriage proposal, which is worth quoting in its entirety:

> Your paragraph 2 was thankfully perused and received as a good advice and with one in mind. I am prepared to leave the girl. I wish to do so if God wishes it. The girl has come out in her true color with stronger love and said that her parents on both sides love me and no contradiction from them. She said that the cause of her past irregularities was only to examine my love. Now that you appear to be against it entirely . . . I cannot at my present age take up anything that will worry me especially in my family because I have no mind for trouble.[79]

Abiọdun continued with a mild critique of his older brother's previous letters on the subject: "Though this was a difficult decision that has caused me great confusion and difficulty, I have decided that I will leave the young woman to comply with your wishes." In doing so, however, Abiọdun was clear that this difficulty resulted from his older brother's position. Abiọdun wrapped up this critical letter with this sentence: "Any way, I wish to impress in pointing out that I will not go against you in this respect, I simply point out the above facts."[80]

Samuel Ariyibi's response to his brother's letter was evasive: "I am writing this to remind you of the house rents you promised to register to me. Will you please do so without further delay? I got your letter and contents were noted. Just continue looking after your work and God will surely help you. It is unnecessary for you to be in a hurry in getting a partner."[81] This response reflects a particular type of "selective hearing" that occurs when someone is confronted with an array of information and chooses to only respond to what they want to, meanwhile ignoring the parts they do not want to engage. Samuel Ariyibi seemed to be using his privilege as the senior in their relationship to avoid the appropriate response to what obviously was a difficult emotional matter for Abiọdun.

The third correspondence on a putative marriage proposal in the S. A. Vaughan files appeared six months later, in January 1935. Before elaborating on the marriage proposal, Abiọdun shared complimentary information about their nephew Bamidele, who recently visited him in Zaria during his holiday from Igbobi College in Lagos and served as the courier of Abiọdun's letter to Samuel Ariyibi.[82] Abiọdun noted that he appreciated "the excellent ways and brotherly dealings of this boy." Abiọdun then discussed the main reason for his letter: "Last time, after my last missive to you, I received a report from home that the hand of my lady had been sought for. Thanks. This is good so far. May God bless the doing and bless the two of us who take it upon ourselves to become good husband and wife. Every success, blessing in this world is in His Mighty

Hand and I pray for it. I believe I will not have cause to regret, if only God and my people are not against me." In the final paragraph Abiọdun wrote, "I humbly beg to call for reply to my letters," and then expressed concern for their brother, Oladunjoye, who had taken ill.[83]

The following month, February 1935, a letter from Abiọdun expanded on the status of the aforementioned marriage proposal. He began the letter by asking about the welfare of Samuel Ariyibi's son, Agboọla, and then moved on to the topic on his mind, pushing the case for a prospective wife from his station in Northern Nigeria. He provided some context for this new plan to secure a wife: "Will you kindly help to thank Ìyàwó ["wife," [presumably, Samuel Ariyibi's wife] for the excellent part she played in the matter of seeking the hand of my lady. May he [God] reward her." Abiọdun went on to mention that he looked forward to "receiving a line" from Samuel Ariyibi since he had not heard from him for three months—an indication that Abiọdun's older brother had not been responding regularly to his letters.

Abiọdun then mentioned that he has enclosed in the envelope letters to and from his prospective wife for his older brother to review, stating, "I think they will interest you." This sentence is immediately followed by, "You may have impression that I am acting against your ruling or advice. Oh no. It is 'Nature' and I hope you will agree with me if I say, it is better for a man to look for a girl and marry her than keeping crooked life with woman of the world and thereby render his life useless and a burden to his family."[84] With this refrain, Abiọdun hoped to prevail on Samuel Ariyibi's indifference to his plan to secure a wife.

In the spring of 1935, after citing a heavy workload as the reason why he had not written in a while and thanking Samuel Ariyibi for the gift of suits he gave him, Abiọdun moved on to "the important part of my writing." He announced to his older brother that he was planning to purchase a plot of land through the assistance of his mentor and "cousin," S. A. Ọlọkọ, in a new residential layout for Nigeria's emerging professional class at Race Course, a small neighborhood adjacent to Ekotẹdo, where Samuel Ariyibi had a house and was completing the construction of a second one. To demonstrate his careful planning, Abiọdun added that he was undertaking this expensive task with his "only friend," J. A. Ayorinde, a classmate at Ibadan Grammar School and colleague at the Department of Agriculture. For Abiọdun, the purchase of this plot of land would be transformative, and he went on to link this action to his desire to start his own family: "My brother after the purchasing of this plot I am determined to marry by 1936 ending or early 1937 and after my marriage I am desirous of concentrating my attention to building [my house]."[85] Significantly, this was the first time in the letters contained in the S. A. Vaughan files that Abiọdun explicitly declared his intention without seeking the approval of Samuel Ariyibi. With the exception of his failed marriage proposal to Ibironkẹ Alalade, most of his correspondence with his brother in the late 1920s and 1930s had revolved around his obligation to his natal family: responding to Samuel Ariyibi's many errands and responding to the essential needs for his mother and siblings.

Far away from home in Northern Nigeria, Abiọdun concluded the letter by sharing his perspective on what he thought was his older brother's growing ambivalence toward him: "I wish to receive your letter in reply to this and many others I wrote to you. If you are not really angry with me, I see no reason why you will not write to me even once in a month or at worse once in three months. But as for me, I take it [writing] as a duty."[86] That Samuel Ariyibi had not written to Abiọdun once in several months, given the frequency with which he wrote in earlier years, was most unusual. The silence suggests that something was awry in the brothers' relationship. But Abiọdun might only be aggravating Samuel Ariyibi's reticence by evoking familial obligations to a much older brother. It is likely that with Abiọdun's growing confidence from his rising professional fortunes and correspondingly higher influence in the Vaughan natal family, despite his status as the youngest sibling, the power dynamics between the brothers were shifting in favor of the younger Abiọdun, with implications for other older members of the Vaughan natal family, notably their mother, Mariam, and three siblings, Ọlayinka Dorcas, Jadesọla Juliana, and Oladunjoye.[87] Despite the significant age gap between them and Samuel Ariyibi's success, Abiọdun was now coming into his own, setting his own priorities, and growing in influence in the family.

A few months later, in June 1935, Abiọdun sent a similar letter to his older brother. This letter further revealed Samuel Ariyibi's waning connection and growing ambivalence toward Abiọdun. It reiterated Abiọdun's plan to purchase the plot of land in Race Course. Once again, Abiọdun requested support for the purchase of an organ. At the conclusion of the request, Abiọdun (referring to himself by his middle name) wrote, "If you simply agree with your poor Alfred and lend him a helping hand, perhaps he will do something good."[88]

This time, Samuel Ariyibi pushed back, refusing to lend support and delivering this paternal condescension: "I thank you for your letter dated 2nd inst. It is my duty to encourage you on a right line and the only advice to give you is to look after your work and save your monies." With regard to Abiọdun's proposal for a wife, Samuel Ariyibi wrote, "Re your girl—when you come home, I shall give you full length of my opinion." And regarding his brother's housebuilding plans, Samuel Ariyibi wrote, "I was glad to hear of the plot you had secured for building. It is a pity you had done this without consulting me first. Houses in Ibadan are not valuable and a waste too. However, do not bother to build now, keep the land there and continue saving, when we see each other, I shall tell you what to do."[89]

Abiọdun's third plan for a marriage proposal did not come to fruition. Fast approaching the age of thirty, he continued his quest for a suitable wife with the diligence required by such an important matter. With at least one emotionally draining marriage proposal behind him and back in his native Yorùbá region after two years of service in Northern Nigeria, Abiọdun was determined to settle down and start his own family.

From his new station in Abẹokuta, about forty-five miles south of Ibadan, Abiọdun penned several letters seeking the support of Samuel Ariyibi in proposing to a new love interest by the name of Dorcas Bolaji. Perhaps mindful of disappointing past experiences with his brother, especially with regard to Ibironkẹ Alalade, Abiọdun introduced the subject in these strong words: "My Dear Brother, As I do not want to become a wretched brother or a regrettable object in our little family, I am appealing for your sympathy. I thank God I have been to the Northern Provinces singly and returned without meddling with a woman or have my blood contaminated with impure blood. This was my determination; I thank God for I carried it out." The letter continued: "Remember, I am now at Abẹokuta and my nature can make me offend people . . . I do not wish to argue things unreasonably or to pull matters with you when you are very strong over it, because you are my father [figure] yet it is my duty to make you understand me." Abiọdun wrote further,

> I wish my people or representative to approach the family as formally arranged. After all, to get a wife is very easy. I can do it alone, even here, but I wish to prove to my people that I am a reasonable fellow. I pour out my feeling, secret and love to you in a *very very short form*. This is the duty of a son to his father and I shall be pleased to hear of your duty early. It is your duty. I do not wish to go against your wish but in this case out of two dangers one is better. . . . A wretched life is a wretched man and poison to the family. I leave all to you and I am sure the above is enough.[90]

After signing off "Yours very obediently," Abiọdun handwrote another plea to his older brother: "I beg most humbly that the matter of my saving is not brought to connection with the above matter."[91] The plea went on, but the message was one-dimensional: Abiọdun wanted to make sure that the fuss he had made over his marriage proposal did not backfire.

Based on the previous marriage discussion between Abiọdun and Samuel Ariyibi and the urgency with which Abiọdun wrote, it seems that he was eager to start a family and marry the woman in question. To make his intentions clear, Abiọdun described, in the above letter, all of the recent scenarios in which he had exercised good judgment in his life choices, especially as a young junior civil servant in the Department of Agriculture, and the pressing need to get married to a desirable woman. From the tone of Abiọdun's letter, his older brother appears to have been tardy in his response to an earlier request for him to initiate the appropriate engagement with the woman's family in keeping with proper Yorùbá marriage customs. This fourth "proposal," recorded in the S. A. Vaughan files, ultimately led to Abiọdun's marriage to Dorcas Bolaji in late 1937 a few months before his thirtieth birthday.

Within the relationship between the two brothers, Samuel Ariyibi dictated the direction of their dialogue. Given this, it was his duty to consider Abiọdun's feelings when making decisions or even when writing to him, for that matter. Samuel Ariyibi was in a position of power within the family, and he used that power to shape the lives of his immediate natal family members who depended on him, but Abiọdun, though constrained by custom, had some leeway in which to maneuver. Now a responsible young man, Abiọdun had a promising career in the colonial civil service, provided financial support for natal family members, and defined a viable pathway for his own future while trying to acquire his older brother's consent, in keeping with Yorùbá customs and traditions. With Samuel Ariyibi's stern personality and Abiọdun's growing confidence, the relationship between the brothers was set for a collision course.

A Note on the Vaughan Family House

A final bone of contention between the two brothers and other senior members of the Vaughan natal family discussed in the S. A. Vaughan files was the control over the Vaughan family house in Gbenla during its reconstruction in the late 1930s. In January 1938 Abiọdun notified his older brother of a meeting he had with his mother and siblings. According to Abiọdun, the meeting was called "to discuss your idea or intention of having Gbenla house as a legacy, before you can offer a helping hand towards the place. I made them understand that you want a surer ground of your people receiving you at any time as a father after the death of our father."[92] At the meeting, family members initially thought that Reverend Okuseinde, a respected St. Peter's Church, Aremọ, vicar, should facilitate their discussion, but after further deliberation they decided that their first cousin Ayọ Vaughan in Alafara—son of J. A. Vaughan, the former personal secretary of the first British Resident in Ibadan, Captain Bower—should be approached to lead the family discussion. If Samuel Ariyibi was in agreement with this suggestion, then all that was left was for his siblings to accept his proposal. Abiọdun concluded the letter by mentioning that he had spent plenty of time "traveling to and fro" to advance this project on behalf of the family, so he would not be pleased to see the plans fall through.[93]

The relationship between Abiọdun and Samuel Ariyibi was further complicated by growing tensions over financial matters in the early 1940s, when the record of correspondence between them in the S. A. Vaughan files came to an abrupt end. The first indication of this financial pressure was expressed in a letter in September 1940, three years into Abiọdun's marriage to Dorcas Bọlaji and two years after the birth of Abiọdun's first child, Lamide, in 1938. In this letter, Abiọdun expressed growing financial challenges and their implications for the Vaughan family: "I am at a loss, I do not know what actually is responsible for the failure as it will not be my pleasure to hear that any of my people is in financial difficulty, especially your good self." In terms of his own personal financial condition, he wrote: "Really, I am in difficulty and I do not know what to do. I am running a course of payment of articles purchased towards my plan of which you have been intimated. I wished to visit home but lack of fund kept me down." Even now that Abiọdun's first child had arrived, he still had to devote the vast majority of his time to his work, which did not allow him to spend time at home in Ibadan with his new family.[94]

The following month, as Abiọdun prepared to return home to Ibadan from Abẹokuta, a series of events intensified the tension between the brothers. Abiọdun requested a loan from his brother, who seemed to be having financial challenges of his own.[95] In his reply, Samuel Ariyibi expressed delight at his younger brother's professional success, then lectured him on the status of their natal family house in Gbenla and Samuel Ariyibi's own financial challenges.[96] Abiọdun, who had expected to have temporary lodging in either the Vaughan family home in Gbenla or his brother's house in Ekotẹdo, was also informed by Samuel Ariyibi that these two options would not be available to him on his arrival in Ibadan because reliable tenants still occupied rooms in both houses. The sentences that follow from Samuel Ariyibi underscore the extent of the tension between the brothers—as well as other members of their natal family—at this critical point: "Stop threatening me. It is your place to know that Gbenla building forms one of the reasons leading to my being out of pocket. . . . It is your affair entirely if you decide to cut yourself from the family and that does not shake me for a minute. I thank God myself for bearing all these difficulties and *dirty words* up to date."[97]

This time, Abiọdun's reply was not conciliatory: "Dear Sir, Yours of 29/10/40 was received and I thank you most sincerely. The letter under reference confirmed a previous one from you suggesting to me to rent a house outside. 2. I am now in financial difficulty, when can I expect that money. 3. With the exception of Sister Jadesọla and the love for my mother, I am prepared to segregate from the family. I thank God for bearing all these difficulties up to-date."[98] For now, this is a full-blown letter of war—or at least these two exchanges are. There is no further correspondence between the brothers in the S. A. Vaughan files until the early 1980s, when Samuel Ariyibi Vaughan, in his nineties and for about forty-five years residing in Lagos, exchanged a few letters with Abiọdun about the status of the Vaughan natal house in Ibadan.

Samuel Ariyibi returned to Ibadan in the early 1980s. He died in Ibadan in 1986 at age ninety-eight and, like his parents and siblings, was buried in the cemetery at St. Peter's Church, Aremọ.

~

With regard to the analysis of the letters contained in the S. A. Vaughan files, it did not take long to understand that what I was observing in the relationship between Abiọdun Vaughan and Samuel Ariyibi Vaughan was not so much the story of a dialogue between two brothers as it was the drama of an upbringing between an elder and his junior in a tightknit Yorùbá family. The story of a father raising a son is rarely magical, and the few magic moments that take place usually begin and end before the child reaches the late teen years. Beyond this age, both in contemporary Western societies and in colonial Nigeria, the learning relationship between father and son is strenuous, as it consists of some trial and error in a world that can be less forgiving with each year the child matures. This certainly was not the nature of the relationship between Abiọdun and Samuel Ariyibi.

When Abiọdun Vaughan began corresponding with his brother, Samuel Ariyibi in 1928, he was twenty-one years old, at which point forty-one-year-old Samuel Ariyibi had assumed the role of a surrogate father and was emerging as the leader of the Vaughan family. As I read these letters, I felt compelled to separate instances in which Samuel Ariyibi acted as a father from those in which he acted as a brother and analyzed them accordingly. What I eventually understood is how little the conventional Western notion of "brother" or "father" mattered in Abiọdun's relationship with Samuel Ariyibi. Abiọdun did not lack a father figure in his life; he simply had to shift his focus as he engaged pressing matters as they unfolded in his life and his changing role in his natal family in his twenties and thirties. Because of the strong bonds in the Vaughan family and his personality, this shift seemed less of a question to consider and more of an order to follow.

When reading these letters, one of the first things I noticed was the vast difference between the kinds of people Abiọdun and Samuel Ariyibi were, the most important being how differently they wrote. When Samuel Ariyibi wrote, it was clear that there was one thing and one thing only on his mind, and that was completing whatever objective or task was at hand. Whether it was fixing houses, collecting rents, distributing financial remittances to family members, outlining school materials, or describing travel plans, he did it with little to no *personal* interaction and consideration. When writing contracts, manifestos, or instructions there is no real need to add any piece of yourself to what you are saying—the personal simply does not matter. Samuel Ariyibi was terse and withholding when questioned on any matter. So why and through what values did he write? His stern, matter-of-fact, and detached writing style was not simply a function of his personality but also a reflection of his older age, access to resources, and professional success relative to his much younger brother and protégé, Abiọdun. Meanwhile, Abiọdun acted as his son, as he was required—and this was simply a template utilized in the dynamic relationship with his much older and uncompromising brother.

But in his twenties and early thirties, Abiọdun was already his own man with his own way of communicating. He was compassionate, considerate, warm, and willing to explain things in detail to ensure that his older brother appreciated the importance of Abiọdun's demands—essentially the opposite of Samuel Ariyibi. Abiọdun enlisted every conceivable emotional tool—especially in the familial and kinship tool kit as expressions of *alájọbí*—to squeeze some concrete reactions out of his older brother, with little success. Samuel Ariyibi was still Abiọdun's surrogate father and the putative head of the Vaughan family, and it was hard for Abiọdun to adjust without undermining the equilibrium of their natal family.

Nevertheless, the responses of both brothers to the pressing material needs of members of the Vaughan family was an essential element of the kinship values system of *àjọbí-alájọbí*, expressed through distributing money, reconstructing the Vaughan family house, building and renovating houses, or collecting rents. The abrupt end to the brothers' twelve-year correspondence in November 1940 is an indelible aspect of an outcome of *àjọbí-alájọbí* on contentious matters because of Abiọdun's professional development, access to financial resources, and growing responsibility in the Vaughan natal family—with a corresponding desire to become his own man—in a dynamic Yorùbá colonial society.

CHAPTER TWO

The Matriarchs' Letters

In my initial review of the files that Abiọdun Vaughan labeled Vaughan Family, I discovered that the letters contained in the files were essentially those of the older women in Abiọdun's natal family, namely, his mother, Mariam O. Vaughan, and older sisters, Dorcas Ọlayinka Brainerd and Jadesọla Juliana Ọdẹbunmi, as well as those of his first wife, Dorcas Bọlaji, from Abẹokuta, to whom Abiọdun was married from 1937 to 1943. Also included are ancillary letters from some close relatives with strong ties to the natal family house in Gbenla. Overall, these letters spanned most of the time period in which Abiọdun worked in various offices of the colonial Department of Agriculture, including Zaria, in the Northern Provinces, in the mid-1930s; Abẹokuta, in the Southern Provinces, from the late 1930s to the early 1940s; Agege, Lagos, in the mid-1940s; and Enugu, in the Igbo heartland, in the Southern Provinces, from the late 1940s to 1950.

After careful reflection on the issues discussed in the letters, I had a better appreciation for why Abiọdun might have labeled these files, dominated by these older women, Vaughan Family. These letters explicitly dealt with matters that were central to the everyday lives of the Vaughan family when Abiọdun was away from Ibadan. The correspondence in this chapter clearly indicates that the "business" of the Vaughan natal family was carried out almost exclusively by the older Vaughan women, who had the responsibility to ensure the safety and security of all family members.[1] In other words, the essence of *alájọbí* for this family was systematically sustained by the everyday labor of the Vaughan matriarchs: Mariam, Dorcas Ọlayinka, and Jadesọla Juliana.

Abiọdun also included the letters of his first wife, Dorcas Bọlaji, in the Vaughan Family files. This was because, while Abiọdun was away working in the Abẹokuta branch office of the Department of Agriculture, Dorcas—for some time—resided in the Vaughan natal family house in Ibadan. Consequently, the affairs of Abiọdun's young nuclear family were not only integrated intimately into the business of the Vaughan natal family but also closely managed by his mother and two older sisters.

Of all the files in Abiọdun's possession during the colonial period, the files labeled Vaughan Family are the only ones where most of the letters were written in the Yorùbá language using the Latin alphabet (with the exception of some letters written by Dorcas Ọlayinka Brainerd and the younger generation in English). These women probably wrote their letters in Yorùbá because of the level of their proficiency in writing and speaking English. This is not to suggest that these women were not literate in English; rather, I feel that at least two of them—mother Mariam and sister Jadesọla—were simply more proficient in writing in Yorùbá. By the standard for women in the first two decades of colonial rule in Nigeria, Abiọdun's two older sisters were well educated, having both attended the CMS mission primary school at Kudẹti, where a major portion of the education was limited to mother tongue (Yorùbá) instruction at the turn of the twentieth century. The situation of Abiọdun's sister Dorcas Ọlayinka and Rachel Ayọdele Akinloye, née Ọkẹowo—mother of Abiọdun's second wife, Gladys Adukẹ Vaughan, and a contemporary of Dorcas Ọlayinka at St. Peter's, Aremọ—was exceptional because in the 1910s they both had a secondary school education. (Rachel, like her only daughter, Adukẹ, after her, attended CMS Girls Seminary School, Lagos—later CMS Girls Grammar School—one of only two schools where young women could obtain a secondary school education in Nigeria in the early twentieth century. Rachel's letters are analyzed in chapter 4.) Since men of Abiọdun's Western-educated, elite pedigree were solely regarded as *akòwé* (literally, "writers of books"), they wrote exclusively in English, the metropolitan language associated with power and status. However, many women of their generation, even when formally educated, would still carry out much of their everyday correspondence and transactions, whether written or verbal, in the Yorùbá language.

To obtain good translations that went beyond mere literal meaning from Yorùbá to English, I sought the help of three outstanding schoolteachers who taught reading and writing in Yorùbá and English in Ibadan.[2] They reflected carefully on the subtle epistemological meaning of the Yorùbá values implicit in the correspondence. I am confident that the English-language translations utilized as quotations for analysis in this chapter effectively capture the essential message that the writers intended to convey in their letters. It should also be noted that I am a native speaker of Yorùbá, and I read and write in the Yorùbá language.

Mother's Letters

A critical message that dominated the correspondence in the files that Abiọdun Vaughan labeled Vaughan Family was expressed through the vibrant and confident voice of his mother, Mariam Vaughan. She was in her early seventies in the early 1930s when Abiọdun started to record his correspondence with most of the members of the Vaughan natal family, including his older brothers, Samuel Ariyibi Vaughan and Ladunjoye Vaughan, and his older sisters, Dorcas Ọlayinka Brainerd and Jadesọla Juliana Ọdẹbunmi.[3] As noted earlier, Abiọdun was the youngest surviving child of Mariam.

As the dominant voice in the letters contained in the Vaughan Family files, Mariam engaged the main issues that shaped the conditions of Abiọdun's life and the lives of his natal family during the time when the letters were assembled in the files. These issues overlap with those discussed in other chapters of this book, notably, the chapters on the files labeled S. A. Vaughan and S. A. Ọlọkọ (chapters 1 and 3) from the late 1920s to the early 1950s. Significantly, the analysis of Mariam's letters—as well as other letter writers in this chapter—illuminates the complexities of Yorùbá kinship ties and interpersonal relations among various members of the Vaughan family, negotiating the boundaries of *alájọbí* and *alájọgbé* while reflecting on the personal qualities of Mariam as a letter writer.

Mariam, whom I remember vaguely in her late nineties as a feisty but quiet matriarch in the late 1960s, was at the core of the Vaughan natal family in the 1930s and 1940s, shaping the interest of family members across generations, premised on the values of *alájọbí*. While her children and grandchildren engaged their vocations from various locations, especially in Ibadan, Mariam held the natal family together with letters providing updates and inquiries predicated on her unquestionable moral authority as the preeminent matriarch whose power and influence connected three generations. While Abiọdun regularly engaged other senior relatives in extensive correspondence on a wide range of pressing family matters, Mariam's correspondence with her youngest child revealed intimate messages that exuded loyalty and trust.

While Abiọdun was away on service tours in branches of the colonial Department of Agriculture in the Northern and Southern Provinces, Mariam updated him on important developments in the lives of family members and relatives in Ibadan. Mariam kept track of the financial remittances that Abiọdun contributed for family support and served as an informal administrator of Abiọdun's business dealings while he was away from home. She called his attention to the pressing needs of close relatives and explored strategies for distributing the resources he provided among family members. The network of Vaughan natal family members and relatives that she coordinated was not only intergenerational but also transregional in character, connecting the Vaughans' native Yorùbá southwestern region to other regions in Nigeria's evolving colonial state.

In 1934, a few months after Abiọdun's arrival in Zaria, Mariam reported on the problem of remittances to address pressing needs. When Samuel Ariyibi withheld the monthly allowance from their mother (see the previous chapter), Mariam registered her strong objection in a letter to Abiọdun:

> My dear son, I want to tell you that your brother is mistreating me. I pleaded with him, but he didn't listen. Also, he is no longer giving me allowance for food. Even if he gives, I will turn it down. He also wrote a letter on 23rd June, 1934, stating that I should relocate to Ekotẹdo. When I told him that the roof of the house [in Gbenla] is leaking, he asked me to tell his siblings [Mariam's other children] to contribute some money to repair it since the family house belongs to everyone [older members of the Vaughan family].[4]

Following Abiọdun's plea to his older brother, discussed in the previous chapter, Mariam informed Abiọdun of Samuel Ariyibi's response later in the year: "I received the letter, the eggs and the money you sent. I have divided it among the people at home and they appreciated it. Dear son . . . your brother sent money to me this month. The money is still intact. I would have rejected it, but I received it because of you."[5]

With Abiọdun away in the predominantly Hausa-Fulani Muslim region of colonial Northern Nigeria—a region culturally and linguistically different from their native Yorùbá region—Mariam's letters, especially in the earlier months, expressed anxiety over the wellbeing of her son. She inquired about his health and offered advice on how to take care of himself. In April 1934, only two months after Abiọdun's arrival in Zaria, for example, Mariam, while discussing the economic challenges of family members at home, wrote about Abiọdun's health: "I received your letter, the money, mattress, and vegetable oil. . . . About the headache that you are having, I will send the medicine for it. Make sure you use it according to the prescription."[6] Later in the year, she continued: "I hope you have fully recovered? Please let me know the condition of your health. Do you have a house maid to assist you with your chores? Please avoid eating groundnut [because of peanut allergies]. I will send elubọ [yam flour, a common Yorùbá staple food] very soon."[7] The following month, Mariam asked Abiọdun about the status of some foodstuff she sent him: "Did you receive the letter and the gari [a common West African staple food made from cassava] I sent through Mrs. Kembi? We wanted to send elubọ along with it but due to transportation problem we couldn't. I will send elubọ through the next available means."[8]

While her son was in Zaria from 1934 to 1935, Mariam kept him informed on a host of pressing family matters, especially Oladunjoye's health challenges and the economic struggles of her children, grandchildren, and other close relatives. Importantly, as one of her two most successful children—along with Abiọdun's eldest sibling, Samuel Ariyibi—Mariam called on Abiọdun to play a significant role in the welfare of the Vaughan family. She operated as a family administrator and organizer, keeping track of resources he sent and identifying how these resources needed to be allocated among family members. This required a great deal of coordination and commitment, derived from her personal capacity and legitimated by her status as the matriarch of the family. Mariam not only kept in regular contact with her son but also served as a bridge between him and family members, on the one hand, and their wider social network, with its foundation in the CMS community in Aremọ, on the other. By sending her son reminders of his obligations to family members, keeping him informed of important developments among their relatives, and advancing his interests back in Ibadan, Mariam served as a sort of "chief operating officer" on behalf of Abiọdun while he was away in Zaria.

Throughout the 1930s, the wellbeing of Oladunjoye, Abiọdun's other older brother, was a major source of anxiety for older members of the Vaughan family. Oladunjoye's protracted health problems featured prominently in Mariam's letters to Abiọdun. In early 1935, about a year after Abiọdun's departure from Ibadan for Zaria, Oladunjoye was admitted to Adeọyọ Hospital, the modern hospital established by the colonial authorities in 1928. Since older family members were morally obliged to lend financial support in times of crisis, Mariam provided a breakdown of the hospital bill to Abiọdun when Oladunjoye was discharged from the hospital.

In another letter a few weeks later, she informed Abiọdun not only about Oladunjoye's health challenges but also about those of one of her grandsons, Agboọla (Samuel Ariyibi's son), and about the support relatives and friends gave their family during the challenging months in late 1934 and early 1935: "Agbo [Agboọla] is also in Lagos because [of health issues] but it is getting better. Ladunjoye is still at Adeọyọ hospital. The doctors said he needs to be operated on this week. Write a letter to Alabi and thank him for his kindness to Ladunjoye and also congratulate him on the arrival of his baby. Also, thank your cousin, Ọla Williams for his effort and concern for Ladunjoye. Ibironkẹ [Abiọdun's fiancée discussed in the previous chapter] has gone to Lagos for her teaching job."[9]

After Oladunjoye's successful surgery at Adeọyọ Hospital the following month, Mariam informed Abiọdun of the hospital bill and the next course of action: "Your brother, Ladun [Ladunjoye], was discharged on Monday. I had written the letter you directed me to write your brother [Samuel Ariyibi] about Ladun's hospital bill. He replied that I should let him know his own contribution towards the bill. I told him to send whatever he can afford out of the twenty pounds ten shillings. It has to be paid in two weeks. Your own contribution should be sent as soon as possible."[10] Oladunjoye himself also wrote to reinforce his mother's request after his surgery: "I appreciate God and all your efforts during the period when I was sick. . . . My hospital bill is as follows: Operation charge 11. 30 pounds. Hospital fees and bed—6. 10 pounds. Beverages, food and milk—1: 0 pound."[11]

Access to reliable information about developments on the home front was essential to being a member of the inner core of the family, a role Abiọdun obviously embraced as an indispensable provider of essential resources. Later in 1935, Mariam wanted to know how Abiọdun was faring in Zaria and informed him that his brother had another child: "How is your eye sight? Hope you are getting better. Also, your brother's wife gave birth to a baby boy on 25th August, 1935."[12] She also expressed disappointment over missing money: "I was sad when I heard that you didn't receive the money. I put it inside the bag of elubọ that I sent through Abiọdun Abọdẹrin. I also sent gari and sponge with the receipt."[13]

With dwindling resources at a time of economic downturn in the mid-1930s, Mariam requested additional relief: "Please kindly send money for elubọ. I would not have asked, if I have money to purchase it."[14] When Abiọdun received a long-awaited transfer to the Abẹokuta office of the Department of Agriculture late in 1935, Mariam wrote him to discuss the idea of sending the son of a friend to serve as his ward: "Fatawu's father want to send Deji's child to stay with you pending the time you will get a housemaid. He wants you to enroll him in school. He will pay his school fees."[15] When Abiọdun returned to Ibadan from Abẹokuta for a brief stay in 1939, Mariam wrote to offer advice on temporary accommodation: "Iya Rasaki has informed me of a good house in her care. Kindly go to Ekerin house at Ago-Owu and ask of Rasaki's mother. She will show you everything."[16] When he returned to Abẹokuta at the end of that year, Mariam expressed gratitude for her allowance and gave Abiọdun the sad news of the death of a close relative: "I received your letter and the money you sent. Thank you very much. . . . Also, Abikẹ is dead. Please encourage your wife to visit Abikẹ's family."[17]

Abiọdun's correspondence with his mother integrated the topics of family and business. It was far-reaching on a variety of everyday issues. For example, in July 1945 Mariam wrote to discuss the supply of essential items: "Elubọ is costly, a bag costs two pounds. I sent chewing sticks, soap and sponge. Tell your wife to take some of them and send what is left to Ẹbun [a niece]."[18] In December 1947 Mariam provided Abiọdun with updates about important developments at home on financial matters: "Mr. Ọlọkọ delivered the money you sent through him to me. I gave the head teacher at Oke-Igbo 5 shillings and he appreciated it. Congratulations on the birth of Dele's child [Mariam's granddaughter in Freetown, Sierra Leone, discussed in chapter 5]. . . . Your friend at Ẹgbẹda also paid me a visit and he gave Lamide [Abiọdun's daughter, who lived with Mariam—more details on Lamide later in this chapter] 2 shillings. Also, Mr. Ayọrinde [J. A. Ayọrinde, Abiọdun's old friend and schoolmate at Ibadan Grammar School and colleague in the Department of Agriculture] always visit me."[19] The social ties referenced in this letter reveal the intricate connection of the Vaughan natal family of *alájọbí* to their wider fictive kinship of *alájọgbé* in Ibadan and beyond.

The sources of material and moral support from Abiọdun to Mariam and, correspondingly, from the mother back to her son continued apace as Abiọdun assumed his postings in Abẹokuta, about forty-eight miles south of Ibadan; in Agege, Lagos; and in Enugu in Igboland from the late 1930s to the early 1950s. In some instances, Mariam utilized close relatives and friends as couriers of food items and other essential supplies. In one case, for example, she informed Abiọdun: "I would have sent chewing sticks and soap but your friend did not pay me a visit. I will send them through any available opportunity."[20]

In keeping with her meticulous attention to her son's business interest and affairs back home in Ibadan, Mariam responded to pressing economic concerns on his behalf. While Abiọdun was away in Enugu in the late 1940s, she reported on the status of a rented room in his new house in Race Course and other important developments concerning his nuclear family: "I received the message and money you sent. Concerning the rent, the house is under lock and key. . . . Also, about Lamide [Abiọdun's daughter], we got the tutor for her. Did you hear from your wife? I don't have her address. I would have written a letter to her."[21]

Earlier in June 1949, Mariam sent information about the cost of basic food items and critical materials for the completion of the construction of Abiọdun's house in Race Course. She wrote: "Elubọ now cost 15 pounds, 5 shillings. If you can afford it, let me know so that Ali can bring it on the 21st June when he is coming there. Concerning the roofing sheets, the price has come down significantly."[22] With Abiọdun struggling to complete the construction of this house on the land he had secured with S. A. Ọlọkọ's assistance in the mid-1930s (see chapter 1), Mariam served as the intermediary between her son and the building contractor, Makanjuọla, and provided critical information on his work while attending to other pressing family matters. "Concerning the building project, two rooms have been completed," she told Abiọdun. "Makanjuọla had collected 21 pounds 10 shillings and he bought two bundles of roofing sheet on 18th May, 1949. I hope your wife's health has greatly improved."[23]

A letter written the following month reiterates the special bond between Abiọdun and Mariam, suggesting interactions more deeply intricate when compared to Abiọdun's correspondence with other relatives. In this case, his mother wrote: "Makanjuọla said he would buy four roofing sheets. He said you asked him to collect money from the driver. . . . Your brother gave Ademọla's father the big parlour, he told him to move in by the end of this month and instructed him to pay 1 pound out of which he asked him to give me 5 shillings [every month] but I will write to tell him that I will collect 10 shillings."[24]

Mariam played a critical role in acquiring essential supplies for the completion of the house that Abiọdun had begun building in Race Course in the early 1940s. She helped him understand the costs associated with the construction project and updated him on the status of the house under construction. These interactions exhibit the deep trust between Abiọdun and Mariam not only as son and mother but also as business partners. Their relationship was mutually reinforcing, relying on the confidence they had in each other's ability to perform their roles. These letters vividly confirm that Mariam diligently carried out critical tasks for Abiọdun, who was now in his early forties, while he was pursuing his career in faraway Enugu.[25]

In October 1949 Mariam provided important information on the status of some close relatives: "Adeyẹmi was transferred to Abẹokuta. . . . All your effort and the money you spent on Adeyẹmi's wife will not be in vain." She then turned to news of the family house in Gbenla: "The wall collapsed and the estimate from the builders to rebuild it was too expensive. Makanju [Makanjuọla, the family contractor] therefore decided to build it himself. It is almost finished now." In closing, she informed him that "Mr Elijah in Itutaba helped Ibidun [Abiọdun's niece] to secure a job in Lagos."[26]

By the end of the year, Mariam had written to express her gratitude to Abiọdun for his financial support and inquire about his wife, Adukẹ, who was expecting their baby the following month after experiencing the loss of three infant children in succession (see also chapters 3 and 4). Mariam wrote: "Do you hear from your wife in Ileṣa? She will deliver safely. Amen."[27]

In response to her son's financial support for family members and the responsibilities he left back home in the late 1940s while in Enugu, Mariam frequently outlined the distribution of the money Abiọdun sent home and updated him on the status of business transactions with mentor and confidant S. A. Ọlọkọ (see chapter 3). In a November 1947 letter, she updated Abiọdun on the money for the upkeep of his daughter, Lamide, and the status of his house in Race Course: "I received your letter on the 13th of this month. Mr. Ọlọkọ delivered the money to me. I gave the tutor [Lamide's tutor] his own. I gave Lamide the money and I paid her school fees. Thank you very much. . . . I went to check the house at Race Course yesterday. The tenants are doing well. I heard that the man will soon be transferred to Lagos. So, write Mr. Ọlọkọ to get a new tenant to occupy the room as soon as possible. Please, thank your friend at Ẹgbẹda."[28] Wherever Abiọdun lived and worked from the 1930s to the 1950s, his responsibilities at home and ties with relatives and friends in Ibadan were sustained by his mother's conscientious work.

As always, Abiọdun's financial obligations toward members of his natal family abounded, especially with the rising needs of the next generation by the mid-1940s. Mariam was the moral voice that encouraged Abiọdun to lend support to these young family members. In one notable case, she wrote about her granddaughter Bisi Ọdẹbunmi, who was Jadesọla Ọdẹbunmi's daughter and Abiọdun's niece. Bisi, a graduate of Queen's College, Lagos, had recently traveled to Manchester, England, for her university education in September 1948. Mariam asked Abiọdun to lend financial support to Bisi and to other young relatives: "Bisi has travelled; send money to her. Also, send money to Jade, Nike, and myself. Dele's father [Bamidele Theo Brainerd's father, John Brainerd] sent 5 pounds to Bisi."[29]

When Samson Ọkẹowo, grandfather of Abiọdun's wife, died while Abiọdun was away in Enugu, Mariam informed her son of the small token she gave her in-laws: "When your grandfather-in-law died, I spent 2 shillings 6 pence to buy biscuits and soft drinks. I also bought kolanuts worth 2 shillings 6 pence for their aged mother. I gave 2 shillings 6 pence to your wife when she arrived. I also gave Abiade [Abiade Ọlọkọ, wife of S. A. Ọlọkọ and daughter of Samson Okeowo] 5 shillings 6 pence. Whatever you can afford, please send to Bisi's mother [his sister, Jadesola, to support Bisi]." Finally, she expressed dismay in the academic performance of two of her grandchildren.[30]

In the late 1940s and early 1950s, Mariam continued to update Abiọdun on important developments back home, including a legal case against Peter Ige (husband of a close relative, Adukẹ) and the departure of Bisi Ọdẹbunmi to England: "This is to inform you that Adukẹ's husband has been acquitted. The judge (Mr. Jibowu) ordered a fine of 20 pounds plus the lawyer's fee. He has resumed duty today, 2nd September, 1948 as a police officer. . . . Bisi will be travelling out of the country on 6th September, 1948. Send the money we discussed as soon as possible."[31]

The Mother and the Marriage Proposal

As we saw in the previous chapter and will observe in chapter 3, an important issue that dominated the duration of Abiọdun Vaughan's service at the Zaria office of the Department of Agriculture was his unsuccessful attempt to marry Ibironkẹ Alalade, a fellow Ọmọ Aremọ and teacher-training student from Oke-Ọfa from 1934 to 1935. While Abiọdun endured a frustrating correspondence with his older brother, Samuel Ariyibi, on this matter, he was having an encouraging dialogue with his mother on the same subject. As in the case of other pressing issues discussed above, such as responding to the serious health condition of his brother Oladunjoye, overseeing the construction of his house at Race Course, and managing financial remittances he sent home to support family members, Abiọdun's marriage proposal to Ibironkẹ Alalade also engaged Mariam's rapt attention. Finding a desirable partner for her son who would take her rightful place as a wife (*Ìyàwó*) in the Vaughan family was evidently a critical question for Mariam.

Mariam's letters on this matter reflected the intricate conversations that undergirded this critical dialogue between Ibironkẹ Alalade and Abiọdun and their families. Before the letters on Abiọdun's marriage proposal to Ibironkẹ appeared in any of the files, there was evidence from the letters contained in the Vaughan Family files that Mariam had been involved in a dialogue with Abiọdun on a possible love interest in November 1931, a month before his twenty-fourth birthday. "The food allowance you sent to me was delivered," she informed him before noting a complaint from a relative: "Ayọ Adebiyi complained that you are no longer writing to him since you have direct contact with the young lady. He said he would have informed you about the girl's character flaw (fighting). Her father is against this bad behavior because he knows you are an easygoing man."[32]

Evidence of Mariam's involvement in Abiọdun's marriage proposal to Ibironkẹ Alalade in the Vaughan Family files was first recorded in a letter Mariam wrote to Abiọdun a month after his arrival in Zaria in 1934. After informing Abiọdun that his brother Oladunjoye had been admitted to Adeọyọ Hospital, Mariam wrote: "The time given for Ibironkẹ is harvest time [to formally introduce the two families, in keeping with tradition]. They insisted that your brother at Kudẹti [Abiọdun's older first cousin Ayọ Vaughan] must be around. They said it is better done during the festive period when many people are back at home. Sorry for not sending gari. It is 5 pounds now. We bought ten 'congos' [a local unit of measurement]. The receipt is attached with this letter."[33]

A few months later, Mariam asked Abiọdun for an update on the marriage proposal while still providing an account of the foodstuffs she had sent to him and other important family matters: "Concerning your fiancée at Oke-Ọfa, let me know the state of the whole matter. I believed you received the foodstuff I sent to you. Write a letter to Mr. Ọlọkọ and ask him if he has good houses for sale at Ekotẹdo or Gbagi because many houses are being demolished in Ibadan now."[34] Several months later, Mariam showed more interest in the marriage proposal: "About the lady at Oke-Ọfa, I got all your messages about her. Make sure that you are keeping in touch with her. Did you know that she was sick? She's getting better. Your brother [Oladunjoye] who was sick and taken to Ijebu for treatment returned to Ibadan. He was later taken to Ido for treatment."[35]

Near the end of 1934, Mariam expressed apprehensions about her son's fiancée. As Abiọdun's mother and the family matriarch, Mariam had a moral obligation to render her considered opinion about her son's bride-to-be. In this instance, she acknowledged Ibironkẹ's presumed deficiencies, whatever they might be, but was measured in her judgment: "About the lady, I don't want to be too forward now until after the introduction.[36] My observation about her failure is not enough to stop the relationship. Those issues can be corrected. I am also praying about it. I want you to join me in prayer. God will have his way."[37]

Two weeks later, Mariam updated Abiọdun on her visit to his fiancée's mother and to St. Peter's Church, Aremọ, to discuss the marriage proposal with the vicar: "I received your letter about the young lady and the contents were well understood. I visited Ayọ, he said he received your letter. I also went to Aremọ. Everything has been discussed with her mother [Ibironkẹ's mother] and the Reverend. I also told them about the date you picked [for the introduction] and they all agreed." She concluded her letter with information about a parcel of food items: "Whenever I see any available opportunity to send gari and elubọ, I will do so. Inform your sister on whatever you are sending her and please be careful. Take care of yourself."[38] In January of the following year, Mariam updated Abiọdun on the visit of members of the Vaughan family to the family of his fiancée in Oke-Ọfa: "I am happy to inform you that we went to Ibironkẹ's house. She has been given to us. They welcomed us warmly. I tried my best and your siblings spent a lot of money. I pray that God gives you both a happy marriage. . . . Write a letter to Mama Aremọ, Nat's wife, and Nike to thank them for all they did."[39]

Despite this positive message, as we have seen in the previous chapter in the correspondence between Abiọdun and his brother Samuel Ariyibi, this marriage was not to be. A few months later, in another letter, Mariam updated her son on news from his fiancée's family: "I'm sorry for not writing you before now. Ibironkẹ's father told me that you would go to Lagos to seek permission to marry your wife but I denied you didn't say that. He informed me that you need to pay 5 pounds 'dowry' but I told him that I'm not aware of it. It is then, he said, it is a new requirement. Ibironkẹ also would be coming around in

June—I believe everything would have fallen into place before you come." This was the last mention from Mariam of Abiọdun's marriage proposal to Ibironkẹ Alalade in the Vaughan Family files.[40]

A Mother's Consolation

The mid- to late 1940s was a tumultuous time in the life of Abiọdun because he and his second wife, Gladys Adukẹ Vaughan, whom he married in 1944, experienced the loss of three infant children in quick succession from 1946 to 1949. (These losses are discussed in detail in chapter 4, which is based on the files Abiọdun labeled Gladys Adukẹ Vaughan.) Not surprisingly, Mariam's letters, through heartfelt condolences, reflected this tragic moment in the life of her son. Despite their somber tone, Mariam's letters continued to engage the quotidian matters in the Vaughan family. It would not be presumptuous to assume that Mariam, a native of Akoko who was already a grown woman by the time the British imposed their colonial rule in Ibadan in 1893, clearly experienced some of the grim consequences of the Yorùbá Wars, which lasted seventy years, and she must have observed recurring problems of infant mortality over her lifetime. These challenges naturally would have given her a unique perspective that her children would not have experienced by the mid-1940s. This is, of course, not to suggest that these tragic events were not troubling to her. Indeed, the sadness she expressed in her letters conveyed the seriousness of these tragic events.

In 1948 Mariam gave Abiọdun instructions on the health of Duro, Abiọdun and Adukẹ's third infant child, who later died in February 1949. She also thanked him for his gift to Mama Agodi (S. A. Ọlọkọ's mother, who lived in Agodi) and updated him on developments in the lives of relatives in Ibadan: "Thanks for your kind gesture towards Mama Agodi. Please pay attention to Duro's health. . . . Write a letter to greet Deji at Ekotẹdo because he had whitlow [a viral infection] three days after your wife's departure. . . . I am sad to inform you that Agbo's sickness relapsed and he was taken to Ijebu for treatment."[41]

In February 1949, after the death of Duro, Mariam wrote to her son to express her heartfelt condolences and offer prayers: "It is with great sadness that I received the news of the death of your child. I pray that God almighty will console you and your wife."[42] After updating Abiọdun on the progress of the construction of his house in March, she shared a prayer on the passing of Abiọdun's infant child: "Mr Ogunṣọla is doing a good job on the building project. I want to implore you not to be discouraged about Duro's death, God will console you."[43] In April she addressed Abiọdun and Adukẹ's concerns about the survival of future children: "Your friend, Akande, promised to write you a letter. Has he done so? He promised to help with herbs for your wife as soon as she conceives."[44] And in May she again expressed sadness over the loss of Duro: "I am writing this letter with sorrow in my heart. I have not been myself since I heard the death of your child. . . . Although I am here but believe me my mind is with you." She informed Abiọdun that she had requested a special prayer at St. Peter's Church, Aremọ, and conveyed the condolences of everyone at home: "I have forwarded a prayer request to the church that God should give you another child. Everyone here sympathizes with you."[45] As the family matriarch, Mariam carried the weight of her son's loss in the words she inscribed in these letters. The pain conveyed in these letters reiterates the importance of children as the beacon of hope and testament to the future. To have such hope ripped away repeatedly leads to deep sorrow.

Mariam Vaughan died in Ibadan in 1972 at about age 107. She was buried with her husband, Solomon Akintọla Vaughan, in the cemetery of St. Peter's Church, Aremo.

Jadesọla Juliana Ọdẹbunmi's Letters

Jadesọla Juliana Ọdẹbunmi, née Vaughan, was Abiọdun Vaughan's immediate older sibling. As in the case of their mother, Mariam, Jadesọla's letters to Abiọdun were contained in the files Abiọdun labeled Vaughan Family, with her letters ranging from the early 1930s to the late 1940s, the period when Abiọdun was stationed in Ibadan, Zaria, Enugu, Abẹokuta, and Lagos. Like others in the inner core of the family, Jadesola engaged the essential issues that affected family members during this period.

Jadesọla was married to Samuel Ọdẹbunmi, a CMS- educated Ibadan man and member of St. Peter's Church, Aremọ. In the 1930s, when Abiọdun started to compile the letters in the Vaughan Family files, Jadesọla and Samuel had three children of elementary school age. Their first child was Tunde, who attended Ibadan Grammar School in the 1940s and then studied law in England in the late 1950s and early 1960s. The second child was Bisi, who attended CMS Kudẹti Girls Secondary School, Ibadan; won a scholarship to Queens College, Lagos, colonial Nigeria's foremost secondary school for girls; and studied nursing administration at Manchester University Teaching Hospital, England, in the late 1940s and early 1950s. The youngest child, Moji, attended Kudẹti Girls School and then studied culinary arts in London in the late 1950s and the early 1960s.

Along with her mother, Mariam, and older sister, Dorcas Ọlayinka Brainerd, Jadesọla was one of the three matriarchs of the Vaughan family. While at various times brothers Samuel Ariyibi and Abiọdun were away on assignment in different parts of the Nigerian colonial provinces from the 1920s to the 1950s, these women held the family together in Ibadan, providing support for close family members, including their brothers' children whom they left behind in Ibadan as they attended to their careers in the colonial civil service.[46] Jadesọla also was a successful trader in fabrics and various consumer items.

The tone of her correspondence with her brother suggests that Jadesọla, like Mariam, had a close relationship with Abiọdun. Additionally, Jadesọla's correspondence with Abiọdun and my interview with Lamide Bakare, née Vaughan, Abiọdun's eldest child, born in 1938, indicate that Tunde, Jadesọla's son, was briefly a ward of Abiọdun before going on to boarding school at Ibadan Grammar School, his uncle's alma mater.[47] Jadesọla was known as Mama Alafara because she lived in the Alafara neighborhood in the core of the city.

Jadesọla's letters to her brother Abiọdun, like those of their mother, started when Abiọdun was transferred to the Zaria office of the Department of Agriculture in 1934. Many of Jadesọla's letters, like Mariam's, discussed the conditions in their natal family, reviewing family illnesses, setbacks, education, vocational training, and employment issues. Shortly after Abiọdun's departure for Zaria, Jadesọla—writing from Ile-Ifẹ, where her husband worked briefly for a European trading company, Paterson & Zochonis—lamented her delayed reply to her brother's letter: "I was not able to write on time because of the sickness of the children. They all had measles at the same time." As a caring Yorùbá elder sister, she admonished Abiọdun to "be careful about your interactions with the girls out there" in Zaria, Muslim Northern Nigeria.[48] In carbon copy replies to his sister, Abiọdun discussed his career and work situations in the Department of Agriculture, especially transfers and exams in the colonial civil service.

In November 1934 Jadesọla discussed her husband's recent transfer, her living conditions, and Abiọdun's transfer to Zaria. It is clear in the tone and substance of Jadesọla's letters that there was a special bond between the two siblings: "My Dear Brother, 'Biodun please bear with me, though you are younger but your character shows you are more mature than your age. We were transferred unexpectedly from Ile-Ife [to Ibadan]. Since then, I have not settled down. We got a rented place at Alafara. We will manage this until we finish building our own house."[49]

Like other important actors in the inner core of the Vaughan family, Jadesọla was aware of Abiọdun's marriage proposal to Ibironkẹ Alalade. She complained that Abiọdun had not kept her properly informed about his fiancée: "You did not tell me about the lady you are planning to marry." Jadesọla implored her brother to thank one Mrs. Adebiyi, who served as the "intermediary" (*alárenà*) between Abiọdun and the woman: "Write to Mrs. Adebiyi, she is the one that helped you so when both of you agree, it is good to carry her along." In her closing remark, Jadesọla was clearly the older sister looking out for her younger brother's wellbeing: "Remember the son of whom you are as you are living in a foreign land [Muslim Northern Nigeria]."[50]

While Abiọdun was working in Zaria, Abẹokuta, Enugu, and Lagos, Jadesọla, like her mother, Mariam, also served as family custodian, forwarding important information to her brother. She too wrote to inform him of their brother Oladunjoye's health and J. A. Ayọrinde's support for their family during this challenging time: "The sickness of Ladun has prevented me from writing, but he is better now. Mr. Ayọrinde supported us."[51] In another letter, Jadesọla told Abiọdun, "The doctor said the sickness of Ladun needs surgery. It has been done and it was successful."[52]

Back in Ibadan, Jadesọla's letters continued to revolve around the welfare of various members of the Vaughan family, her personal conditions, and those of her husband and children, as well as the special bonds between her and her younger brother. In May 1935 she wrote about her health challenges, expressed gratitude to her brother for his support, and admonished him to look after himself in Zaria: "Sorry for not replying on time, it was due to my sickness. All the money I have for business has been spent on my illness. Thanks to God that all the amount you spent was not wasted. God will continue to bless you. . . . Biodun, take care of yourself. Continue with your spirit of humility."[53] In another letter, Jadesọla, presumably because of their closeness in age, underscored the strong bond with her brother: "The issue between you and I is quite different from others. I want to tell you that you are more special to me than any other person, though we belong to God our creator." She then informed him that their older brother, Samuel Ariyibi, "sent 1 pound. May God bless him."[54]

At a moment of family crisis starting in mid-1935, Jadesọla bared her mind to her brother and confidant, Abiọdun. Her tone in these letters is reticent and sad. She expressed strong opposition to her husband's desire to take another wife: "I think Baba Tunde is having a relationship with another woman. . . . Anyway, I will stop him from marrying her."[55] She continued in the same letter: "I asked him to give me money and when he refused, I told him to give me out of the money he is owing me and that was when we had a fight. . . . You should have found out things from me before writing to him."[56] As Jadesọla's challenges persisted well into the following year, she continued to acknowledge her brother's support while reflecting on God's grace: "Thanks for your love and care throughout my trials. I committed everything into the hands of God and I believe he will make things work out for me very soon."[57]

In the late 1940s, with Abiọdun now back in the Yorùbá region and on tour in Abẹokuta, Jadesọla highlighted the academic progress and professional development of the next generation of the Vaughan family and requested financial support. She wrote about employment opportunities, educational advancement, and vocational training for a nephew and niece, Ladele and Ibidun: "Ladele spent one and a half weeks in hospital. He has started work anyway. My Dear Brother, I will need your assistance if Ibidun passed her examination at the end of January. The expenses of Christmas and new year, with the money I told you I am refunding has been the reason I am short on fund."[58] As the economic challenges persisted, several letters revealed that Jadesọla continued to reach out for her brother's financial support not simply for herself but also for the advancement of her nieces and nephews. An illustrious and accomplished trader in the 1940s and 1950s, Jadesọla wrote about the slowdown in her trading business and the need for relief in September 1949: "This time is tough, brother. There is no sales at all. The goods I received since July are still in stock. There is no money on hand at all. Please lend me 5 pounds 10 shillings by all means."[59]

Jadesọla's special relationship with Abiọdun was further reinforced by the important role her brother was playing in the life of her eldest child, Tunde, in the late 1940s and early 1950s, following his graduation from Ibadan Grammar School. During this time, Tunde lived briefly with his uncle Abiọdun, who continued to mentor him as a young man. "Thanks for all the care you are giving Tunde. Please don't relent on him," Jadesọla told Abiọdun. "Don't forget that he is the only male child I have. Please do all you can for me." When Abiọdun eventually got a long-awaited promotion as senior clerk in the Department of Agriculture, making him one of the highest-ranking Nigerians in this bureaucracy by the late colonial period, Jadesọla wrote, "We give the glory to God for the promotion you have in your place of work. May God continue to lift you higher." She then pleaded with him to pay close attention to Tunde: "Continue to counsel Tunde. You know all my effort on him."[60]

Information about notable events in the family was regularly transmitted from Jadesọla to Abiọdun in the late 1940s. When Jadesọla, while briefly in Lagos with her family, was robbed in October 1947, Abiọdun and his wife wrote to express their concern. To show her gratitude, Jadesọla replied, "I got your letter and that of your wife to sympathize with me when I was robbed in my house." To help reinforce her business as a trader as the Nigerian colonial economy suffered another downturn, Jadesọla informed Abiọdun of a loan she had secured from a relative: "Brother Deji has given me the 20 pounds and he said I should pay it back in four instalments." She then informed him that their nephew, Samuel Ariyibi's son Agboọla, who was having a challenging time after his studies at Abẹokuta Grammar School, had traveled to Lagos without anyone's consent.[61]

With family issues always at the center of their correspondence, Jadesọla informed her brother of the announcement of the engagement of their niece Ibidun in 1949. She noted her dissatisfaction with the marriage plans but was resigned to her niece's decision: "Ibidun said she will marry the man from Ikire. He has a wife already and she will be the second wife. I tried to convince her not to be a second wife, but it seems her mind is already with the man. I don't know him but we cannot force her to do what we want. May God lead her and be with her, if that is her choice."[62]

In early 1950 Jadesọla continued to apprise Abiọdun of the progress of the next generation of their natal family. Jadesọla called the financial burden of another niece's illness to her brother's attention: "Oyinlọla is sick, the bill is high, but she is better now." She also briefed him on another marriage proposal to their niece Ibidun, this time from a single man: "Concerning Ibidun, it is Elijah's son at Itutaba that wants to marry her. I have done some investigations about it. He is a good person and he is also doing well. . . . Ibidun has agreed to learn the trade of sewing. . . . I told the man not to rush their wedding. If she learns this trade, it will be for the benefit of both of them in the future."[63]

We will recall that Abiọdun's mother, Mariam Vaughan, shared several painful moments with her son on the passing of his infant child Duro in 1949. Not surprisingly, Jadesọla also acknowledged this tragic event during this time. Convinced that this recurrence of the loss of Abiọdun and his wife's infant children is a manifestation of *àbíkú*, a phenomenon pervasive in Yorùbá beliefs at the time, even among Western-educated Christians, Jadesọla wrote of Duro's death: "That will tell you that the child is a wicked child. With all the care given to him he died at last."[64] Writing further, she pleaded with her brother to console his wife, Adukẹ: "Please take heart and console your wife. She is a woman and the way she will react to it will be different from yours." Jadesọla's special relationship with her brother is reflected in this statement: "I would have come to console you, but you are far away from me. . . . God will provide the child that will live with us forever. . . . I am the one taking care of the two older women at home. The death of this child saddens me."[65] In another letter in early March, Jadesọla wrote again to sympathize with her brother: "It is painful that Duro died, that is not the end of life, your other children will care for you [in your old age]."[66] As she had done consistently, she concluded with this advice: "Please take care of yourself and remember you are in a foreign land." This time the "foreign land" was Enugu, in the Igbo heartland.[67]

After the passing of Abiọdun and Adukẹ's third infant, Jadesọla outlined strategies that close relatives and friends were exploring to respond to these tragic events. During Adukẹ's fourth pregnancy, Jadesọla wrote that J. A.

Ayọrinde (Abiọdun's best friend, schoolmate from Ibadan Grammar School, and colleague at the Department of Agriculture) would take Adukẹ to Ileṣa for special prenatal care: "I saw Mr. Ayọrinde. He told me that he has written you to send Adukẹ to him so they can take care of her in Ileṣa. . . . Rev I. C. [an Anglican clergyman] also said he will give us something about this issue of Abiku. If it is the will of God, it will work for our good." She concluded: "May God bless all the medication and prayers we are making towards what we want Adukẹ to have."[68]

In August 1949 Jadesọla continued to engage the crisis confronting Abiọdun and his wife on the survival of their infant children. She wrote to remind Abiọdun that he had yet to reply to her about Adukẹ's trip to Ileṣa to seek medical care that would help address the crisis. She continued to extend her good wishes and prayers: "You told me that Adukẹ will go to Ileṣa to meet Mr. Ayọrinde and since then you did not reply me. Whatever the case, May God continue to have mercy on us. May we not experience the death of a young child again."[69]

With Adukẹ in the eighth month of her fourth attempt to have a child in November 1949, Jadesọla wrote, "I pray for safe delivery for Ìyàwó ["wife"]. . . . I do not think I can go to Ileṣa now [to visit Adukẹ] because there is nobody to take care of the house as thieves are common now in Ibadan." She expressed dissatisfaction with a nephew and his wife who relocated to Lagos without informing older relatives: "I heard Deji and his wife are now in Lagos but his mother did not tell anybody."[70]

In the latter months of 1949, with Adukẹ's delivery fast approaching, Jadesọla told Abiọdun of an unspecified health problem that she had recently experienced. Alongside the anxiety that accompanied this unexpected ailment, Jadesọla informed her brother of the many relatives and friends in their Ibadan CMS network who, in the spirit of *alájọgbé*, came to her aid, providing financial assistance for the cost of her medical care: "We got assistance from many people but I want you to thank these people especially—Brother Bukuru gave us 5 pounds, Ladele Ọlọkọ gave us 1 pound, Rev Akingbehin gave us 2 pounds. . . . Sister and her husband also tried," she wrote, referring to Dorcas Ọlayinka and John Brainerd. She concluded by reassuring Abiọdun, "Be at rest with my sickness. I am now getting over it."[71]

In the late 1940s, Jadesọla also discussed the maintenance of the Vaughan natal family house in Gbenla, a contentious issue we discussed briefly in Abiọdun's correspondence with his mother, Mariam, earlier in this chapter, and his brother Samuel Ariyibi in chapter 1. Jadesọla reported, "I hope mama has informed you about the fence built at the back of the house at Gbenla."

She concluded the same letter with the good news that her older daughter "Bisi started work on 5th February."[72]

We will recall in the correspondence between Abiọdun and Samuel Ariyibi in the previous chapter that contentious family matters, alongside personal temperaments, had strained the brothers' relationship by 1940, when their correspondence came to an abrupt end. In a letter a decade later, in August 1951, Jadesọla called attention to the ongoing feud between the brothers and played peacemaker: "Please settle the problem between you and Brother [Samuel Ariyibi] once and for all. If he does not answer you, let me know when you come back so I can also go and see him as well." She briefed Abiọdun on her lingering health problem: "If you collect the medicine, please bring it when you are coming home. I am still having stomach pain."[73]

Similar to the letters of her mother, Mariam, and older brother Samuel Ariyibi, Jadesọla's letters engaged extraneous issues that were not directly connected to the major themes that typically dominated the lives of Vaughan family members. These issues were nevertheless relevant to the relationship between the two siblings because they reveal the intimacy between Jadesọla and Abiọdun. In one noteworthy case, Jadesọla informed her brother of a treatment someone gave her when she was ill: "I was given a concoction to drink. Since then, I have been unable to sleep at night. The medicine has made me thinner and if care is not taken, one can die."[74] In another instance, Jadesọla informed Abiọdun about her excitement over the planned visit of a close relative, Baba Bukuru, to Lagos. She went on to tell him that she would not inform their brother Samuel Ariyibi, who now resided permanently in Lagos, "because he may say why should you hear of this before him. . . . Take care of yourself and be punctual at your place of work."[75] There was something special about Jadesọla and Abiọdun's relationship that reflected deep care and mutual respect. Sometimes Jadesọla came across as an older sister who gave counsel to a younger brother, but at other times she revealed her vulnerability, soliciting Abiọdun's support and advice.

Jadesola Juliana Odebunmi died in Ibadan in 1996 at age ninety-four. She was buried in the cemetery of St. Peter's Church, Aremo.

Dorcas Ọlayinka Brainerd's Letters

Dorcas Ọlayinka Brainerd was the elder of Abiọdun's two older sisters. She was affectionately known as Mama UCH, for University College Hospital, Ibadan, the teaching hospital established by the colonial authorities during decolonization, where she worked as matron for indigent mothers and children in the latter part of her life in the 1950s and 1960s. There was a significant age gap of thirteen years between her and Abiọdun. Lamide Bakare, Abiọdun's eldest child, informed me that Dorcas Ọlayinka, a disciplinarian of sorts, was more of a maternal guardian to Abiọdun while he was a student at the CMS elementary school and the CMS secondary school, Ibadan Grammar School.[76]

Like many of the more talented young Ibadan CMS members with links to St. Peter's Church, Dorcas Ọlayinka had her elementary school education at the CMS parish school at Kudẹti in Ibadan and then attended CMS Girls Seminary School. As discussed earlier, Dorcas Ọlayinka married a Sierra Leonean Anglican man, John Brainerd, who came to Nigeria at the beginning of the twentieth century to work in various clerical and administrative capacities for the colonial railway system. This system linked the vast regions of the northern and southern Nigerian provinces together when the Lagos Government Railway and the Baro-Kano Railway were amalgamated in 1912.[77] Dorcas Ọlayinka and John had one child, Bamidele Theo Brainerd. The correspondence between Abiọdun and Bamidele, along with Bamidele's wife and children, is the subject of chapter 5.

Like the letters of her mother, Mariam, and sister Jadesọla, Dorcas Ọlayinka's letters dealt with the quotidian issues of the Vaughan natal family life, starting when Abiọdun took up his appointment at the Zaria office of the Department of Agriculture in 1934 and ending with his last major posting back at the head office in Moor Plantation, Ibadan, in the early 1950s. Dorcas Ọlayinka's letters also briefly discussed vicissitudes such as the loss of Abiọdun and Adukẹ's infant children, also encountered in the letters of the two other Vaughan matriarchs. Unlike those of Mariam and Jadesọla, however, Dorcas Ọlayinka's letters were somewhat detached in tone and matter-of-fact.[78] Her maternal feelings toward Abiọdun, however, were expressed in reaction to a serious eye infection that her brother called to her attention a year after his arrival in Zaria: "Sorry about your eyes. Make sure you don't use herbs on it because the eye is a very sensitive part of the body."[79] The following month, Dorcas Ọlayinka acknowledged her brother's material support for her and a niece: "Nike's trip was successful and I saw all what you sent to me. The 2 pounds and the gold. I appreciate them all. I was even surprised to see what Baba gave Nike. I am grateful."[80]

While Abiọdun was away in Zaria, Bamidele Theo Brainerd, Dorcas Ọlayinka's only child and her pride and joy, had landmark academic accomplishments, which his mother proudly shared with Abiọdun. In May 1935, one year into Abiọdun's service in Zaria, Dorcas Ọlayinka informed him of Bamidele's success at Igbobi College, Lagos, one of Nigeria's leading secondary schools, which was noted in Nigeria's foremost national newspaper: "Dele did excellently well in his junior Cambridge Examination which I believe you might have seen in the *Daily Times*."[81] A few months later, after Bamidele returned from vacation with his uncle in Zaria, Dorcas Ọlayinka thanked Abiọdun for "spending [money] when Dele came to you. At the same time, I thank your two friends. . . . Thank you for the eggs you sent to me. May God bless you." With Bamidele's senior Cambridge examination fast approaching, his mother wrote the following year, "It's quite painful when I heard about the money you lost, but then I still give thanks to God for he knows everything. . . . On the issue of Dele, which we discussed, the time is so close. 3rd December is the examination."[82]

Several years later, in September 1940, when Dorcas Ọlayinka fell on hard times, she sought help from the brother to whom she gave so much when he was a young man: "I would not have come to you and I don't want to disrupt other responsibilities you have, but I need 5 pounds to buy the drug." She concluded with a prayer for Bamidele on an unspecified matter: "God will touch Dele so that he will listen to what his Dad wants to tell him."[83]

Bamidele graduated from Igbobi College with distinction, went on to graduate from the University of Sierra Leone, took up a civil service position in the Sierra Leonean colonial government, and married a Sierra Leonean woman, Viola, in 1947. "I thank you for the telephone call I received on the day of Dele's wedding," Dorcas Ọlayinka wrote to Abiọdun shortly thereafter. "I am happy to say that I received the caftan. Viola proved good and chaste. May God grant them success in their marriage." In closing, she asked about Abiọdun's wife: "Hope Gladys [Adukẹ] is doing fine?"[84]

Dorcas Ọlayinka's letters, like those of Mariam, Samuel Ariyibi, and Jadesọla, unsurprisingly, discussed their brother Oladunjoye's serious health problems. In December 1934 Dorcas Ọlayinka penned her first letter to Abiọdun about the challenging medical condition faced by her younger brother Oladunjoye: "I got your letter. I would have replied but I know you would have heard about Ladun's admission to the hospital at Adeọyọ."[85] As Oladunjoye's health deteriorated the following year, Dorcas Ọlayinka informed Abiọdun: "Concerning Ladun, there is nothing we can do. I don't want the trouble to be too much on the people in Aremọ. They all did well on their visit to Adeọyọ [Hospital]. . . . For four days, Ladun could not recognize anyone. They said it was something that was worrying him to the extent that they want to perform surgery on him."[86] Two days later, she sent another report on Oladunjoye's health, this time to underscore the help provided by J. A. Ayọrinde, Abiọdun's boyhood friend: "Write to appreciate Ayọrinde for Ladun. He went to Adeọyọ Hospital again to see him."[87] Later in the year, in October, Dorcas Ọlayinka expressed her anxieties over Oladunjoye's surgery and her dependence on God: "May God make the surgery a success."[88] In April 1941, while Abiọdun was away on assignment in Abẹokuta and Dorcas Ọlayinka was on official duty in

Jebba, in the southern region of the Northern Provinces, Oladunjoye succumbed to his illness. "I would have replied the letter but each time I want to do it, tears rolled down my face," Dorcas Ọlayinka wrote. "That is why I could not do anything but now I have accepted my fate." She asked Abiọdun to encourage his wife to attend to their mother: "Please take care of Mama. Tell Bọlaji to go and stay with her for some time."[89]

The saga over Abiọdun's proposal of marriage to Ibironkẹ Alalade, amply discussed in Abiọdun's correspondence with his mother, Mariam, and two other siblings, Samuel Ariyibi and Jadesọla (and briefly with S. A. Ọlọkọ in chapter 3), was also discussed in Abiọdun's correspondence with Dorcas Ọlayinka. A few months into his tenure in Zaria, Dorcas Ọlayinka wrote: "Concerning Ibironkẹ. . . . Though her mother is ready to support her, even when the issue of fight in the church came up, the mother of the child that engaged in the fight was ready to go to court without even informing the vicar. . . . Abiọdun, I am so surprised that after all these, she refused to inform me."[90] When the marriage proposal collapsed later in 1934, Dorcas Ọlayinka wrote: "Mama and the rest of us have taken it off our mind and you too should do the same because you still have a lot of good things ahead."[91]

A year after the unsuccessful marriage proposal to Ibironkẹ Alalade, Dorcas Ọlayinka was involved in an unsuccessful attempt to secure the hand of an unspecified woman in marriage to her younger brother (also briefly discussed in Abiọdun's correspondence with his mother and brother). Dorcas Ọlayinka wrote: "I have been the one going from one place to another. . . . I have been making enquiry on this girl, though I don't know her but those who know her are saying good things about her."[92]

As revealed in the other letters analyzed from the Vaughan Family files, Dorcas Ọlayinka's letters also acknowledged the critical role Abiọdun played in providing financial support to meet the essential needs of family members. When Abiọdun sent a gift of money to Dorcas Ọlayinka in December 1934, she wrote to express her gratitude on New Year's Day of 1935: "I got the letter you wrote to collect money from Mr. Laleye. He gave me the money. Thank you very much. May you also eat the fruit of your labor, Amen."[93] When an elderly relative died in Lagos in July 1937, Dorcas Ọlayinka not only wrote to share the news but also requested financial help so she could meet the obligation associated with the celebration of life of an elderly relative: "It is with regret I am telling you about the death of our cousin, F. T. Vaughan of breadfruit Street. The expenses will be too much for me. If there is any amount you wish to provide, please do so."[94] In 1938 Dorcas Ọlayinka wrote to thank her brother for "all the provisions you sent to me and I use them accordingly. I am now healthy."[95] Similarly, in another letter almost seven years later, Dorcas

Ọlayinka thanked Abiọdun "for the drug you sent to me. May the Lord continue to bless you, Amen. . . . My food can digest properly and there is improvement now."[96]

The tension that we saw in the correspondence between Abiọdun and his older brother Samuel Ariyibi in the S. A. Vaughan files and expressed intermittently in Mariam's letters took center stage in Dorcas Ọlayinka's correspondence with Abiọdun. In one instance while Abiọdun was in Zaria in 1934, Dorcas Ọlayinka updated him on a contested family property with Samuel Ariyibi: "I got your letter on the issue of Brother [Samuel Ariyibi]. I am happy that he eventually surrendered our house to us and we have collected our money as well. The lawyer has intervened, but we are trying all we can so that it would not become a court case, provided he hand over the remaining money."[97] The following month, she wrote to Abiọdun to inquire about the outcome of his correspondence with Samuel Ariyibi and inform him about their brother's new house in Yaba: "How is your discussion with Brother on the house in Gbenla? I discovered that he has a house in Yaba and is planning to have another one in Eko [Lagos Island]. Please keep this a secret between us."[98]

In another letter at the end of the year, Dorcas Ọlayinka expressed disappointment with Samuel Ariyibi's treatment of their mother, Mariam, which Mariam had discussed with Abiọdun (see their letters earlier in this chapter) and Abiọdun had discussed with Samuel Ariyibi (see chapter 1). "The most painful thing I want to tell you is that Brother did not give Mama money for food," Dorcas Ọlayinka wrote to Abiọdun. "His wife was the one that sent money to Mama. Imagine. What can someone's mother do that would warrant such treatment?"[99] The following year, Dorcas Ọlayinka's antipathy for Samuel Ariyibi's position continued in this reply to Abiọdun: "I was angry when I read the letter you wrote. . . . Biodun, could you believe that I did not eat anything when I went to Lagos. He only dropped money two times for all the period I spent there. . . . I have heard all what you said about the land you intend to build your house but Brother said you should stop it. Please don't discuss everything with Sammy [Samuel Ariyibi]."[100] Dorcas Ọlayinka's final letter about her disagreement with Samuel Ariyibi appeared in the Vaughan Family files twelve years later, in 1947. It reads in part: "I was called by my brother but it was quite unfortunate that I am not satisfied with the reason he sent for me. He wanted to buy a house which is too costly. The house is between 4,000 to 4,500 pounds but he wanted to price it for 900 pounds. Before I got to Lagos, he has made advance payment of 500 pounds."[101]

One distinctive 1937 letter in which Dorcas Ọlayinka reprimanded Abiọdun confirmed her reputation as a no-nonsense disciplinarian among the Vaughan matriarchs. Regarding an indiscretion from her younger brother, Dorcas Ọlayinka wrote: "I thought you are responsible and wise but you are not. I was informed you came to town and you did not stop at home to see your mother, elderly, and younger ones. This is your usual habit. I want you to know that bad company corrupt good manners. Remember that you have a wife and you know the condition she is in [pregnant]."[102]

While Abiọdun was on tour in Abẹokuta in the late 1940s, Dorcas Ọlayinka underscored pressing family matters. In one instance, she reminded him of the renovation of their natal house in Gbenla: "We are to balance two carpenters 200 pounds but the remaining money with me is 162 pounds. Please let us plan on how to balance them. If not that Dele is going back, he would have helped you out. All I know is that there is God." She then informed him of their mother's recovery: "I am happy to tell you that Mama is doing well now and so thanks be to God." Finally, she notified him of her own health challenges: "I have to see the doctor for my health. . . . I ought to write more than this but I am very weak."[103] A few months later, Dorcas Ọlayinka informed Abiọdun that she had paid off her debt to a close relative and that their niece had had a baby: "Ebun has given birth to a baby boy on the 1st of November. May God protect the baby."[104]

Dorcas Olayinka Brainerd died in Ibadan in 1973 at age seventy-nine. She was buried in the cemetery of St. Peter's Church, Aremo.

Dorcas Bọlaji Ajibose-Vaughan's Letters

Dorcas Bọlaji married Abiọdun Vaughan in 1937. They were married for six years, from 1937 to 1943, and had a daughter, Olamide (Lamide), in 1938. During much of their marriage, Abiọdun was away working at the Abẹokuta office of the Department of Agriculture while Dorcas lived for some time with Mariam, Abiọdun's mother, in the Vaughan natal house in Gbenla. From a careful review of the letters contained in this section of the files, I arrived at the conclusion that the story line of Dorcas's marriage to Abiọdun, documented in Dorcas's letters and Abiọdun's carbon copy replies, revolved around her relationship with the three matriarchs in the Vaughan natal family; her experience living in the Vaughan family house; her two pregnancies, with the second leading to the birth of Lamide; care for Lamide; and health challenges she experienced in her last year of marriage to Abiọdun. As in most of the letters analyzed in this chapter, the letters in this section of the Vaughan Family files were translated from Yorùbá to English.

Abiọdun met Dorcas, a kind and gentle Ẹgba-Yorùbá woman with some formal Western education, while he was working out of the Abẹokuta office of the Department of Agriculture in 1937. Dorcas's letters open with her status as a new wife to Abiọdun and, by extension, as a "wife" in the Vaughan natal family. With her husband stationed in Abẹokuta, Dorcas wrote to update him on her health and acknowledge the support of Abiọdun's close relatives following her move to Gbenla. In her first notable letter to Abiọdun, Dorcas, who was pregnant when she arrived in the Vaughan natal house, expressed gratitude to family leaders, most of them the Vaughan matriarchs, for their kindness and generosity: "When I got to Ibadan, Mama Agba ["the senior mother," Mariam] took care of me in all areas concerning my pregnancy. Mama Ekotẹdo ["the mother who lives in Ekotẹdo," sister Dorcas Ọlayinka] visited me every day."[105] In another letter written later in the month, Dorcas reported, "I want you to thank Mama Alafara ["the mother who lives in Alafara," sister Jadesọla], Baba Alekuro, Mama Ekotẹdo [sister Dorcas Ọlayinka], Mama Agba [mother Mariam], your friend at Oranyan and others for their kindness during my sickness. May God bless them all. I am happy to tell you that I am okay now."[106] Unfortunately, Dorcas lost the pregnancy by the end of the year.[107]

The next round of correspondence between Dorcas and Abiọdun did not occur for another year because Abiọdun returned to Ibadan to work briefly in Moor Plantation from the end of 1937 to the end of 1938. The resumption of the letters in September 1938 coincided with Abiọdun's return to the branch office of the Department of Agriculture in Abẹokuta. The first letter was from Abiọdun to Dorcas (a carbon copy appears in the Vaughan Family files). In it, Abiọdun discussed a medical prescription for Dorcas during the pregnancy that ultimately led to the birth of their daughter, Lamide, in November 1938: "I sent a drug to you to be used every day. It is carefully packaged in 6 places; use them as prescribed. Prescription: Take one and divide it into four, then take it, the first early in the morning before food, it continues like that until everything is finished at twenty-four times."[108] Writing from Ibara Omiọla, in the Ẹgba-Yorùbá region, Dorcas replied incisively: "I want to inform you that I am taking my drug regularly and I am fine now, except for the cold."[109] The following week, Dorcas wrote to remind Abiọdun to attend to some essential needs: "I expect you to send money for mattress and some other things to me; send them through your friend."[110]

As Dorcas prepared to deliver her child, Abiọdun, despite his CMS Anglican upbringing, made reference to what appears to be a prenatal Yorùbá traditional religious practice: "I have discussed with Mr. Alabi that we shall come home on 15th October. I don't want to come twice because of the cost of transportation. . . . You might give birth at the end of October. Remove the beads from your waist at the end of October. . . . I hope you are using the drug I sent?"[111] A week after Abiọdun's letter of instructions, he wrote: "I pray you will deliver safely and that God will keep the child for us."[112] In the weeks before her delivery, Dorcas wrote Abiọdun a flurry of letters, requesting supplies of essential items ranging from clothing to medication, and she provided updates on her health: "Please when are you coming. . . . [D]on't forget to send the soap you promised. I have used all the ones at home."[113] A few days later, she wrote: "You need to see how big my pregnancy is now; please don't forget the sweater because it is so cold here. Thank you for your love," and again, in the following week, she reminded him: "Please don't forget the sweater you mentioned and the money you promised to give me."[114]

With Dorcas's due date around the corner, Abiọdun anxiously awaited the arrival of his first child. He wrote to check on Dorcas's health and pray for the safe delivery of their baby: "I did not hear from you. Hope all is well? Anyway, everybody is fine here too. I thought you will deliver your baby in October. Anyway, no problem, the baby will be delivered successfully, Amen. Just let me know when it's time; I am getting ready."[115] A week later, Dorcas gave birth to a girl, Ọlamide (Lamide). Following the receipt of a telegraph announcing the arrival of the baby, Abiọdun's carbon copy letter inserted in the Vaughan Family files congratulated Dorcas and expressed joy and excitement at this special news: "Congratulations on your safe delivery. May God continue to bless the baby and bless us too. I was so happy when I received the message. My friends and I started rejoicing over the special gift God has given us. I will be coming home in two weeks with some of my friends."[116] For her part, Dorcas wrote to inform Abiọdun: "Congratulations, I have delivered safely. The labor was too painful because the baby was so big. . . . When you are coming, make sure you buy things to take care of our baby."[117]

A letter in the Vaughan Family files indicated an anxious moment in the condition of the newborn as Dorcas got postnatal care with the help of the family matriarch, Abiọdun's mother, Mariam. On November 29, only two weeks after the delivery of the baby, Dorcas wrote Abiọdun of Lamide's challenging health condition while again requesting essential supplies: "What I am facing concerning your child's health did not allow me to see your letter. The sickness got worse. She was coughing repeatedly, but recently she is getting better. . . . Ensure you send something to us quickly."[118] Abiọdun arrived a few days later to meet his baby daughter. When he returned to Abẹokuta in early December, he instructed Dorcas: "Please I want you to write me two or three times a week so that I will be assured that you are in good health."[119] Lamide resided in the Vaughan family home in Gbenla while her father continued to work in Abẹokuta.

There was no more correspondence between Dorcas and Abiọdun in the Vaughan Family files until a few letters surfaced in early 1943 and one final letter from Dorcas in August 1944.[120] In February 1943 Dorcas experienced what appeared to be a serious illness while she was in Abẹokuta: "Concerning my health, I am getting better after taking the drugs including the ones in my brother's place. So let your mind be at peace."[121] The following month, she wrote, "I want to inform you that my sickness is getting worse. . . . Please pray for divine healing. Pray that I will see my child in peace."[122] Writing from Karo Division, Northern Provinces, the following month, Dorcas expressed concern over the severity of her illness: "The reason I write you again is that I want you to bring my child to me. This ailment is so terrible that it can take away my life. Please bring my child to see me."[123] A final letter in August 1944 reveals that Dorcas was back with her family in Abẹokuta.[124] The couple were divorced in 1943. Dorcas Bolaji Ajibose-Vaughan died in 1976 at age sixty. She was buried in the cemetery of St. Peter's Church, Aremo.

Ancillary Correspondence from the Vaughan Natal Family

Many scattered letters from several voices in the Vaughan natal family, including those of Abiọdun's older brother Oladunjoye and younger family members, were also contained in the Vaughan Family files from the 1930s to the 1950s. Many of these letter writers benefited from remittances Abiọdun sent to older family members, especially his mother, Mariam, who distributed the funds to meet their essential needs. Through their letters, they, like the three matriarchs, stayed connected to Abiọdun while he was attending to his professional duties in various offices of the Department of Agriculture. On their own, they sought financial support from Abiọdun, kept him informed about developments at home, and ran important errands for him while he was away from Ibadan.

Abiọdun's older brother Oladunjoye, who had severe health challenges that led to his untimely death in 1941, wrote several letters while Abiọdun was in Zaria from 1934 to 1935. In January 1935, after the illness that resulted in his surgery at Adeọyọ Hospital (discussed in Abiọdun's correspondence with his mother and sisters above), Oladunjoye wrote to thank his younger brother for his financial support.[125] Oladunjoye was also an important source of vital information for his brother while he was away in Zaria. For example, in August 1935 Oladunjoye informed Abiọdun of the death of their infant nephew: "I want to inform you that Ìyàwó [probably Samuel Ariyibi's wife] lost the baby she gave birth to on 2nd June, 1935. May God console her. Amen."[126]

From the 1930s to the 1950s many Vaughan family members from the next generation sent good wishes, requested essential items, shared important information, and sent condolences. For example, Bamidele Theo Brainerd (while a student at Igbobi College, Lagos), Agboọla Vaughan (at Abẹokuta Grammar

School), Tunde Ọdẹbunmi (at Ibadan Grammar School), and his sister Bisi Ọdẹbunmi (at Queens College, Lagos) wrote their uncle many letters during this period to discuss a variety of personal and family matters. Specifically, in August 1934 Kehinde Vaughan, a niece, wrote to her uncle Abiọdun: "I am happy to write this letter to you. Hope you are fine and everyone at home? Adukẹ and Akin [Abiọdun's niece and nephew] send their greetings to you."[127] Another niece, Ẹbun, wrote to ask after Abiọdun: "Hope your work is moving on smoothly? May God continue to grant you promotion in your work."[128] Yet another relative, Adeoti, reminded Abiọdun to bring herbs when he returned home to Ibadan from Abẹokuta: "Concerning the herbs, please don't forget to buy them for me."[129] In April 1943, while Abiọdun was working in Abẹokuta, a relative named Adenikẹ thanked him for supporting her child and apologized for an unspecified disagreement: "I thank you for caring for my child. May God keep your own too. . . . I want to apologize for everything that happened. Please tell Mama [Abiọdun's mother, Mariam] not to be upset with me."[130]

In February 1949, when Abiọdun and Gladys Adukẹ lost their third infant, Duro, heartfelt condolences and expressions of grief poured in from these younger Vaughan family members. Adukẹ Ige, a relative, wrote: "I just heard about the death of your child after my arrival from Akure. It saddens me but take heart and console your wife. God will give you another child. Amen."[131] Abiọdun's nephew Akinola Vaughan sent condolences: "I was very sad when I heard about the death of our younger brother [cousin]. Please encourage yourself and your wife. God will give you another child. Amen."[132]

Last but certainly not least, Abiọdun's nine-year-old daughter, Lamide, in December 1947 expressed gratitude: "My Dear Daddy, Thank you very much for the money you sent to me."[133]

~

From a critical analysis of the letters that shaped major story lines in the Vaughan Family files, it is evident that the three matriarchs nurtured a moral order that sustained the tightknit Vaughan natal family, firmly connecting three generations in Ibadan from the 1930s to the 1950s. As the elderly matriarch, Abiọdun's mother, Mariam, through major issues consistently discussed in her letters, accounted for both the material resources and the moral framework needed to sustain family members at a time of dramatic social change in colonial Nigeria. As diverse communities evolved into southern and northern Nigerian colonial provinces by the 1930s, the network that Mariam coordinated connected an expanding social world in which Abiọdun and other members of the Vaughan family were destined to navigate. At the epicenter of the Vaughan family, Mariam kept Abiọdun, away on professional duties in various branches of the colonial Department of Agriculture, mindful of vital issues that connected him to his home in Ibadan: his responsibility to provide regular financial remittances to meet pressing needs of family members; his moral obligation to contribute to the maintenance of the natal family house in Gbenla; and his need to be attentive to a complicated marriage negotiation with prospective in-laws. Equally important, Mariam lent support to the construction and maintenance of Abiọdun's house in Race Course while providing maternal comfort for her son in a moment of grief and loss.

It is notable that the matriarchs were in varying degrees deeply invested in Abiọdun's unsuccessful attempt to marry Ibironkẹ Alalade while he was away in Zaria in 1934 and 1935. Their insightful letters reiterated their investment in Abiọdun's personal life, potentially through a marriage to a socially desirable Omo Aremọ. Unlike Samuel Ariyibi, these women as optimists observed traditional protocols of interaction with Abiọdun's potential in-laws, especially through dialogues with key figures in Ibironkẹ Alalade's family. Similarly, during Abiọdun's tours of duty in Abẹokuta, Lagos, and Enugu, the Vaughan matriarchs in the tumultuous 1940s, especially Mariam, were primarily responsible for the care of Abiọdun's child, Lamide, along with other grandchildren in their natal home in Ibadan. Moreover, these women were at least initially important sources of support for Abiọdun's first wife, Dorcas, during their marriage from 1937 to 1943. Finally, when Abiọdun and his second wife, Gladys Adukẹ, experienced the tragic loss of their infant children in the late 1940s, these Vaughan matriarchs were important sources of comfort and advice.

It is apparent that Abiọdun's relationship with his two older sisters, though intimate and trusting, still differed in terms of their style, tone, and purpose, reflecting the siblings' proximity in age, personalities, and childhood interactions. Abiọdun's oldest sister, Dorcas Ọlayinka, perhaps because of the maternal role she was credited with playing when he was a student at St. David's Primary School, Kudẹti, and Ibadan Grammar School, exuded through her letters Yorùbá maternal authority. Though different in temperament and tone, Abiọdun's relationship with Dorcas Ọlayinka is reminiscent of his relationship with his older brother Samuel Ariyibi, who performed a similar role during the adolescent phase of Abiọdun's life. Consequently, Dorcas Ọlayinka's letters are at once commanding, admonishing, and cajoling. Conversely, the letters of Jadesọla Juliana, Abiọdun's immediate older sibling, reflect a different type of sibling relationship. In both tone and substance, Jadesọla's letters are reassuring, collaborative, intimate, and respectful. Her letters, like Mariam's and

Dorcas Ọlayinka's letters, provided concrete solutions to pressing problems, such as the loss of Abiọdun and Adukẹ's infant children, and solicited financial support to meet the essential needs of family members.

In short, these special relationships between Abiọdun and the Vaughan matriarchs defined the foundations on which the structure of the Vaughan natal family was ultimately consolidated. They were sustained not simply by Yorùbá custom, norms, and tradition but also by concrete material conditions that advanced the personal and corporate interests of members of the Vaughan family. Through the medium of letter writing at a moment of great socioeconomic transformation in colonial southern Nigeria, these relationships existed at the intersection of tradition and modernity, defining the moral essence of *alájọbí*.

CHAPTER THREE

Ibadan CMS Men

Kinship and Yorùbá Civic Life

THE LETTERS CONTAINED IN THE FILES Abiọdun Alfred Vaughan labeled S. A. Ọlọkọ, unlike the letters discussed in other chapters in this book, are not from Abiọdun Vaughan's direct relatives or in-laws. Instead, they are from Abiọdun's mentor and "cousin," S. A. Ọlọkọ, as well as other friends and associates in a network of Ibadan Christian-educated men. However, these letters underscore Yorùbá kinship bonds, Christian social orientation, and aspirations for social mobility, dominant issues in other chapters in this book.

Consistent themes in the letters contained in the S. A. Ọlọkọ files include information and strategies through which this group of local men, most of them graduates of CMS secondary schools in the region (notably, Ibadan Grammar School, CMS Grammar School in Lagos, Abẹokuta Grammar School, and Ijẹbu Ode Grammar School, as well as a teacher training school, St. Andrew's College, Ọyọ), advanced their pioneering careers in an emerging Yorùbá colonial society. While some worked as schoolteachers, the majority were clerks and junior administrative officers in the Department of Agriculture or in European trading companies. As many of these young men served in far-flung areas of colonial Nigeria, their letters reveal the strong bonds among them. Finally, the correspondence indicates that the letter writers were members of two local civic groups, the Ibadan Brotherhood Fund Association and the Ibadan Cooperative Savings Society, that connected the economic interests and professional advancement of their members with those of the civic progress of the local community.

Recurring themes in the files revolve around social mobility, job security, and the perspective of the principal letter writer, Ọlọkọ, who served as a mentor to a group of men of similar social experience, including Abiọdun. The letters also underscore the important civic values of the writers and many of the men who were referenced as members of this small social network. In these files, the letter writers are constantly searching for and working toward professional advancement in the Department of Agriculture, other colonial bureaucracies, educational institutions, and European trading companies.

Since these Ibadan CMS men served as junior civil servants throughout colonial northern and southern Nigeria, their letters reveal a sense of displacement as they navigated alien social landscapes in Nigeria's heterogeneous society. For example, they felt anxious about professional opportunities and advancement in the Department of Agriculture, and because of this, they checked in regularly with Abiọdun and Ọlọkọ to discuss their concerns and explore viable solutions to their problems. Accordingly, the letters reveal how sustained connection with the network through letter writing was beneficial to these men. Affirming Akiwọwọ's concept of *alájọbí-alájọgbé* in a dynamic Yorùbá colonial society, the letters analyzed in this chapter show how these civic and mutual aid groups provided the institutional node for collective social action that enhanced the lives of these men as compatriots.

It is notable that although these men claimed Ibadan as their hometown, many of them did not have firm roots in the city. In many instances, their parents or they themselves arrived in Ibadan as children in the late nineteenth century or at the turn of the twentieth century. By this time, the city was a critical destination for many refugees and immigrants from the consequences of the final stage of the seven-decade-long Yorùbá Wars, following the fall of the Old Ọyọ Empire in 1836.[1] For example, as noted earlier, Abiọdun traced his family's origin on his father's side to the Ẹgba-Yorùbá town of Oke-Ọna, near Abẹokuta, itself a town that was the direct product of these wars, and on his mother's side to Akungba-Akoko, an Ondo-Yorùbá town about 210 miles northeast of Ibadan.[2] His mother arrived as a young woman in Ibadan, having recently married his father, Solomon Akintọla, in Ilorin during his travels as a trader with strong CMS connections in the early 1880s.[3] Although S. A. Ọlọkọ cofounded the Ibadan Progressive Union, the city's most influential civic organization during the colonial period, was later Ọ̀tún-Ààrẹ of Ibadan (a distinguished chieftaincy title), and was one of the city's most renowned men of his generation, he was Ijeṣa in origin (from the Ijeṣa capital city of Ileṣa, fifty-eight miles northeast of Ibadan), his parents having arrived in the city in the late nineteenth century.[4] As discussed earlier, the CMS mission stations in Aremọ, Kudẹti, and Ogunpa had served as focal points for many of the families of these emergent Christian-educated men with no connection to the old military lineages on which Ibadan's innovative Baálẹ̀ (later Olubadan) and Balogun chieftaincy lines were based earlier in the nineteenth century.[5]

In his letters, Ọlọkọ came across as an able mentor to Abiọdun and many of the other young men in their social and professional network. Additionally, the letters of these men served as updates on their lives and careers, as well as accounting documents for the contributions that the men made to their mutual aid organizations. Ọlọkọ and Abiọdun's letters, along with sprinkles of letters from the various associates that constituted this network, shed light on how these men exchanged valuable information through letter writing to navigate their novel world as pioneering clerical and junior administrative officers in Ìgbà Òyìnbó, or "the era of the white man." In colonial Nigeria, at least before World War II, these Western-educated Christian elite men, as salaried professionals, were a unique group at the intersection of tradition and modernity.[6] Focusing attention on the extensive correspondence about mutual aid, self-help, and associational life in these men's letters, I underscore the dialectical interaction between tradition and modernity, revealing how a traditional Yorùbá mutual aid system, known as the *èṣúṣú* system, was adapted into a Western mode of economic advancement and civic engagement. In this context, tradition and modernity were not mutually exclusive; the letters reveal the imaginative way these men blended old and new forms of social and economic mutual aid together.

This chapter also focuses on the correspondence between Abiọdun, Ọlọkọ, and their associates in the Ibadan Brotherhood Fund Association and Ibadan Cooperative Savings Society.[7] Revealing bonds of friendship with deep roots in Ibadan CMS education and training and emphasizing the interconnections between *àjọbí-àjọgbé*, these letters exhibit the vibrant associational life of the men and their commitment to these civic groups during the three decades in which Abiọdun assiduously filed their letters.[8]

During the period of decolonization, many of these men actively supported the Ẹgbẹ́ Ọmọ Odùduwà (organization of the descendants of Odùduwà, progenitor of the Yorùbá people), the pioneering sociocultural organization that provided the institutional foundation for an ethnonational Yorùbá political movement. This movement, in turn, culminated in the formation of the dominant Yorùbá party, the Action Group, in the Western Region, following the major constitutional reforms of the late 1940s and early 1950s.[9] Significantly, a detailed eight-page copy of the minutes of the inaugural meeting of Ẹgbẹ́ Ọmọ Odùduwà in Owo, in the eastern Yorùbá region, was handwritten by Ọlọkọ and labeled "Ibadan Brotherhood Association."[10] This indicates that the civic organizations to which Abiọdun, Ọlọkọ, and members of their network belonged not only participated actively in the Ẹgbẹ́ Ọmọ Odùduwà's inaugural meeting but also had a strong affiliation with the organization after it was founded in 1949. With firm foundations in the CMS communities in Aremọ and Kudẹti, many of these men later developed deep commitments to the progress of Ibadan under colonial rule.

The Ibadan Brotherhood Fund Association

The activities of the Ibadan Brotherhood Fund Association (IBFA), one of the two civic groups in which these Ibadan CMS men were active, embodied the values evident in the letters in the S. A. Ọlọkọ files. What became the IBFA in the late 1930s emerged out of a loosely defined group of friends, many of them old students of Ibadan Grammar School in the 1920s and the 1930s. S. A. Ọlọkọ, the CMS stalwart, was not among the men who founded the IBFA; he became its leader later on, in the 1940s. However, Ọlọkọ had provided leadership for the younger CMS men who formed the IBFA as an informal group earlier in the 1930s, and he had coordinated the activities of the Ibadan Cooperative Savings Society (discussed below), a group that might have inspired the founding of the IBFA. The letters of the IBFA men not only discuss the official business of the group but also shed light on the professional and private lives of the small network of friends and associates that constituted its membership.

The record of the IBFA in the S. A. Ọlọkọ files starts with a welcome message from Abiọdun Vaughan and three other prominent Ibadan CMS men to new members of this mutual aid organization. In a typed memorandum, IBFA secretary J. A. Ọjẹrinọla announced the election of three new members:

> I am directed to inform you that Messrs. S. A. Ọlọkọ of the Agricultural Department, Ibadan, J. L. Ogunṣọla, former headmaster of the Central School, Ibadan, and S. A. Akinrinade of the American Tobacco Company, Osogbo, have applied to become members of the Ibadan Brotherhood Fund Association. The applicants were respectively recommended by Messrs. A. A. [Abiọdun Alfred] Vaughan, E. A. Ogunṣọla and J. A. Ayọrinde and the association has received the approval of all the members in Abẹokuta center. . . . In this connection, I am to point out that as the first two applicants [S. A. Ọlọkọ and J. L. Ogunṣọla] mentioned in my paragraph 1 are respectable gentlemen of experience they would be of appreciable usefulness to the association in all ways possible.[11]

Letters in the S. A. Ọlọkọ files from officials of the group advised IBFA members on financial literacy, money matters, and professional advancement. There is a plethora of valuable information from association members. Soon after Ọlọkọ was elected an IBFA member in 1940, he became president and regularly wrote to Abiọdun, who served as treasurer of the organization in the early 1940s. Ọlọkọ frequently requested from Abiọdun updates about the receipt of dues from members and the management of association funds.

The letters reveal the significance of the IBFA passbook in the management of the funds contributed by the members. In a letter written in November 1942, an IBFA member, for example, apologized to Abiọdun: "I return herewith the passbook. I am sorry for the little delay caused in sending back the book."[12] Despite limited resources and extensive financial obligations, many letters show that members worked hard to pay their dues on time: "By how much is he in arrears? I think I am at fault. So let me know before the end of the week. I have just settled my accounts on the cement purchased. By June I shall be in position to take another serious step."[13] A letter from E. A. Ajani, a founding IBFA member, to Abiọdun is indicative of the passionate commitment of IBFA members:

> I have to acknowledge the receipt of the sum of 4 pounds and 6 shillings sent to me in February. . . . The three young men with me are doing well. I have been eagerly expecting the passbook. I understand it is not yet back from Ileṣa. That is awful. I hope the secretary has written to Ileṣa members. After we have got it, it should definitely stay at Ibadan, to punish the Ileṣa members by making them meet the cost of remitting their contributions to you at Ibadan. I send through Mr. Lawson the sum of 1 pound being my contribution for November, December (1940) January and February (1941).[14]

To reconcile the dues of two members, Ajani and Ọjẹrinọla, a senior member of the association, G. O. Ogunṣọla, senior schoolmaster at Baptist Boys High School, Abẹokuta, founded by the Southern (USA) Baptist Convention in 1923, wrote to Abiọdun in 1942: "Mr. Ajani has sent me his own share of the contribution to the IBA [IBFA]. I shall send it to you through Mrs. Ayọrinde when she is returning. Mr. Ọjẹrinọla's share is likely to accompany if I am able to get in touch with him today or tomorrow."[15]

When members were tardy in the payment of their dues, some colleagues expressed dismay. G. O. Ogunṣọla, for example, decried a prominent IBFA member's delinquent dues: "I shall be calling Mr. Ọjẹrinọla this morning. I shall speak with him about his delinquency in the payment of dues to the Ibadan Brotherhood Association. He as a foundation member ought to take a manly pride in all affairs of the union." Ogunṣọla then reported on some students whom the IBFA was supporting with scholarships: "We have invited the students to come for a feast and some pleasant afternoon. I shall express the opinion of the promoters of the Higher Education scholarship fund to the house. We shall forward our contributions in due course."[16] A few months earlier, Ogunṣọla wrote from the Provincial Office in Ijẹbu-Ode, about forty-five miles south of Ibadan, where he was on assignment as an educational officer: "I have today deposited into the passbook of our IBA [IBFA] the sum of 1 pound 5 shillings which I shall contribute up to November month. The postal clerk's entry and his official date stamp are the conclusive evidence of the payment."[17]

Another active Ibadan CMS man, A. A. Akinrinade, wrote in June 1941 from Ogbomoṣo, where he was working as a clerk for a European trading company, to discuss his account in the passbook. He asked Abiọdun to relay a message to a close friend and old Ibadan Grammar School student: "Please help inform Mr. Ayọrinde that I forgot to leave my post office passbook the other day with that paper I gave him, as the passbook will be required on the day he will withdraw the money, as the amount withdrawn should be entered into the book. I therefore sent it through Ọ̀gá [master] at Ọyọ. He might have received it, I hope."[18] A year and a half later, Akinrinade wrote again from Ogbomoṣo to reconcile his IBFA dues: "Enclosed please find a 10 shillings postal order which you should please take as my contributions for November and December (1942) and credit to my IBA account." He also thanked Abiọdun for logistical assistance with the house he was building back at home in Ibadan: "Even before the proposed transfer came to our knowledge, you were indirectly shouldering the burden of my building arrangements, so I was gratified to learn of the proposed handing-over to the very right man. Now, in advance, I wish you long life, more wisdom and prosperity in this coming New Year."[19]

E. O. Alayande, a staunch Ọmọ Aremọ who became the principal of Ibadan Grammar School and a prominent educationist in Nigeria from the late 1940s to the 1980s, wrote from Ondo, about seventy miles southeast of Ibadan, where he was a teacher at the CMS's Ondo Boys High School: "The IBA passbook was received this morning and I have constrained myself to get money to make a deposit in time so that I do not occasion a disappointment."[20] Alayande then observed, "We are experiencing the fate of all mission teachers. Our April salary may not be paid until the close of next week. . . . I expect you will send the passbook only at the end of the month when I shall be able to pay my dues."[21]

Letters of IBFA members also reveal their commitment to the professional advancement of fellow members. Many of the letters provide critical information on employment opportunities, economic assistance, and related topics. In this context, the role of examinations in career advancement was discussed repeatedly. "I am glad to tell you that I took senior promotion examination on 4/2/43 [February 4, 1943] and out of the 27 candidates only 7 passed and I am one of the successful candidates," E. A. Bọlaji, Abiọdun's close friend and fellow IBFA member, wrote to him. "My s.p. e badges are issued to me this morning but I do not know to where I will be transferred yet. . . . I am now a fully qualified senior produce examiner and to be trained as sub-I of P [subinspector of produce]. As a result of this examination, I think I will be transferred to

Ibadan or elsewhere." Bọlaji went on to comment on his marriage: "You will remember that my wife always said that she would marry a higher and better man than myself and she had fulfilled her promise and I am not interested in the affairs anymore."[22] In another letter, Latidoye Ayọọla, IBFA member and Abiọdun's Department of Agriculture colleague, wrote to inquire about the results of his examination for promotion: "I shall be very grateful if you would please enlighten me on the following points. 1. We still have not been informed officially about the result of our exams. Therefore, I would be grateful if you can tell me why the delay. 2. I would be glad if you can advise me on how I can obtain the result officially."[23] In another instance, an IBFA member awaiting the results of an examination for promotion in a clerical position sought Abiọdun's help.[24] A few months later, he told Abiọdun about the outcome of his examination and requested a meeting with a senior official in the department.[25] A junior clerk in the Department of Agriculture in Ibadan and a member of Abiọdun's wider social network wrote in June 1941, "Once more, I beg you, sir, to let me know why the result is kept dark to us."[26]

In addition to the question of professional advancement, IBFA men expressed anxiety over their transfers to branch offices far away from their hometowns, especially Zaria and Kano in the Muslim North and Enugu in the Southeast. Indeed, Abiọdun himself had extensive discussions with his mentor, Ọlọkọ, on strategies for obtaining a transfer to a more desirable location within the bureaucracy of the Department of Agriculture. In a letter to Ọlọkọ, Abiọdun sought advice on a transfer back to the headquarters in Ibadan from the branch office in Abẹokuta in July 1941.[27] While on a service tour in Zaria, an IBFA member informed Abiọdun that his request for a transfer from Zaria to the Yorùbá region had been denied. "Home Home Home again from a foreign shore," the man wrote, quoting the lyrics of a mid-nineteenth-century song. "I usually move with fear whenever I think of the future condition of the following generation. . . . [T]here is much hope for you to come up but you will not mind if you are given a station in a district. Upon enquiry from Mr. Ọlọkọ, I was made to understand that the petition you put up was not successful."[28]

In another instructive case, Ọlọkọ provided insight on the strategy that Abiọdun and another IBFA member, Ogungbe, should adopt to secure their transfer. With both men planning to swap transfers in opposite directions—Ogungbe planning to move from Ibadan to Abẹokuta, his hometown, and Abiọdun hoping to return home to Ibadan from Abẹokuta—Ọlọkọ explained a roadblock to their plan to Abiọdun in November 1939: "I am sorry to hint you that your exchange with Mr. Ogungbe may not come just as planned and anticipated. Sometime last week Mr. Fabunmi had to submit an unsatisfactory report on Mr. Ogungbe. In fact, the young man is not performing his duties with necessary satisfaction. The report will certainly affect Mr. Ogungbe's transfer to Abẹokuta next month." Referring to a higher-ranking British agricultural specialist, Ọlọkọ added, "Mr. Trotman will not like to have a man whose service was considered unsatisfactory. It is a great pity that Mr. Fabunmi did not let me know before he submitted it. . . . If I had seen it, I would have persuaded him not to submit it."[29] In the context of the discussions of transfers, Ọlọkọ provided further information on the professional status of several men in their social network. "About Ogungbe's transfer, there is hope of its materialization but I cannot say when, as experience is showing that it is not for the Head Office to send out an incompetent clerk," Ọlọkọ wrote.

> Mr. Bamiṣaiye who was posted to my branch for over nine months before he was transferred to Benin is being terminated in his appointment for inefficiency. I had expected this and had always warned the young man as he was grossly inefficient and was either incapable or unwilling to learn. He was engrossed in the "foolish idea of once a schoolmaster" and centered his mind much on importance of himself. The [British] Head clerk in fact seemed to have some interest in the fellow and he appeared to wink at his faults. He never called for my report on him any time and I found it unwise to report on his inefficiency. You will be given sufficient notice before the transfer takes effect. I will find out tomorrow the probable time and let you know.[30]

Several months later, Abiọdun reiterated his request for a transfer: "Further to my letter of recent date regarding the possibility of the proposed exchange transfers this coming December, I beg to find out from your end how far our success may be, for I am very anxious to know the ultimate position of this long talked [about] transfer."[31]

Earlier in his career, in Zaria in 1934, Abiọdun expressed concern for the position of an associate in their social network: "It is an unpleasant news that Mr. Fashọgbọn has gone out of favor with Mr. Gibberd [a British agricultural specialist]. I advise that you try your best to see that Mr. Fashọgbọn is transferred to Ibadan. It is better to separate them and the quicker this is done the better."[32] In August 1937 S. Alabi, a friend of Abiọdun who was a clerk in the Ibadan headquarters, wrote Abiọdun to express interest in a transfer from Ibadan. "I am growing tired of HQ [headquarters] and wish to make a little change—a change that will not make much of a difference i.e., that will not take me too far away from home. There are only two stations that appeal to me and that is AB [Abẹokuta] or Agege [in Lagos]," Alabi wrote, referring to two stations in his native Yorùbá region, "and if there is no way to either of them, I shall have to stick myself down here and make the best of the present. The object of my letter therefore is to sound you and if for any personal reason you may prefer to be here."[33] In January 1943 another IBFA member sought advice from Abiọdun on how he could secure a transfer from the branch office, where he worked as a cotton examiner, to another office where he would have liked to work as a cocoa clerk: "I really want a change of appointment no matter how small the monthly salary is. I am fed up with the present one. Do you think, sir, that it is still possible for the Snr. Bot., to give me that appointment of Temp. Cocoa Asst.?"[34]

Early in 1949 when Abiọdun, while stationed in the Enugu branch of the Department of Agriculture, asked Ọlọkọ about his own application for promotion, Ọlọkọ replied: "I am sorry I cannot give any reason for the delay in promotion. . . . The promotion to first class clerkship [senior clerks] are first released. Others must come out sooner than later. Just let us be patient."[35] With regard to his own professional progress, Ọlọkọ wrote: "Mr. Priddy [a senior CMS Aremọ compatriot] came over a week ago to congratulate me openly in the office that my acting appointment as Accountant has been approved and that the paper for gazetting was then being dispatched. He thought Beattie [a British senior administrative officer] must have informed me as he obtained his permission before coming to congratulate me."[36]

Abiọdun's recommendation for promotion to senior clerk was denied by the Office of Head Clerk in November 1949. "I regret to inform you in confidence that the recommendation of your promotion and that of Mr. Abudu was turned down by the selection board," Ọlọkọ wrote to him, but he then offered words of sympathy and encouragement: "This pained everyone who knows about it here and I should console you not to get disturbed. The fact that you were strongly recommended should put you in good stead for future occasion. I know this will be a saddening news for you but you have to bear it and do not show any despair. You should do as if you heard nothing about it. You know it is a risk for me to tell you the matter being reached but I feel I should rest your mind. Do keep it absolutely secret to yourself alone."[37] Two years later, when Abiọdun was promoted to senior clerk, one of the most senior positions for a Nigerian in the Department of Agriculture, after almost two decades of service, Ọlọkọ extended warm greetings: "Accept our congratulations for your promotion. We wish you long life, good health, and happiness to enjoy it. Mr. Adeyemi would appear to have lost his chance due to his inordinate ambition and shifting from one department to another."[38]

These letters providing advice, moral support, or simply reports on the professional advancement of IBFA members and associates were far-reaching and multivalent. In one form or another, the values and social bonds of these men were reflected in many of the letters contained in the S. A. Ọlọkọ files. Within months of Abiọdun's arrival in Zaria in 1934, his close friend who was an elementary schoolteacher in Ibadan, E. A. Akintola, solicited Abiọdun's support for a more reliable employment opportunity in Zaria, but not before praising his sensible behavior:

> You know Zaria is full of all sorts of vice action, and perhaps you have not fallen in love with any lady before your departure, hence you are to be cautious and think of many other good things before you. Of course, you never give yourself up to such habits. It has of late been known to you that I am anxious to get another employment which is of regular payment. And Zaria there is perhaps better, so you may please investigate for me either under firms or any other department. Trusting that you will gladly render me any possible assistance that lies within your power.[39]

While Abiọdun was in Zaria, several friends also wrote him to provide professional advice, moral support, and information about happenings back at the Ibadan headquarters of the Department of Agriculture. Josiah O. Keleko, a colleague who provided such information, is worth quoting in full: "I hope you are getting on nicely over there. If you can only follow my words of advice to you i.e., that you should cling more to Mr. Obiesie than anyone else, you will feel at home in Samaru [a neighborhood in Zaria]. As I have told you, Mr. Obiesie is a nice fellow, very Godly and sympathetic." Keleko went on: "It would be stale news to you to learn that Mr. Fashọgbọn has regretted his transfer to Agege [Lagos]. You will remember he childishly worked out the transfer in the early part of 1933 because the lady he was then keeping was at the Catholic convent, Ebute-Metta [a neighborhood of Lagos]. He had not spent two months in Agege before he was fined 5 shillings and has been informed that he will be transferred to the Cameroons next month." After the "stale" news, Keleko described a scandal: "It would surprise you that Mr. Adeyinka's successor (Mr. Adeyẹmọ) has again misappropriated a greater amount than Mr. Adeyinka. The following drama happened in connection to his case: When the magistrate wanted to check him, he said he forgot the safe key in his house. The magistrate at once offered to drive him to his home for the key and they both went. Mr. Adeyẹmọ entered his room and locked the door. He drank caustic soda and fell down hopelessly."[40]

A. A. Akinrinade, who had written to discuss his IBFA passbook account with Abiọdun in 1941 while working for a European trading company in Ogbomọṣọ, shared this information about his new employment with his old friend Abiọdun in 1946:

> I am sure it will interest you to learn that I have had a departmental transfer from the post of instructor to a clerk and typist. As far as typing is concerned I do not know how and I confessed it to the general manager. . . . The general manager has bought a portable Underwood [typewriter] for the office which I am instructed to practice. I have thus started to practice about a week ago. Practice touching. Now I need some typing papers, carbon papers, and a ruler and eraser for which I enclosed please find order for 10 shillings.[41]

There is also evidence to suggest that some of the letters contained in the IBFA section of the S. A. Ọlọkọ files were written by junior clerical officers. These were recent secondary school graduates, some of whom were making their way into the CMS social network that came under Ọlọkọ's leadership by the mid-1930s, especially at the Department of Agriculture. Olu Osikalu, a junior clerk in the department working out of the Abẹokuta office, provides an example of such men who sought the assistance of Ọlọkọ, Abiọdun, and other senior CMS men in the IBFA. In April 1941 Osikalu, soliciting Abiọdun's support for career advancement, wrote, "According to your advice, I shall try my level best to gain the favor of S.A.O. [S. A. Ọlọkọ] if and when his assistance is required and I do trust also that you will do your best for me as you have been doing in the past, when time permits. May God help you, sir."[42] A year and a half later, in December 1942, Osikalu informed Abiọdun of new developments in his professional condition:

> The result of my last exam in "Group Diplomas" in bookkeeping and accountancy from the London Chamber of Commerce has not been published yet and I am really tired with the present appointment. I wish to try my luck in the mercantile houses. I shall be grateful if you could assist me to find out from friends over there [in Ibadan] or outside of town how I can find my way in with or without a certificate. I do not mind how much it will cost me. I just want a place where I shall be able to make use of my knowledge in accounts.[43]

Similarly, in November 1942 G. O. Ogunṣọla, an elder in the social network and an IBFA member, sought Abiọdun's support for the son of a compatriot: "A few days ago Joseph's last application to your department was honored. He was called up for interview which will take place on Monday. His father and I are very much obliged to you for the past assistance you have rendered and we shall ever remain so knowing that you will still do your best to give him the necessary direction at this time also."[44]

IBFA men also used their membership in the association to advance their standing in society. Beyond utilizing the IBFA for personal and professional advancement, some IBFA letter writers (and Ibadan Cooperative Savings Society members, discussed below) underscored the civic values of a rapidly evolving Yorùbá society in the 1940s. In one notable case, IBFA and Cooperative Savings Society member J. A. Ọjẹrinọla provided a straightforward African nationalist statement to his Ibadan CMS compatriot Abiọdun: "We here are not forgetful of our duties to our fatherland and we are not leaving any stone unturned to help achieve the aim of the mother union. Your efforts have greatly assisted to awaken the voluptuous spirit of our people at home both literate and illiterate. They are now being taught the value and importance of education, they are being shown the light and the way. I pray the creator of the universe will crown our efforts with success."[45] Similarly, in another letter to Abiọdun, this IBFA member wrote, "With regard to this, I would like it to be included on the agenda the subject 'Possible educational assistance to the town by the Association and the ways to effect it.'"[46]

Several letters from IBFA members further underscored the importance of administrative rules, regulations, procedures, and processes, noting the group's orderly commitment to "meeting schedule, agendas, goals, meeting attendance, and membership." These letters articulated the mission, objectives, opportunities, and challenges confronting an organization that represented a group of young men who saw themselves as the future of their local community in a moment of rapid social change.

Ọlọkọ and Abiọdun, along with other associates, though stationed in various towns in an evolving colonial Nigeria, aspired to contribute to the civic virtues of Ibadan. In earlier sets of letters in the S. A. Ọlọkọ files, in the spirit of civic commitment expressed through their dedication to their alma mater, Ọlọkọ wrote about a celebration that occurred while Abiọdun was in Zaria in 1934: "I am enclosing herein for your information the programme of the Founders Day of Ibadan Grammar School. Yesterday service was impressive and largely attended."[47] Four years later, after his transfer from Zaria to Abẹokuta in the Yorùbá region, Abiọdun circulated an article he had published in a local newspaper to IBFA members and other members of the Ibadan CMS social network. Abiọdun's article outlined the events of the Founders Day of Ibadan Grammar School at a celebration at Abẹokuta Grammar School, a sister CMS school. Abiọdun wrote that "during the course of the delivery, the lecturer opened the eyes of the listeners to the natural wealth of the country, saying that Nigeria could be a self-maintained country and great manufacturing area.

Every kind of mineral wealth was to be found in the country. Revd. Kuti [principal of Abeokuta Grammar School, legendary educationist, and father of famous musician Fẹla Anikulapo Kuti], chairman of the event, in summing up made many impressive and soul-stirring remarks on unity, self-help, and cooperation. . . . He said that true patriotism should be taught in our schools."[48]

The Ibadan Cooperative Savings Society

In addition to letters from members of the IBFA, the letters in the S. A. Ọlọkọ files that shed light on the collective identity of these Ibadan Christian-educated men were those from members of the Ibadan Cooperative Savings Society, another mutual aid union that advanced the economic interests of the men in this socioreligious network. Although there were a few distinguishing features between the Cooperative Savings Society and the IBFA's money system, there were also many similarities between the two groups. Information obtained from the letter writers suggests that membership overlapped between these two mutual aid societies.

The Cooperative Savings Society emphasized greater economic advancement for its members. They took more concerted effort to pool their resources for the benefit of all. They worked intensely to save their resources in a manner that assisted fellow members and looked more intentionally toward one another's fortunes. An early statement in the S. A. Ọlọkọ files written by Ọlọkọ in December 1934 captured this mission: "As I hinted to you before, the year-plan of the Cooperative Savings Society closes end of this December, and members have decided to share the savings according to individual contributions. The accounts have been made up to end of November, 1934."[49] Although references in the letters to the Cooperative Savings Society seem to be fewer in comparison with those to the IBFA, the Savings Society's objectives were more clearly focused. The Savings Society provided a framework for saving and money management to which members more strictly adhered—though, in some special conditions, flexibly.

Although much of the work of the group focused on regular contribution of dues from members, there is evidence in the letters to suggest that membership transcended narrow financial considerations. Ọlọkọ's letter in March 1934 to Abiọdun, following Abiọdun's transfer to Zaria, reflected an important consideration of kinship ties in this civic group: "You seem to have cut your monthly estimate too dry. I will rather like you to gain more experience before you are sure of what will suffice for you living over there."[50] Similarly, in another letter written in the earlier years of the Savings Society, Ọlọkọ commented on Abiọdun's account: "I have the pleasure to inform you of the closing of the Christmas fund and I send you herewith the annual report which shows the statement of accounts for perusal and early return. . . . I am writing this in the office, so I cannot quote your balance from last year. I have to congratulate you for this steady savings and I pray they will be utilized on lasting monuments."[51]

Much of the extensive correspondence between Abiọdun, who for many years served as treasurer of the Savings Society, and Ọlọkọ, the leader of the group—as well as other members—was meticulously documented in the S. A. Ọlọkọ files. The information includes basic inquiry on the payment of dues and careful accounting of the funds contributed by members. The Savings Society's painstaking accounting is reflected in about forty-five letters spanning a decade from the early 1930s to the mid-1940s. To demonstrate the critical role the Savings Society played in the professional and personal lives of its members, I will draw from notable letters that typify the dedication of these men to this mutual aid society, as well as the strong bonds of solidarity among Savings Society members.

E. O. Alayande, a teacher at Ondo Boys High School, wrote in February 1943: "The copy of the minutes of the last meeting has reached me and I expect that Mr. Ayọrinde [his friend] will make my account good up to the end of February at least before he comes over here. I hope other members acquit themselves credibly. I hope that immediately after the war [World War II] is over we shall find avenues of spending the money profitably."[52] In May 1943 another member wrote from the Bida office of the Department of Agriculture in the Northern Provinces: "When Mr. Ayọrinde was leaving Ibadan for Ondo on transfer, he wrote to inform me of it as well as to hint that my arrangements about the Xmas fund contributions . . . had been passed on to you [Abiọdun]."[53]

From Abẹokuta, Savings Society and IBFA leader G. O. Ogunṣọla wrote to account for his dues and those of another member: "Mr. Ajani sent the sum of 15 shillings to the IBA and Savings Society through me. In case I fail to come at the end of the month, I shall remit it to you. I hope to be able to pay for four or five months in advance." Ogunṣọla also explored opportunities to purchase cement for the construction of his house in Ibadan, asking Abiọdun, "Please remember me when the cement season returns. I hope you will consider my case when the ban is lifted. If license is needed you could get someone to obtain it on my behalf."[54] Two weeks later, Ogunṣọla wrote again to reconcile Ajani's IBFA dues in a letter that may have been mistakenly filed in the Cooperative Savings Society section of the S. A. Ọlọkọ files: "I send herewith the sum of 15 shillings being Mr. Ajani's contribution to the IBA [IBFA] as already reported. The balance of 10 shillings goes to pay my own part for two months. Since you reported that I had paid for January in advance. . . . I hope to come to Ibadan on Saturday, April 10th to witness the finalists display at the next Grier Cup Sports taking place at Government College, Ibadan. Please help me arrange for the cleaning of the grounds around my building."[55] A. A. Akinrinade, Abiọdun's friend who was working as a clerk in Ogbomosho in March 1943, wrote: "Enclosed please find the money order for a sum of 2 pounds to square up Mr. Joseph."[56] Another Savings Society member, Okunola Idowu, based in Lagos, wrote to reconcile his monthly dues in May 1943: "Enclosed herein the sum of 10 shilling in the form of postal order. This is to cover my dues from March to April ending."[57]

In August 1938 Ọlọkọ balanced Abiọdun's contribution to the mutual aid society with financial obligation to a close relative, Ajeigbe: "I enclose herewith money order for 1 pound 1 shilling, 6 pence to which please join the 15 shillings due from you towards the savings account here which I have paid on your behalf. This brings the total to 1 pound 15 shillings and 6 pence to be disbursed as follows: 1 pound 6 shillings 6 pence, Ajeigbe's school fees etc. 10 shillings for Ajeigbe's subsistence for August."[58] Later, in 1940, Ọlọkọ reminded Abiọdun of a small arears in his dues: "The amount you have to remit to balance up your account is 1 pound 9 shillings and 11 pence. If you find it inconvenient to do this, I will manage to cover it up till the end of October."[59]

Included in Abiọdun's payment of dues to both the IBFA and the Savings Society were many other financial obligations he left behind in Ibadan while working in Zaria from 1934 to 1935. This comprehensive statement of financial remittances forwarded to S. A. Ọlọkọ to meet Abiọdun's family and Savings Society obligations in Ibadan while he was working in Zaria in 1934 and 1935 revealed the overlap between records of Abiọdun's Savings Society accounts and accounting for funds for family matters:

> A. A. Vaughan, January 1 pound, February 1 pound, March 1 pound, 10 shillings, April 1 pound 10 shillings, May 2 pounds, June, July 2 pounds, August 2 pounds, September 2 pounds, October 2 pounds, November 2 pounds, December, interest 9 shillings, Balance in December 19 pounds and 9 pence. A. A. Vaughan accounts, 1935. December 1934, by first payment, credit 19 pounds 6 shillings 3 pence, balance 19 pounds 6 shillings 3 pence; February 1935, by second payment, credit 2 shillings 8 pence, balance 19 pounds 8 shillings 11 pence, March 1935 to Ladun's hospital fees debt 1 pound [a contribution to Abiọdun's brother Oladunjoye's surgery at Adeọyọ General Hospital, discussed in chapter 2], balance 18 pounds 8 shillings 11 pence; April 1935 to supplement March contribution debit 15 shillings, balance 17 pounds 13 shillings 11 pence; May 1935, purchase of building plot debit 6 pounds [Abiọdun's plot to build his house in Race Course, discussed in chapter 1], balance 11 pounds 13 shillings 11 pence; June dash [gift] to Akadiri for above plot debit 5 shillings, balance 11 pounds 8 shillings 11 pence; 15/6 cost of blocks, 4 shillings balance 11 pounds 4 shillings 7 pence; Transport and fixing 4 pence,

> balance 11 shillings 4 shillings 7 pence; June clearing the bush 5 pence, balance 11 pounds 11 shillings 2 pence; August to Mama [Abiọdun's mother, Mariam] for provisions 7 shillings 6 pence, balance 10 pounds 16 shillings 8 pence; to Ayọrinde for shirts 15 shillings, balance 10 pounds 1 shilling 8 pence; November Christmas funds credit 20 pounds 9 shillings 5 pence, balance 30 pounds 11 shillings 1 pence.[60]

In addition to remittances for essential amenities for close relatives, the accounting for the payment of dues also included important costs such as the purchase of plots of land on which to build houses, the construction of houses, and the payment of debts. This connection between Savings Society contributions and the provision of financial resources to meet a variety of familial obligations further underscores the strong kinship bonds of *alájọgbé* that undergirded the tightknit social network of these men.

Purchasing Land and Building Houses

In modern Yorùbá society, one of the notable achievements an aspiring young man starting a family can attain is to purchase a plot of land in a desirable neighborhood on which to build his own house. In the correspondence contained in the S. A. Ọlọkọ files, many of the formal discussions dealing with the official business of the two civic groups discussed above were interspersed with queries about the purchase of land on which to build houses, as well as the construction of the houses themselves.

Ọlọkọ, who had set the bar for other members in this tightknit network by embarking on the construction of a modern two-story house in the early 1930s, informed Abiọdun of the status of his house: "The time of opening my house is not under consideration at present. Though the plastering and the cement work is almost done, there are ceiling and painting remaining to be done. If I can go as far as doing the ceiling now, I have to apply a brake as there is no more funds to carry on at present. I think I will be moving into it before I would paint it and this is not going to happen until about November as I would like my wife to deliver [our baby] in Agodi, DV [Deo volente, "God willing"]."[61]

The correspondence below provides insight into how Abiọdun Vaughan purchased a plot of land on which he ultimately built a house in Race Course, a new residential layout that was established by the colonial authorities in the mid-1920s (also discussed briefly in chapter 1). Interestingly, notable members of Abiọdun's Ibadan CMS socioreligious network, such as S. A. Ọlọkọ and J. A. Ayọrinde, also built their houses in this neighborhood in the 1930s and 1940s. Given the importance of this landmark project, with its significant financial commitment, it is not surprising that Abiọdun sought the support of Ọlọkọ, influential Ibadan CMS stalwart and the most senior Nigerian in the colonial Department of Agriculture. These letters engage the intricate business and logistical planning involved in the purchase of the plot of land and the construction of the house. Additionally, the letters also contain the plans of other members of the network to acquire the plots of land on which they constructed their own houses.

When Abiọdun concluded the purchase of his plot of land in May 1935 while stationed in Zaria, Ọlọkọ wrote to extend good wishes: "I will arrange to walk-mark the plot for you and will give you the statement of total cost. I pray that the land may be yours and your descendants forever and that you make use of it to the best advantage. By this you are building a plan for your future and you should look forward to erecting a building on it to fulfill the purpose for which you acquired the land."[62] Noting the significance of the venture, Abiọdun, in a letter to one of his IBFA associates, wrote: "Mr. Ọlọkọ has done a great deal of good in the matter, but for this effort we could not have got it so cheap and so early. I cannot thank him sufficiently and even if I should say I would thank him I cannot do so according to my heart. . . . You need to write him and express this desire of mine to him."[63]

Several months later, Ọlọkọ, in another letter, wrote to Abiọdun to discuss the maintenance of his plot of land in Race Course: "The following expenses have been run on your land. Agreement fee 6 pounds, land owner's representative fee 5 shillings, weeding out the plot 5 pence, four cement blocks 4 shillings, transport and fixing of the blocks 4 pence. Total 6 pounds, 9 shillings, 9 pence."[64] Abiọdun did not start to build on this plot of land until the early 1940s, after saving enough money to begin the construction of a two-story house. In July 1944 Ọlọkọ outlined an estimate of the cost for initial labor for the construction of Abiọdun's house. The government contractor's statement reads:

> I agree to carry out the following works in the above building.
>
> 1. Making front verandah concrete decking and hand railings as directed.
> 2. One concrete step or stair case, one wooden staircase and every remaining bricklayer's work therein.
> 3. Making doors and windows of the downstairs and upstairs and glass windows of the upstairs.
> 4. Making wooden floor of the upstairs and ceiling.
> 5. Making fence wall to the backyard, with kitchen, and bathroom and all other carpentry works therein.

> To supply all necessary materials with one already got by the owner and labor for the sum of one hundred and eighty pounds. . . . Signed Owner of the house. To Government Contractor.[65]

A year earlier, E. O. Alayande, Ọmọ Aremọ and teacher at the CMS Ondo Boys High School, had written his old friend Abiọdun to congratulate him on his plans to build his house: "How about the building? I guess you have nearly completed the mud-raising. May God Himself help you in this noble venture. This bid is an impetus to me personally but as you would guess the teacher's means are so lean that to do such a thing should be fairly remote. I wish you happy realisation of your plan."[66]

As the construction of Abiọdun's house progressed in the late 1940s while he was stationed in Enugu, Ọlọkọ, back in Ibadan, wrote to inform him of the rising cost of building materials: "I am afraid iron sheets are rather scarce and dear. I understand a bundle cost something above 10 pounds and was as much as 25 pounds which will buy only two bundles and few sheets. I wish to contact Mr. Makanju [the contractor] and see if he can get them more cheaply."[67] The following month, Ọlọkọ provided more detailed information for the construction of the house: "I have got the 25 pounds which can only cover the cost of two bundles of iron sheets. We succeeded in getting a bundle at 10 pounds 5 shillings and I gave 21 pounds 10 shillings to Mr. Makanju to buy two bundles, leaving with me a balance of 3 pounds 10 shillings. I wanted to delay the purchase for a little while as it is rumored that prices would go down soon but Mr. Makanju was very anxious as he said he had started and no iron sheets enough to protect the walls."[68] Earlier in January 1948, Ọlọkọ had provided insight into and encouragement for the construction of Abiọdun's house:

> I note what you said about buying planks and making frames. I am not having Ayọrinde's plan here now as I cannot calculate what number of planks will be required. You cannot, of course, buy planks too much for your requirements. Whatever amount you said will be utilized to the best advantage. Mr. Ayọrinde's building is proceeding on well. It is just in the foundation and is costing highly because Ayọrinde chose to make the foundation with stone and cement. This indeed will make the house very strong but in my own opinion the soup does not require the extra salt. The foundation is strong enough.[69]

Many letters written by IBFA and Ibadan Cooperative Savings Society men reveal that Ọlọkọ's role in this housebuilding venture in the 1940s was far-reaching among members of the social network. Ọlọkọ provided moral leadership and practical assistance to many of these men, many of whom were away on service tours, in the construction of their houses back home in Ibadan. With regard to the construction of the home of Ibadan CMS compatriot E. A. Ajani, Ọlọkọ wrote to inform Abiọdun: "Mr. Ajani's house is continuing. The builders have not been regular with the work. . . . We are a bit handicapped about money and Mr. Ajani looks much to you for help. He has himself tried to forward money to carry on."[70] Ajani, who was away on official duty in Meko (seventy-five miles from Ibadan on the Nigeria-Dahomey border) in the early 1940s, wrote to Abiọdun: "I am sending per bearer the sum of 20 pounds as part payment for the house. I shall be thankful to you if you will kindly get all documents in respect to same and please keep same in your custody until I come."[71] Nine years later, Ajani continued:

> I also want to thank you for the picture of your house showing the additional apartments which contribute to the beauty of the house. I had written you a letter of congratulations on this noble move which I trust you have received now. Will you call on a bricklayer to give you the estimate. I would also like to know what the foundation of the kitchen including the latrine would cost us. See the plan. If these two works could be done this year or early next year, the task would be lighter. If we are spared, we can jump on the remaining [tasks] in 1952 i.e., building of kitchen and roofing, plastering house-inside, door and window.[72]

In March 1943 another IBFA and Savings Society member, A. A. Akinrinade, stationed in Ogbomosho, acknowledged Abiọdun's support for the construction of his house: "I cannot by words express my gratitude to you and your friend for the benefit I received from you; you have really helped me indeed to become one of the house owners now at Ibadan. I fully appreciate all that you do for me and I am grateful to you indeed. Please make Joseph the carpenter to understand that I do not for a minute forget that I owe him a sum of two pounds and I hope to square him up through you, of course, as early as possible."[73]

In March 1941 S. A. Ọlatundun, a clerical officer with a trading company in Abẹokuta who was building his house in Ibadan, wrote: "I shall be glad and thankful if you are looking out for me about building materials which you may find cheap, especially from builders who may fail to use same for their proposed building aims." He continued, "Mr. Adegbite has been able to assist me in the purchase of the fifteen bags of cement. Kindly let him have that two pounds and I shall send something for the water that must be used on the floor."[74]

While issues surrounding the acquisition of plots of land, the construction of houses, personal improvement, economic wellbeing, and civic engagement dominate the correspondence in the S. A. Ọlọkọ files, Ọlọkọ made a notable reference to traditional Yorùbá cosmology in a letter to Abiọdun in 1940. Although there is no evidence in the files of what specifically prompted Ọlọkọ's curious letter, his categorical expression on this subject, especially as a CMS man, is worthy of note. In an apparent response to a letter from Abiọdun, Ọlọkọ wrote, "Yes, I presume you are a mind reader. There is nothing I loathe more than these native medicine men. It is not only the monetary side of their contract but the fear their endless discovery incites in people who allow them to have control of their lives."[75] From the tone of this quotation, we can guess that Abiọdun must have shared some information on a challenging matter with Ọlọkọ that led to this reference to a Yorùbá diviner. Ọlọkọ was clear in his denunciation of "native medicine men" not because of their trade but because of the effects he felt they had on the people who consulted them, especially the alleged "fear" and anxiety they incited and the "control" they commanded among local people. While Ọlọkọ did not find the work of "native medicine men" desirable in a modernizing Yorùbá society, it is evident from this letter that they still retained an important role in the lives of Western-educated Ibadan Christian men such as Abiọdun, who dominated the IBFA and the Ibadan Cooperative Savings Society.

Moreover, the issue raised in this letter is at the intersection of Yorùbá traditional beliefs and Ibadan CMS Anglicanism, a subject that resonates in many of the letters compiled by Abiọdun Vaughan. Whenever they arise, these issues reveal the dialectical tensions between tradition and modernity, continuity and change—and between Yorùbá customary ways and Western Enlightenment ideas. This is an essential question for the letter writers in the colonial moment, starting with the growing influence of the CMS in Ibadan at the turn of the twentieth century.

Kinship Matters

The correspondence in the S. A. Ọlọkọ files, in contrast to that in the other files analyzed in this book, is decidedly formal—even containing some official documents of the Nigerian colonial state, such as receipts of accounts for purchases and minor debts. Nevertheless, these letters also engage a plethora of familial and kinship matters, such as the allocation of financial remittances for the provision of essential goods and services for close relatives, analyzed in other chapters in this book. Additionally, these letters reflect landmark events in Abiọdun Vaughan's life, some of which we have explored from the perspectives of members of his natal family, notably, his mother, Mariam Vaughan, and siblings Samuel Ariyibi Vaughan, Dorcas Ọlayinka Brainerd, and Jadesọla Juliana Ọdẹbunmi in chapters 1 and 2. Therefore, we can place the S. A. Ọlọkọ correspondence at the intersection of ideas of *alájọbí-alájọgbé* that sustained the trust in the intimate relationships between Abiọdun, Ọlọkọ, and the other Ibadan CMS men who wrote the letters—men who embodied the nucleus of the social network expressed through the institutional framework of the IBFA and the Cooperative Savings Society.

In letters dominated with talk of education, professional advancement, and social uplift, Abiọdun and Ọlọkọ also sustained an organic correspondence that reveals strong kinship ties through the powerful medium of letter writing. In one instance that underscores this strong kinship ties, Ọlọkọ wrote in regard to two close relatives, "I am very much obliged to you for the great help you have done for Ajeigbe in seeing him through his school period. May the Lord reward you. Popo is now back to finish his year two and arrangement is made to finance him through the year. He will remain with you until such time as you are transferred. I thank you most sincerely for the help you have been giving him." Ọlọkọ went on to tell Abiọdun, "I wish to continue the same arrangement in respect of Ajeigbe. From the end of this month, I shall allot 10 shillings for his subsistence. You should therefore hold back 10 shillings out of your subscription towards Provident fund. I understand you want to contribute 20 shillings this year and leave off Xmas fund. I do not expect Popo to be as tamed and cultured as Ajeigbe but I want us to help him and leave him to his own."[76]

While Abiọdun was stationed in Abẹokuta, Ọlọkọ asked him to inquire about the possible enrollment of Ajeigbe in the CMS secondary school for boys there:

> I want you to make an inquiry for me about what it will cost to send a boy to Abẹokuta Grammar School. Ajeigbe will pass out from class four middle at the Ibadan Grammar School end of the year. The school does not have a higher standard [at that time] and at present class four is not a qualifying standard for government clerical appointment any more. Unless one passes at least class five he cannot be considered, much less appointed. I understand Abẹokuta Grammar School goes up to class six and that boys receive very sound training. I wish to compare with Lagos and I want you to give me the following information:
>
> A. School fees payable.
> B. Boarding fees.
> C. Are boys prepared specifically for foreign tests? If so, what are the facilities and what foreign examinations standards intended for each class.
> D. What will do for a home-staying pupil as maintenance at Abẹokuta.
> E. Other school requirements—books, uniform, etc.[77]

The following year, Ọlọkọ sought information about a good secondary school education for his daughters:

> Mr Ayọrinde told me that Baptist Girls' School there [in Abẹokuta] is very good. I want to know more about the school. Will you get me the prospectus and any other necessary information. I want this for the future plan of my girls. The Kudẹti Day School is not running again standards above the infant classes and as I cannot afford to board them, I have to arrange for mixed school. I would have chosen Catholic convent where Ibidun is attending. . . . I shall be glad if you will let me have the information as soon as possible.[78]

Turning his attention to financial accounting to meet family obligations and the payment of dues for mutual aid groups, Ọlọkọ wrote, "I enclose herewith money order for 1 pound 1 shilling, 6 pence to which please join the 15 shillings due from you towards the savings account here which I have paid on your behalf. This brings the total to 1 pound 15 shillings and 6 pence to be disbursed as follows: 1 pound 6 shillings 6 pence Ajeigbe's school fees etc. 10 shillings for Ajeigbe's subsistence for August."[79]

From the letters analyzed in chapters 1 and 2, we will recall that financial obligations were central to Abiọdun's relationship with his natal family, as was his unsuccessful attempt from 1933 to 1934 to secure the hand of Miss Ibironkẹ Alalade as his wife. The S. A. Ọlọkọ files indicate that when Ọlọkọ was not giving advice on career advancement and financial literacy or presiding over the finances of the IBFA and the Cooperative Savings Society, he was advising Abiọdun on his obligations to family members. There was an intense talk about a misunderstanding between Abiọdun and a cousin in which Abiọdun rescinded an offer of financial assistance. "I do not want to interfere much in the matter as I feel within me that she has not been weighing matters as I think she should. But notwithstanding this, she deserves all the help that you can give," Ọlọkọ wrote to Abiọdun. "It is in my own opinion not right for you to be indifferent to her on this account. As far as it lies in your power you should do what you can to help her. . . . If you wish to give her any help it is better to do it when it is not late and if she gives you a cold reception you should not mind but consider it as an obligation on your part."[80] The letter ends with Ọlọkọ himself asking for a short-term loan to address an unexpected financial obligation.

The distribution of financial remittances that was discussed at length in our analyses of the correspondence between Abiọdun and senior members of the Vaughan family in chapters 1 and 2 (and will be discussed in subsequent chapters) also featured extensively in the S. A. Ọlọkọ files. Alongside the formal accounting for Abiọdun's payment of his dues to the IBFA and Savings Society, Ọlọkọ consistently disbursed Abiọdun's remittances to his close relatives in Ibadan while Abiọdun was away in Zaria from 1934 to 1935. For example, Ọlọkọ wrote in one notable letter in June 1934:

> I thank you for your letter of the 3rd ultimo and have to acknowledge receipt of the 2 pounds 10 shillings which I have distributed as directed. Although one month notice is necessary, yet I have paid in the two pounds which brings your capital to seven pounds, May ending. I gave five shillings to Ayọrinde, telling him to credit you with six pence for subsequent expenditure. Five shillings went to Mama [Abiọdun's mother], who expressed thanks. She added that she would prefer you sending an allowance to your sister in Ekotẹdo just to help her in her time of need.[81]

In one letter written earlier in 1934, Ọlọkọ had discussed the distribution of Abiọdun's remittances and allocation of mutual aid funds while he was stationed in Zaria: "The letter which contained your last remittances is now misplaced. Will you give statement of disbursement of the sum of 6 pounds 3 shillings sent? I remember quite well of 1 pound 7 shillings 6 pence to Mama. The statement of funds sent to me falls short of June remittances by 1 pound 9 shillings and I wonder whether this was for other purpose or purposes. Prob fund 2 pounds 7 shillings 6 pence; Solade 13 shillings, Christmas and provident funds 15 shillings, Mama [Mariam Vaughan] 5 shillings, Lesson [academic tutor for young relatives] 2 shillings 6 pence."[82]

In one instance a year later, in 1935, Ọlọkọ distributed two pounds and five shillings to Abiọdun's close relatives while he was still in Zaria.[83] Months after that, Ọlọkọ noted in another letter that he had delivered Abiọdun's remittance to his mother. In another instance in the previous year, he wrote that Abiọdun's mother had again requested financial assistance for his older sister Dorcas Ọlayinka.[84] Another letter discussed giving "Mama her allowance," although this time, Ọlọkọ did not account for the amount in his letter.[85] In July 1934 Ọlọkọ "acknowledges receipt of 2 pounds and 5 shillings and distributed accordingly, including to Mama, contribution to cooperative sharing is 9 pounds and allowance to sister."[86] In January of the following year, Ọlọkọ continued to account for the allocation of remittances to Abiọdun's close relatives while updating him on his mutual aid contributions: "I have to acknowledge receipt of your letters and the 2 pounds 10 shillings sent in one and I have distributed the money as requested. . . . The Christmas fund has been deposited with the same Barclays Bank under another bank passbook. The provident fund is going to the post office savings account. I moved into my new house on the 29th of January, 1935."[87]

Well into the late 1940s, whenever Abiọdun was away working in various stations of the Department of Agriculture, including Zaria, Abẹokuta, Lagos, and Enugu, Ọlọkọ distributed remittances to Abiọdun's close relatives and continued to serve as the conduit between Abiọdun and pressing financial obligations in Ibadan.[88] In January 1948 Ọlọkọ wrote of seeing Abiọdun's mother and discussing school fees for Abiọdun's daughter:

> Mama visited us yesterday and informed me that Lamide's school fees came up to 11 shillings as against 8 shillings and 3 pence estimated and that barring this, the money sent was sufficient. I have given the 2 shillings and 3 pence which you should not bother to return. Yes, you sent 1 pound for books etc. This sum was used to purchase books and uniforms and the cost just tally except the cost of sewing the uniform [Lamide's school uniform]. Arrangement is being made for it to be sewn by Ibidun [Ọlọkọ's daughter] at no cost to you.[89]

Along with this breakdown of remittances to cover fees for Lamide and a monthly allowance for "Mama," Ọlọkọ provided information about the academic progress of his daughters, Atinukẹ and Nikẹ. He concluded his letter with one of his favorite subjects of correspondence with Abiọdun: the working conditions of the Ibadan CMS men employed in the Department of Agriculture.[90] At the end of 1948, Ọlọkọ sent another message of developments at home: "Adukẹ [Abiọdun's wife] and her child are quite well. So is Mama who has just left me here about 20 minutes ago. Duro [Abiọdun and Adukẹ's child] was baptized last Sunday."[91]

Beyond the strong Yorùbá kinship values and CMS training that tied the network together, there is extensive evidence from the letters of Abiọdun and Ọlọkọ that suggests that there was a special personal relationship between these two men. Although they were not blood relatives, Abiọdun in most of his letters addressed Ọlọkọ as "Dear Cousin," a fictive kinship designation from a younger Ọmọ Aremọ to a reliable older compatriot with a strong connection to Abiọdun's natal family. Additionally, the activities described in Ọlọkọ's letters, especially in fulfilling many errands for Abiọdun while he was on service tours from the early 1930s to the early 1950s, reflected a strong affinity between Ọlọkọ and members of Abiọdun's natal family.

Finally, although the letters do not explicitly acknowledge it, Gladys Adukẹ Vaughan, née Akinloye, Abiọdun's wife, was Ọlọkọ's niece-in-law, since Adukẹ's mother, Rachel Ayọdele Akinloye, née Ọkẹowo, was the older sister of Ọlọkọ's wife, Abiade Ọlọkọ, née Ọkẹowo. These marriage ties exemplify the types of kinship interconnections that were common among Ibadan CMS socioreligious networks, especially Àwọn Ọmọ Aremọ (CMS children of Aremo) and Àwọn Ọmọ Kudẹti (CMS children of Kudeti), as colonial rule was consolidated in Ibadan Division.

These special kinship ties of *alájọbí-alájọgbé* are vividly reflected in Ọlọkọ's letters on three major incidents central to Abiọdun's life during these years. These issues were the tragic loss of Abiọdun and Adukẹ's three infant children (discussed in chapter 2 by the three Vaughan matriarchs), Abiọdun's unsuccessful courtship of Ibironkẹ Alalade (discussed in chapters 1 and 2 by Abiọdun's mother and siblings), and the tense relationship between Abiọdun and his brother Samuel Ariyibi Vaughan (discussed in chapter 1). Since I have provided contextual analyses for the information teased out of these letters in chapters 1 and 2, I will limit my discussions to the textual analyses of Ọlọkọ's response to these three major events in the life of Abiọdun Vaughan.

In 1949, just a few months after noting the baby's baptism, Ọlọkọ received the sad news of the passing of Abiọdun and Adukẹ's third infant child: "It shocked me to read in your telegraph handed to me in the afternoon of the 22nd, of the death of Duro. This is pitiful and I have to repeat our sympathy for the painful loss. May the Lord God bestow His mercy and replace the child with those who will live long and survive you, their parents. I went up that afternoon to break the news to Mama [Abiọdun's mother] who was very sad over the event."[92]

In an apparent reply to Abiọdun, who was confounded by the passing of his third infant in succession, Ọlọkọ offered the sage advice of an older compatriot: "I feel I should not condemn your idea about finding a premature medicine for the premature death of Gladys' [Adukẹ's] child. Whatever you do may it please God to support it or give it His blessing. What I think is generally responsible is hereditary convulsion. I would suggest we concentrate more on simple remedies for this during the gestation and childhood. When the time comes, I will write out for you some prescription." Ọlọkọ then noted, "I saw Gladys' mother [Ọlọkọ's sister-in-law and Abiọdun's mother-in-law] here last Sunday [at St. Peter's Church]. She said she came with the Emir of Abuja who is attending the legislative council meeting at Ibadan here. She may go back [to Abuja, where she was the head nurse and midwife in the Abuja Welfare Center] next week. She is looking healthy."[93]

To further underscore the close personal relationship between these two men, Ibidun, Ọlọkọ's daughter, sent heartfelt condolences to her godfather, Abiọdun: "My Dear Godfather, with sorrow I learned that Dada [Duro] passed away recently. The bad news gave me a severe shock. May he Rest in Peace. Amen. May God comfort you, and bring back a nice baby for us. Amen. I told my mother about it and she feels it too much, and sympathize with you. Please sir help to greet the mother well and carry my sympathy to her."[94]

Four months later, Ọlọkọ seemed to have changed his mind from his modern "medical" diagnosis to the Yorùbá traditional belief of *àbíkú*, discussed in chapter 2, for the death of Abiọdun and Adukẹ's infant children. In search of a solution to this painful event, Ọlọkọ, in a reply to Abiọdun in July 1949, wrote:

> I have since met the young woman I spoke about and I consulted her. She confessed she no longer gets visual contact with the "mates" [infants believed to occupy the liminal space between the spirit and temporal worlds], but recommends that the mother should show kindness always to little children and give them occasional presents and little feastings. She advises getting someone also to prepare medicine to get any new babe out of the "mates" fold or "blind" it from their doings and company. She believes that the circumstances of the death of your late child were of "mates" characteristics.[95]

At the time when we observed rising tensions between Abiọdun and his older brother Samuel Ariyibi in the mid-1930s, it is notable that Abiọdun was also engaging Ọlọkọ in a different type of correspondence on challenging matters with serious implications for the Vaughan natal family. As Samuel Ariyibi redefined his obligations to the family, Ọlọkọ's letters reflected many of the sentiments Abiọdun expressed in his interactions with Samuel Ariyibi in the file he labeled S. A. Vaughan, discussed in chapter 1. This reply from Ọlọkọ to Abiọdun, which encapsulates the sentiment expressed in several letters, is worth quoting in full:

> I have to acknowledge receipt of your letter of the 18th instant and note under what passion it was written. There is not much for you to regret about, only you have to make the effort to work out the salvation as far as it lies in your power. By this I mean that as your position in order of birth, in the family, you have to realize that you have to virtually shoulder a greater responsibility than your natural obligation. Now as a right you ought not to mind building your father's house, but now if others fail—I apologize to use the expression—through foolishness, you, with foresight may possess will and realize that it is glorious to perpetuate the memory of your family. If you are of this opinion, may the Lord God help you bring it to pass. Dear Abiọdun, I must confess that I cannot follow the trend of opinion of your eldest brother [Samuel Ariyibi]. He seems to think it not inglorious to neglect the natural family obligations on account of individual behaviors. I wonder, if in a Yorùbá family life, he would not have failed as the head of a family. He is so opinionated that it is useless trying to convince

> him. I do not intend to exacerbate your passion but I write in this strain to open to you my mind and to make you reflect in case you are capable of such idea.[96]

Similarly, with regard to another matter that generated much tension in the correspondence between the Vaughan brothers, the unsuccessful attempt of Abiọdun to secure the hand of Ibironkẹ Alalade in marriage, Ọlọkọ chimed in with this opinion at the initial stages:

> Mr. Alalade is no more opposing and when my mother interrogated him lately, he has left uncontrolled his daughter's mind about the love for you. So, it appears that everything is smooth now. I am not of the opinion that the parents should be approached until the girl makes the suggestion or we learn they so desire, because it is already known to both families and the rest is a mere and unimportant formality. Whatever suggestion you desire to make you can make it to the girl and whatever you both agree upon that we should do. I hope to discuss the matter with elder cousin [Samuel Ariyibi Vaughan] this week.[97]

Two weeks later, Ọlọkọ was less optimistic: "That their differences can spoil your relationship is not possible of eventuality except the parents of the girl are still unwilling. When next I meet Mr. Adetoun [an older relative of Miss Alalade] I will speak to him about the proposal and ascertain his view."[98]

While Abiọdun was away in Zaria in Northern Nigeria in the mid-1930s, in nearby Abẹokuta in the early 1940s, and in Enugu in the Igbo region in the late 1940s, Ọlọkọ gave general-interest information such as updates on who was getting married, who came to visit, who had passed on, who had a child, who did well in school, who was struggling in school, and who had family finance, welfare, and health conditions.[99] For his part, Abiọdun occasionally complained about not receiving enough information about conditions at home from close relatives in Ibadan.

While Abiọdun was away in Zaria, other members of his Ibadan CMS network served as important links between Abiọdun and home. For example, immediately after Abiọdun's departure for Zaria, E. A. Bọlaji, an old Ibadan Grammar School student, wrote: "I am pleased to inform you that this time I am able to go and see Mama [Abiọdun's mother] personally in order that I may give a true report of her health. It was on the second that I went there and I spent about 30 minutes with her. She forced me to take some morsels of gari [staple food made from cassava] which she had prepared."[100] Two weeks later, Bọlaji reported: "To know of the health of mama, I sent my boy to her last Sunday to see her condition for me but sorry she was away in church. The following afternoon I went to Sister [Abiọdun's sister] who told me she is well together with your family. As regards Mama going to Kano [in Muslim Northern Nigeria], I am not sure of it yet and I do not think it will be so."[101] And a few months later, he wrote, "This morning it was Mama who woke me up from bed. I was much surprised to see her that particular time in the early morning. . . . She said that since about two weeks that she has not got your letter her mind is not settled; and therefore, I should write and ask you the cause of your long silence."[102]

Several letters also show that Bọlaji sent parcels of foodstuffs to Abiọdun in Zaria: "As I told you before your departure about your foodstuffs. If your food is getting finished please let me know as early as possible so that the necessary arrangements can be made. . . . I privately heard that Nike [Abiọdun's relative] will have a parlor marriage [a formal Christian elite marriage] with her husband soon."[103] Two weeks later, Bọlaji provided valuable information about the transportation of foodstuffs to Abiọdun in Zaria: "As you instructed me to go to Mama to get your foodstuffs to station for the purpose of transport, I sent my boy to her on Sunday and the boy was told that the gari and the yam flour has been taken to Brother [one of Abiọdun's brothers] who had sent them to you."[104]

Letters from family members and CMS compatriots were a critical source of emotional support for Abiọdun, who, from the perspective of people in Ibadan in early 1930s colonial Nigeria, was in Ile Hausa, the distant land of Hausa people. For his part, Abiọdun worked hard to connect himself to important issues back home. For example, as Ọmọ Aremọ, Abiọdun retained active membership at St. Peter's Church, Aremọ, the CMS church on Oke Aremọ (Aremọ Hill) that served as the religious nucleus for the children of Aremọ: "I wish to convey my desire to subscribe towards Aremọ Native Pastorate Fund [St. Peter's Church], 1934–35, to the members of Parochial Committee. Despite the fact that on my honor I have made a promise to subscribe a few shillings towards the Native Pastorate Fund of St George's Church, Zaria, I shall be very glad to send in my quota."[105]

Regular correspondence would continue when Abiọdun was transferred to Abẹokuta in the Yorùbá region in the late 1930s. But when family members and others in the network do not stay in regular contact, relatives on the receiving end who see them as essential to the kinship system are likely to express their misgivings. For instance, Ọlọkọ wrote to Abiọdun about having spoken with two of such relatives: "I expressed your difficulties to them and told them not to take much offence at you not writing them. I also told them why it was impossible for you to visit them during your last vacation leave. Neither of them seemed to be satisfied with your silence of indifference."[106] Writing from Meko, Ajani, an Ibadan CMS compatriot, quibbled, "This is my second letter. There is no reply to the first one."[107] In one instance, he wrote, "As God sees everyone's heart, I have to confess to you that your long silence did pain me."[108] On another occasion, it was Ajani who explained the tardiness in his own reply, noting, "I hope you would not mind my keeping so late to attempt the reply of your letter."[109]

Although many of the letters in the S. A. Ọlọkọ files revealed a deep personal relationship between Abiọdun and Ọlọkọ, many also showed the strong affinity among other members of the civic groups. In addition to the support provided by the members of the two organizations, I highlight two incidents discussed in the S. A. Ọlọkọ files that further illustrate this important point. First, I discuss the period in mid-1941 when Abiọdun experienced the loss of an infant son who was born in March of that year and the loss of his brother Oladunjoye. In addition to the importance of recording these tragic events in the life of our primary protagonist, Abiọdun, the brief correspondence among IBFA and Savings Society men provides an insightful perspective into the depth of kinship that characterized the relationship among the men in the CMS networks, especially Àwọn Ọmọ Aremọ and Àwọn Ọmọ Kudẹti.

In April 1941 Olușọla, son of Abiọdun, was admitted to a hospital in Abẹokuta immediately after his birth. While Abiọdun was in Ibadan, it was G. O. Ogunșọla, an elder in the Ibadan IBFA and Savings Society based in Abẹokuta who coordinated the care for the infant while Abiọdun was away on a service tour. Ogunșọla wrote: "I went to the hospital to see how the baby was getting on. Thank God. The lady in charge is doing all she can to play the part of a mother. The baby is doing well and on the road to normal development. Miss Akinyemi is going to the place every day. It is very kind of her. Besides she is well known to all the female nurses so that my frequent visits to the place have not given any trouble to them or me."[110] Two weeks later, however, Ogunșọla wrote, "This afternoon I called at the hospital and found that the baby was not doing so well. A rapid change for the worse set in yesterday according to the nurses' story. The Lord is good and great. With him nothing is impossible."[111]

When the infant died, IBFA and Savings Society associate G. Amosun expressed condolences.[112] Writing from Otta, a Yorùbá town about one hundred miles north of Ibadan on the southernmost boundary of the Northern Provinces, G. Obasa, another member of the network, told Abiọdun, "Thanks very much for your congratulations. The time of my marriage synchronized with the time you were bereaved. Please accept my sympathy though too late. I am pleased to observe that you had taken things with calm and fortitude befitting one who professes and acknowledges Christ as Lord. My wife joins me in sympathetic feeling."[113]

D. O. Ilori, another old friend and mutual aid group associate, wrote, "As soon as I had my leave I went away to my farm and to my house in Lagos it was when I learnt of the loss of your child as well as your elder brother. Please have my sympathy and extend same to the family."[114] IBFA and Savings Society member J. A. Ọjẹrinọla sent a message of condolence: "The news of the staggering blow caused by the death of our beloved brother [Oladunjoye] was like a thunderbolt to us. Surely, it is a heavy blow. A loss which the family and well-wishers can never recover. . . . It is just Godly to bear bereavement of this kind with calmness."[115] Many other IBFA and Savings Society men and friends at the Department of Agriculture sent heartfelt condolences to Abiọdun over the loss of his brother.[116]

The second incident I address is the saga surrounding Abiọdun's plan to marry Ibironkẹ Alalade, discussed above in the correspondence with Ọlọkọ and in chapters 1 and 2 in dialogues between Abiọdun and the senior members of his natal family. While Abiọdun was engaging in these dialogues, old Ibadan Grammar School student and mutual aid group member Moses Gbenro served as intermediary for Abiọdun with Ibironkẹ. In a letter penned in July 1934, Gbenro wrote, "I am still making enquiry about your intended lady Miss Ibironkẹ Alalade in which I found out that she has not secured any gentleman more than my beloved Vaughan. Therefore, my prayer on our proposal is that if it may please God that she may be yours in which I know you will take her to hymeneal."[117] A few months later, Gbenro continued with the same positive message: "Please all family at home are quite well. Mrs. Gbenro is well also and she heartily joined me in greeting you. The enclosed letter is from your sweetie, Miss Alalade. According to your letter I have set watch on her if there is any private man on line, but she is all around in love with you, therefore you should always be on alert about her, and I pray that both of you may be spared with long life and prosperity. Amen."[118]

Finally, in 1939, back in Ibadan, this reply to one of Abiọdun's CMS compatriots in Ibadan further demonstrated the supportive involvement of these men in each other's personal life. Responding to Ajani's responsibility for the pregnancy of a young woman, Abiọdun wrote, "I think the only thing to do is to give subsistence allowance to the girl monthly until she delivers. . . . We shall be prepared to take care of the girl in any way possible in her house. . . . It will be pleasing to arrive at this mutual agreement."[119]

A few letters revealed occasional ambivalence among the men in this tight-knit network. However, whenever such antipathy arose, it was expressed with the discretion that their Yorùbá kinship norms demanded and the medium of letter writing afforded. In one interesting instance, E. A. Bọlaji, an old Ibadan Grammar School student, shared misgivings about Ọlọkọ to Abiọdun:

> In the case of Iyabọ [Bọlaji's wife], I have to thank you again for your keen interest in me. You have not once failed to carry out your duties as a real friend and you never once failed to give suitable and better advice. . . . Continue this without weary and later on you will become undetachable part of my body my dear Vaughan. . . . As you have said in yours it is a real mistake to have chosen her as my wife. The cause of the mistake is due to the failure of your so-called cousin that is Ayọ Ọlọkọ. If she had not failed nothing would have induced me to get a thoughtless wife as the one I get at present. . . . I will give her a long rope leading to a great regret when I shall be compelled by necessity to get another wife who will adhere to my saying.[120]

In another case, an active member of the network and close friend of Abiọdun, J. A. Ọjẹrinọla, expressed misgivings about a compatriot named Ajani: "Our disobedient Ajani will be left behind with all his evil practice. I thank you heartily and also Mr. Bọlaji for warnings to Ajani."[121] E. A. Akinpẹlu's commentary on trust and friendship suggests a concern about an undisclosed matter between him and Abiọdun in January 1939: "I note with interest and care your remarks on certain tendencies on our part as regards our wives as strangers to ourselves! Much as I agree and see all the points you raised, I would like to see you act according to your sermon. . . . Personally, I prefer the present [gift] of a penny with true love behind it to many pounds with darkened mind on it. After all what is money in the absence of real love."[122]

A Discourse on Colonial Administration

The messages contained in the S. A. Ọlọkọ files seldom refer directly to the formal instruments of the British colonial state, despite the roles of many of the letter writers as career civil servants in major colonial bureaucracies such as the Department of Agriculture. However, on a few notable occasions, some of these men explicitly wrote to each other about their encounters with British colonial policies or the administrative aspect of their work as clerical and administrative officers.[123]

In a reference to the subject of race and colonial bureaucracy, Abiọdun Vaughan, upon his arrival in Zaria in 1934, wrote to Dẹjọ, a colleague back at the Ibadan headquarters of the Department of Agriculture: "After about 3 to 4 hours rest, I got up, dressed and reported for duty in the Assistant Director of Agriculture, Northern Provinces office. Well, here I am. We are on the Sokoto Road. African staff in one side and European in the other. Agricultural department have many staff here which compose Europeans, including specialists, and Africans of various capacity. In addition, we have Hausa agricultural assistants and clerical staff."[124]

Back in Abẹokuta in 1938, in a letter to Ọlọkọ on a contentious matter between Abiọdun and a colleague named Akilapa in the Department of Agriculture, Abiọdun again gestured in the direction of race within this colonial bureaucracy: "As Africans to Africans, I use to maintain the policy or idea of helping my African fellows in any affair between the white and the black, if even I have cause or causes to blame the black afterwards. . . . [A]part from being a member of my race and rank, Mr. Akilapa will take no heed. My principle is to refrain from any matter that may cause or result in the termination of appointment of my fellow [African] man."[125]

Abiọdun's most notable carbon copy letter on the conditions of Nigerian employees and colonial administration was written during an incident when the British district officer came to the Abẹokuta office of the Department of Agriculture to discuss the potential recruitment of Nigerian workers into the colonial military force at the initial stages of World War II. In a letter to Ọlọkọ in July 1940, Abiọdun described his ambivalence about this colonial policy. The letter is worth quoting in full:

> The Monday following the Saturday you left me, D. O. [District Officer] Blair came to the office and asked that members of Agric. should come forward to join Abẹokuta Volunteers Force. I told him we were for food production scheme. He then said that the staff resident in Abẹokuta ought to come forward and that if there was war in Abẹokuta or elsewhere, offices would be closed down. He regarded Mr. Ilori as too old for the game and asked me, Akinfe, and messenger to present ourselves on the field in the evening for medical examination. In the evening, myself and messenger were found fit and suitable, Akinfe was not examined—observed undesirable.[126]

Abiọdun continued:

> I wished to join the Police Volunteer Force, but the D.O. advised I should join Defence Force. I was registered in the Defence column. . . . It was known that the Defence Force was not confined to Abẹokuta alone but a Unit of Defence Volunteers at any place could be asked to defend in anywhere within Nigeria. . . . Today the 25, I went to the D.O. to tell him I am not brave as to level a rifle against any human being and I prefer changing to Police Volunteer or serve in Food Organisation. I have not taken the "oath"—I will not take it—I will not commit myself. The D.O. agreed I should discuss it with the A.D.O. [British assistant district officer] on 5th August and that he would let me know if there is any necessity for a letter of resignation.[127]

This subject did not come up again in the S. A. Ọlọkọ files.

As World War II intensified, G. O. Ogunṣọla, senior schoolmaster at Baptist Boys High School, Abẹokuta, and elder in the two mutual aid associations, wrote that the war had prevented the Southern (United States) Baptist Convention missionaries—founders of the Baptist Boys High School, where he was senior schoolmaster—from returning home on vacation: "They are prevented from traveling by water or by air now. Miss Perry is five years in the country and yet cannot go home on account of the new regulation."[128]

While Abiọdun was serving away from home in various offices of the Department of Agriculture, important Ibadan divisional and provincial administrative activities were called to his attention by several friends in the Ibadan CMS network. In one lighthearted moment, E. Fabunmi, an old Ibadan Grammar School student, informed him about a major civic event in Mapo Hall, the provincial headquarters, while Abiọdun was in Zaria: "Last Saturday, at the Mapo Hall, the Ibadan Progressive Union with the Ogbomọshọ Progressive Union gave a welcome to H. L. Ward-Price, Esq. [British Resident, Ọyọ Province]. At the concert stage, Mr. Ayọrinde played a very vigorous and interesting part," Fabunmi wrote, referring to the old Ibadan CMS student who was Abiọdun's best friend. "You must know that Mr. Ayọrinde is now famous throughout the length and breadth of Ibadan as a local comedian. In fact, the young man is a very good actor and everybody, white and black, enjoyed him and encored him several times. It is a pity that you were not here to enjoy the sight. Oh, Vaughan, hasten home to the South and drink more of the milk of enjoyment. May your two years swiftly run over and then we shall have you among us once more, Old Boy."[129]

Additionally, while Abiọdun was in Zaria, Ọlọkọ updated him on important policy decisions at the Department of Agriculture in Ibadan. In March 1934 Ọlọkọ informed Abiọdun of colonial policy on the smallpox epidemic in the province, and a week later he reported that the colonial authorities had permitted African clerks to wear native attire—*agbádá* and *ṣòkòtò*—to work.[130] In February 1948, while Abiọdun was working in Enugu, Ọlọkọ wrote to inform him of his (Ọlọkọ's) appointment as acting accountant in the department.[131] Four years later, as he reported on administrative reforms in the department, he proudly informed Abiọdun of the admission of his daughter Atinukẹ to University College, Ibadan, Nigeria's first university, founded in 1948.[132]

Several other IBFA and Savings Society men kept Abiọdun informed about developments in the Ibadan headquarters of the Department of Agriculture while he was away. For example, while he was in Abẹokuta, D. J. Ogungbe, a clerk in the Ibadan office, told him: "You might have been informed (I believe) that Mr. Trotman [the British agricultural officer] has received a sort of promotion as marketing adviser to Trinidad and in course of three months hence he will be released by the head of agricultural department in order to go and assume his new post. In this case, another agricultural officer shall have to be posted permanently to agricultural station Abẹokuta; but nobody knows who and when. Do you know exactly the probable time Captain Poynter will return to the head office?"[133]

In early 1951, at the onset of the constitutional reform that led to Nigeria's decolonization, S. A. Ọlọkọ, G. O. Ogunṣọla, and E. A. Sanda—three stalwarts in this Ibadan Christian-educated network who were also members of the Ibadan Progressive Union, an influential civic organization with strong membership among Ọmọ Aremọ and Ọmọ Kudeti—were named members of the Order of the British Empire (MBE) by the British Crown for meritorious service in their respective professional endeavors.[134] In September of the following year, while Abiọdun was away on a service tour in Lagos, Ọlọkọ reported on the upcoming event to celebrate the award: "This is to inform you that the ceremony of presentation of the insignia of the honor of MBE conferred on me in January 1951 will be performed by H.H.L.G [His Honour, Lieutenant Governor of the Southern Nigerian Provinces] on Monday the 6th October at 10 am at Mapo Hall. Sanda and Chief Ogunṣọla too will be invested with their own."[135]

These Ibadan Christian-educated men were firmly dedicated to their personal professional development and the advancement of their city during a moment of social, economic, and political ferment. It is fitting to conclude our discussion of their correspondences with a quotation from an eight-page document written by Ọlọkọ (and contained in the S. A. Ọlọkọ files) on the historic inauguration in 1949 in Owo of the Ẹgbẹ́ Ọmọ Odùduwà, a panethnic movement that articulated the interests of the Yorùbá people in Nigeria as decolonization intensified after World War II.[136] While there was no discussion of this topic among the letter writers in the S. A. Ọlọkọ files, Ọlọkọ's meticulous account indicates that these Ibadan CMS men, like many of their Western-educated counterparts in other Yorùbá communities during this period, were actively engaged with this transformative event in modern Nigerian history.[137] In a document titled "Inaugural Conference of the Egbe Omo Oduduwa, 1949," filed under the Ibadan Brotherhood Fund Association section of the S. A. Ọlọkọ files, Ọlọkọ—in reference to the dominant nationalist party, the National Council of Nigeria and the Cameroons—referred to the perspective of Obafemi Awolowo, who was the secretary-general of the Ẹgbẹ́ (Group) and soon became the leader of the Action Group, the dominant Yorùbá political party, and premier of the Western Regional Government during the decolonization process in the 1950s.[138] Paraphrasing the statement of the Ẹgbé, Ọlọkọ wrote:

> Individual efforts had helped us to the present point, but the result can't compare formally with that of a united group like all-embracing Ẹgbẹ́ Ọmọ Odùduwà. Assuming all Yorùbá cheerfully contribute their quota, however small into the [Ẹgbé's] Endowment Fund, it is too certain that our progress is assured in all aspects we consider. Let it be clearly understood that we did not inaugurate the Ẹgbẹ́ to fight any individual or group as some arch-propagandists say. We want to face our problems and find solutions to them to enable us [to] take our rightful place in the scheme of things to come. . . . The Ẹgbẹ́ believes that the best of our national characteristics and institutions (and there are many) should be carefully preserved and treasured. Many people envy them and care not a fig for their absolute destruction.[139]

S. A. Ọlọkọ died in Ibadan in 1984 at age ninety. He was buried in the cemetery of St. Peter's Church, Aremo.

~

As civic, social, and economic actors, Abiọdun, Ọlọkọ, and their compatriots kept up multilayered and multivalent correspondences, cutting across a variety of pressing issues of personal advancement, financial security, and social mobility. Their letters reveal strong interpersonal relations sustained by Yorùbá kinship ties and Western Christian training to navigate pathways of development, advancement, and social change in Yorùbá society. Much of the content of the letters analyzed in this chapter, reflected through the central role of the two formidable mutual aid and civic groups, was based on concepts of *ọ̀làjú* (the enlightened), *ìlọsíwájú* (progress), and *ìdàgbàsòkè* (uplift), which were gaining momentum in many Yorùbá cities during the colonial period.[140] These mutual aid and civic groups led by CMS elites were not unique to Ibadan; similar groups were active in major Yorùbá cities during the decolonization process.[141]

Ọlọkọ was the towering figure at the center of this tightknit Ibadan socioreligious Christian network. Because of his senior position in the Department of Agriculture, exemplary leadership qualities, temperament, and personal fortitude, Ọlọkọ embodied the mission and objectives of the two mutual aid and civic groups that sustained remarkable kinship ties among these Ibadan CMS men.[142] Many of the letters suggest that Ọlọkọ was a mentor to most of the letter writers and was considered a knowledgeable elder by his younger compatriots.[143]

Since many of these Ibadan CMS men served as junior civil servants throughout colonial northern and southern Nigeria, their letters reveal a general sense of displacement as they navigated Nigeria's diverse society. For example, these men were anxious about employment opportunities and professional advancement in the Department of Agriculture, and because of this, they consulted Abiọdun and Ọlọkọ to explore viable solutions to their problems. Accordingly, the letters consistently reveal how sustained connection with the network through letter writing advanced their professional development as well as their kinship ties. These letters also reveal how the civic and mutual aid groups provided the institutional node for collective social action that was vital to the advancement of the lives of these men as friends and compatriots, affirming Akiwọwọ's concepts of *alájọbí* and *alájọgbé* in a dynamic Yorùbá colonial society.

CHAPTER FOUR

The Gladys Adukẹ Vaughan Files

THIS CHAPTER IS A COMPREHENSIVE ANALYSIS of the correspondence between Abiọdun Vaughan and his second wife, Gladys Adukẹ Vaughan, née Akinloye, a schoolteacher and Ọmọ Aremọ.[1] There are about 345 letters and documents in the file that Abiọdun dedicated to his correspondence with Adukẹ from 1943 to 1961.

Adukẹ's maternal family had deep roots in Aremọ's CMS mission station going back to its inception in the early 1870s, following the arrival of her grandfather Samson Ọkẹowo as a young man from Ijebu-Ode. Her grandmother Hannah came to Ibadan from Ilesa as a girl at the tail end of the Yorùbá Wars in the 1870s. Estranged from her family in Ilesa, about fifty-five miles from Ibadan, young Hannah was raised by the Akinyele family, an influential CMS family in Aremọ in the last quarter of the nineteenth century. By the turn of the twentieth century, Samson had firmly established himself as an affluent trader and influential benefactor of Aremọ's CMS community, providing the first building—a two-story house in Alekuso—that housed Ibadan Grammar School when it was established in 1913.[2] Samson and Hannah had a daughter named Rachel Ayọdele Akinloye, née Ọkẹowo, born on July 17, 1898, who in turn gave birth to Adukẹ on July 18, 1920.

Adukẹ Akinloye's father was Akanbi Akinloye, a prominent commercial cocoa farmer and produce buyer in Ibadan by the time British colonial rule was consolidated in Ibadan Division in the 1910s and 1920s. He had been a student at Ibadan's first elementary school, St. David's (CMS) Primary School, Kudẹti, at the turn of the twentieth century and was a mentor to Abiọdun Vaughan in Aremọ's small CMS community.[3] A Christian convert from Islam with connections to Aremọ, Akanbi was a direct descendant of one of the powerful Ọyọ-oriented lineages that had established the novel political order in Ibadan by the 1830s.[4] Over the years, Akanbi, unlike other descendants of these "traditional" lineages, became a Christian by virtue of his connection to Ibadan CMS socioreligious and educational institutions.

Although the families of Adukẹ and Abiọdun were well acquainted in Aremọ's small, tightknit CMS community, the correspondence between thirty-six-year-old Abiọdun Vaughan and twenty-three-year-old Adukẹ Akinloye formally began in the files Abiọdun labeled Gladys Adukẹ Vaughan in 1943, while Abiọdun was on assignment in the branch office of the Department of Agriculture in Abeokuta and Adukẹ was working as a primary schoolteacher at the Alake School, the *ọba*'s (king's) school, also in Abeokuta.[5] Although Abiọdun and Adukẹ's marriage and family life had unique qualities and challenges, their correspondence for two decades addressed many of the issues we have discussed in previous chapters. These issues include married life, family health challenges, family tragedies, family obligations, financial remittances for family support, family wellbeing, social mobility, professional advancement, socioreligious life, and personal development. Specifically, the letters revolved around four major events in the life of the two protagonists from 1943 to 1961: negotiation of a marriage proposal from Abiọdun to Adukẹ from 1943 to 1944, the painful loss of Adukẹ and Abiọdun's first three infant children from 1945 to 1949, Adukẹ's strategies and plans for professional advancement as a primary schoolteacher in the late 1940s and early 1950s, and the experience of Adukẹ as a mature student and mother of five children pursuing advanced professional training in nursery and primary school administration in London from 1958 to 1961.[6]

This chapter also analyzes the extensive letters from Adukẹ's mother, Rachel Ayọdele Akinloye, nurse and midwife at a CMS hospital in Abeokuta and later at the Abuja Welfare Center, Northern Provinces, in the late 1940s, and Adukẹ's brother Adisa Meredith Augustus Akinloye, a law student at the London School of Economics and Inns of Court from 1946 to 1950 (all contained in the Gladys Adukẹ Vaughan files). In addition, this chapter includes about fifteen letters (also contained in the Gladys Adukẹ Vaughan files) from another brother of Adukẹ, Ọlayinka Odumosu, who was a student at Ibadan Grammar School and St. Andrew's College, Ọyọ, in the 1930s and a law student in London in the late 1940s and early 1950s.

The Courtship

The marriage that resulted from the courtship of Adukẹ Akinloye and Abiọdun Vaughan is mentioned in the letters between Abiọdun and older Vaughan family members, notably, his mother, Mariam, and elder sisters, Dorcas Olayinka Brainerd and Jadesola Juliana Ọdẹbunmi, and in letters contained in the files Abiọdun labeled S. A. Ọlọkọ, discussed in chapters 2 and 3. In the first batch of letters in the files labeled Gladys Adukẹ Vaughan, Abiọdun's main objective was to secure Adukẹ's hand in marriage by presenting a logical argument reminiscent of the kind his older brother Samuel Ariyibi had put forth in letters to him about a decade earlier. However, Adukẹ's response to Abiọdun's authoritative tone was confident, despite her much younger age. (Abiọdun was thirteen years older and already had a daughter, Lamide, from his first marriage to Dorcas Bolaji Ajibose-Vaughan.) Adukẹ reflected on Abiọdun's reasoning and seemed to understand it as an expression of his strong desire to marry her, but she would not yield until she was ready. Throughout the courtship, Adukẹ tolerated Abiọdun's unrelenting arguments and responded concisely with reasons why the time was not quite right with questions unresolved. Her effective engagement with Abiọdun's position proved her to be a good match for the more experienced Abiọdun.

This quotation from one of Abiọdun's many carbon-copied letters documenting his courtship of Adukẹ in the Gladys Adukẹ Vaughan files sets the stage for the series of exchanges in which the courtship of thirty-six-year-old Abiọdun and twenty-three-year-old Adukẹ commenced. "I have to confirm my discussion with you during your short stay in Ibadan. I am very sincere with every word I expressed that day and I maintain the love I have for you since 1937," Abiọdun wrote, alluding to a previous conversation and the idea that he harbored feelings for Adukẹ while married to his first wife, Dorcas. Abiọdun further noted:

> This is rather strange but I think if nature, as I believe, has natural communication . . . you will agree with me without any question. A fact remains to be settled. Why holding up till now? I have the courage that should it come to pass if it has been so destined. I therefore concentrate upon the question of my economic development and I thank God, I have set up a standard [I am successful]. Of course, circumstances may come into one's way in life and I think if you agree with me, I assure you that I can right the wrong through your cooperation. The question I need to ask you is are you actually in love?[7]

In comparison to Abiọdun's letters on his unsuccessful marriage proposal to Ibironkẹ Alalade about a decade earlier, the tone of this marriage proposal is clear and authoritative. Abiọdun addressed Adukẹ with a stern voice, in sharp contrast to his incessant pleas for the support of his older brother Samuel Ariyibi in his marriage proposal to Ibironkẹ. He continued, telling Adukẹ, "My visiting you at Abeokuta depends entirely upon the way you handle this matter." Abiọdun noted, "Time is precious and should be used on concrete affairs. Childish way and childish mind have gone, therefore let us play the game of man."[8] As was the case in his letters to his older brother on Abiọdun's proposal to Ibironkẹ Alalade, persuasion remained the central goal in this letter, but this time persuasion was done on Abiọdun's terms, with less emotion and sentiment. Thus, Abiọdun chided Adukẹ for what he considered a waste of his time.

These were tough words, but evidently Adukẹ was a tough woman, and on some level, Abiọdun's determination may have attracted her attention. Rather than respond with equally stern language, Adukẹ's tone was conciliatory but firm. Instead of fighting Abiọdun's "fire with fire," she seems to have neutralized him with contradictory statements in her letters, so much so that the following letter from Abiọdun explained why her statements were confusing to him. The letter shows how determined Abiọdun was not just to woo Adukẹ but also to prove to her why she should be wooed. Abiọdun's letter, listing his location "As Known," an indication of familiarity between the couple, gave a humorous tone to their correspondence during this early stage of their courtship: "I feel I should not write much but only make a remark that your letter is not definite. The same thing occasioned in your former one hence I gave you the benefit of the doubt and continued to press the matter." This implies that Adukẹ had doubts about Abiọdun's marriage proposal. But in that quest Abiọdun was rising to the occasion, based on the statements in this letter: "So far, the world is liable to change . . . and a closing remark of love, gave me the encouragement and deepest love. . . . Let us help ourselves in prayer that God will guide our footsteps." He added a quote from Alfred, Lord Tennyson ("More things are wrought by prayer"), revealing the strong Anglican teaching from the CMS training that shaped the socioreligious experience of Abiọdun as a CMS grammar school student.[9] He concluded, "Gladys, be simple and do not mix. . . . Yours lovingly."[10]

However, as is often the case in such Yorùbá courtship matters, important family interlocutors intervened to shape the dialogue between the two protagonists. Adukẹ's mother, Rachel Ayọdele Akinloye, a nurse at Miss MacCourth Hospital, a missionary hospital in Abeokuta, was that voice in the margins, shaping the contours of Abiọdun and Adukẹ's correspondence. Rachel Ayọdele's interventions, filtered through her daughter to Abiọdun, reveal a major concern of Adukẹ about Abiọdun's marriage proposal. This quotation from Adukẹ's letter reveals the sticking point: "First of all, I must break the news that I told my mother yesterday of this matter. . . . I decided yesterday to tell her in a simple way—that you proposed to me but I am not so serious about the matter." She continued: "She raised no objection, but she is somewhat afraid of the condition of your wife, though I told her that I heard you are no longer with her. Still she said I should mention something about the woman. . . . If you know that the condition is a simple one as you have been saying [that you are now single], I wish you [to] write a letter that can prove that you are serious and about the definite assurance of my safety." Adukẹ concluded the letter: "I am a little bit tired. I can't write much, but at the same time I am ready to write as much as I can to please you. . . . I like to see my people about the matter before touching this matter of marriage. . . . I prefer a quiet marriage, but church marriage though, this I can do in a place that I am not known. Let us leave the rest of this discussion till we meet."[11]

As stated by Adukẹ, the letter was inspired by her mother's response to hearing of Abiọdun's proposal and subsequent "negotiations," having just been informed of the matter recently by Adukẹ. For this reason, a bone of contention may have been exposed in ways not altogether apparent in their previous correspondence, as Rachel Ayọdele's expectation for her daughter was the assurance that Abiọdun was in fact the divorcé that he had claimed to be. Adukẹ's specific line of questioning and Abiọdun's further clarification that he was now single were consequential, referencing a request for a small wedding in an Anglican church, emphasizing their proposed union as acknowledged by English common law along with the religious sanction of the Church of England. In short, Adukẹ alluded to the fact that these concerns were not hers alone to address. As a fellow Ọmọ Aremọ, Abiọdun had to have been conscious of them and had to assist her in managing them properly before they could proceed with their marriage plans. Adukẹ had to wait for indicators from Abiọdun that he not only was thinking of his own interests but also was mindful of her expectations, as well as those of her family, amply underscored by the intervention of her mother.

Abiọdun's persistence is also omnipresent in this specific set of letters, especially when it is analyzed chronologically. Several other letters written by Abiọdun to Adukẹ during the courtship continued to underscore the desire of Abiọdun as a man who had come into his own in the early 1940s. With the desire to marry a man from her world, though thirteen years her senior, Adukẹ sent a letter that broke the stream of Abiọdun's pleas. Sent while on a brief holiday at her maternal grandparents' house in Aremọ, Adukẹ's message was firm and not so sweet, but it is worth quoting in its entirety: "My Dear, Your letter was received. You are a brother to me. I would have known what to give as a reply to your strong letter. I observe that you are very strong in mind and with determination against my leisure. Dealing with me in such a strong way can't help us. I wish very much to see you today if you please round about 5 o'clock. I have seen my Dad. I have some words for you. Your Dear, Gladys."[12]

This extenuating personality issue was evident in Adukẹ's letter after Abiọdun visited her in Abeokuta later in February 1944. In it, Adukẹ objected to a correspondence between Abiọdun and G. O. Ogunsola, a senior member of the Christian-educated men's social network discussed in chapter 3, and his wife, both of whom were Adukẹ's informal guardians in Abeokuta. Adukẹ rebuked Abiọdun: "I wonder why you're so serious about what happened here during your visit. I am greatly surprised to read in Mr. and Mrs. Ogunsola's letter that you reported me to them, after all that I have done on Sunday to satisfy you, but you are very queer." Exactly what Abiọdun "reported" to the older couple is not specified in the letter, but she continued:

> I am now studying you and I know the sort of person you are. You cannot easily forget and forgive. That is bad. You are older than I am so you ought to take my offer as lightly as possible. Do not form the habit of giving report. It is better we settle things amicably between us. I do not want to start the love with dispute because of a very simple matter. What I care much for is your understanding and true love, after that comes the rest. I want you to understand me and know when I am serious and when I am not.[13]

The letter goes on to describe Adukẹ's travel plans to Ibadan, noting family members she notified about their engagement and that she would only have a brief moment to discuss their wedding plans when they eventually met. She signed off: "I remain. Your Love. Gladys."[14]

When Adukẹ's older brother, Adisa Akinloye, an old Ibadan Grammar School student and fellow Ọmọ Aremọ, received the news of his sister's engagement to Abiọdun while working as a health officer in Zaria, Northern Provinces, he expressed resounding approval in a letter to Abiọdun: "The love that exists between you and Gladys has been brought to my knowledge, and it has received my approbation and consent."[15] With this formal tone, Adisa, the leader of the next generation of the Akinloye clan, affirmed their engagement: "She will not fail to be a good and dutiful wife to measure up to your expectations."[16]

Finally, Abiọdun received the blessing of Adukẹ's father, Akanbi Akinloye, and her mother, Rachel Ayọdele Akinloye. To Adukẹ's father, Abiọdun wrote on March 13, 1944, about ten months into their courtship:

> My Dear Father, I wanted to write to you the day I returned home, but problem of transmission of such communication confronted my effort, and I therefore concluded to hold on until I see you at home where and when I give you THANKS for the kind fatherly treatment you accorded me and a friend when we visited you [at his cocoa farm in Araromi Village on the outskirts of Ibadan]. More thanks also for freely giving me the hand of your dear daughter in marriage. I beg to express that I admire your frank disposition and ready consent and for

> regarding me as your son and that we two are your children. I pray to live and measure up to this expectation and give you no cause to regret. May God bless you and give you grace to be able to accomplish your lofty aim and idea and give you sound, healthy and long life to enjoy the result of your labour.[17]

On the same day, Abiọdun penned a similar letter to Adukẹ's mother, attempting to alleviate any reservations she might have: "My Dear Mother, I went to Dad at the farm for discussion and I am too pleased to inform you that I was well received and my request granted without hesitation or question. I am therefore happy to note that I am a son in your hand as well as Gladys your daughter. For this and other reasons, I wish you not to doubt our sincerity of purpose and I wish you trust and hope that our happiness is sure. I am, Your son."[18]

Given the strong Ọmọ Aremọ connection of the three families—Vaughan, Akinloye, and Ọkẹowo—the ringing endorsement of Akanbi Akinloye and his eldest son, Adisa, was enough consent from Adukẹ's natal family to Abiọdun and Adukẹ's engagement. At this junction Abiọdun had achieved his objective to secure Adukẹ's hand in marriage, but Adukẹ would continue to assert her perspective, raising queries about Abiọdun's idiosyncrasies and, in one instance, about the venue and type of wedding ceremony.[19] Adukẹ, now twenty-four years old, was meticulous with her plans, and thirty-seven-year-old Abiọdun was ready to pick up the pieces of his life with a young woman rooted in Aremọ's CMS community.

Marriage, Kinship, and Family Life in Troubled Times

For fourteen years before Adukẹ's departure to England, letters contained in the Gladys Adukẹ Vaughan files reveal that Adukẹ and Abiọdun's marriage experienced challenges that centered largely on health care, financial pressure to meet pressing needs of Abiọdun's nuclear family, and the devastating loss of three infant children in quick succession. The letters in this section of the file outline not only the resourcefulness of the two protagonists but also the intervention of two of Adukẹ's close relatives, her mother, Rachel Ayọdele Akinloye, and her older brother, Adisa Akinloye, who actively intervened through the medium of letter writing with Abiọdun and Adukẹ from the mid-1940s to the early 1950s. As we have seen in chapters 3 and 4, Abiọdun's close relatives were also actively engaged with important issues in the couple's lives, especially the painful loss of their third infant, Duro.

Letters from Adukẹ's Mother

The first notable issue in the letters in the Gladys Adukẹ Vaughan files after the couple's marriage in 1944 was Adukẹ's prenatal and postnatal challenges from 1945 to 1950. Adukẹ's mother, Rachel Ayọdele, a nurse and midwife, persistently intervened to ensure that her daughter obtained adequate health care in a moment of family crisis.[20] A three-way dialogue among Abiọdun, Adukẹ, and Rachel Ayọdele centered on Adukẹ's wellbeing during this period.

From her new base in Abuja in the Northern Provinces, where she worked as head nurse and midwife in the divisional welfare center, Rachel Ayọdele's letters underscored the relationship between a confident and socially prominent Yorùbá mother-in-law and son-in-law, Abiọdun. Rachel Ayọdele's letter to her only daughter, Adukẹ, also contained in the Gladys Adukẹ Vaughan files, provided instructions on general healthcare issues as well as prenatal and postnatal advice. At the arrival of Adukẹ's first child in May 1945, a year after her marriage, Rachel Ayodele congratulated her daughter, noting, "I was glad when I got Tiwalolu's photograph. May God keep the child for us. The clothes and other materials you bought [for me] were very good. May God bless you."[21] Tragically, Adukẹ and Abiọdun lost Tiwalolu a few months later.[22]

In a letter written early in July 1946 to Abiọdun just before her daughter's twenty-sixth birthday, Rachel Ayọdele called Adukẹ's health challenges to her son-in-law's attention and offered advice on how to respond to them. She noted that Adukẹ's persistent fatigue resulted from anxiety over the loss of her first infant child, stress over her current pregnancy, and demands on her as a professional woman. Rachel Ayọdele stated emphatically that "pregnant condition is no joke" and encouraged her daughter and son-in-law to obtain medicine from the modern government hospital in the New Reservation area of the city, where British administrators, civil servants, and other European expatriates resided.[23]

When Adukẹ had her second child the following week, Rachel Ayọdele congratulated her daughter and son-in-law and provided important information on postnatal care: "Congratulations for the new born baby. My main message is to appeal to you to take good care of yourself. I want you to use hot water to bathe from head to toe for quick recovery. . . . Also, you can put Dettol [a popular disinfectant] in every water you use, collect it from the nurse your friend."[24] Several weeks later, Rachel Ayọdele continued with advice to Abiọdun on how to provide health care for his wife. In keeping with Yorùbá customary ways, she forwarded a list of names for the newborn.[25]

Then the couple was struck with their second tragedy: Adukẹ and Abiọdun lost their second infant two weeks later.[26] In this moment of intense grief, Rachel Ayọdele, a devote Christian, consoled her daughter, relaying the advice of Abiọdun's friend and fellow Ibadan Grammar School student J. A. Ayọrinde: "Mr. Ayọrinde said you should take your heart off giving birth [for a while]. . . .

It will soon be over by God's grace and God will fight the battle and make you victorious."[27]

When the family experienced an unspecified loss in November 1948, Rachel Ayọdele, holding on to her strong Christian faith, wrote: "I received the letter you sent to me concerning the death and the money you sent to me (1–1-0 pounds). Thank you so much. I have accepted my fate and I thank God for everything."[28] Rachel Ayọdele's resignation to a loved one's death provides an important subtext to reflect on these successive tragedies for Adukẹ, Abiọdun, and their families. These tragic outcomes, whatever their modern scientific explanations, cannot evade an age-old Yorùbá cosmological explanation, including Ibadan CMS Christians. These questions at the intersection of the Yorùbá belief system and Christianity were an important discourse among various characters in this book.

Rachel Ayọdele's letters to Abiọdun and Adukẹ also engaged everyday issues from an older Yorùbá woman of status to her son-in-law and daughter in the latter decades of colonial rule. For example, in one instance, she told her daughter, "I want you to do me a favor: kindly get me a special woven basket, it's very good when you embark on a journey. Please let me know the cost so that I can send the money. Get me the one with a big size."[29] In the same letter, Rachel Ayọdele informed Adukẹ that her older brother, Layinka (Olayinka), would be visiting her before traveling back to London, where he was pursuing a law degree: "Layinka wrote to me that he will be coming home before going back to England. . . . Please when he is around, I want you to lend me your big kettle for boiling water to bathe and to drink before he returns to England."[30] When Rachel Ayọdele was ill in Abuja, Abiọdun and Adukẹ sent money to meet her healthcare expense. When she recovered, she wrote to them, "Thank you for your care when I was not well. . . . I know God will bring me back home [from Abuja, Northern Provinces]. . . . I also received the palm oil you sent to me. May the Lord bless you with good children."[31]

In September 1949 Rachel Ayọdele continued to discuss everyday issues and the pressing concern of Adukẹ's health care. She also beseeched Abiọdun: "Please, I implore you to get me enough palm oil as it's very costly and scarce here [in Abuja]. The one you bought for me has finished. Kindly buy enough and send to me. Thanks."[32] In another letter the following month, after giving Abiọdun detailed instructions on how to properly care for his wife in the latter months of her fourth pregnancy, Rachel Ayọdele thanked her son-in-law for the palm oil: "I received your letter and also heard all what you have said about Gladys, let us continue to pray that God will grant her quick recovery. I am grateful about the palm oil and the container."[33] In September 1950 Rachel

Ayọdele again wrote to express her gratitude: "I am happy to tell you that I saw the palm oil you sent to me. May God continue to replenish you. Amen."[34]

Adukẹ's aforementioned fourth pregnancy spanned from February through December 1949. While on leave in Ibadan from her service in Abuja, Rachel Ayọdele wrote to Abiọdun imploring him to pay careful attention to the pregnancy, and she provided critical instructions on prenatal care. "I received the letter you wrote on 9–5-49 [May 9, 1949] today and I understand everything you said," she wrote. She then referred to Adukẹ's stated desire to travel from Enugu, in the eastern region of the Southern Provinces, where her husband was working, to Ibadan: "As for Gladys who insisted that she is coming here, if she's pregnant, let the pregnancy grow to five months [before she travels] because of the long distance."[35] In October Rachel Ayọdele suggested a good place of special care for her daughter as she approached the crucial final weeks before childbirth: "On the issue of Gladys, it is good that she is with my younger brother [cousin P. C. Priddy] but at the same time, it is better she stays with her friend she spoke about for proper care."[36]

When Adukẹ finally gave birth on Christmas Day of 1949, Rachel Ayọdele continued to advocate for her daughter, appealing to Abiọdun to hire a maid to provide postnatal care: "I was glad when I heard that Gladys had given birth, may God keep the child and all of us together. Ensure you get a helper to stay with her. She must not stress herself at all. Somebody should be there to take care of both the child and the mother."[37] The baby girl was named Abiọdun, a namesake of her father, who was born on Christmas Day of 1907.

Eight months after the birth, while on leave in Lagos, Rachel Ayọdele asked her daughter to inquire about the price of kola nuts: "Anyway, I would be very happy if you can help me find out how much they sell kola nut in bags at one hundred in a bale. Ensure you get the big ones. They prefer the big ones at Goriya while the small ones by Sasa [near Abuja, Northern Provinces]. If you eventually find out, please let me know." She then pivoted to her favorite topic of health and wellness for her daughter:

> Concerning your condition, I want to recommend a drug for you which is very effective. It's called cod liver oil. It's good for every ailment. This is how it's written on the bottle 'fresh pure cod liver oil B.P' bottled by commercial medicine stores 10, Victoria Street, Lagos, New Court Road, Ibadan. There is another powerful tonic for digestion. It is good for all ailments too but make sure you show it to a doctor for proper prescription. Make sure you reply my letter soonest. . . . When your brother is coming to Lagos, let him bring yam flour for me in the bag I used to send rice to you.[38]

Adukẹ's older brothers, Adisa Akinloye and Ọlayinka Odumosu, were anxious about their sister's conditions and kept in touch with her through their letters.[39] "I am not suggesting that you should be very suspicious, but you should exercise good care in everything and everywhere," Olayinka wrote to caution her in 1947. "London is dark by 3:30–4:00pm, on foggy days all traffic stops and even pedestrians cannot see, the extreme cold etc." He also encouraged her to pray regularly.[40]

Rachel Ayodele Akinloye died in Ibadan in 1993 at age ninety-five. She was buried in the cemetery of St. Peter's Church, Aremo.

Letters from Adukẹ to Abiọdun

During this period of great anxiety in the late 1940s, Abiọdun was stationed in the Enugu office of the Department of Agriculture in the Igbo heartland of southeastern Nigeria. Adukẹ, back in Ibadan and briefly in Ilesa wrote to her husband frequently. In late 1948 Adukẹ's letters to Abiọdun often mentioned their third infant child, Duro.[41] She wrote, for instance, about Bisi Alalade's daughter's (Jadesola Odebunmi's granddaughter) and Duro's christening at St. Peter's Church, Aremọ, and she asked Abiọdun to send a thankyou note to a man in his Ibadan CMS network who gave Duro money after the christening.[42] In another letter, Adukẹ requested more money from her husband, claiming that the last family allowance was insufficient. She noted that Duro was in good health and that their new house in Race Course now had a tenant.[43] In October 1948 Adukẹ continued to provide news of important developments at home, including this update about the daughter of Abiọdun's mentor, S. A. Ọlọkọ: "About four days ago Ibidun Ọlọkọ's fiancé's people came to Agodi to ask the hand of Ibidun [in marriage]. Today the fiancé and friends came to Agodi to thank the family. I was there also." She concluded that "Duro and everyone are well at home."[44] Tragically, as previously discussed, Duro passed away in February 1949.

As discussed above, Adukẹ's fourth pregnancy began soon thereafter. Because she had to temporarily suspend her career as a primary schoolteacher to seek prenatal care in Ilesa, about sixty miles from Ibadan, Adukẹ explored opportunities for petty business while staying with her uncle J. C. Priddy, a civil servant who worked for the divisional marketing board. In a typical letter while residing in Ilesa, Adukẹ thanked her husband for a money order he enclosed in his previous letter and informed him that she would be staying with her uncle for an unspecified reason. She went on to reassure him that she was taking her medicine as instructed and looking after her health. She made these assurances with hope, especially for a young woman who had tragic experiences with her previous infant children: "You need not have any doubt about my using the medicine as ordered. You know I am no more a babe, and I know what I am about. I know the purpose of my coming here [to get proper prenatal care]."[45]

A month later, in October 1949, as she approached her delivery date, Adukẹ wrote Abiọdun a letter that provides some insight into her state of mind during this difficult time: "I thank you for your advice about the trade I mentioned in my letter, but I will like to do some petty trade as from now. I have been thinking myself of the possibility of getting the goods here from Oshogbo but that is a simple thing, if I can get some amount to start with. That is the only problem. I am so sorry that I have bought that kola. Had I known I would have used the money in another way." The letter continued: "At any rate, I am waiting for God's help. I am trying to fry something with flour for sale. I wish you try and send me the address of Mrs. Adejokun so that I may write her and discuss about the price of things in Kano [the preeminent northern Muslim city]. My uncle's mind is not settled at all at Ilesa. He wishes to travel back to the North. He is always saying this and he is a man that can leave at any time."[46]

Adukẹ then addressed her prenatal health: "I am attending the hospital every week and we are to pay 2/- every week for the hospital fee. These are the reasons why I wish to get something to do. I wanted to buy something for Mr. Kupoluyi's mother," Adukẹ added, referring to the woman who served as a temporary guardian in Ilesa. "I have already used two kinds of medicine, and I think I will [also take one of them] four times before I deliver. By the Grace of God all will be well."[47] Although vulnerable, Adukẹ was ambitious and restless. She would have liked to channel her energy into a productive enterprise that would augment the limited allowance from her husband.

While many of Adukẹ's letters conveyed critical information, some merely served to maintain contact with her husband. In one such letter, six months into her critical fourth pregnancy, Adukẹ thanked Abiọdun for his financial support but was more inclined to engage in a simple dialogue between a wife and her husband.[48] In another letter, she thanked Abiọdun for complying with her wishes from a recent request, then quickly requested a mortar and pestle for pounding yams. Adukẹ reminded Abiọdun to inform her mother in Abuja of her welfare.[49] And in another letter the following month, Adukẹ, after asking about Abiọdun's wellbeing, requested *aṣọ ìró*, a Yorùbá wraparound cloth, from her husband.[50]

Adukẹ spoke frankly about her objectives and expectations. Many of her letters followed a consistent format in which she expressed her hope for a desirable outcome. Even when her letters during this difficult time seem mundane, as discussed above, they were nevertheless intentional in their purpose. In a notable case where she sought her husband's financial support for petty trade "in onions and beans," she made sure to remind him, "There is no need wasting time. . . . I could see that I am still far behind."[51] In October 1949 J. A. Ayọrinde, Abiọdun's close friend, paid her a visit in Ilesa and gave her a small gift of money. In her letter to Abiọdun, Adukẹ acknowledged Ayọrinde's kindness. She then updated Abiọdun on the status of her health and the medicine that she had been prescribed. Adukẹ's letters to Abiọdun during this difficult time are not intimate, sentimental, or emotional; instead, they are transactional, harking back to their courtship in 1943 and 1944.[52]

As Adukẹ approached the time for the delivery of her fourth child, the tone of her letters belied their businesslike language, revealing a vulnerable emotion not usually reflected in her letters to her husband. The first such letter was written in late November 1949, only a month before her delivery date. In it, Adukẹ was positive about the future, affirmed the promotion her husband had been awaiting, and hoped for Abiọdun's transfer home from Enugu.[53] Two weeks later, she added levity to her message: "I thank you for the efforts made about a house maid. It is very difficult to get housemaid nowadays. I wish you can get a boy over there before we get a good girl as our wife to do the better work (Laughter)."[54] Adukẹ's last letter before delivering Baby Abiọdun on Christmas Day of 1949 was emotional but resolute: "Dear, I am pleased to tell you that I am pretty well and I am happy always as the time is near and I am looking to God for an easy delivery, and I know He will surely hear my prayers. . . . I know your mind is always with me as mine is with you. My Love, what we are eager about will come to happiness one day."[55] After the deaths of their first three infants, we can assume that what they were "eager about" was finally having a child who would survive.

Following the birth of their daughter, a telegram was sent to inform her husband: "Child born on Christmas day—will be named Abiọdun, her father's name."[56] A week later, on New Year's Day of 1950, Adukẹ updated her husband about her health and that of the newborn and stated that she expected him to visit them in the coming weeks. Before signing off, she wrote: "Buy anything that is necessary for us when coming or you bring us something that is good."[57] After Baby Abiọdun, Adukẹ would have four other healthy children.

However, the hope of a new beginning that accompanied the arrival of Baby Abiọdun in Adukẹ's letter was short-lived. Without providing a reason, Adukẹ asked to spend some time with her mother, who had moved back to the Yorùbá region after her service at Abuja. After a brief stay in Enugu, where her husband was still in service, Adukẹ wrote to him on assignment in Lagos: "I will be very pleased if you agree to my going to my mother after the treatment here. I will like to go and rest for some time. You know we have discussed this before I left Enugu and this is the right time for it. You cannot feel my absence at home now. So I wish you allow me to go and have some months rest." She ended the letter with this complaint: "There is nothing from you for my Xmas and New Year present [gift]. Why is it that you always treat me like that from time to time? Is this a punishment from you or from God?"[58] A few more letters reveal a growing strain on Adukẹ and Abiọdun's marriage. This letter from Adukẹ in March 1950, only three months after the arrival of Baby Abiọdun, shows the tension: "The brevity of my last letter was not through lack of interest. I see no reason why I should be less interested in you now. As for me I will see that I try my best to make things alright but the major part of it is in your hand."[59]

Writing from Ibadan to her husband, who was on assignment in Lagos by the time of the birth of their second daughter, Ibironkẹ, in February 1952, Adukẹ penned a candid letter that further highlighted the growing tension in their marriage. In a reply to one of her husband's letters, Adukẹ noted that "a wife is always happy to be together with her husband but under some circumstances this is not always the case." She underscored the stress of another transfer on her family as she cared for a toddler and a four-month-old baby with the help of her mother. She insisted that she did not want to leave close relatives who provided support, and she planned to earn "my own money to help myself and *my* children" while "always at your [her husband's] service even though I am here." Adukẹ ended her letter complaining about the limited amount of money Abiọdun sent her, about her husband's failure to express "sympathy to me or to my people" on the death of her uncle Adeyemi Ọkẹowo, and about the overdue christening of the children at St. Peter's Church, Aremọ.[60] Adukẹ was calling Abiọdun to task, claiming that he was not holding up his part of the bargain and not living up to her expectations.

Nevertheless, these letters reveal the personality of Adukẹ as a determined woman who knew exactly what she wanted. Her relationship with her much older and professionally established husband was largely transactional. For Adukẹ, Abiọdun's main role was to provide the essential resources to raise a family. Strategic in approach but clear in language, Adukẹ was forthright about her expectations of her husband. She knew her worth and was clear about Abiọdun's obligations to her and their children, a project that required a balancing act between the needs of the Vaughan natal family, discussed in previous chapters, and Abiọdun's growing family. As a woman of industry, Adukẹ wrote letters that were not emotional or sentimental; rather, they were direct, practical, and functional. It was clearly understood from the beginning that it was Abiọdun's duty to provide the bulk of the essential resources for the sustenance of their family. That is what was expected of him not simply as a husband but as an Ọmọ Aremọ in Yorùbá colonial society.

However, as Adukẹ was direct in her request of resources from Abiọdun, she was also aware that she might be stretching her husband thin, given his obligation to Lamide, his daughter from his previous marriage, and other close relatives. The sentiment behind these words from Adukẹ is instructive: "I know it's unfortunate and might anger you, but this is what you signed up for when you got married and had kids, and as your wife, I have no problem reminding you of your responsibilities."[61] The clarity with which Adukẹ made her case complicates the idea of Yorùbá patriarchal values and reified notions of traditional Yorùbá marriage and family norms during this dynamic moment in colonial southern Nigeria.[62]

Letters from the London School of Economics

The files that Abiọdun Vaughan labeled Gladys Adukẹ Vaughan also contain letters written by Adisa Meredith Augustus Akinloye, Adukẹ's older brother, while he was a law student at the London School of Economics and the Inns of Court from 1946 to 1950. In addition to illustrating familial and kinship ties, as well as the marriage dynamics discussed above, these letters capture important trends in colonial Yorùbá society starting immediately after World War II.

By the mid-twentieth century, Atlantic Nigeria had a track record of at least eight decades of missionary primary and secondary school education, as well as a handful of postsecondary schools in teaching and vocational fields, such as St. Andrew's College in Ọyọ, Wesley College in Ibadan, and Yaba Higher College in Lagos. But in the period immediately after World War II, many Yorùbá educated elites were beginning to aspire for more advanced postsecondary education in the modern professions such as law, medicine, engineering, allied health, science, technology, administration, and education, mainly in British universities.[63] A small group of Yorùbá elite had obtained university educations before the war from West Africa's first Western-oriented university, Fourah Bay College, Freetown, Sierra Leone. These people, such as Abiọdun's uncle J. A. Vaughan, private secretary of Resident Bower in the 1890s, and E. O. Alayande, Abiọdun's close friend, later in the 1940s, trained to become secondary schoolteachers, administrators, and Protestant theologians. After the war, a relatively small but notable group of southern Nigerians, including products of Yorùbá Christian mission and colonial government schools, took the demanding Cambridge examination to study in leading British universities.

Adisa Akinloye was among this cohort of Nigerians to explore highly sought-after training in the modern professions in British universities. He arrived at the London School of Economics, one of Britain's foremost institutions of higher learning, in August 1946. He wrote Abiọdun and Adukẹ from London until January 1950, when he returned to Nigeria to become the first native of Ibadan to pass the English bar and qualify as a barrister. After establishing one of the first law firms in Ibadan with his half-brother, Ọlayinka Odumosu, in 1951, Adisa became a prominent politician in the Yorùbá region during this transformative period in Nigerian colonial history.

Adisa Akinloye's letters had entered the Gladys Adukẹ Vaughan files while he was working in Zaria as a health officer in the colonial provincial council, before he traveled to the United Kingdom in August 1946.[64] Recall that he had provided a ringing endorsement of his sister's engagement to Abiọdun in 1944.[65] Immediately after his admission to study law at the London School of Economics, Adisa sent his sister a letter to inform her that he had resigned his position in Zaria and would "travel light to bring [his] belongings back home—selling old items," and would then prepare to travel to London. He then commented on how Adukẹ's silence had made him "uneasy."[66]

It is clear in the tone of Adisa's letters to Abiọdun that the relationship between the two men predated Abiọdun's marriage to Adisa's sister. Although Adisa was eleven years younger than Abiọdun, the men had much in common: they were both Ọmọ Aremọ, having grown up as members of St. Peter's Church, Aremọ, and attended elementary school at the CMS parish school and secondary school at Ibadan Grammar School. The detailed information contained in the many letters Adisa wrote to his brother-in-law—along with their consistency—reveal the high level of familiarity between the two men.[67] Additionally, Adisa wrote his sister, Adukẹ, forty-two letters that were contained in Abiọdun's Gladys Adukẹ Vaughan files. Why did these three people sustain such intentional correspondence while Adisa was a law student in London?

Although Adisa consistently expressed great interest in the affairs of family members back home in Ibadan, it is clear from the onset that what sustained Adisa's letters were important business transactions in which Adisa's brother-in-law and sister served as intermediaries between Adisa and his father, Akanbi Akinloye, the commercial cocoa farmer and produce buyer, to provide financial resources for Adisa's legal education and cost of living in London.[68] After I reviewed most of Adisa's letters to Abiọdun and Adukẹ, it was apparent that the couple facilitated the financial transactions that helped sustain Adisa while he was a law student in England. Many of Adisa's letters admonished Abiọdun to help collect rent from one Mr. Sanda, a tenant at a store in Gbagi, the commercial district of Ibadan that Adisa's father, Akanbi, had passed on to him to help defray the cost of his law education and maintenance in London. Additionally, Abiọdun and his wife ran errands for Adisa to his father at his cocoa farm in Ararọmi Village, in the outskirts of Ibadan. But Adisa, as the older brother of Adukẹ and emerging leader of the Akinloye family, also inquired about his sister's condition as she confronted the tragic loss of her infant children, discussed above. These traumatic occurrences experienced by Adukẹ and Abiọdun from 1945 to 1949 coincided with the years when Adisa was in England.

In terms of form, presentation, and substance, Adisa's letters reflect the consistent clarity that we have seen in most of the letters analyzed in previous chapters. Adisa's letters convey at least two important interrelated elements: the writer's disciplined bureaucratic and businesslike mission as he asks for a prompt response from the recipient of the letter, and a deliberate desire to sustain the bonds of kinship with Abiọdun and Adukẹ back in Ibadan. Adisa wrote formally and with clear intention and a monochromatic tone. As a letter writer trying to stay connected with physically distant family members, Adisa earns high marks. He was resolutely engaged with these close relatives' concerns without intruding on their privacy or dictating actions of his own. He kept his brother-in-law and sister updated about the progress of his legal studies and shared information about his health and that of his young family with them.[69]

Covering a variety of emotional and concrete matters of importance in his correspondence, Adisa endeavored to draw Abiọdun and Adukẹ into a thought process of shared interests and values, regardless of their relevance to the central themes of his letters. His letters show a consistent sense of genuine care, thoughtfulness, and empathy for the wellbeing of Abiọdun, Adukẹ, and other close relatives in Ibadan, making him actively engaged with important family matters, despite his apparent long distance from home. This method of engagement was not underhanded; Adisa was simply doing everything he could to stay in Abiọdun's and Adukẹ's minds as an active family member, despite the enormous challenges unfolding in their lives during this time. Through these letters, Adisa was aware that nothing separates family more than the feeling that important family members are uninterested in significant developments in one's life.

When Adisa arrived in London in 1946, he shared his initial impression of the city with Abiọdun:

> Anybody who expects to see wonderful things will be disappointed by the outward appearance of London. But one must admire the skill, cleverness, and ingenuity of the Englishman. There is much to say about London, but I cannot do justice to it in this small space of paper. The train service is superb in speed and comfort and at the same time costly. Trains travels 60 miles an hour, and the

> third class coaches are better than first class in Nigeria. . . . London is too costly. I stay at the above address, being an hostel and I am paying 4/6 per day and breakfast. . . . Rooms cost 1 pound 15/- per week here. Imagine![70]

By staying in the loop, especially with specific requests in mind, Adisa was gently asking Abiọdun and Adukẹ to consider his interest a priority among the many family responsibilities that they were obliged to address, especially during this traumatic moment in their lives.

Equally important, Adisa was concerned with his sister's health, since this was the period when Adukẹ was confronting the loss of her infant children. After the death of Adukẹ's second infant in the summer of 1947, Adisa penned two letters, contained in the same envelope, to Abiọdun and Adukẹ. To his sister, he wrote, "Why is this world such a sorrowful world." With no answer to this question, Adisa noted that Adukẹ should "resign to God's good care and never be disheartened." He admonished her to "buck up" and pray that "God will deliver children to you."[71] Adisa's care for his younger sister was further expressed in these strong words the following year when his sister lost her third infant, Duro. While expressing heartfelt condolences, he encouraged Adukẹ to look for a hopeful future: "It will serve no useful purpose to reply to the recent shock you had and the loss you encountered. It was a surprise as it was sorrowful. But I am sure you will hold yourself together, and we all pray fervently that God may comfort you. Perhaps a holiday away for one or two months will surely do you good. Why don't you go to mother at Abuja."[72]

At the center of Adisa's letters to Abiọdun and his wife were questions revolving around access to financial resources for the payment of his fees at the London School of Economics and his maintenance in London. In a letter to Abiọdun in the earlier stage of his studies in February 1947, Adisa had reason to be optimistic about access to these resources: "About ten days ago, I received a letter from CM Ltd, Ibadan, that my father transferred 150 pounds to me, and that I should demand the 150 pounds from their York office. You know what that means, that my indebtedness to Dad is great indeed. It is worth great appreciation that he could get such an amount and entirely independently. I should expect that Dad expects me to use this amount judiciously. . . . But I have devoted the money to the Inns of Court."[73] Several months later, Adisa's letters indicated that he was experiencing financial challenges to meet the cost of his legal training and living in London. In order to pay his examination fee, Adisa urged Abiọdun to collect the rent from Sanda, the tenant in Gbagi: "I shall be grateful if you will make all efforts to collect the money from Mr. Sanda in time for me."[74]

A year later, when financial resources were not keeping pace with the cost of his education and living, Adisa explained in detail the dimensions of his financial problem to Adukẹ. A May 1947 letter that captures the extent of Adisa's financial challenge is worth quoting in full. He began by telling his sister, "I am very moved indeed by your letter and words of encouragement. We need entertain no fear. By the grace of God, it will be alright."[75] But things were not yet alright.

> I have written exhaustively in your husband's letter of the critical condition of things for me. Things are not rosy at all. Throughout last year I worked for my living, maintenance, clothing, books, etc. Even my enrollment fee in the Inns of Court, Dad was unable to meet it completely. This year is perhaps the most important year for me. As I have to do the finals both for the LLB and the Bar, I had written long before, say in September last year to Dad, stressing upon him the necessity of having my full time on studies. To work and study is not too pleasant.[76]

Adisa then went into mathematical detail:

> Last year Dad was able to give me 130 pound, which I used as part of enrolment fee. This year with the price of cocoa being higher I expect something more, say 150 pounds. With this I can live upon and leave off working in order to be sure in my examination attempts. All I receive however is 30 pounds, and which was only received last week!! Imagine. In fact, in December Dad sent 35 pounds which was for my university fees for the session. And even then, it was 45 pounds. I needed for the fees not 35 pounds. I had to make up the balance.[77]

Adisa then told Adukẹ what he needed her husband to do: "I trust Mr. Vaughan will make efforts for the collection of the rent arears. In fact, it has grown up to a substantial amount something around 12 pounds. If the rent could be collected then I can use it for the payment of my exam fee."[78] Correspondingly, Adisa underscored the implications of his challenging financial condition in this letter to his brother-in-law, Abiọdun:

> Regards to the rent from Mr. Sanda, I am thankful that you are making a move to ask Mr. Ayọrinde to do something about it. I have found the rent so useful and even now I should find it more useful still. The situation of things is rather critical I am sorry to say. . . . The task before me is very heavy indeed. Undoubtedly, the high standard I am desirous of setting is seriously impeded. My

> maintenance, my cost of books, housing, etc. have all been borne by my sole and lonely struggle in an English office in the unkind and acute winter climate. I am at the office at 8 am and sometimes do not close until 4: 30 pm. I rush to school to start lectures from 5–8: 30. I rush to the library to go and read until 9: 30 and then to my room. And so it goes on clockwise. I am only relieved by the holidays I give myself when I am on the verge of breaking down.[79]

Several months later, to rectify his difficult financial condition, Adisa further counted on Abiọdun as a reliable intermediary with Adisa's father and his connection to the store rented by Sanda in Gbagi:

> I hope you will be able to visit Dad during your leave [from Enugu]. There are various thoughts arising now as my course is nearing completion. I have been extremely in financial strain and my letter to Dad brings no response whatsoever. The silence makes me understand that he cannot afford it. But then, adequate provision is necessary in order to be able to carry out successfully the course one is pursuing. An undisturbed mind, undisturbed by financial strains is absolutely necessary to a good persecution of studies. I am sure I wrote to tell you that Mr. Ayọrinde [Abiọdun Vaughan's compatriot] has forwarded to me the rent he collected from Mr. Sanda. There are still arears which by now has increased. I wrote also that Mr. Ayọrinde should make another effort. I have not heard from Mr. Ayọrinde as regards this.[80]

Adisa's letters also conveyed the warm messages and expressions of concern that family members expect to hear from their close relatives, especially when they are separated by a long distance. Adisa's expressions of his feelings in these letters were detailed and thorough. He addressed pressing issues, acknowledged those in the recent past, and anticipated those looming on the horizon. In a notable case following the birth of Adukẹ and Abiọdun's third child, Duro, in the summer of 1948, Adisa congratulated his brother-in-law and sister while inquiring about the welfare of family members at home and informing them of the rigor of his legal studies.[81] Several months later, Adisa inquired about his sister and the baby's welfare:

> How is Gladys [Adukẹ]? I hope she is now there with you at Enugu. I am sure my dear sister will be much annoyed at me because I have not written her for so long. This portion of the letter goes to her. She should please not be annoyed, because I did not know at what address to write her at Ibadan, particularly to express my sympathy for the death of grand pa at Aremọ [Adukẹ's maternal grandfather, Samson Okẹowo]. May he rest in peace. . . . I have not got any picture of

> Duro. I hope you will please send me one soon. May God always watch and protect the young child so that he may grow up full of grace and blessings.[82]

As discussed above, Duro tragically passed away in February of the following year.

In January 1950, just before his return to Nigeria, Adisa extended a congratulatory message to his brother-in-law and sister for the birth of their baby girl, Abiọdun (discussed above) while expressing apprehension, given previous losses suffered by the couple. "My joy knows no bounds hearing that Yetunde [Adukẹ] has put to bed [given birth to] a female child on Xmas day. We received the news with joy and mixed feelings of fear; but we pray earnestly that our joy may be full, that God may in his mercies spare us this child. The past experience has made us to fear. God will answer our prayers and spare this child. . . . Now that you are at home, you will be in position to handle personally all arrangement as to my return home."[83]

While Adisa was studying at the London School of Economics, he married Miss Nkpa Eke (also known as Adia), from Calabar in Nigeria's Cross Rivers region, whom he had met in Zaria while working as a health officer. They had a daughter, Olufunmilayọ (also 'Funmilayọ), in 1949, a few months before Adisa's return to Nigeria with his family in February 1950. In November 1947, fourteen months after his arrival in London, Adisa informed his sister of his plans to have Nkpa Eke join him and announced his plan for marriage: "I have got the parents' permission and consent. I have paid the dowry, and plans have been finalized that she should sail for the U.K. at a short time. This is entirely my own plan, and the parents have no contribution in it whatsoever. Dad has approved of it and has given a formal undertaking. Her presence here will be a wonderful help. I have secured for her admission where she will study and financially, she will not cost me more than I am [currently spending]."[84]

When Miss Eke set sail for London, Adisa informed his brother-in-law that his fiancée "left Lagos on the 12th instant for this country. She is expected here round about 5th of March. . . . Apart from the fact that I look ahead to the future, I also realise this place is not too safe for a young man. Don't blame some of the boys bringing home English wives. Even there are scores of others already gone home leaving issues [children] in this country. We must pray that our own country does not degenerate into such immoral state as this country now!"[85] Adisa then picked up on his favorite issues of financial resources for his law studies and living expenses:

> It is desirable if anything can be done in relations to the rent arears and that I may get it in time to meet payment of exams fees and also to buy some books

> which I so much need. The last rent was for the month of April. . . . I hope you will not keep long before you write to me, and also to make all effort as to how to collect the rents that I so much now need. I am sure when you go home on leave, you will see Dad and be able to make very good arrangements as regards the store rents etc.[86]

During Nkpa Akinloye's two-year stay in London from March 1948 to February 1950, she occasionally included short notes in envelopes containing her husband's letters to Adukẹ, indicating she had established at least a friendly, if not trusting, relationship with her sister-in-law before she left Nigeria. In one lighthearted letter to Adukẹ, she wrote that "your brother is sitting directly across from me." When she took a trip with her husband, she reported that she and Adisa were two of eleven "blackies" on board the ship, so "the eleven of us got to know each other as though we'd been friends before." One highlight of the trip was a narrow escape from whales that nearly damaged the ship. Nkpa mentioned seeing "dolphins and mighty sharks." In the same letter, she shared the wonders and mundane aspects of the city of London with Adukẹ, addressing her as "Sister" to show respect and kinship: "Sister, there is really nothing very strange in London as I see a little bit of her. The buildings are magnificent and old. These people are still using horses as means of transport. The only strange thing here is the underground and electric trains, bus, trams and escalators." She wrapped up her letter, noting that she and her husband were "living very modestly but happily."[87]

Unlike the letters from Abiọdun's older brother Samuel Ariyibi Vaughan, in which there are clear hierarchies of information, Adisa's letters, though clear in their purpose and intention, are always respectful and measured in tone, and they arrogate equal value to prevailing issues. Adisa's correspondence addressed quotidian family matters as well as the vicissitudes of life—childbirths, marriages, weddings, education, deaths, and so on. However, business matters were also brought up in Adisa's letters; they were the central theme that prompted the consistency of his letters in the first place. Much of Adisa's preoccupation revolved around his central mission in the United Kingdom: strategizing for the funding of a prestigious law degree, studying for rigorous legal examinations, meeting living expenses for himself and his family, passing the English bar, and returning home to Ibadan as soon as possible.

In August 1948 Adisa announced in a letter to Abiọdun, "I am very pleased to inform you that I passed the part 1 LLB finals in the second class honours. The result was released about 2 weeks ago."[88] In January of the following year, Adisa shared the good news of another landmark academic success with Abiọdun and Adukẹ by revealing that he had passed his English bar examination:

"I know this will please you both and hence I hasten to inform you. It was a clean good pass." He went on to mention that very few people from his class passed, and he shared his initial doubts about his success in the examination: "When I left my job about two and a half months ago, I had barely 5 weeks to prepare intensively for the exam. I was hesitant and almost discouraged. But I pushed on. I am happy that I have passed and a good pass without any of these conditional passes which I hate and detest so much." After sharing this news, he provided some insight into the significance of his accomplishment: "But if there is opportunity shall we not strive at the best? . . . But degrees do give one consideration and put a premium upon one so that people will regard you in esteem, they will expect that you stand a better chance of efficiency and success."[89]

Adisa's declaration about his success in passing the bar exam is significant, in that only a small percentage of Africans were acquiring university degrees and professional training in the British metropole during this time. Obtaining a university degree—especially a coveted law degree from the prestigious London School of Economics—and passing the English bar in 1949 separated Adisa from the vast majority of even the most privileged educated elite in the Yorùbá society of the time. These distinctions allowed him to attain unique power and influence in Ibadan during a time of great political transformation when Nigeria was embarking on the decolonization process in the early 1950s and the subsequent transfer of power from colonial rule to independence in October 1960.

As it would later turn out for Adisa, there would be important benefits associated with such notable legal training and academic success at this transformative moment in Nigerian history. Adisa knew this, Abiọdun knew this, Adukẹ knew this—as did countless members of the Akinloye and Vaughan families and their extended Ibadan CMS community and kinship network. In a Yorùbá society where the great fortune of an individual radiates out to ignite the pride of their kin, Adisa's remarkable achievement soon became the crowning glory of one of Ibadan's most prominent families, the pride of his father, Akanbi, and even a credit to the great Yorùbá city of Ibadan as a whole.

As mentioned above, Adisa Akinloye would go on to have a brief but distinguished legal career as a pioneering barrister in Ibadan and eventually as a politician. He cofounded the Ibadan People's Party in 1951 with the charismatic Ibadan politician Adegoke Adelabu.[90] In the 1950s and 1960s Adisa was a prominent figure in the dominant regional political party, the Action Group; regional and federal minister in the Western Nigerian government and the Federal Nigerian government; and a leader within the Nigerian National Democratic Party, following the Action Group crisis of 1962.[91] During Nigeria's second attempt at a civil-democratic government, the Second Republic, Adisa Akinloye was the national chairman of the ruling party, the National Party of Nigeria, from 1979 to 1983.[92]

Adisa Akinloye died in Ibadan in 2007 at age eighty-nine. He was buried in the cemetery of St. Peter's Church, Aremo.

Gladys Adukẹ Vaughan's London Years

Adukẹ Vaughan continued to work as an elementary schoolteacher in Ibadan in the 1950s. She secured the support of her husband, Abiọdun, in August 1958 to travel to England and train to become a nurse. With her mother, Rachel Ayọdele Akinloye, moving into Adukẹ's home in Race Course to look after her five children, Adukẹ embarked on a lifechanging trip to London at the age of thirty-eight.

The late 1950s, two years before Nigeria's independence from Britain in 1960, was a time when many more educated Nigerians, mostly from the Southern Provinces, were pursuing university studies and professional training in the United Kingdom in far greater numbers than those in Adisa Akinloye's cohort immediately after World War II. Most of these younger Western-oriented Nigerians were products of Christian mission secondary schools and a handful of colonial government secondary schools that had been established before the war.[93] Many of the men trained in professions such as law, medicine, engineering, and academics, while most of their female counterparts trained in what were traditionally defined as women's professions, notably, nursing, elementary school education, hairdressing, catering, cosmetology, and so on.[94] Although Adukẹ was a product of two prominent Ibadan CMS families—Akinloye and Ọkẹowo—and married a member of Ibadan's pioneering CMS men, she did not fit neatly into this group of women because of her older age and status as a mother of five children.

With limited financial support from Ibadan, Adukẹ's transition to life in London was challenging. Many of her initial problems revolved around finding affordable accommodation, adequate employment, and admission to a nursing school. On arrival in London, Adukẹ shared her experience with her husband: "This place is terribly cold. My hands and feet are always cold, despite that I put on my gloves and stockings. I am trying all I can to protect myself from this terrible cold." Despite her troubles, though, she remained attentive to and concerned about her faraway relatives and the bakery business she and Abiọdun had established to supplement the family income, writing in the same letter, "I am happy to hear about [ten-month-old son] Fẹmi's effort in trying to walk. Please don't forget about [older children] Biọdun and Ronkẹ's schooling. How is the bakery work going? Greetings to the people in Gbenla, my children and Mama [her mother]."[95]

Adukẹ received support from Ibadan CMS relatives and friends studying in London. For example, S. A. Ọlọkọ's daughter and Adukẹ's first cousin, Atinukẹ Ige, née Ọlọkọ, and J. A. Ayorinde's daughter, Bisi Apata, arranged a rented room for Adukẹ in a house in Hammersmith, London, owned by Ibadan CMS man S. L. Durosaro, who later became a prominent politician and Osi-Olubadan, a senior Ibadan traditional chief.[96] "I have moved to Mr. Durosaro's house. . . . It was Tinukẹ and Bisi who suggested my moving here," Adukẹ wrote near the end of 1958. "The rent here is 2 pounds 10 shillings a week. I have been looking for a job. I should start on December 29th. This will help a bit in paying my rent and I can manage with the foodstuff I brought from home. . . . Tinukẹ and Bisi helped a lot. They do not allow me to cook yet. Tinu said I should manage on with them until I start working. I am alright with them. They take me around everyday."[97]

A week later, Adukẹ reported:

> I am happy here with Tinukẹ and Bisi, but the difficulty I have now is to get a hospital [to train as a nurse] and the elaborate expense of the rent. I have paid a week's rent and in about two days' time I will have to pay another. I wish to get a job quickly. I hope to start one on Monday 29th December. . . . I have written over twenty applications [for nursing school] but you could imagine how difficult things are now, only two sent forms and one of these have sent for my references, the other hospital has written back to me that they regret they cannot accept me so I have only one hope and that is from the hospital that wrote to my employer from home. I wish you remember me always in your prayers for God's help. . . . You may ask Mr. Durosaro for some reduction from the rent, for I don't know how long I shall have to stay in the house.[98]

A few months after arriving in London, Adukẹ realized that, at her advanced age, opportunities for admission to a nursing school were limited, so she shifted the focus of her training back to her professional experience as an elementary schoolteacher. In February 1959 Adukẹ enrolled in an advanced certificate professional training course in nursery school teaching and administration at Wandsworth Technical College in Wandsworth, London. Adukẹ documented her experience in many letters to her husband. She wrote candidly about adapting to a difficult life in England, adjusting to the rigors of her professional training, and coping with the painful separation from her children.

For his part, Abiọdun, in many carbon-copy letters filed neatly in the Gladys Adukẹ Vaughan files, offered words of encouragement and support. In one instance, he wrote: "I know it is not easy to study at your age. You possess matured brain and ideas, the only hindrance in the way of an elderly person in the field of learning is the thought of responsibility and worldly matters and since you can set this trouble off your mind, you can learn better than younger people."[99] About a year after Adukẹ's arrival in London, Abiọdun designed a plan to provide modest financial support for his wife's professional training and living expenses in England. He wrote to her, "I shall be able to send you 10 pounds every month except January, May, and September, when Lamide's school fees will come up and the amount may be reduced to 5 pounds in each case. 2. My next letter, say next week, will convey the beginning of the promise. I wish you to act according to your suggestion of getting a house nearer your work place."[100] The letters contained in the Gladys Adukẹ Vaughan files indicate that Abiọdun was unable to fulfill this promise because of his extensive financial obligations back in Nigeria.

In many of her letters, Adukẹ wrote candidly about the impact of demanding working conditions on her health, especially during her first year in London: "The work in this country is very strenuous but is something one must bear. I have to work 8 ½ hours a day from 8am till 5: 30pm with only one-hour break. I have reduced in weight now, but still I am happy that I am receiving some amount to maintain myself."[101] Adukẹ also documented the discrimination in housing and employment that many African, Afro-Caribbean, and Asian immigrants experienced in the United Kingdom after World War II. For example, after a year of living in London, she wrote, "I have been looking seriously for a house and I should have moved in, but unfortunately it is one of our problems here to get a house for rent from these white people. They discriminate greatly. Most of them don't like to take us in their houses. . . . You cannot easily imagine what I am saying unless you are here and see the difficulties I encounter."[102]

Amid these challenges, Adukẹ worked hard to secure the essential financial resources to meet the cost of her professional training and living in England. Only months after her arrival in London, Adukẹ, like many students from Britain's African, Asian, and Caribbean colonies during this time, took on a low-paying and labor-intensive job to support herself. In one letter, she wrote, "I have been called for an interview which I will go for on Feb 3rd all being well. I wish the interview is successful. . . . I am still getting on with my job and with this I can strictly manage my living."[103] After taking up an unspecified job in Bournemouth, on the south coast of England, a train ride of about two hours from London, Adukẹ wrote: "You should not be very surprised to hear that I have left Bournemouth. The work is very strenuous. I started the work with strong determination, but it is a pity I am not physically strong enough for the job. I made up my mind to leave without telling anybody because it was so difficult."[104]

Adukẹ meticulously outlined the difficulty of reconciling living, working, and studying conditions in London with her anxiety over the welfare of her children back in Ibadan. While striving to cope with a demanding professional training, Adukẹ continued to work to support herself in London. She documented her typical workday in London in September 1959, slightly over a year after her arrival in England: "I usually return home late for it is a whole day's work from 7 o'clock am to 7 o'clock pm and it takes me about one-hour journey to this place. You can imagine how tired I am now at this hour of the day writing." But then she revealed her preoccupation with her children's wellbeing: "I got a letter from Lamide [Abiọdun's eldest child from his previous marriage] as well today telling me of the children's illness before she left home. I am worried about this. What is wrong that they all fell sick at the same time? Could you please let me know their condition as early as possible and the cause of such illness? This is the reason of my writing this letter tonight."[105]

In addition to her challenging working and living conditions, Adukẹ repeatedly complained about London's cold and gloomy winter. In a letter written in January 1960, she described her first winter in London the previous year: "I felt home sick during that time."[106] More importantly, many of her letters continued to show how much she missed the children she had left behind in Ibadan, heightened by her condition as an older West African woman with limited social support in London. In retrospect, Adukẹ, several months before her return to Nigeria in 1961, summed up her three years of studying, working, living, and professional training in London: "You can imagine what a sorrowful time I had here every end of each year missing my children, the condition was awful, imagine me alone on my own every time and still have to work very hard for an achievement."[107] Similarly, earlier on, Adukẹ opined, "I want you to know that my children are the big and pleasant tie between us. . . . I am the oldest and the only coloured student and I am one of those still struggling to reach the goal."[108] However, Adukẹ recognized that she had to endure these challenging conditions: "It appears to me that this is the most tedious time I have during my course. I get weary and tired always. It is getting too much on my nerves, however it may be I must bear it to the end."[109]

If Abiọdun was not always able to provide financial support, he provided encouragement for his wife's laudable mission. He expressed concern for Adukẹ's health: "I ask this question because myself and your people need you and your welfare. I believe that should be our concern, particularly myself because I realize the responsibility God has given us." He concluded with this paternal admonition: "I trust you are thrifty; but do not manage against your health."[110]

Adukẹ's letters to her husband underscored her persistent financial challenges, especially in her last two years in England. After she wrote to explain her challenging financial situation and lack of adequate support from Abiọdun six months after her arrival in London, he replied: "I am getting over my financial problem. . . . I was awfully bad financially, but gradually I am getting out and I will soon be able to play my part to help you."[111] Adukẹ's reply was swift. She chided Abiọdun for what she considered his indifference to her condition: "I am happy you are getting over your financial problem. I know you should be alright now but it seems you have forgotten all about my conditions here, that is why you keep on promising without fulfilling it and it is not wise to expect things to come to crisis before you help me."[112] In March 1959 Akanbi Akinloye, Adukẹ's father, died in Ibadan. After the funeral ceremony, Adukẹ wrote to thank her husband: "I thank you . . . for all that you did during the burial ceremonies of my Dad. . . . I know the death is a release to the poor old man who was in bed for some years, but I am not so happy I am unable to pay him back the last honour as a loving and dear father."[113]

In August 1959, in response to his wife's difficult living conditions, Abiọdun wrote to Supo Morondiya, an Ibadan CMS barrister based in Jos, Northern Provinces, to negotiate an affordable rented room for Adukẹ in a house Morondiya owned in London: "I have written to my wife to inform her that you have been very kind to us to agree to allow her to live in your house in London while running a course of training and this step will surely help us a great deal in solving our problem. I received a letter from her expressing her thanks and joy for your kindness. She stated that she would prepare to live in any portion of the house according to your direction."[114] But the negotiations for the room remained unresolved, so Abiọdun, two months later, appealed to Morondiya: "I have to remind you of your promise to me and I wish you let me know your final decision so that I can make arrangement for my wife. Her position now requires your help."[115] When Abiọdun received a concession from Morondiya, he wrote to Adukẹ, "My dear wife, I attach herewith for perusal and return a letter written by Mr. Morondiya. It appears he has reconsidered the matter of accommodation. I advise you to go to the house again and see Tunki and the room mentioned in his letter. If the room is convenient and the half rent is 1 pound 5 shillings i.e., half of 2 pounds 10 shillings, I advise you to take it in order to cement friendship between the two families."[116]

Abiọdun continued, turning his attention to other financial matters on the home front, including, the payment of outstanding taxes on the family bakery business the couple established a few years before Adukẹ's departure for England: "The following day I despatched my last letter to you, I received Inland Revenue [taxation office] summons paper for 30 pounds, 14 shillings, 4 pence which is tax on bread business. I have been dragging out this matter with them for a considerable period. I made them to understand that the business was bad and I dropped it over a year ago. To shorten the whole matter, I agree to pay 15 pounds in order to withdraw the matter from court." But Abiọdun reassured his wife, "Despite my plight if I collect rent, I will send some money this month. Apart from this unexpected and compulsory demand on my pocket, my promise will always be fulfilled because I will not be happy if I neglect my duty and see you suffer there. I believe you are not really bad financially now. . . . I shall send the 'ata' [pepper] you required through post if I fail to get somebody leaving for U.K. from this side. . . . We are well. Femi [youngest child] is becoming a gentleman—full of strength, etc."[117]

Ultimately, Adukẹ opted for a more suitable accommodation near her college, writing to Abiọdun, "I am happy to inform you that I got a room to live in very near my training centre and it is 3 pence ride to the College, just a stone throw to the centre, no need to go by bus. I am quite happy about this. It is 2 pounds a week for the rental. I paid the money in advance this morning and I hope to move there on Saturday the 28th November." Adukẹ continued:

> I learnt that Mr. Durosaro is coming down next week. If you get this letter before he leaves home, I shall be too happy if my pepper could be sent through him with some ground edé [Nigerian crayfish]. Please tell Mama [her mother, Rachel Ayọdele] about this as well and please tell her there are some pins in the children's dresses with which I attached the under wears and the dresses together. This should be taken off before trying them, and in [fourth child] Ṣubu's shoes there is a stuff which could be taken off if the shoes are alright, but if a bit loose it can be fixed to make it fit. I am in need of pepper. I haven't any at present.[118]

In December 1959 Abiọdun sent another reassuring message to his wife, reaffirming his commitment to her educational and professional objectives.[119] But Adukẹ's financial challenges would continue well into her second year in England. A few months after Abiọdun's promise to lend assistance, Adukẹ expressed her frustration: "I cannot agree under any circumstance your failure to help me since I had left home. What I can consider it to be is lack of interest and sympathy. Whatever the conditions maybe I think you can first consider someone who is far away from home and who needs help. I want you to realize that what causes most of the mental trouble of our people in this country is financial problem."[120] Several other letters from Adukẹ to Abiọdun underscored her challenging financial situation in 1960. For example, in January of that year, a year and a half after Adukẹ's arrival in London, she wrote: "I really need your financial assistance as early as possible and something not less than £10 will suit my condition. You know that I have been left alone without any help from anybody for the past thirteen months."[121]

One letter describing her challenging financial condition, which she penned in January 1961, the year she returned to Nigeria, is worth quoting in full. She began by addressing her older husband by a fictive kinship title:

> Uncle, but I wonder why there is no money sent to me all this time. Do you think I do not need your help? Please think seriously about this question, and do what you think is right. . . . What surprised me most was about the English girls in my class asking me what you sent me for Xmas. I couldn't say you sent nothing but I kept telling them that you sent a reasonable amount to buy what I want. Let us forget about what I want, but think of what I need. . . . In this country, one needs good food to keep life going, good clothing for protection against this terrible cold and good heating, and what effort have you made to see that I have all these in two years that I have been here.[122]

Abiọdun's reply to Adukẹ fell short of her request:

> It is quite unreasonable for me to write a lengthy letter on the point you raised regarding lack of financial support. I can only leave the matter to God and conscience and tell you in short that you knew of my financial entanglement before you left home. I have not entirely taken out my name from the mess but I should not tell you that side of the matter but tell you the bright side of it. . . . You should also realize the fact that now that you are not home, I take great care of your children. . . . In short, let us forget this matter, and let us sing praises on both sides for God is merciful. I know all will be well very soon; you may regard me otherwise, but my mind and love is for you because you have set a good example.[123]

In an attempt to reconcile his wife's challenging condition in London with his financial obligations in Ibadan, Abiọdun explained his difficult financial conditions, emphasizing his desire to support his wife's laudable professional advancement, which he believed would contribute significantly to their family's wellbeing once she returned home to Ibadan. In a letter later in the year, Abiọdun wrote:

> I wish you to be practical in your expression. I want to know everything in detail without hiding things from me. . . . I want you to state (a) if you have free house

plus your present allowance you are now receiving; how much you feel can help you to face the course without hardship that can give you any set back or derangement . . . ; (b) if you are paying rent at the present rate plus your allowance, what additional amount you will require to face the course. Give answer to (a) and (b) per month. I ask these questions because myself and your people need you and your welfare. I believe that should be our concern, particularly myself because I realize the responsibility God has given us.[124]

He ended with the same advice that he had given his wife in at least one previous letter: "I trust you are thrifty, but do not manage against your health."[125]

At the end of the many letters Adukẹ wrote to her husband, she took ample time to enquire in some detail about the condition of the five children she had left behind in Ibadan. It would be reasonable to assume that her main source of information about her children would have been her mother, Rachel Ayọdele Akinloye, their primary caregiver while Adukẹ was away in England. Nevertheless, Adukẹ's letters to her husband provide insight into her emotional state on this critical issue. In many of her letters to him, she insisted on parenting despite being a continent away, providing specific instructions on a wide range of issues, especially on her children's education, health care, safety, and overall wellbeing. Only a few months after her arrival in London, Adukẹ wrote: "I believe my children are quite well? Will you please write immediately [when] you receive this letter and let me know the condition of things at home."[126] The following month, she reminded the father of her children, "Please don't forget about their coaching [tutor] after school, as school work alone cannot get one anywhere now-a-days."[127]

Adukẹ would continue to express anxiety over her children's wellbeing, especially given the fact that I, her youngest child, was only ten months old when she left for England. In April 1959 she asked Abiọdun, "How are the children? I am very anxious to hear about them especially about my small boy Olufẹmi. Please tell me more about these children."[128] In a similar vein, six months later, she reminded her husband of why she had made the sacrifice to further her education and acquire professional training: "Fẹmi will be 2 years on the 18th of October. . . . Time will soon come when I will be back home to do my duty as a mother."[129] Several months after that, she commented on the academic performance of her older children, Abiọdun and Ibironkẹ: "Thank you for your letter and the children's report sent. The reports are fair, but they should try harder this year being their first year in the class."[130] In one unusual but interesting letter, Adukẹ wrote that their "pen-friend's mother told me that the children have replied to the letters and they sent photographs as well. They hope to send Christmas cards and presents next month and I wish you could help the children in sending a native thing with Christmas card. I know they will appreciate this."[131]

In August 1960, a full year into her course in nursery school administration and teaching, Adukẹ wrote about the implications of her professional training in England for her family: "I pray that God may crown my efforts with brilliant success so that I may be able to carry out my work successfully as a mother and a helpful wife."[132] Nine months later, in a letter to her eldest child, Abiọdun, now eleven years old, that found its way into the Gladys Adukẹ Vaughan files, Adukẹ wrote: "I always think of you all and I am anxious to see you, your brothers, and sisters. Pray that the time might quickly come when I shall come home to join you with joy. Biọdun, be a good girl and do your best in school."[133]

But despite her anxiety over her children back home in Ibadan and her feelings of alienation in London, Adukẹ succeeded in making London more than a tolerable abode by assuming the role of an "auntie" or "older sister" to the emerging generation of Ibadan CMS men and women—Àwọn Ọmọ Aremọ and Àwọn Ọmọ Kudẹti—who were pursuing university degrees and professional training in England at the time.[134] Virtually every major character in the preceding chapters—namely, Abiọdun Vaughan, Samuel Ariyibi Vaughan, Jadesọla Ọdẹbunmi, S. A. Ọlọkọ, J. A. Ayọrinde, G. O. Ogunṣọla, E. O. Alayande, S. A. Fajẹmbọla, and so on—had at least one grown child pursuing a university degree or professional training in England in the late 1950s and early 1960s. Additionally, many of these grown children would marry men or women who were directly connected to Ibadan's CMS community or its affiliates in other Yorùbá cities.[135] The marriages of these Ibadan CMS men and women reveal self-perpetuating kinship and socioreligious ties among this Ibadan Anglican elite network in the second half of the twentieth century.

In many of her letters, Adukẹ informed Abiọdun of these relatives' visits, marriages, childbirths, graduations from universities, and completions of professional training, indicating the strong kinship bonds between Adukẹ and this small but formidable network of Ibadan CMS relatives and friends in London during this time. These bonds were self-perpetuating over three generations because of the depth of their Yorùbá kinship values, their strong CMS roots, and the scope of their connection to the wider world. As the social dynamics of southern Nigeria expanded considerably immediately after independence, the relationship of the next generation could not be neatly contained within the narrow confines of their Ibadan CMS network. Nevertheless, in the context of decolonization in metropolitan London, Adukẹ was held up as an elder in a loosely defined Ibadan CMS "kinship" network of *alájọgbé* based in

London to counter the alienation she evidently experienced during her three-year stay in England.

It is instructive to conclude the analysis of Adukẹ Vaughan's correspondence with a detailed discussion of her professional training in nursery school administration and teaching. Following her frustrating experience with nursing mentioned above, Adukẹ explored other professional training, such as elementary school education and catering, common among educated women from Britain's many colonies in the 1950s and 1960s. This quote from one of Adukẹ's letters to her husband on this subject reveals her dilemma in her earlier months in England: "I am still on with the arrangement for my studies but I haven't been able to get one course as yet. I have been able to get a job now, and I am managing on with this. . . . Catering is another course which will be in demand in Nigeria and some other courses as well, but all these need much money. All I wanted to do is look for a short course which wouldn't cost much and would at least fetch me something when I get home."[136]

Two weeks earlier, Adukẹ had expressed her preference for a course in nursery school administration and teaching because she thought it would be "alright for a woman of my age," but she noted that it would require significant financial resources.[137] Abiọdun encouraged his wife to seriously explore "the nursery course which is in the line of your former duty—teaching," asking, "But where is the money for the course. I need at least about six months to settle up. I need to get myself out of some debt. . . . I quite appreciate your remark that old losses are returning to us; but where is the money to feed and educate them [our children], especially at this age of journey to the end of life. When one is about 50, he should realize that the remaining journey is not up to the past. However, the old age will be happy and pleasant after the clouds have cleared away."[138]

Many of Adukẹ's London letters focused on how her professional training would shape viable career paths for her when she returned to Nigeria. When she switched from nursing to nursery school teaching and administration, the school she applied to, Wandsworth Technical College, required a testimonial from her previous place of employment as a teacher in Nigeria. After Adukẹ requested a letter of reference from the school where she had worked as a teacher for eight years, the school headmaster sent the document to Wandsworth College. A carbon copy of the headmaster's testimonial Abiọdun included in the Gladys Adukẹ Vaughan files reads:

> Reference to the District Administrative Officer, London County, Children Department, the County Hall, Westminster Bridge, London S.E.1. With reference

> to your No. CH/NEDOF of May 1959, I inform you that Mrs. Gladys Adukẹ Vaughan was a teacher in Sabo Memorial School, Ibadan, Nigeria for eight years (1950–58). During this period, she was found to be honest, diligent, intelligent, sympathetic, promising, exemplary in character and a devout Christian. 2. She seldom absented herself from the school and when it happened, it was under serious and unavoidable circumstances. She gave her best to the school, especially her class in preparation and delivery of her lesson. She is also good in infants' methods, care, management and mother of five children. 3. She left the school with ambition to further her education in the United Kingdom. Therefore, it affords me great pleasure to recommend her to anyone who may need her service.[139]

Several months after her application and ten months after her arrival in London, Adukẹ was admitted to the advanced diploma (certificate) course in nursery school administration and teaching at the college. She reported the good news to Abiọdun: "I received the result of my interview from London County Council today which says that I have been selected for nursery student training under the council."[140] Shortly thereafter, Adukẹ wrote: "I am happy to tell you that I have started my training since Sept. 7th and that was about two weeks ago. . . . I have been used in the practical side of the work now. It is not difficult and I pray I may be able to do well in the academic part of the work."[141] A year later, Adukẹ registered a major milestone in her professional training: "This is to inform you of my success in my last exam. We were told of this good news yesterday by our Matron. I am now one of the second-year students."[142] The quest for this professional training was arduous, as Adukẹ continued to report in her letters. However, now forty years old, she was aware of the gamble she took and the need to focus on the long game.

In May 1960 Lamide, Abiọdun's eldest child from his previous marriage, set sail for England to train as a registered nurse at Oxford University's Radcliffe Infirmary Hospital. Abiọdun's announcement to Adukẹ of Lamide's arrival in England is worth quoting in full:

> [1.] Your stepdaughter leaves Lagos on the 3rd instant. I sent one letter to you through her. All your requirements were despatched to you. I even sent you elubo [yam flour] and other people sent you foodstuffs. 2. Lamide will reach you on the 16th May according to shipment schedule and she will remain there with you until 21st instant when she will report at Oxford Radcliffe Infirmary Hospital. She will show you a copy of the letter written to her from the hospital authority. 3. I managed under thick and thin to cover her passage fees. Her mother also

> tried and finally members of our family came up with the usual presents [gifts]. 4. I gave her 20 pounds travelers' cheques together with 2 pounds Nigerian money which she could exchange in the boat. I also sent 5 pounds through her to you. I instructed her to exchange this before reaching you. 5. I am also sending to you herewith 10 pounds in postal order. This amount with 20 pounds travelers' cheques will help her to purchase her immediate requirement. The last 10 pounds was presented to her by her people. She received 42 pounds, 7 shillings, 6 pence financial help from different members of the family. The whole expense in this connection have gone above 150 pounds and this has given me some financial difficulties; but I think it will be very easy this time to get over.[143]

Abiọdun and Adukẹ's correspondence also featured information about simple events, such as regular delivery of parcels of Yorùbá foodstuffs and visits with close relatives, especially Lamide, as well as notable celebrations, such as family weddings and the baptisms of children in London. For example, Abiọdun called Adukẹ's attention to the gàrí and èlùbọ́ he sent "through Mr. Adeyemo whose address in London is as follows: Abiọdun Adeyemo, 60 Church Road, London, S.E.19."[144] The following month, Adukẹ requested "fine gari or elubo whenever you get people coming down."[145] When, in September 1959, Mojisola Ọdẹbunmi, Abiọdun's niece and daughter of Jadesọla Ọdẹbunmi, married Ọlaniyi Ọladeji—an Ibadan CMS gentleman from Abebi and engineering student at Queen Mary College, University of London—Adukẹ reported back to her husband and sent him a copy of "Mojisọla and Ọlaniyi's Wedding Reception Programme."[146] Finally, early in March 1961, while putting finishing touches to her professional training in London, Adukẹ reported on one of Lamide's several visits to her: "Ọlamide came here about two weeks ago. She is pretty well. I had time to talk with her about her work and advised her not to be very serious about that matter you mentioned in your letter sometimes—I mean the question of boyfriend." Adukẹ then addressed plans for her own return home: "Thank you for informing me about the nursery schools now in Ibadan. I would prefer to work in one of the three you mentioned in your letter which is St. Mary's School [Maryhill Convent School]."[147]

As if to predict what was to come when Adukẹ established a pioneering nursery and primary school in Ibadan in 1962, a year after her return to Nigeria, Abiọdun had forwarded to her an article from the *Nigerian Daily Times*, Nigeria's preeminent newspaper, on a proposed nursery school in Ibadan in 1959, several months after she enrolled at Wandsworth Technical College. The article read: "The Women's Improvement Society, Ibadan, plans to open a day nursery [school] at Ibadan early next year. Mrs. F. A. Ogunsheye, president of the society, announced in Ibadan." For his own part, Abiọdun wrote, "This move by some women will interest you: Apart from this, the Government too will soon do something and finally it is a business one can establish if he or she has the means. . . . The course you are running will surely prove useful because of the rapid development that is going on in our country."[148]

In the summer of 1961, Adukẹ took the final written examination for her nursery school course. She reported: "There were about two hundred candidates who took the examination in that centre alone and I was the only coloured lady in the whole lot."[149] A few weeks later, Adukẹ informed her husband, "The result of my final examination came out this morning and I am happy to inform you of my success. I couldn't believe my eyes when I read my name in the list of successful candidates. Praise be to God. It is now certain that I shall be coming home any time this year if I could get an accommodation on the boat. . . . I went to Oxford yesterday. Ọlamide [Lamide] was quite well. Love to my children."[150]

What was now left for Adukẹ was to complete the requirement for the practical component of her course at the end of September 1961. As she prepared for her final practical examination, Adukẹ saw the light at the end of the tunnel. With the success she attained in her professional training and academic work, Adukẹ, aware of life's many challenges, found joy in her accomplishments. In a letter before the practical examination, having overcome all odds, she wrote triumphantly: "If I pass my examination, it will be necessary to work first under any nursery school or if my people can help to create a post for me under the government, I can work in a child's welfare centre. I wish you can discuss this with some influential people whom you know is interested in our affairs. . . . I am now with four letters behind my name as a professional lady."[151]

Two weeks later, as Adukẹ prepared for her practical examination, Abiọdun discussed arrangements for her return to Nigeria:

> I forward herewith the sum of 20 pounds for deposit towards your passage home. I wish you arrange to travel by M. V. Apapa. Third Class will cost only 49 pounds. As soon as I hear about your success, I will send money to cover up. It is necessary that I renovate the house and equip it with some [new] furniture. In the event of your success and you finish the practical side in September, when do you hope to return home? . . . I hope you have returned from Oxford and that your daughter [Lamide, Adukẹ's stepdaughter] is doing well there.[152]

For her part, Adukẹ set in motion meticulous plans in her new areas of professional training once she returned home to Ibadan. With regard to employment opportunities in Ibadan, she informed her husband,

> I have sent in my application form and I chose Rev. Alayande [E. O. Alayande, now an ordained Anglican minister] and Mr. Durosaro [a regional politician] to be my referees. I have seen Rev. Alayande on his way from America. He was pleased to see me and gave me one guinea. Could you please tell Mr. Durosaro about the same and have a discussion with him about our plan? He might be in the position to help as this is a new course; my application will be sent to the Public Service of the Western Region of Nigeria. I don't mind working in a nursery school, but I prefer working in the Government Service for some time before establishing my own [school]. God's will be done.[153]

When Adukẹ left Nigeria for England in 1958, Nigeria was undergoing a major political transformation. The country had experienced about a decade of political reforms starting with the consequences of the historic 1947 Local Government Despatch, instituted by the British Labour government, and several national constitutional reforms imposed by colonial authorities, notably, the Richards Constitution of 1946, the Macpherson Constitution of 1951, and the Lyttleton Constitution of 1954.[154] All these major political reforms ultimately led to the independence of Nigeria in October 1960. Abiọdun and Adukẹ engaged in a discussion of the implications of these transformative national development issues for their family. While Adukẹ was away in England, Abiọdun, on several occasions, called his wife's attention to the ascendancy of her brother, Adisa Akinloye, in national politics following his political success in local, regional, and national politics under the constitutional reforms during decolonization in the 1950s. In 1959 Abiọdun wrote: "Registration for election to the [federal] House of Representatives (centre) is going on and your brother will contest one of the Ibadan seats. I wish him good luck. He has my cooperation."[155] As the capital of the Western Region, one of the three regional administrative headquarters of Nigeria's emergent federal government, Ibadan grew in political and economic prominence in the country. Abiọdun noted the city's growing significance in a letter to his wife in April 1960, six months before the country's independence from Britain: "Ibadan is now a special place for people's settling that one might not be able to get a vacant land to buy in the future."[156] Several reference points such as these in Abiọdun's letters were not simply to inform Adukẹ about notable developments in the country while she was away in England; they also portended the trajectory for their family upon Adukẹ's return to Nigeria.

When Adukẹ completed her practical examination in September, a younger member of the Ibadan social network who was pursuing professional training in London, Moyo Ọdẹlusi, and her husband invited Adukẹ to stay with them before she set sail for Nigeria in late October. After Adukẹ's departure from the

Ọdẹlusi household, Moyo wrote Abiọdun, expressing the hopes and aspirations of the thousands of young Nigerians in universities and technical colleges in the United Kingdom during these transformative years: "[This] is just to tell you that Auntie [Adukẹ] left us about a week ago and to be with you D.V. [Deo volente, "God willing"] by next Wednesday say 7th Nov or so. We really miss her, but we can't help her going away. We hope that she can meet you all in good state of health. . . . We shall always remember her and we too look forward to that glorious day when we shall step into that lovely country of Nigeria our fatherland. How happy shall we be. Our love to everybody at home."[157]

In her final letter from London, Adukẹ made this notable assertion to her husband: "I would like to stop having children. I am now advanced in age and moreover I would like to have the number of children that I could manage to help. I have seen my doctor about this and he sent me to the family planning centre where I could be helped."[158] As she sailed back to Lagos in October 1961, Adukẹ wrote, "This is just to say hello and to inform you of my voyage back home. We left Liverpool on the 26th October. The sea was rough the first two days on sea and most of us were sea sick but thank goodness the condition is alright now and we are having a smooth sailing back home. We shall reach Freetown [Sierra Leone] on Saturday the 3rd November and I will have to post this letter there. . . . I am looking forward to seeing you all in good condition."[159]

To conclude on a note on style and presentation, Adukẹ's letters are fascinating to analyze. Unlike that of her brother Adisa Akinloye, Adukẹ's writing style shows interesting variations in her sentence structure, phrase succinctness, and word choice, depending on the importance of the message she was trying to convey. While this style seems unintentional, it is nevertheless effective in conveying each distinct message, especially in comparison to Adisa's letters, who wrote as though he knew that I, his nephew, would try to pull apart his words decades later and decided to lock me out with consistency. Adukẹ's letters are direct and enjoyable. They consistently reveal the intentions of a woman who was determined and focused in the quest for her objectives.

A critical distinction of Adukẹ's letters in comparison to many of the letters from major characters in this book is the wide spectrum of human conditions and emotions that she engaged. Along with the letters of her mother, Rachel Ayọdele Akinloye, and brother Adisa Akinloye—all letters analyzed in this chapter—Adukẹ's dialogue with her husband, Abiọdun, effectively described in detail pressing issues at the core of the construction of their nuclear family. In reference to the range of issues discussed in other chapters that focus on Abiọdun's natal family, Adukẹ was firmly focused on her nuclear family—herself, her children, and her husband.

Along with her five biological children, Adukẹ Vaughan adopted four more. She built a pioneering private nursery and primary school of distinction in Ibadan, Omolewa Nursery and Primary School, and worked as a board member (and chair) of the city's Home for Motherless Babies, as well as various other charities, mostly for indigent children and women, in Ibadan. She rose through the ranks of Ibadan's influential women traditional chiefs to earn the title of Ọ̀tún-Ìyálóde, the second-highest women's chieftaincy title in Ibadanland. She died at the age of ninety-three in Ibadan in April 2014. Like almost all the other major characters in this book, Adukẹ was buried in the cemetery of St. Peter's Church, Aremo—which became Cathedral Church of St. Peter's, Aremo, in 2005.[160]

~

The analysis of the letters in this chapter is multilayered not simply because of the overlapping and intersecting subjects addressed by the two protagonists, Adukẹ Vaughan and Abiọdun Vaughan, but also because of the mediating voices of Rachel Ayọdele Akinloye and Adisa Akinloye. The important issues analyzed in the chapter, like those in the correspondence analyzed in previous chapters, were shaped not only by prevailing Yorùbá values and norms but also by the dramatic social and political transformations in the last two decades of colonial rule, the 1940s and 1950s.

Discussed against the backdrop of distinctive social values that emanates from the original CMS stations embodied in the ethos of Àwọn Ọmọ Aremọ, Àwọn Ọmọ Kudẹti, and Àwọn Ọmọ Ogunpa, the ideas and issues articulated in the letters in this chapter further underscore Yorùbá modernity at a moment of heightened social change in late colonial Ibadan. As evident in the story lines analyzed in this chapter, these letters reveal the moral obligations of Abiọdun as a socially mobile Yorùbá Christian man, husband to Adukẹ, son-in-law to Rachel Ayọdele Akinloye, and brother-in-law to Adisa Akinloye. The discourse on the moral order on which obligations are negotiated is predicated on the mutually reinforcing Yorùbá kinship system and reciprocal marriage relations in this moment of great social change.

It is instructive at this point to reflect on earlier letters in Abiọdun's possession, notably the letters contained in the S. A. Vaughan, Vaughan Family, and S. A. Ọlọkọ files, analyzed in the previous chapters, in which Abiọdun sustained intense dialogues with close relatives and compatriots. In the S. A. Vaughan correspondence, Abiọdun, then in his mid- to late twenties, poured his heart out to his older brother Samuel Ariyibi, revealing depth of emotion and imploring his older brother "to do the right thing." Fast forward in a sustained correspondence from his late thirties to his early fifties, and Abiọdun's actions, though more attentive, are somewhat reminiscent of the authority his older brother exerted over the Vaughan natal family in the 1930s. At various stages of their marriage, Adukẹ pleaded with her husband to be more favorably inclined to her concerns.

Interestingly, the nuances of the story lines in the Gladys Adukẹ Vaughan files are evident when compared to how some of these stories were discussed by the main characters in the files labeled Vaughan Family and S. A. Ọlọkọ, discussed in chapters 2 and 3. As discussed in the letters of some relatives—specifically, Jadesọla Juliana Ọdẹbunmi, Abiọdun's immediate older sister, and S. A. Ọlọkọ, Abiọdun's "cousin" and mentor—the traditional Yorùbá belief in *àbíkú*, the "supernatural" infants who inhabit the liminal space between temporal and spirit worlds, operated in the background of some of the letters in this chapter.[161] Despite their strong Yorùbá Anglican and Western training, Abiọdun and Adukẹ, along with their relatives, seem to have been drawn to the idea of combining their Christian beliefs and aspects of Yorùbá traditional beliefs to help explain and respond to the tragic losses of their first three infant children. Consequently, from what is explicitly stated in the letters of close relatives and from vague ideas and courses of action that are roughly discernible from some of their letters, I observe a more nuanced and subtle account in the letters of the major characters in this chapter to these tragic events.[162]

The letters contained in the Gladys Adukẹ Vaughan files also provide greater insight into the transregional evolution of Nigeria as a colonial society with its connection to metropolitan Britain through the lens of Adisa Akinloye immediately after World War II and Adukẹ from the late 1950s to the early 1960s. These letters provide an opportunity to interrogate the experience of Western-educated Africans in metropolitan Britain as colonial subjects striving for professional advancement in the shadows of racism and alienation in the United Kingdom. This direct focus on the social contradictions of the colonial condition was surprisingly absent from much of the writings of Abiọdun and his compatriots, despite their proximity to British technical specialists in the Department of Agriculture back in Nigeria. In metropolitan Britain, however, the issue of race was omnipresent, mediating various aspects of Adukẹ's experience.[163] Given Adukẹ's passing references to the racial prejudice she encountered, especially in housing, her response to these evidently painful conditions was nevertheless cavalier. Although Adukẹ occasionally reported these racial prejudices in her letters, her strong engagement with her small network of Ibadan CMS relatives and compatriots studying in London during this time provided an essential "kinship" network as an expression of *alájọgbé* to counterbalance the alienation she experienced in England. More importantly, rather than excessively focus on London's many challenges, Adukẹ, who was well aware that her stay in England was temporary, focused her attention on obtaining the resources that would ensure her educational success and professional advancement as she anticipated her return to a better life with her family, especially her children, in Ibadan.

It is clear from Adukẹ's letters on both quotidian and challenging life issues that her objectives revolved around personal advancement and the progress of her children. She focused on the future, regardless of the physical and emotional toll and cost. Despite the trauma she experienced from the loss of her infant children, Adukẹ placed much of her attention on personal progress, professional advancement, and social uplift. In many regards, it is appropriate to characterize Adukẹ as a pragmatic feminist in the context of the Yorùbá society of her time because of the ways she asserted her agency to acquire the material resources for professional advancement and personal development. Consistently asserting her agency and tactfully appropriating the transactional relationship with her much older husband as an Ọmọ Aremọ, Adukẹ did not hesitate to remark on his shortcomings as she engaged her duties as a mother, wife, and professional woman.

The letters contained in the Gladys Adukẹ Vaughan files, like those in the chapter on the Vaughan matriarchs, thus provide a critical window into gender dynamics outside its preconceived Western notions. In this chapter, gendered conditions were complicated by other salient social variables, notably, kinship, motherhood, family, social status, and social mobility. Consequently, Adukẹ's interests and actions were shaped by her ability, ambition, and *choice* as she asserted her position as a wife, mother, daughter, and sister. Adukẹ was clear in her quest for what she needed in her relationship with Abiọdun. This was initially observed in their courtship, as Adukẹ expected Abiọdun to continue in his pursuit of her, even as she took her time to ensure that she was making the right decision. Similar to chapter 2, where the matriarchs in Abiọdun Vaughan's family sustained the moral order for the Vaughan natal family in a dynamic Yorùbá colonial society, the issues raised in Adukẹ's letters—alongside those of Rachel Ayodele Akinloye and Adisa Akinloye—in this chapter provide an important conceptual framework on which to interrogate shifting gender relations and the changing role of the family, at least in this particularly social context during a moment of rapid change from the mid-1940s to the early 1960s in Ibadan.

CHAPTER FIVE

From Freetown with Love

THE LETTERS ANALYZED IN THIS CHAPTER are contained in the files Abiọdun Vaughan labeled Freetown. They were written by Bamidele Theo Brainerd, the only child of Abiọdun's older sister Dorcas Ọlayinka Brainerd; Bamidele's Sierra Leonean wife, Viola; and three of their children. These letters were written to Abiọdun from Freetown, Sierra Leone, starting in 1956, four years before Nigeria obtained its independence from Britain. The final letter in these files was registered in 1994, thirty-four years after Nigeria's independence; it marks the end of Abiọdun's decades-long practice of compiling letters from Vaughan family members and their Ibadan compatriots.

Among West Africa's British colonies, Sierra Leone has a unique history, having been founded as a resettlement colony for thousands of Black people liberated from Atlantic slavery from the late eighteenth century to the late nineteenth century. During this period, Sierra Leone was home to many descendants of free Black people from England and from across Britain's Atlantic colonies, such as Jamaica and Nova Scotia, Canada.[1] Sierra Leone was also populated by descendants of liberated West Africans, including many people from Yorùbá communities who were freed from Portuguese and Brazilian slave ships by British squadrons off the coast of West Africa during the Yorùbá Wars in the nineteenth century. Indeed, while the Yorùbá region—and, by extension, the southern Nigerian region—would later become the epicenter of CMS missionary activities in West Africa, the Sierra Leone colony, founded by the British Crown in 1787, was the launching platform for the CMS in the region at the turn of the nineteenth century. The unique historical conditions of Sierra Leone in Atlantic West Africa made this colony the focal point of British culture and civilization in the region.[2]

This is, in part, the social context for the values articulated in the letters analyzed in this chapter. Specifically, the values reflected the Ibadan CMS heritage in which Bamidele Brainerd and his children defined their aspirations in their letters to Abiọdun from 1956 to 1994, overlapping with the first three decades of Nigerian and Sierra Leonean independence from Britain. Bamidele's family in Freetown affirmed the link between Sierra Leonean and Yorùbá Anglicanism, so vividly expressed in the CMS community that had been consolidated in Ibadan by the turn of the twentieth century.

As noted earlier, Bamidele was the son of Dorcas Ọlayinka Brainerd, Abiọdun's sister. Dorcas Ọlayinka was thirteen years older than Abiọdun and had married a Sierra Leonean man, John Brainerd, who came to Nigeria at the turn of the twentieth century to work as a clerk in the colonial Department of Railway, the rail transportation system that connected Nigeria's Northern and Southern protectorates at the beginning of the twentieth century.[3] John and Dorcas Ọlayinka presumably met through her (Dorcas Olayinka's) brother Samuel Ariyibi Vaughan, a colleague in the colonial railway clerical staff (see chapter 1).[4] Bamidele was raised by his mother in Ibadan and then attended Igbobi College, Lagos, an Anglican-Methodist secondary school and one of colonial Nigeria's foremost secondary schools, in the mid- to late 1930s (see chapter 2). Following his graduation from Igbobi College, in the early 1940s Bamidele attended the University of Sierra Leone (Fourah Bay College; at the time, it was British West Africa's only university), where he met his bride-to-be, a Sierra Leonean woman named Viola. After graduating from the university, Bamidele married Viola, and they had five children: Fọlakẹ, Rotimi, Ọlaolu, Olufẹmi, and Gbemi.

The letters analyzed in this chapter cover the correspondence among three generations: an older generation represented by Abiọdun; a middle generation represented by Bamidele and his wife, Viola; and a younger generation represented by three of Bamidele and Viola's children, Fọlakẹ, Rotimi, and Ọlaolu, who wrote letters to their granduncle Abiọdun. Since Mariam—Abiọdun's mother and Bamidele's grandmother—was an important point of reference in these letters, they incorporate her generation, the foundational first generation gesturing back to the 1880s, when Mariam and her husband, Akintọla Solomon, became active members of Aremọ's emergent CMS community. Significantly, the letters also mention Fọlakẹ's son, so they connect the lives of five generations of the Vaughan family.[5]

Kinship Bonds: Freetown and Ibadan

Letter writing was Bamidele Theo Brainerd's medium for connecting the unfolding narrative of his life in Freetown with the lives of his family back in his hometown, Ibadan, after his departure for Freetown in the early 1940s. Beyond his mother, whom he evidently stayed in contact with, it appears that Bamidele's other sustained correspondence with the Vaughan family was with his uncle Abiọdun, with whom Bamidele had established a strong relationship during his youth. As Bamidele embarked on his life's journey in Freetown, studying at the University of Sierra Leone, taking up a civil service position with the government of Sierra Leone, marrying Viola, and raising a family, his letters to his uncle reflected a myriad of unfolding family issues in Freetown and Ibadan. During the duration of the letter-writing experience analyzed in this chapter, Bamidele expressed the desire to hear regularly from Abiọdun. Occasionally showing some frustration, he implored Abiọdun to reply to his letters in a timely manner. Bamidele was writing not just to be heard but also to obtain information about the conditions of close relatives back in Ibadan, to connect with his mother's family, to disseminate information about the conditions of his family in Freetown, and to solicit his uncle's support on a range of pressing issues.

Bamidele's letters were active in tone. They suggested a longing for home. In one notable instance early in the Freetown files, he wrote, "I sincerely hope this will not be the last letter [you will write me]. . . . I hope to hear from you regularly."[6] This certainly was not Abiọdun's last letter, nor was it Bamidele's. More than a decade later, in 1969, Bamidele complained that "since I wrote you last, I have not heard from you."[7] Toward the end of the year, he quibbled: "It is a long time now since I heard from you."[8] But overall, Bamidele and his family heard from Abiọdun for thirty-eight years, from 1956 to 1994, making this the longest family correspondence filed by Abiọdun.

To establish the connection between his evolving life in Freetown to that of his uncle Abiọdun back in Bamidele's hometown in Ibadan, Bamidele announced the birthday celebration of his fourth child, Olufẹmi, in December 1958: "Praise the Almighty and kindly extend my hearty thanks to mother for the trouble she took. I am writing her but I want you to please express this in person on my behalf, thanks, especially for the presents she sent to the baby. I appreciate it highly and may the Almighty lengthen her days. Amen."[9]

The first major story that linked Bamidele's family in Freetown to his mother's family in Ibadan, as documented in Abiọdun's files, was the trip Lamide, Abiọdun's daughter, took to London to study nursing in England, discussed in chapter 4. In May 1960, several months before Nigeria's independence from Britain, twenty-two-year-old Lamide, on her way to London, sailed via the Freetown port and was charged by her father to deliver a letter and package to her cousin Bamidele. Bamidele's report of Lamide's stopover in Freetown revealed the ties between him and his uncle. "I was not fortunate to see your daughter on her way to the U.K.," he wrote to Abiọdun. "I remember vividly the short time I spent with you at Ibara, Abeokuta [in the early 1940s], but to be honest

I cannot recollect this lady's face nor her mother's. . . . [S]he left a package of gari and elubo and a letter from you."[10] As he continued in the same letter, Bamidele provided greater detail about Abiọdun's package, linking the food items to himself, his Sierra Leonean wife, Freetown, and Ibadan: "She [Lamide] was wise to have left the parcel of gari and elubo together with your letter at the customs Baggage Room and sent an officer to inform me. I highly commend her for this act of wisdom. . . . My wife knows how to prepare the gari, but I will have to teach her about the preparation of amala [*èlùbó*, "yam flour"] which is almost on the same line as foofoo the favorite dish in Freetown."[11] Despite his paternal connection to Sierra Leone, Bamidele, who grew up in Ibadan and attended secondary school in Lagos, in the Yorùbá region, referenced *àmàlà*, a distinct Yorùbá food, unlike *gàrí*, which is derived from cassava and widely consumed across West Africa. Bamidele noted that Viola, his Sierra Leonean wife, was unable to prepare *àmàlà*, highlighting the distance between Freetown and Ibadan.

Whether through food or other everyday items, Bamidele, over the years, continued to reflect on his homeland. It is clear from the extent of Bamidele's letters and the letters written later on by his children that Abiọdun served as the conduit between Freetown and Ibadan. Although Bamidele had migrated to his father's native Sierra Leone, his letters evinced a longing for Nigeria, especially Ibadan, the land of his youth. He could not wait to return to Nigeria, even though he had no plans to do so at the time. This quote from a letter written in September 1963 is poignant: "I yearn for the day I will return to Nigeria, the land of my birth and boyhood. But I have no plans at present as regards my change of residence."[12] While Bamidele never returned to live in Nigeria, this sentiment captures his ambivalence about being away from the Yorùbá region of southwestern Nigeria. Three weeks later, Bamidele was connected once again to his relatives in Ibadan, this time through the marriage of his first cousin Lamide to Lokun Bakare, a fellow Ibadan CMS, graduate of Ibadan Grammar School, and engineering student in London. Bamidele wrote, "I hope she is married to a good man who will be a real brother to her."[13]

After returning to his native Sierra Leone, John Brainerd—Abiọdun Vaughan's aged brother-in-law and Bamidele's father—retained connection with Abiọdun. With Bamidele now living in Freetown, much of Abiọdun's correspondence with John concerned the welfare of his aging wife, Dorcas Ọlayinka. In the summer of 1962, Abiọdun informed John that his wife was seriously ill at University College Hospital, Ibadan, where she was a matron for indigent women and their children.[14] Abiọdun wrote, "But the money order was received towards the end of October when my sister—Mrs. Brainerd—was seriously sick. . . . We should not allow mama at Gbenla [Dorcas Ọlayinka's mother] hear of her illness. . . . I had no other business besides office and her house every day. . . . I refrained from writing to Dele [Bamidele] on this."[15] John replied, "Well if I were you, I should have written to Dele of his mother's illness and perhaps we all should have joined in prayer for her quick recovery. I hope you would do so in [the] future. Nevertheless, we are divided in body but we are one in spirit and prayer does lots of good."[16] There is no evidence in the Freetown files that Abiọdun informed his nephew Bamidele of his mother's illness.

Several years later, the question of Dorcas Ọlayinka Brainerd's failing health surfaced again as a major dialogue, this time between Bamidele and Abiọdun. In many letters from the late 1960s to the early 1970s, Bamidele lamented his inability to properly attend to his mother's care, not simply because he was away in Freetown but also because he had to balance the cost of such care with the needs of his growing family in Sierra Leone. In several letters, Bamidele called on his uncle to lend support for his mother's care. On one occasion in May 1968 when Abiọdun provided support for Dorcas Ọlayinka, Bamidele was appreciative: "Many many thanks for your services to my dear mother. May God bless you and let your children do more for you. Amen." He then explained, "I really know it is my duty to do what you are doing for her. But God knows all. I am still in the junior service and my commitments are many, especially now that the children are becoming big. If I were in senior service, I would have been too glad. However, that is providence all over and one should not murmur but persevere."[17] In another letter written in February of the following year, Bamidele again thanked Abiọdun and other family members for supporting his mother back in Ibadan. It is clear in several letters that limited resources prevented Bamidele from sending enough money to meet his mother's needs. However, Bamidele, the only child of his parents, did not shy away from his obligations to his ailing mother, always striving to gather enough resources to meet his mother's pressing needs: "Mama has appealed to me to help her but believe me dear, since I took up no employment and trade is so bad, I can hardly think of doing so. But whatever be the case and circumstance since it is Ma who has asked me, I shall send to her later D.V. [Deo volente, "God willing"]."[18] In another letter two years later, Bamidele expressed concern for his mother's failing health. "I received a letter from my mother last week informing me that she fell ill and was unconscious for a few hours," he wrote to Abiọdun. "I thank you very much for the help you rendered and the care you and your wife took of my mother during her illness. Please give my love to my grandmama and other relatives and friends especially your friend Mr. Ayọrinde."[19]

A few years before the second serious setback in Dorcas Ọlayinka Brainerd's health, Bamidele's father, John Brainerd, died in Sierra Leone late in 1967.

This sad event revealed the strong kinship ties among the natal family of Abiọdun that we have seen in countless letters analyzed in previous chapters and will feature prominently in many of the letters analyzed in this chapter. After John's death, Bamidele received support from his mother's relatives in Ibadan. He expressed gratitude to Abiọdun for the money he sent to support the cost of John's funeral: "Apart from the material assistance which the money will be to me, the gesture alone had had a psychological effect on me thus alleviating the heavy burden on my shoulders. I thank God that after all is said and done, I come from a family where there is love and a spur of altruism which is one of the cardinal principles of Christianity. I pray that that spirit may continue and pass on from one generation to another." Bamidele then gave his uncle the details of his father's death and information about the funeral: "Actually dad had been sick for the past three or four months but he did not tell us in Freetown. . . . Dad died at 3:30 a.m. on the 19th [of October] and was buried on the 22nd. . . . We have already performed the seventh day ceremony on the 25th and intend on going to church for a memorial service in accordance with custom on 12th November 1967. . . . We are planning to celebrate the 40th day of Dad's death on the 27th November 1967."[20] Although far away in Ibadan, Abiọdun not only was an uncle but also performed the role of a surrogate father to his nephew Bamidele away in Freetown on the celebration of his father's life. A strong affirmation of *alájọbí*, this sense of obligation from Abiọdun to Bamidele is a reflection of the reciprocity of care Dorcas Olayinka extended to her much younger brother, Abiọdun, when he was a boy growing up in Ibadan in the 1910s and 1920s.

In March 1972 Mariam Vaughan, Abiọdun's mother, passed on at about age 106. Bamidele conveyed his condolences to Abiọdun: "I received a letter from my mum only two days ago informing me about grandma's death on 24th March. The news came as a surprise to me because I never heard about her illness at all. Was she sick for some time before she died? How old was she before she died? Although grandma was of very ripe age before she died yet her departure will be felt by all who were endeared to her."[21] When he did not receive a timely reply from Abiọdun, Bamidele, in typical fashion, followed up with another letter, further extending condolences for his grandmother's death and expressing gratitude to Abiọdun for his mother's care: "I have no doubt you have received my last letter in which I expressed my sympathy for the irreparable death of our dear mother and grandmother. May her soul rest in perfect peace. . . . Thank you very much for all your work and interest in the family in general and in my mum in particular."[22]

Bamidele's letters to his uncle were dominated by important developments in the life of his wife and children in Freetown. He consistently provided reports of his children's educational accomplishments, professional training, travel plans to visit relatives in Ibadan, engagements, marriages, and births. A diligent father who took his parental obligations seriously, Bamidele at some point in 1967 sought financial support from his uncle to meet his children's pressing needs. In August of that year, he wrote to express gratitude for previous support and requested a small loan at a time of severe economic downturn in Sierra Leone: "I am much grateful to you sir for all the assistance you are rendering. I know it is my duty to do it but for reasons known to you I am not [always] in a position to do. Believe me, Uncle, if I were in a position to do so I would not have given you the worry because God knows it is my duty." To underscore the pressing need for the loan, Bamidele continued: "Much as I appreciate your help in respect of this loan, if it will *not* be possible for me to get it this very month [August] or first week in Sept I am afraid, Sir, it will not serve the purpose for which I badly need it. As I explained earlier the schools reopen in mid Sept and school fees, books, and uniform must be bought and paid for before opening of schools."[23] When the funds arrived later in the month, Bamidele was quick to acknowledge receipt with deep gratitude: "The money came just at the right time as schools open on the 12th instant. . . . I am really deeply touched by your prompt action taken in order to effect transfer of this loan."[24]

Celebrating the Life of Dorcas Ọlayinka Brainerd

As the only child of his parents, Bamidele wrote letters to his uncle Abiọdun that revolved around discussions of family obligations he left behind in Ibadan, the most important of which were to provide proper care for his aging mother, Dorcas Ọlayinka Brainerd, and manage the estate he inherited from her after her death in July 1973. Many of the letters discussed the last years of her life and the immediate aftermath of her death, further affirming the strong family ties that typified most of the correspondence in the Freetown files.

Bamidele, his wife, and their children expressed gratitude to Abiọdun, since he and other Vaughan family members in Ibadan had lent support to Bamidele in Freetown by taking care of his ailing mother and celebrating her life when she died. Bamidele's eldest child, Fọlakẹ, now in her midtwenties, wrote: "I must also thank you very much for all the care you took of Grandma while she was alive. I know you'll say it is your duty but at the same time it is my duty to thank you and say how appreciative I am."[25] Ọlaolu, Fọlakẹ's younger sister, wrote, "Thank you for all the care you took of grandma during the course of her illness. The good Lord himself would reward you."[26] Although Abiọdun expected these expressions of gratitude from his grandnieces as *ọmọlúàbí* (persons committed to a just community), he brushed their thanks aside, insisting that he had simply discharged his duty. His response points to the strong sense of familial obligations in the Vaughan natal family and the reciprocity of care exemplified in *alájọbí*, apparent in the correspondence among older Vaughan relatives and their social network, discussed in previous chapters. Nevertheless, the letters from the Brainerd children provide insight into what was expected from the next generation—at least those with their type of CMS Yorùbá social orientation. In one of his many carbon-copied letters to his grandnieces and grandnephew in the Freetown files, Abiọdun underscored his sense of duty and admonished them to do their part: "You need not thank me about your grandmother who is my sister. I am doing my duty. I wish you all long life and prosperity to do your duty to the end."[27]

During this time of loss and family transformation, many of Bamidele's and his children's letters reflect the integration of West African religious beliefs into the Anglican CMS upbringing that has shaped the Vaughan family now going on several generations. These letters, with their numerous references to a supreme being and the spirit world in a variety of contexts, appealed to spirit forces, especially those of the departed, to protect family members in Freetown and Ibadan. Although unable to meet all his financial obligations, Bamidele expressed gratitude through prayer for his uncle, especially for Abiọdun's help during Bamidele's mother's funeral.

Bamidele's Sierra Leonean wife, Viola, in a rare letter to Abiọdun, expressed special gratitude for his support for her family during her mother-in-law's funeral. She provided vivid insight into the place of ancestral spirits in the West African Christian ritual of the "forty days," the celebration of the life of a departed parent, noting that "Mama's [Dorcas Ọlayinka] forty days was yesterday. Theo (Dele), and myself decided to observe the day, so we talked to her on Monday night by putting water and kola on the table for her and told her that we are going to cook a big meal for her and the other families who had gone to the other world. On Tuesday was the forty days we prepared beans, and we cooked rice. Also, we killed fowls and bought meat to cook the soup."[28] Viola went on to describe how the "guests" eagerly participated in this special ritual:

> You want to see when they came to visit us, they came as a school. You want to see them devouring the food we prepared for them. That showed that they were pleased with the ceremony (I mean vultures). Everything went smoothly and quietly. There was no rain till we finished everything. We thank God for His goodness towards us. Amen. . . . I know by God's grace she [the deceased Dorcas Ọlayinka] will make provisions for everybody who has contributed to make her ceremony a success. . . . May God bless you for all that you have done and may He allow you to reap the reward of your labour. Amen.[29]

Bamidele, in a notable letter, acknowledged the many relatives who called on his family when they visited Ibadan for his mother's funeral. He expressed pleasure in what he called the "African way of life," in which family members rally around one another to lend moral and financial support in times of need. Bamidele and his family consistently expressed gratitude for good deeds rendered to them by their relatives in Ibadan, especially at this time. They wrote to ask questions about the welfare of their relatives in Ibadan. They expressed the wish to connect with family members, despite the obvious constraints of time and distance, and insisted on keeping strong kinship ties through the medium of letter writing. For Bamidele and his family it was essential that family members care for each other, but it was even more important for them to show gratitude for the support rendered by their relatives. Bamidele wrote to Abiọdun: "I do not think I can sufficiently thank you for all that you did to make the burial rites of my dear mother a success and also make our visit, though short, an enjoyable one. I pray that the link between us in Sierra Leone and you and your children will be stronger than before."[30]

Similarly, Bamidele's eldest son, Rotimi, in his early twenties, accompanied his parents to the funeral in Ibadan and then wrote to his granduncle: "Well grandpa, I must now extend my sincere gratitude to you and everyone for all you did for us during our stay at Ibadan. We were very homely, and indeed, it was a very sad moment when we had to leave. My heart was full that I could not say much at that time. Once again, grandpa, I say many, many thanks for all you did for us. We really appreciate your efforts and we shall always remember our visit."[31]

The following month, Bamidele wrote again: "After exerting much energy on the recent funeral of my Mum, I would not advise you to task your energy on anything now. You need some rest or else you may suffer a break down in health. . . . I am not surprised that distant relatives were still visiting you up to last week knowing how numerous the branches of the Vaughan family tree are. I hope you are now having a respite. On our arrival here, relatives and friends have visited us and are still visiting us to express their sympathy for our loss. That is the African way of life all over which Europeans cannot understand."[32] Bamidele also offered these cryptic words after returning from his mother's funeral in Ibadan: "I hold the few who hold this incident as a good result to the judgment of God and to the knowledge of men and to the many who sympathise with me and share in my grief and difficulty, I say pray for them still, and all will be well with you and me."[33] Viola concluded: "Let us pray that God will grant us our heart's desire to see each other frequently. Amen."[34]

Various facets of Christianity fused with West African traditional religious beliefs were evoked to positively shape family members' temporal experience.

These spirit forces were called upon as Bamidele and his family expressed gratitude for the good deeds and goodwill of their Vaughan relatives such as Abiọdun; to wish relatives and loved ones well; and to give glory to God for his grace, mercy, and favor. Most of the letters from Bamidele and his family after his mother's funeral consistently referenced their gratitude to God for his grace. They prayed for each other on paper as if they were standing together in real life. In these letters, religious expressions and practices were evoked to make sense of the family's circumstances, whether the passing of Bamidele's mother in 1973 or the passing of Bamidele's grandmother Mariam the year before. The letters also credit God's grace for the financial and moral support from family members and for landmark accomplishments in children's education and professional training, discussed in great detail later in this chapter. When Bamidele's daughter Ọlaolu suddenly fell ill and the Brainerds experienced the loss of Viola's aunt only a month after their return from Dorcas Ọlayinka's funeral in Ibadan, Bamidele reported the incidents to Abiọdun and acknowledged God's grace: "She [Ọlaolu] has already started to prepare to arrange for departure [to England] when she took ill early this month. However, she is improving gradually and we thank God for this. . . . In addition to this worry, my wife lost her aunt who was trading in Gambia on 11th August. The past three months have been a bit tough for both of us, but we thank God for His mercies."[35]

These letters demonstrate the coming together of a family in times of loss and triumph and even over those mundane activities of everyday life. The Freetown letter writers wrote to Abiọdun to show gratitude, offer themselves as grieving partners, and express sympathy. "I know God's will must be done. Grandma lived a Christian life and died the life of a Christian," wrote Fọlakẹ. "So Papa once again let's take heart and ask God for his mercy on us remaining ones."[36] Similarly, Ọlaolu, Fọlakẹ's younger sister who had visited Ibadan the previous summer, wrote: "I would like to extend my sympathy to you and all the other members of the bereaved family. It was a shock to us. The Lord knows why he does anything and we must not question his works. I know grandma is with the angels now. And her spirit will be with us all. . . . May God bless you and your family, and may He strengthen your days so that you will enjoy the fruits of your labour. Amen."[37] Bamidele's brother-in-law who was working in Northern Nigeria also extended his condolences: "It is with deep regret that I receive the news of your sister's death from my brother-in-law. It indeed came as a shock as no one was anticipating such at that particular time. However, such is fate which is beyond man's control. As a man, I am sure you will take consolation and I do pray that the Almighty will grant you strength to carry on through your days."[38] Bamidele and Viola's son Rotimi would continue to write his granduncle in the months and years after the funeral of his grandmother in Ibadan. In one interesting letter, he called for divine support and inspiration in his pursuit of professional training and educational success: "Anyway, I want to work on a plan so that I could start a postgraduate course at the start of the 74/75 session. I hope God will help me so that everything will work out well."[39]

On March 1, 1974, Viola lost another aunt in Freetown. This unexpected death coincided with the planning of the one-year anniversary of Bamidele's mother's passing in 1973. Once again, the strong faith of the Brainerd family was evoked in their letters. Rotimi's discussion of his mother's preparation for her aunt's funeral rites revealed how deeply held West African customary practices and religious beliefs, infused with Christian doctrines, shaped family traditions to celebrate the life of older relatives who were believed to have joined the ancestors. In March 1974 Rotimi informed his granduncle, "Mummy lost her aunt on the 1st of March. The one whose elder sister died in the Gambia last September. She died after a week's illness. Her death was a real shock to us because there was no indication that she was frail. Anyway, it is God's will and it must be done. The funeral service was well attended and all the arrangements for the funeral went on smoothly."[40] The following month, Rotimi continued: "Mum is now through with all the funeral rites for the death of her aunt. The forty-day ceremony was on the 9th of April, and everything went on quietly and peacefully. It was a relief for her because all throughout this period she has been actively engaged with the arrangements. Now she can take time off to relax."[41] In these letters, Bamidele and his family in Freetown were deeply engaged with the passing of their older relatives, whether locally or back in Ibadan. "We have remembered the one-year anniversary of the departure of Grandma Dorcas from the world. May her soul rest in peace," Bamidele's son Rotimi noted in a letter to his granduncle Abiọdun in July 1974.[42]

The first anniversary of Dorcas Ọlayinka Brainerd's death was the occasion for the celebration of life that is expected from close relatives for a family member who was blessed with a good life, worthy personal accomplishments, and successful progenitors. This anniversary also provided Bamidele with a unique opportunity to reaffirm his kinship connection of *alájọbí-alájọgbé* not only with his Vaughan relatives but also with his mother's wider CMS socio-religious network back in Ibadan. Thus, to mark this special one-year anniversary, Bamidele asked Abiọdun to take out an "in memoriam" announcement in a Nigerian newspaper: "Please I am asking you to do me a favour by publishing an 'In Memoriam' on behalf of myself, my wife, and the children in Sierra Leone. Thank you in advance." Bamidele continued: "We hope to attend service in the morning and cook some beans and fry akara [bean cakes] which the immediate members of the family will eat. According to the custom here we shall put some of the cooked beans and fried akara and plantains in a plate and put it on a table with a glass of water in a room. This is intended for the deceased who is expected to come in the spirit and partake of the food on the table."[43] Though these family members were thousands of miles apart, they celebrated the lives of their ancestors together. Bamidele's description of this custom that involved cooking food for the deceased in Freetown connected the Sierra Leonean custom of his wife and father with the Yorùbá customary ways he grew up with in Ibadan.

In the previous month, Bamidele had requested his uncle to search for a tombstone: "I am really anxious about making a tablet and placing it on my mother's grave. I wonder how much a decent one (which is not elaborate) will cost."[44] In another letter, Bamidele continued with his quest: "I never knew that it is very expensive to erect a tablet at the grave of a deceased relative in Nigeria. It is not so expensive here although individual craftsmen who do the job do not use marble. We have no companies who do that kind of job. It is done by private craftsmen that may be why it is not so expensive [in Freetown]. However, I shall take your suggestion and write to the company (Carrara Marble Company) at Ebute Metta [in Lagos]."[45] In a follow-up letter about a month later, Bamidele queried the monument company that his uncle had recommended: "I have received a reply from Carrara Marble Co. Ltd. They did not send me a catalogue or price list but simply informed me that their tombstones cost 1200 [naira] in Lagos and they are made of marble. The Manager even suggested that I should go and visit their workshop as the company does not issue catalogues. . . . Is there any other company that does this type of job in Nigeria as I consider the Carrara Marble Co. products expensive. I shall later on contact them to find out if it is only one type or size of tombstone they sell."[46]

Following the publication of the "in memoriam" in a Nigerian newspaper the following month, Bamidele expressed his gratitude to his uncle: "Many thanks for your last letter dated 25th June in which you enclosed newspaper cuttings of the 'IN MEMORIAM' published in memory of my late mother. Thank you very much for your efforts in rallying members of the family round to celebrate the occasion. It is a pity my request to you to have an 'in memoriam' inserted in the newspaper on my behalf and on behalf of the children here (Sierra Leone) must have reached you late hence it was published late. However, that will be corrected next year by the Grace of God."[47] In this West African tradition, the letters from Bamidele and his family reveal that the death of an elderly relative is not a feared end but rather a celebration when descendants give glory to God for a life well lived and for his grace on their family.

An important aside: In 1974 Bamidele, in keeping with shared kinship values of *alájọgbé*, in faraway Sierra Leone acknowledged the news of the passing of the mother of E. O. Alayande, one of his uncle's close friends during his youth in Ibadan, long-term compatriot, and principal of Ibadan Grammar School in the 1960s and 1970s. "I am sorry to learn about the death of Canon Alayande's mother," Bamidele wrote to Abiọdun. "Please extend my condolence to him."[48] The following year, Bamidele continued to discuss the resting place of his mother. He made a request to Abiọdun for the beautification of his mother's grave: "I had wanted to suggest it long ago before you brought it up in your letter. The money in my mother's savings bank book which is not much could be used also for the purpose of decorating her grave."[49]

The final correspondence between Abiọdun and Bamidele on the remembrance of the life of Dorcas Ọlayinka in the Freetown files included a discussion of the cost of the decoration of the tombstone for her grave twelve years later, in 1987. Bamidele wrote, "Consequent to the discussion I had with Fọlakẹ, I have arranged that $900 (nine hundred US dollars) be paid to the London account of Lamide your daughter who is my cousin. The amount was remitted about seven days ago to the under mentioned address. . . . I hope this will defray all expenses on Mama's tombstone."[50] In another letter, Fọlakẹ confirmed the transaction to pay for the cost of her grandmother's tombstone back at her resting place at St. Peter's Church, Aremọ: "Well Papa since my return I have discussed the subject of Grandma's grave with Daddy and other members of the family and we are all agreed that it is time the grave was properly made so we have already remitted $900 by cheque to Sister Lamide's bank account in London."[51]

It is fitting that Bamidele would have the last word on the remembrance of his mother: "I am not too fussy about the wording on my mother's tombstone so long as it is appropriate. In the first place it is generally written in Yorùbá language and I am not good at writing the Yorùbá language again although I can still speak it intelligently. So I can only suggest this form: 'In loving memory of our dear Mother, Sister, Grandmother, and aunt, Dorcas Ọlayinka Brainerd who changed life for eternity on 23rd June 1973. Age 79 years. At the rising of the sun and going down of the same we will remember you.'"[52] Finally, in 1992 Bamidele reported one last death of an elderly relative to Abiọdun: "My wife's mother, who was my mother-in-law, changed this life for eternity on Sunday 15th March 1992 and she was buried on 19th March 1992. She died at the ripe age of 105 years."[53]

Family Matters, Family Transactions

The letters of Bamidele on the celebration of his mother's life, heartfelt as they were, merely interrupted a well-established pattern in which everyday family matters overlapped important business transactions. Bamidele inquired about the welfare of his uncle and close relatives while discussing pressing business matters, notably, the maintenance of a rented house that belonged to his mother and new business opportunities for his aging uncle back in Ibadan. For example, many of the letters after his mother's death discussed the maintenance of a house in Oke-Ado, a socially mobile neighborhood in Ibadan, that Bamidele eventually inherited from his mother. Bamidele wrote in one notable case in 1975, "In the circumstances prevailing now in Nigeria I can understand your explanation in connection with the repairs at the house at Oke Ado. I hope however that the tenants are not giving any trouble or defaulting in the payment of the monthly rents."[54]

A few months later, Bamidele discussed more efficient strategies of maintaining the house: "I am very grateful for your interest in seeing that adequate repairs are carried out on the house at Oke Ado. . . . I agree with your suggestion to hand over the collection of rents in the Oke Ado house to Lawyer Adisa Ọlọkọ who I believe is the son or nephew of Pa Ọlọkọ [S. A. Ọlọkọ, former mentor of Abiọdun]. This will relieve you of the worries of calling at the end of the month for rent. With a reliable and honest lawyer, one is sure to get his money without any worries."[55] However, in keeping with Bamidele's strong ties to the Ibadan of his youth, important family matters with some financial rewards such as the management of this house could not be entirely separated from Bamidele's memory of his hometown: "Are there two lawyers in the Ọlọkọ family? I only knew that Pa Ọlọkọ's daughter is a lawyer [Atinuke Ige, née Ọlọkọ, who became a judge of the Nigerian Federal Court of Appeals]. I did not know that there is another Lawyer Ọlọkọ."[56]

About three years earlier, right after the death of his mother, when the recurring flood from the Ogunpa River ruined a section of the house, Bamidele expressed frustration with the failure of the Ibadan City Council to address this perennial drainage problem during the rainy season in this section of the city:

> I am sorry to learn that the usual flood at Oke Ado has done damage to the property in Mummy's house. Please convey to the gentleman, his wife, and children [the tenants] my profound sympathy for their loss. I am really very sorry to learn about the plight of the tenants at Oke Ado. Please convey my sympathy to them whenever you see them. I wonder whether Ibadan City Council can afford to sit down idly after collecting rates and taxes and see the inhabitants around

> Oke Ado suffer like this every year. It is indeed inhumane if nothing is done to stop the yearly flood. I agree with you for not worrying the tenant about the rent when he is already suffering from a flood disaster.[57]

Though he was in favor of leniency toward the tenants regarding rent after the flood in 1973, Bamidele took a very different position in June 1980, telling Abiọdun, "I agree entirely with the decision arrived at by the family about the increase in rent and rate. The proposal to effect major repairs in the house is also a good idea, but the question is money. To be candid I do not think I can raise that amount now. Things are difficult here for us with regards to cost of living and I am a pensioner who manages life with the pittance given us at the end of the month."[58] Discussion of the maintenance of the house in Oke Ado, complicated by the failure of successive Western (later Ọyọ) State Governments to resolve the flooding problem from the Ogunpa River, would remain a major issue in the correspondence between Bamidele and his uncle until the mid-1990s, when Abiọdun stopped compiling letters in the Freetown files.

As discussed above, what sustained Bamidele's protracted dialogue with Abiọdun was an abiding trust that naturally affirmed business transactions such as the maintenance of the house in Oke Ado. But Bamidele's letters also reflected genuine care from a devoted nephew for a trusted uncle and confidant. In several letters written before the passing of his mother, Bamidele expressed concern about Abiọdun's health, encouraging him not to overwork, especially as he advanced in years: "I learnt from my mum that your work is so arduous that you are almost fatigued by the time you return home in the evening. I know from experience that those who work in commercial enterprises do very hard work. I hope however that you will not overstrain yourself especially now that you are advancing in age."[59] Bamidele wrote to express concern when armed robbers broke into Abiọdun's office in 1970: "I hope you were not seriously wounded. I would like to humbly suggest to you that in the future when you want to work very late you ask for police protection."[60] A few months later he added: "I hope you are not getting any difficulty in your work. Please take things easy so as not to strain yourself."[61]

At the time of the above letters, Abiọdun was the manager at West African Breweries in Ibadan, a position he had assumed in the late 1960s after working in a managerial position in the Western Regional Government's Cooperative Union. He retired from this managerial position and announced plans to establish his private company as an agent for West African Breweries at the age of sixty-six in 1973. In response to the news, Bamidele wrote, "I am happy to learn that you have now finally retired. I pray that God may give you long life so that you may enjoy the fruit of your labor. . . . I have no doubt that with your experience you will soon build a good business which will benefit you more than the drudgery of office work. The only snag in business is that one should have more initiative. Please don't give too much goods on credit."[62]

The following month, Bamidele continued with his usual words of encouragement and prayers: "I am pleased to learn that you are settling down to business. I am quite sure that with good organization and the help of God your business will succeed."[63] Finally, Rotimi echoed his father's sentiments, reiterating his goodwill and prayers for his granduncle's business plan: "How are you getting on with the business. I hope you are doing well. I pray God to guide and direct you so that the business will continue to thrive."[64]

Bamidele and his children wrote Abiọdun to inform him of major developments in their lives and to inquire about close relatives in Nigeria. When Bamidele lost contact with two first cousins he grew up with in Ibadan, Bisi Alalade, née Ọdẹbunmi, and her brother Tunde Ọdẹbunmi, he wrote to Abiọdun to inquire about them in January 1968: "Please may I know whether Bisi and her brother Tunde are in Nigeria. I have not heard from them for ages. Even when dad died, I never received a line from them although their mother (my dear aunt) wrote me."[65] Bamidele occasionally shared thoughts on returning to the country of his youth. In 1971, for example, he told his uncle, "I wish I could get a job in Nigeria. I would have liked to go over after retiring if even for a short time. I am yearning to see what the new Nigeria looks like and also to renew acquaintanceship with old school friends who are still alive."[66]

There is a consistent reciprocity of care in the correspondence between Bamidele and Abiọdun—a tone that suggests a desire for mutual consideration that sustained the long duration of correspondence between the two main protagonists in this chapter. When Abiọdun announced his plans to build his retirement house on a plot of land adjacent to the Vaughan natal house in Gbenla in 1974, Bamidele sent his enthusiastic support and prayers: "I pray that God may help you in the new building you are putting up at Gbenla. I can imagine the work involved in the supervision of the building especially at your age. May God give you health and strength to enjoy the fruit of your labour. Please don't overwork yourself."[67]

Connecting with the Homeland: The Brainerd Children and Ibadan

The letters of Bamidele Brainerd and three of his children, Fọlakẹ, Rotimi, and Ọlaolu, largely revolve around the deliberate manner in which the children, as individuals, sustained kinship ties not only with their granduncle Abiọdun Vaughan but also with other close relatives in Ibadan. These important correspondences consolidated mutually reinforcing dialogues over several decades, linking four generations, starting with Mariam Vaughan, their great-grandmother. These letters not only reveal the interpersonal commitment of Abiọdun, Bamidele, and Bamidele's children to sustain strong kinship bonds but also incorporate wider ties with relatives in Ibadan. The letters weave tapestries of *alájọbí* between distant geographical locations, not only Freetown and Ibadan but also the United Kingdom and the United States in the 1970s and 1980s.

As previously discussed in this chapter, a special relationship based on trust between Abiọdun and his nephew Bamidele was the catalyst for the fascinating dialogues among the younger generation of the Vaughan family in Sierra Leone, Nigeria, the United States, and the United Kingdom during this period. Initially, the relationships that sustained these dialogues were conceived in the Brainerd children's visits and discussions of plans to visit their relatives in Ibadan.

The concerted efforts the Brainerd children made to visit their Vaughan relatives started with an unsuccessful attempt by Bamidele's eldest child, Fọlakẹ, to visit Ibadan in 1963. In the summer of 1963, Bamidele wrote his uncle Abiọdun to explain the disappointing news that Fọlakẹ was unable to visit her grandmother Dorcas Ọlayinka despite his best efforts: "Ị have written my mum to allay her anxiety re: Fọlakẹ's proposal to spend her holiday with her grandmother. I had already written to my mother and explained the difficulty of sending the girl during this long vacation. I told her my wife is pregnant and this as you know entails a lot of financial expenses."[68]

The following year, Bamidele explained another failed attempt for Fọlakẹ to visit her grandmother and close relatives in Ibadan:

> What happened was that we had already prepared Fọlakẹ, my daughter, to sail on the 26th July. She had already got her traveling certificate and her luggage had been prepared. Her passage was booked with the Elder Dempster Agencies who at the last moment disappointed us. We were told that all third-class cabins had been booked from Liverpool to Lagos and that she would either travel on the 1st class cabin or deck. As the 1st class is too expensive and the deck is not safe for such a young and inexperienced girl, we had to abandon the idea.[69]

In 1966 Fọlakẹ traveled from Freetown to Ibadan to visit her grandmother Dorcas Ọlayinka, great-grandmother Mariam, granduncles Abiọdun and Samuel Ariyibi (who now resided permanently in Lagos), grandaunt Jadesola Ọdẹbunmi, aunties, uncles, and cousins along with their children in Ibadan. This was the first of three visits Fọlakẹ made to Ibadan in the 1960s and the 1970s recorded in the letters contained in the Freetown files. When she returned home to Freetown after her visit to Ibadan in 1966, a new medium of correspondence opened up between Fọlakẹ; two of her siblings, Rotimi and Ọlaolu;

her Sierra Leonean mother, Viola; and her father, Bamidele, to Abiọdun and other relatives in Ibadan. In his letter to his uncle Abiọdun after the return of his daughter to Freetown, Bamidele discussed the photos she took with her many relatives. His description of the photos demonstrates intergenerational bonds that were made more dramatic because of the passage of time and geographical distance between Freetown and Ibadan.

Bamidele also described Fọlakẹ's appreciation for the kindness of her relatives in Ibadan. Her vivid descriptions of the people she met and the places she visited connected her father to these relatives as well. Bamidele wrote, "She related to me and her mother all your kindness and help you gave to her as a father. We thank you all for all the trouble you have taken to make her stay at Ibadan an enjoyable one. . . . My special thanks to your amiable wife (formerly Miss Akinloye) who passed here some years ago to the U.K. . . . Fọlakẹ spoke so highly of her interest in her welfare that I wish I could fly to Ibadan to express my personal gratitude to her." Bamidele revealed that he only recognized older relatives in the photos but felt connected to his boyhood through all the beautiful photos and the news his daughter shared with him. "Having left Ibadan for so long I can only boast of knowing my near relatives. Can you believe me that in the picture Fọlakẹ took with Grandma and her great grandchildren, I could recognize such ladies like Bisi, Ẹbun, Taiwo, and Kẹhinde. I could not recognize others like late Uncle Ladun's children and Auntie's other daughter."[70] In another letter, expressing his gratitude for his uncle's hospitality, Bamidele wrote: "I am pleased to learn that our Fọlakẹ (for she is yours as she is ours) had a wonderful time with you and the entire family in Ibadan."[71] It meant so much to Bamidele that his eldest child was overwhelmed with such love and hospitality from his relatives in Ibadan. For her part, Fọlakẹ wrote to her granduncle, "Well Papa everybody was so happy to see me and when I showed them the pictures, they were so happy to see them. I tried to point out to them all the people who were there and all my brothers and sisters and mummy were so happy to see you all because they don't know you and they didn't know we had such a large family in Nigeria. . . . I cannot write grandma by this mail as I am pressed for time. Please tell her I shall write her soon."[72] Without any coordination, Fọlakẹ, her siblings, and their father were writing to family members in Ibadan. Conversely, family members in Ibadan were busy writing to Bamidele and his family in Freetown. Focusing on the wide range of issues that the Freetown letter writers responded to from their Ibadan relatives, one can imagine maps with dotted lines jumping from one location to another, each representing a different family member connecting with another.

After a second visit to Ibadan in the summer of 1970, Fọlakẹ wrote her granduncle when she arrived back home in Freetown: "Daddy, mummy, and all my other brothers and sisters send their love and we all thank you very much for caring for Grandma."[73] Fọlakẹ's letters underscored God's grace, revealing the strong CMS traditions of her family in Freetown and those of her relatives in Ibadan going back several generations. In one instance, she wrote: "May God bless you and spare your life to enjoy the fruits of your labour. May he let you see many more of that Big Day in your life, Amen."[74]

Fọlakẹ's visits also opened up a medium to convey the educational progress and professional success of Bamidele's children in Freetown to Abiọdun and their relatives in Ibadan during a critical time in the evolution of Bamidele's family in the 1960s and the 1970s. As we have seen in previous chapters, Western education has always been the barometer of success for the letter writers in this book, and it would continue to define the aspirations of the next generation. But with the generation emerging out of decolonization in the 1950s and 1960s, the attainment of a university degree was now the ultimate yardstick of success for a young person of their social background, so Bamidele wrote to Abiọdun with great pride when his eldest child, Fọlakẹ, graduated with a bachelor's degree in economics in 1970: "I have no doubt my mother has informed you about the success of our daughter in her final exams for the degree of B.A. Econ (Durham University). May praise and glory be to God who has helped her throughout her course. She is working temporarily now at the Barclay's Bank until she makes her final decision. You see she wants to continue the course consequently she is hunting for scholarship which will enable her to do the M.A. Econ."[75] In the same letter, he recorded the educational progress of Fọlakẹ's younger siblings: "Rotimi is reading for a degree in science. My third child Ọlaolu has just sat for the G.C.E. 'O' level examination and is awaiting the result. May God crown her efforts. Amen."[76]

Bamidele later told Abiọdun the good news of the academic success of his younger daughter: "I am pleased to inform you that my second daughter Ọlaolu who sat for the G.C.E. 'O' level examination in June 1970 passed. She now intends to continue her studies at another secondary school in preparation for the G.C.E. 'A' level examination."[77] Three years later, after completing her general certificate of education, advanced level, Ọlaolu received a government scholarship to study at a university in the UK.[78] And in the summer of 1971, Bamidele proudly announced, "I am happy to inform you that my second child Rotimi by name succeeded in his B.Sc. examinations which he sat in June 1971."[79]

Reconciling his family obligations in Freetown with a longing for the land of his youth in Ibadan and Lagos, especially the desire to provide a solid foundation for his children in Sierra Leone, however, proved challenging. In this one of several letters, Bamidele lamented: "I hope you will realize the difficult position I am placed because of family ties. Much as I would like to go to Nigeria after retiring, yet the family ties here prevent me from doing so. I still have three children going to school—one is only 8 years old. To leave them will be a problem for me."[80]

Bamidele's younger children also kept their granduncle informed about their educational accomplishment and professional training. Following his return to Freetown from their grandmother's funeral in Ibadan in 1973, Rotimi, who had taken up his father's habit of providing detailed information about the family and matters of general interest in his correspondence with his granduncle, recounted his experience as a science teacher in a government secondary school after graduating from the University of Sierra Leone: "I have now started teaching at one of our secondary schools. I have been waiting for the fisheries job since we returned, but the people kept promising and that seemed to be the end of it. When schools reopened, I decided to secure a teaching appointment, I am getting used to it now and it's also quite an experience. I don't mind it at all, since I only hope to teach awhile. I am hoping to proceed to further studies towards the end of next year if all goes well."[81] Reporting further on his professional progress and the wellbeing of his siblings at the end of 1973, Rotimi wrote:

> I am happy to say that I am getting on well with the teaching job. There is no cause for complaint. I am still hoping to get the other job as I am keeping my fingers crossed. Yes, I do find time to do some studies. In fact, you have to be reading in order to teach efficiently, especially when I have to teach up to the G.C.E. O Level classes. . . . I am trying to get the prospectus for Ibadan University, so that I could see whether I can do some postgraduate course there. . . . I received letters from Fọlakẹ and Ọlaolu first week, and they say they are well and doing fine.[82]

In a letter written the following month, Rotimi continued where he had left off: "I am getting on well with work. The children [Rotimi's students] are now having their exams, and school is expected to close for the Christmas vacation on 18/12/73—next Tuesday. Fọlakẹ and Ọlaolu are doing fine in Britain. In fact, I got letters from both of them last week. . . . When I write them next, I shall mention that you enquired about them."[83] Rotimi continued to provide his granduncle Abiọdun with detailed information about his experience as a secondary school science teacher in Freetown along with his future professional plans the following year. In one instance in March 1974, Rotimi wrote,

"I have to do a lot of work preparing the students for their G.C.E. exams," and in the following month, he wrote: "We have reopened for the third and also the last term of the present school year, which is the most important. All students are now thinking about examinations. . . . I shall do my best to help them as much as I can."[84]

A month after that, Rotimi informed Abiọdun not only about his progress as a teacher but also about the educational progress of his siblings in Sierra Leone and England: "I hasten to reply because soon I will be engaged earnestly with preparing questions for the end of school year exams. In fact, the G.C.E. exams have already started. Olufẹmi [his younger brother] has started his as he is doing some supplementary subjects this year. I heard from Fọlakẹ and Ọlaolu about a fortnight ago and they are getting on nicely and also doing fine. They too will be having their exams early next month. I pray that God will help all of them in their studies and he will crown their efforts with success."[85]

Shared family values premised on the wellbeing of the next generation continued as an important theme in the Brainerd family letters in the early 1970s. These letters focused even more intentionally on professional training and employment opportunities for the children, with requisite updates on their educational accomplishments. As we have seen, these discussions cut across generations, from Abiọdun to Bamidele and from Bamidele's children back to their granduncle, connecting the long distance between Ibadan and Freetown and now following the Brainerd children as they moved on to the United Kingdom, where Bamidele's two daughters were pursuing undergraduate and graduate degrees, while Rotimi continued his quest for professional advancement.[86]

In January 1974 Bamidele announced happy news: "You will be pleased to learn that Fọlakẹ was engaged to a former colleague of hers at the Fourah Bay College in London in December last year. Her fiancé is Mr. Thomas a law student in London. I shall inform you when the marriage will take place. Fọlakẹ is still carrying on with her studies and she expects to complete her course even after her marriage by the Grace of God. She has passed parts I and II of the A.C.C.A. exams. Her sister Ọlaolu is also trying in her studies."[87]

When Fọlakẹ became pregnant later in the year, Bamidele again announced the good news to his uncle, with the inevitable spiritual affirmation: "Since then I have heard news from Fọlakẹ that she is expecting a baby soon for the gentleman who engaged her last December. This piece of news was not revealed to me until lately. . . . I only pray fervently that God and the spirits of the departed may help her deliver her baby safely when the time comes."[88] And in May 1974 Bamidele announced the birth to Abiọdun: "You will be pleased to learn that Fọlakẹ gave birth to a baby boy last month. I understand that both of them are well."[89] As the baby was the first grandchild of Bamidele and the first greatgrandchild of Dorcas Ọlayinka Brainerd, the arrival of Fọlakẹ's baby in London was an important turning point not only for the Brainerd family in Freetown but also among their Vaughan relatives in Ibadan.

In preparation for Fọlakẹ's wedding, Bamidele reported: "I have to inform you that Rotimi will be leaving by air tonight to visit his sisters in London and to take part in Fọlakẹ's wedding as it is not financially convenient for me and Viola to go. Please tell Auntie that the wedding will take place in London on the 31st August—the last Saturday in August."[90] Similarly, Rotimi wrote: "I must inform you that I should be leaving for Britain around 15/7/74 to witness Fọlakẹ's wedding. I guess dad would have informed you about that by now. Actually, I was not planning all this time to go, but since she is the only one there with her sister, I had to assist them."[91] After Fọlakẹ's wedding, Bamidele distributed portions of the wedding cake to his uncle, relatives, and close friends in their wider CMS social network in Ibadan: "About three weeks ago I sent a chunk of Fọlakẹ's wedding cake by air to you to distribute to relatives and close friends like Mr. Ayọrinde and Pa Ọlọkọ. I hope you have received it by now because our postal system here is sometimes unreliable."[92]

Later, in October 1974, Rotimi continued along the common theme of family welfare, educational progress of the next generation, and spiritual affirmation for the family's advancement: "No doubt you would have heard from dad that the wedding was quite a success," noted Rotimi in a letter to his granduncle. "May God give them a happy home and long life to enjoy their offspring. . . . Fọlakẹ and Ọlaolu have returned to their colleges now. May God give them strength and courage to go through their studies successfully. . . . I have also resumed teaching since the Tuesday after my return. I am having quite a hectic time now, since this is the beginning of the school year."[93] The following month, Rotimi continued: "I got a letter from Fọlakẹ and Ọlaolu last week and they are doing fine in their studies. They are only complaining about the rising cost of living which of course is worldwide. Now I don't bother to talk about it, because it is a waste of time. It seems endless, so I have come to accept it. . . . Teaching is very tedious and it needs a lot of patience and understanding. There is very little reward in it, because only a few of the children are serious these days."[94]

In addition to the happy news of Fọlakẹ's wedding and the birth of her son, Bamidele continued to focus on the importance of Western education for human advancement, which features prominently in the letters of the major characters in this book. Bamidele, in one of his letters, explored the question of academic integrity when informing his uncle of a BBC report of the "dishonest practice of University students forging the G.C.E. exam certificate to gain entry into Lagos University." On this subject, he concluded: "This is really bad and a stop should be put to it or else Nigeria will lose her respect in the outside world."[95]

As Bamidele navigated life's opportunities and challenges, especially through the lens of his children, with education at the forefront, his letters and those of his children continued to provide updates on the accomplishments of various cousins and siblings in their academic and professional training not only in Sierra Leone and Nigeria but also increasingly in the United Kingdom and the United States, where the younger generation were beginning to pursue advanced education and professional training. In Abiọdun's and Bamidele's families, this started with Abiọdun's eldest child, Lamide, in the United Kingdom in 1960 and continued with his second child, Abiọdun, in the United States in 1968, followed by Bamidele's eldest child, Fọlakẹ, as a postgraduate student in the United Kingdom in 1970. The contents of these letters thus reveal how the new generation of the Vaughan family—including their cousins in Sierra Leone—were making headway, despite economic downturns, limited resources, and political instability in these two newly independent West African countries.

One of the most notable of these academic accomplishments occurred in 1972 when Fọlakẹ, following her undergraduate degree in economics at the University of Sierra Leone (with a bachelor of science in economics conferred by Durham University), completed her postgraduate degree from Durham University, one of Britain's oldest universities. In August 1972 Fọlakẹ announced her milestone achievement to her granduncle: "I guess you've heard of the news of my success from Grandma but I know it's my duty to write and inform you especially as I know how much interest you've showed in my affairs."[96]

For the Brainerd family, 1975 opened with the good news of Rotimi's appointment as a fisheries officer in the Ministry of Agriculture and Natural Resources. No longer a schoolteacher, he was finally pursuing the professional path for which he had trained at the University of Sierra Leone a few years before. Immediately after his appointment, Rotimi announced the news to his granduncle:

> I am happy to inform you that I have been appointed a fisheries officer. I received the letter of appointment just yesterday, and I hope to assume duty by the end of the month. The appointment has been long outstanding. At least, I have waited for about 18 months for this appointment. May the Almighty be praised. I am leaving the teaching field to enter into another field, which I hope will be interesting, because I will be doing a lot of research work which would involve reading a lot of scientific journals and publications up to and even beyond my level of qualification.[97]

The following month, Bamidele shared the news of his son's appointment with his uncle: "You will be pleased to learn that Rotimi has succeeded in getting appointment into the Civil Service. He was appointed as Fisheries Officer in the Ministry of Agric and Natural Resources late last month and he started to work in the Ministry early this month."[98]

With the steady progress of Bamidele's and Abiọdun's children in the mid-1970s, letters from Bamidele and Rotimi continued to provide updates on the educational advancement and professional training of the next generation of the Vaughan clan in Sierra Leone, Nigeria, the United Kingdom, and the United States. With the deeper engagement of correspondence between the Brainerd children and their granduncle, information about happenings in Ibadan and from their cousins now traveling to the United Kingdom and the United States for higher learning filtered through to Bamidele and his children. In one instance, Bamidele wrote to Abiọdun that he was "pleased to hear from Fọlakẹ that your daughter Kumbi went to the United States recently. I wish her good luck and pray that she may return to meet you and render assistance to the family."[99]

While a graduate student at Durham University in 1972, Fọlakẹ expressed apprehension about living conditions: "There are only two black girls in the hostel—a Nigerian girl and myself. Some of the white girls are friendly but some are very snobbish and just don't care about black people. The Yorkshire people are very nice and helpful. They treat me nice. I have not encountered any problems so far thanks to the Almighty and I do hope I don't have any till I finish my studies."[100] In a perspective reminiscent of the reaction of older Nigerians to racial prejudice in the British metropole immediately after World War II, her granduncle Abiọdun wrote: "I am very happy indeed to receive your letter of the 10th Feb 1972. I realize that it takes time to settle down in a new country especially when you are on your mission. No doubt you will meet with so many characters—some good and some bad—you will have to bear them all."[101]

In another letter written in May 1976, Bamidele wrote: "I hope Kumbi will remember to tell her cousin, Fọlakẹ, about her intention to return home as she will be anxious to hear from her. Praise be to God that she has completed her course. Fọlakẹ and her sister are still in the United Kingdom trying hard at their studies."[102] Several months later, Bamidele in an apparent reply to information from his uncle observed:

> I never knew that Subu [Abiọdun's daughter] had gone to the U.S.A. I thought that she is at Ibadan because when we were there in 1973, she was then a student at Ife University. It is really a good experience for students to go abroad and

> study. The change of environment alone broadens their view of life in general. . . . Rotimi expects to go to U.K. on a year's course soon. This is being arranged by his Ministry (Agriculture and Natural Resources) and the British Government. As a fisheries officer, he is to study how the fishery industry here is like [that] in the U.K.[103]

In October 1976 Bamidele wrote: "Fọlakẹ is trying in her studies. She passed the final examinations of the A.C.C.A. with reference in only one subject which she hopes to sit later this year by the grace of the Almighty God. Her sister [Ọlaolu] has also passed her exams and obtained the diploma in medical secretaryship. We give praise to God for his help and mercies."[104]

Bamidele's and his children's letters in the 1970s also discussed everyday family matters such as the impact of Sierra Leone's economic downturn on their family and news of the passing of older relatives back in Nigeria. When the Brainerd family received the news of the loss of Lamide's maternal grandfather, Bamidele sent his condolences to Abiọdun and the Vaughan family in Ibadan: "Please accept our sympathy, though belated, for the death of Lamide's grandfather at Abeokuta. I do not think I met the old man during the time I visited you at Abeokuta. However, please extend our sympathy to Lamide and her mother."[105] Rotimi also added his condolences: "I am so sorry to hear of the death of Lamide's mother's dad, please extend my deepest condolences to the bereaved family. May his soul rest in perfect peace."[106]

When Lamide's mother—Abiọdun's first wife, Dorcas Bolaji Ajibose-Vaughan—passed on only a few months after her own father's death, Bamidele expressed heartfelt condolences: "I am sorry to hear that Lamide lost her mother. I remember her quite well when I spent my holiday with you at Abeokuta in 1936 or 1937 [while in secondary school at Igbobi College]. . . . I remember also that she came to visit me and my wife when we were at Ibadan [in 1973 during Bamidele's mother's funeral]. Please accept my heartfelt sympathy and confess the same to Lamide and her husband."[107] By recounting the past spent with Lamide's mother, Bamidele signaled that this was someone he had not forgotten, someone whose memory he could recall, and someone whose loss mattered to him. The expression of such intimate sentiments to his uncle regarding the death of Dorcas Bolaji Ajibose-Vaughan and her father was essential to Bamidele's connection to his mother's natal family in Ibadan. Because of Bamidele and Abiọdun's special relationship over the years, going back to his youth, the correspondence with Abiọdun by the Brainerd family in Freetown served as another affirmation of Bamidele's enduring connection to Ibadan.

As with the announcement of Fọlakẹ's engagement in 1974 in London, Bamidele responded with joy to the announcement that his uncle Abiọdun's daughter Ibironkẹ had gotten engaged in New York City two years later. "I am happy to learn that Ibironkẹ has been engaged," Bamidele wrote to Abiọdun. "I wonder whether she is the lady who resembles you very much. I remember she passed through Freetown once when she went to Nigeria on holidays. May God give her a happy marriage home."[108] And when Ibironkẹ got married a few months later, Bamidele sent congratulatory messages: "I am happy to learn of the marriage of Ibironkẹ. I wish her and her husband a happy matrimonial life."[109]

When his uncle's other daughter, Abiọdun, got married in Ibadan in 1978, Bamidele wrote him to say that he sent "a congratulatory cablegram to your daughter, Abiọdun and her husband on the day of their wedding—at the Greenspring Hotel. I hope they received it. I wish them God's blessings in their married life. Please accept our heartiest congratulations from all of us here. It is indeed a blessing to be alive to see one's children settling down in life after spending so much on their upbringing and training. May God give Abiọdun and her husband a happy home."[110]

From late 1970s to the mid-1990s, when the last letter entered the Freetown files, Bamidele's letters focused on connecting his younger children, Ọlaolu, Olufẹmi, and Gbemi—all born in Freetown from the early 1950s to the early 1960s—to their relatives in Nigeria. With the passing of their grandmother Dorcas Ọlayinka in 1973 and with Abiọdun advancing in years, Bamidele was even more intentional in this effort. As we observed in the 1960s and early 1970s, when he arranged visits to Nigeria for his older children, Bamidele again explored travel plans to Ibadan for his third child, Ọlaolu, in August 1979. "My daughter, Ọlaolu, has expressed her wish to visit the land of her grandmother in October or early November this year," Bamidele told his uncle. "She was born after Rotimi and works in the Office of the United Nations Development Programme here. I would be grateful if you could let me know as soon as possible if you think it will be advisable for her to go to Nigeria at that time of the year to spend her holiday."[111]

The following month, Bamidele followed up on his request to Abiọdun by first relaying important family news: "I am pleased to inform you that Olufẹmi our fourth child left for the UK on the 26 instant on a course in telecommunications. He works for the Sierra Leone External Telecommunications Limited. He will be away for two years. May God go with him and help him in his studies. Amen." He then explored Ọlaolu's travel plans to Nigeria at the end of 1979: "Ọlaolu likes to know some places in Nigeria so I hope you will afford her the opportunity to know towns like Benin and Ife. I have written Auntie Gladys [Gladys Adukẹ Vaughan] about her visit as Ọlaolu is anxious to meet her again after a long absence."[112]

Four years later, in 1983, Bamidele's youngest child, Gbemi, a student at the University of Sierra Leone, like her older siblings, Fọlakẹ, Rotimi, and Ọlaolu, visited Ibadan. When she returned, her father expressed gratitude, as he did after Fọlakẹ's visit to Ibadan in the 1960s and 1970s, to his uncle and other relatives who hosted her: "Thank you very much for making Gbemide's [Gbemi] stay at Ibadan memorable and pleasant. She told us about her visit to Auntie Alafara [Grandaunt Jadesọla in Alafara], Lamide, Auntie Gladys. . . . I am going to write Auntie Gladys and Taiwo in Lagos to thank them for the warm welcome given to Gbemi."[113]

Later in the year, Bamidele reported on the success of Gbemi at the University of Sierra Leone: "I am happy to say that Gbemide was successful in the examination she sat for in early September and she has already started work in the second-year class in the economics and social sciences faculty at the university. Although scholarships are not easily awarded to students here at the University, but thanks be to God the Almighty she has been lucky to be awarded one at the beginning of this academic year which started on 1st October 1983."[114]

In June 1984 Bamidele shared more happy news about the progress of the next generation with his uncle: "You will no doubt be pleased that Ọlaolu my daughter who visited you in 1980 was engaged last Friday 29 June to a Mr. Leslie Thomas. It was a quiet affair as the cost of living nowadays does not warrant any unnecessary expense."[115] At the end of the year, Bamidele, as he had done with Folake ten years before, reported on Olaolu's wedding plans: "The preparation for Ọlaolu's wedding which took place here on 15 November has engaged part of my spare time. Thanks be to God the Almighty everything ended well." In the same letter, Bamidele acknowledged receipt of an invitation to a different wedding, that of Abiọdun's son. "Unfortunately," he wrote, "none of us here will be able to attend the wedding of your son, Wọle. However, I hope my brother-in-law will be able to make the journey to Ibadan to represent us. We sincerely wish Wọle and his future partner all the best in their marriage life. May God the Almighty bless them with children who will be good citizens in His kingdom."[116]

In 1986 Bamidele's son Rotimi finished a PhD in marine resource economics at the University of Rhode Island. Bamidele informed Abiọdun that Rotimi, "who accompanied me and my wife to Nigeria in 1973 [for the funeral of Bamidele's mother] has completed his studies in the USA and he is working for an international organization in Senegal. He visited us with his wife a few days ago and enquired after you and Chief Ayọrinde."[117]

Several letters from Bamidele to Abiọdun in the late 1980s indicate that, at least in Bamidele's opinion, there was growing strain in the transnational communications between Bamidele's family and their relatives in Ibadan. This was expressed in mild lamentations, such as "Please give my regards to my dear auntie at Alafara. Her daughter has broken contact with us altogether. Even my cousin Wọle who used to communicate with Gbemi before has stopped. I hope he is not living overseas."[118] Additionally, later in the year, he quibbled, "It is a pity that our children don't communicate with one another to keep in touch in case of eventuality. Olugbemide [Gbemi] at one time was communicating with Wọle but once he got married the chain of communication appears to have been broken. However, I hope he (Wọle) and my other cousins are well."[119]

To wrap up family news in Ibadan and Freetown in the late 1980s, Bamidele in 1987 told Abiọdun that he was "shocked to learn from your letter the dastardly attack of those barbarous armed robbers on the house of Lamide and her husband. Thank God her life and those of her husband and children have been spared. In the whole of West Africa, I believe Nigeria is the worst for armed robbery."[120] Two years later, Bamidele expressed "heartfelt condolences" at the passing of Abiọdun's son-in-law [Ibironkẹ's husband, Adebayọ Adefọpẹ] and conveyed his gratitude to his "dear Auntie at Alafara. . . . for the beans she sent to me by Fọlakẹ" and stating, "It is a long time since I ate that type of brown beans. We have more of the white beans here. The elubo (yam flour) Fọlakẹ bought was also delicious."[121] In 1993, the year before the final entry of letters in the Freetown files, Bamidele informed Abiọdun that his youngest child, Gbemi, "who visited you in July 1983 and worked for a short spell at the Nigerian Institute of Social and Economic Research has gone to New Delhi to do a short course in computer technology."[122]

Political Discourse

In sharp contrast to many of the letters contained in the files analyzed in this book, many letters in the Freetown files were decidedly political, with Bamidele and his son Rotimi actively engaged in sophisticated discussions on virtually every major political and economic development in Nigeria and Sierra Leone in the first three decades after the attainment of independence from the 1960s to the 1990s. Bamidele wrote extensively about political instability, military coups, economic downturns, droughts, and insecurity, alongside the resilience and resourcefulness of local communities—all prevalent issues in these two West African countries in the early decades after independence.

Opening his discussion on politics with a passing reference to a military coup in Sierra Leone in March 1967, Bamidele told Abiọdun, "I would have written you long before now but the political uproar and the military coup, which you no doubt have heard about, had hindered me. For the past few weeks, we were in danger for our lives."[123] In the same letter at the onset of the Nigerian Civil War in 1967, Bamidele made a casual reference to a war that would have a devastating impact on southeastern Nigerian communities by the time it ended in January 1970. "This is efficiency par excellence," he stated sarcastically. "At this rate of doing business, I am afraid Nigeria's economy will suffer terribly during this civil war."[124]

As Bamidele engaged the tragic consequences of the Nigerian Civil War (also known as the Nigerian-Biafran War) and the negative outcomes of the economic crisis in Sierra Leone, he continued to report on the educational progress and professional training of his children. He wrote in one instance: "How is the civil war affecting life over there? I hope there is not much hardship. Rotimi was successful in the G.C.E. examination ordinary level which he sat for in June 1967. . . . Please give my regards to my grandma, your wife, and your children."[125] After the cessation of hostilities from the Nigerian-Biafran War in January 1970, Bamidele wrote: "I'm glad that the war is now over in Nigeria. I pray most sincerely that God may give the country serious and true leaders and not a bunch of opportunists who are out to feather their nests."[126] Bamidele consistently underscored Nigeria's special place as Africa's most populous country while African countries constructed pathways in governance after decades of colonialism. Despite his embrace of Sierra Leone, his father's homeland, Bamidele saw Nigeria as home and expressed concern about the country's recurring political crises since independence in 1960, exemplified in the Nigerian-Biafran War.

Despite the serious challenges confronting emerging African states, Bamidele, a standout cricketer and sportsman at Igbobi College, Lagos, in one of his letters took respite in a detailed discussion of the biannual West African University Games in Freetown in 1969. Athletes from universities across West Africa gathered in Freetown to compete in a recently established sporting event. He wrote with great excitement that these young men and women were the future of the new Africa. For Bamidele, this sporting event was a welcome break from the instability that many African countries were experiencing at that time. "Early this month students from the Universities of Ibadan, Ife, Lagos, Ahmadu Bello at Zaria together with those in Ghana, Liberia, and Senegal met in Freetown for the biannual Sports or games. We had a thrill in seeing the young men and women showing their prowess in sports," he wrote to Abiọdun. "Currently visiting us is the Nigerian Cricket Team which has started to play a test match against the Sierra Leone Cricket Team since Friday 18th April 1969. The match will end today and the Nigerian team expect to proceed to Bathurst [the name of the capital of the Gambia until 1973] where they will play another test match next Thursday."[127]

Following his penchant for drawing conclusions on the consequences of political and economic crises in Nigeria and Sierra Leonne, Bamidele was concerned about the image of Nigeria in the outside world. He noted that many other Africans were closely following political events in Nigeria and asked for firsthand information from his uncle, despite his extensive consumption of news on Nigeria from the Sierra Leonean press, the BBC, and Voice of America. Bamidele wanted to understand the Nigerian story not only from the perspective of Sierra Leonean and Western journalists but from the perspective of relatives in Ibadan such as Abiọdun. For example, he was interested in how Nigerians were responding to the historic national election of 1960:

> Nigeria has indeed become the cynosure of all countries, especially Africa. Believe me, you cannot imagine the interest with which many people here follow events, especially political events, in Nigeria. Everybody was interested to see how the Nigerian politicians would behave after the election results especially as there were reports of disturbances and arrests during the election campaign. . . . Dr. Nnamdi Azikiwe seems to be the favorite Nigerian politician here and not a few were surprised and disappointed when he failed to be [elected] Federal Prime Minister. . . . I am keenly interested about events at home and I hope whenever you find it possible you will give me some titbits of home news.[128]

With Nigeria moving into its second decade of independence in the 1970s, Bamidele's letters continued to explore political and economic development in the country, though now drawing greater comparison with the situation evolving in Sierra Leone. As he followed the news in Nigeria, he sought to understand how Nigeria's oil boom, strikes by labor unions, and worldwide inflation were affecting his relatives in the country. Both he and his son Rotimi struggled to reconcile increasing inflation in Sierra Leone and the news of the oil boom in Nigeria in the mid-1970s. In November 1974 Bamidele wrote: "I heard over the BBC some time ago that Nigeria's balance of payment is very healthy due to the boom in crude oil. With Nigeria having millions of naira on reserve I have no doubt that business is good and that there is no cause for complaint. I wonder whether Nigeria is experiencing the seemingly worldwide inflation." He then described the effects of inflation on the Sierra Leonean economy: "Costs of imported [goods] as well as local foodstuffs soar almost every week. However, we are managing with what we have. As you may know we have not got much variety of native foodstuffs in Sierra Leone hence you have to buy only staple food which is rice at any price you can get it. A thing like beans is a luxury."[129]

When discussing two important political events in the region in the 1970s, notably, the return to civil-democratic government from military rule in Nigeria and the consequences of the failed military coup in Sierra Leone, Bamidele wrote:

> I heard over the BBC on Tuesday last that the Military Government [in Nigeria] has abolished the idea of handing over the reins of government to civilians in 1976. This must be a big disappointment to many aspiring politicians in Nigeria. I am sure General Gowon [the Nigerian head of state, 1966–75] and his advisers must have had good reasons for making such a statement. However, the longest lane has a turning and in God's own time the civilians will assume power after they have properly learnt their lesson of working together for the good of the country.[130]

Turning to Sierra Leone, Bamidele reported: "Some disgruntled ex-politicians and some junior army officers attempted to assassinate a few ministers of state and overthrow the Government of the day. They actually bombed a minister's official residence one early morning in July but fortunately he escaped with his family. The people involved in the attempted coup are now facing treason trial."[131]

Bamidele's letters discussed in some detail the Gowon regime's contentious civil service salary reforms, the Udoji awards, in Nigeria. He wrote about a BBC report on the subject: "It appears that since Udoji Report on salary structure of the civil service was implemented, Nigeria has been in a labour unrest. We hear over the BBC of strike action here and there, and even recently learnt that three universities—Lagos, Ife, and Ibadan have closed down. The Military Government is indeed finding things tough and I can imagine some of them longing to go back to the barracks instead of continuing as governors. I hope and pray that the dispute over salaries will be settled as early as possible."[132]

Bamidele's son Rotimi weighed in on the controversial Udoji salary awards and Sierra Leone's economic crisis. His perspective on the Udoji awards and rising inflation in Sierra Leone was succinct: "It is nice to hear that there has been a revision of salaries leading to increases in various government sectors. Though this has led to a corresponding increase in the cost of living, people can still adjust their standards of living appreciably. Here, we are only experiencing a continuous rise in the cost of living. It is indeed a wonder how people still continue to survive."[133]

Bamidele and Rotimi were astute commentators on African political, economic, and social conditions, especially those in Nigeria and Sierra Leone immediately after independence in the 1960s and 1970s. Along with writing insightful reports about the Nigerian-Biafran War and the attempted military coup in Sierra Leone, Bamidele and Rotimi consistently discussed the rising cost of basic commodities in Sierra Leone, drought in northern Nigeria, and student unrest in Nigerian universities. In one letter, Bamidele wrote that he "heard over the radio some time ago that parts of Nigeria were affected by the drought that is now raging over Africa. I hope the Western State [the Yorùbá region] has not been affected."[134]

The following month, Rotimi reported on the severe economic conditions in Sierra Leone: "Over here, prices are rising at a very fantastic rate, that I wonder whether we shall ever get things stable again. Everyone now is crying about the rising cost of living. Today you will buy something at Le. 2, next week it will cost Le. 4 Le. 5. Nowadays, it's 100% and over increase."[135] In another letter written the following month, Rotimi told his granduncle Abiọdun that he was "sorry to hear that the drought in Northern Nigeria is affecting you. . . . We have not had much rainfall this year too, so we are wondering whether there would not be scarcity of some common foodstuffs next year. Right now, we do not have enough rice to meet demands."[136]

Rotimi's letters continued to provide insightful analysis of the implications of the deepening economic, political, and environmental crises for the citizens of both countries, especially his family in Sierra Leone and relatives in Ibadan. In 1974 he wrote: "We are all doing fine at this end, except that the rising cost of living is giving some cause for concern. In the next few years, it would become extremely difficult to cope with this situation if nothing is done and if salaries remain the same."[137] As the condition of local people became more precarious in Sierra Leone and Nigeria, Rotimi expressed concern about the impact of the economic recession of 1974 and the Sahelian drought of the same year on his relatives in Ibadan and his family in Freetown:

> I noted with regrets the losses you incurred due to the reduction in prices on some commodities. I heard about it sometime ago on the radio. Let us hope that it will be advantageous to you all in the long run. I also hope that the drought problem in the North has eased now. We have not got any serious rains since the year started. We are wondering what will happen if this situation continues, because we do not have any surplus foodstuffs in store to supplement. Anyway, God will help us find a solution. Here, there is just continual increases in prices. It is very difficult to make assessment in advance.[138]

When the rain finally returned to Freetown two months later, Rotimi noted with joy: "We have started to get rains seriously this month and we hope it will continue so that the crops will thrive."[139]

As Bamidele and Rotimi relayed the challenging economic and political conditions in Sierra Leone to Abiọdun and reflected on the news coming out of Nigeria, they underscored the implications of these challenging conditions for their relatives in both countries.[140] As the months rolled by, Bamidele continued to inquire about development in his homeland: "I hope the trouble at the Nigerian universities has now been settled and that normal work has returned once more there. When I heard about the closure of the universities over the radio, I was a bit concerned about Subu who is at Ife University. However, I have confidence that wiser heads at the universities will not let the innocent students suffer with others and will soon reopen the universities." He then returned to the topic of inflation: "I wonder whether the gradual but steady rises in the prices of essential commodities are hitting you in Nigeria as they are doing here. Petrol is available right enough but it costs one naira per gallon now and I understand the price will go up in March or April. Rice the staple food is sold at 28 [naira] or 30 [naira] per bag of two bushels. Prices of goods change so often that one is at a loss what to do and how to budget one's salary."[141] Amid his description of the economic and social turmoil, Rotimi included a message of hope about his sister: "Ọlaolu is trying hard in her studies and she is well although the rising cost of living is giving us some problems."[142] These letters reflect strong familial ties during a moment of hardship in Sierra Leone and uncertainty in Nigeria, emphasizing the Brainerd family's resolve as the pathway of *aláj̣ọbí* connects the Brainerd family in Freetown to Bamidele's homeland in Ibadan through the medium of letter writing.

Bamidele, however, was not content to simply complain about the economic downturn in Sierra Leone and Nigeria. He offered insightful ideas on how to tackle both countries' economic problems. With the arrival of the tourist season in early 1975, Bamidele explored the idea of generating revenue for Sierra Leone's depressed economy by transforming the country's tourism industry. He called his uncle's attention to the opportunities that the industry had to offer Sierra Leone and Nigeria with progressive government policies and forward-thinking state authorities:

> It is tourist season now in Sierra Leone. Almost every week tourists from different parts of Europe and America arrive either by planes or steamers to visit the country. The Government here has put a lot of premium on this trade, that is tourism and has a separate Ministry of Tourism and Cultural Affairs to deal with problems on such matters. I wonder if the Nigerian Government encourages tourism and whether it has a department that deals with such an important trade. Ibadan alone, not to talk of other towns and cities has a lot of interesting

sites for tourists to visit. When these tourists visit places, they spend a lot of money.[143]

As the economic crisis deepened in Sierra Leone and with growing political tensions in Nigeria over the country's transition to a civil-democratic government in the late 1960s and early 1970s, Bamidele evoked the spiritual forces at the core of West African religious belief, emphasizing his faith in God to lead Sierra Leone and Nigeria through the challenging years immediately after independence. He followed developments in both countries closely, constantly reporting on what he had read in Sierra Leonean newspapers or heard on national and international radio channels. The political crisis that led to the tragic demise of Nigeria's first civil-democratic government in January 1966 and subsequently the outbreak of the Nigerian-Biafran War in July 1967 loomed heavily in memory, and Bamidele hoped that the recent political instability would not cause the country to degenerate into the type of crisis Nigeria experienced in the 1960s.[144] Bamidele was thankful that the military government had demonstrated to the world that Nigeria still had "Godly and decent men" capable of constructing a pathway to good governance and development.[145]

When General Yakubu Gowon was toppled in a "palace coup" in 1975, Bamidele gave his assessment of political developments in the country:

> Yes sir, we were shocked when in the early morning of 29th July, BBC announced over the wireless or radio the change of government. Our fear at first, when we heard of the news was that there should not be a repetition of the civil crises of 1966. Thanks be to God that the soldiers are more sensible this time. Credit should be given to General Gowon who by his open declarations of loyalty to the new government has shown the world that there are Godly and decent men in Nigeria who are prepared to serve their country not for the acquisition of power and wealth but for selfless service to the Fatherland. General Gowon has by his action made a name for himself in the history of Africa. If only the Nigerian civilian leaders could copy the example of this decent gentleman when they assume power then there will be no cause for soldiers to interfere in the country's political affairs.[146]

A few months later when a group of junior officers carried out an abortive countercoup that claimed the life of the country's new military ruler, General Murtala Mohammed, Bamidele shared the concern of many Nigerians: "I was sorry to hear about the abortive coup d'état that took place in Nigeria on the 13th instant. I understand that apart from General Mohammed who was assassinated in Lagos other state governors were also killed. I hope and also pray that this incident will not spark off more trouble in the future as a similar one did in 1966."[147]

Bamidele situated his perspective on political and economic developments in Sierra Leone and Nigeria in the broader context of the economic downturn around the world in the mid-1970s. He believed that it was the responsibility of Western industrialized countries to address the worldwide recession, which had devastating effects on the economies of poor African countries such as Sierra Leone. He drew a sharp contrast between Nigeria and Sierra Leone:

> While the Nigerian government is faced with the problem of dissension among the ranks in the [armed] forces, here [Sierra Leone] is faced with economic problems. Trade is not as brisk as before and therefore government finds it difficult to get sufficient revenue to run the country. Inflation is mainly the cause of the trouble. One big mining company which engaged thousands of workers and had been mining iron ore for over forty years had to close down business last year October and paid off all workers. However, we hope one day the big and powerful countries of the world will find a solution to this economic nuisance—inflation—which is causing a lot of havoc to most governments of developing countries.[148]

As was typical of his perspective on Nigerian state affairs, Bamidele related the national developments in the country to the specific conditions of his family in Ibadan: "I hope the congestion of Lagos has now eased and you are now able to get materials (especially cement) to carry out repairs to and building of houses."[149]

Bamidele's brilliant son Rotimi astutely commented on the grim economic conditions of Sierra Leone in a letter to his granduncle in 1975: "The budget for the 1975/76 year is now out and we are in another tough time. No avenue was left untouched. Little wonder how people in the lower income bracket manage to survive. Business people are taking advantage of the situation as there is no price control whatsoever. Anyway, the Lord will provide for us, and we hope that the situation will not continue like this indefinitely."[150]

Slightly less than a year earlier, Rotimi had evoked a spiritual perspective to explain the uncertainties of his world, hoping that time would bring peace and stability to Sierra Leone. He wondered about Sierra Leone's future and seemed resigned to the precarious economic conditions and volatile political upheavals that were common in many African countries. "I got a letter from Fọlakẹ and Ọlaolu last week and they are doing fine in their studies. They are only complaining about the rising cost of living which of course is worldwide. Now I don't bother to talk about it, because it is a waste of time. It seems endless, so I have come to accept it," Rotimi wrote before updating Abiọdun on the verdict of Sierra Leone's attempted coup, which his father had reported to his uncle several months before: "The sensational treason trial which you might have heard of has ended last Saturday and all fifteen people were found guilty of the charges and sentenced to death by firing squad. We are hoping and praying that peace and tranquility will prevail in our country. Things are so difficult nowadays. Anyway, we are keeping on the right side of the law."[151] A few years later, Bamidele reported on the lingering inflation and growing food shortage in Sierra Leone: "The cost of living is terrible here at present but I want to think that it is better over in Nigeria where farmers produce more food than here. You have a variety of foodstuff to choose from, but here the staple food is rice, although you may with a bit of luck buy yams, cassava, or cocoyams but they are expensive."[152]

As previously observed, the image of Nigeria outside of the country mattered a great deal to Bamidele. The tone of his letters revealed that he felt a personal stake in Nigeria's political evolution and image around the world. When several Nigerian businessmen were arrested for bank fraud in Sierra Leone, Bamidele reported the event to his uncle in Ibadan: "It may surprise you to learn that four Nigerian young businessmen were arrested here a few weeks ago for forging travelers' cheques. They had as a matter of fact used some of the forged cheques to buy goods in shops to the value of 1000 [naira] before they were detected and apprehended by the police. They are now awaiting trial in the High Court."[153]

Significantly, Bamidele was deeply engaged with the far-reaching reform policies imposed by General Mohammed's successor, General Olușẹgun Ọbasanjọ, in Nigeria from 1975 to 1979. He applauded the military government's universal primary school policy: "I read in the *West Africa* newspaper some time ago that the Nigerian government has inaugurated the free universal primary education (U.P.E.) in the whole of the country. That is a laudable achievement and a feather to the cap of the Military Government. There is a rumour around the town here that owing to the great demand for primary schoolteachers for this project there is the possibility some teachers may be recruited here by the Nigerian Government to work in Nigeria."[154] And a few months earlier, Bamidele made an interesting observation about the military regime's Operation Feed the Nation campaign: "I think one of the ways by which the Military 'feed yourself' campaign can succeed is for the soldiers themselves to set an example by cultivating their own farms. It is not useful telling people to do something without your showing them how to do it."[155]

The Ọbasanjọ administration's most important policy, the 1979 transition to civil-democratic government (and one of the most important in postcolonial

Nigerian political history), did not miss Bamidele's attention. "I was pleased to read from a newspaper that the Military Government is doing their best to put Nigeria back on her normal political footing," he wrote to Abiọdun in 1976. "I understand that elections into local state councils will take place not very far from now and that the target date for handing over [to a civilian government] is 1979."[156]

When the constituent assembly elections for the military-imposed transition to constitutional democracy finally arrived in 1977, Bamidele reflected on the role of some of the old politicians such as Adisa Akinloye, Abiọdun's brother-in-law, in the emerging liberal democratic government:

> I have been following the political trend of events in Nigeria. The result of the constituent assembly elections is interesting in that names of many of the old-time politicians are not prominent. Is it that many of them are tired? I was expecting to see the name of Chief Akinloye on the list of contestants for the Ibadan Municipal seat. I observe that Chief Fani Kayọde former Deputy Premier, Western Nigeria lost the election for the Ọranmiyan seat. I understand he is going to quit politics for the church to be a preacher. I pray that the new crop of politicians will put away selfishness and avarice and work consciously so as to evolve the constitution that will enable Nigeria to prove that multiparty democracy can work successfully in a Black man's country.[157]

Several months later, in June 1978, Bamidele continued to hold up hope for Nigeria's transition program to democracy: "We have been following with keen interest the proceedings of the constitutional assembly. I hope and pray the politicians will listen to the advice of Lt. General Ọbasanjọ and carry out their duties with sincerity and the true spirit of patriotism so as to produce a constitution worthy of the name Nigeria abroad. May God guide them in their deliberations."[158]

When gubernatorial elections were held in August of the following year, Bamidele suspected correctly that the new governor of Ọyọ State—the new state created by the military government with Ibadan as its capital—was the son-in-law of Abiọdun's former mentor, S. A. Ọlọkọ. "I read in *West Africa* that a gentleman by the name of IGE was elected as governor of Ọyọ State. Is this gentleman related to the husband of Pa Ọlọkọ's daughter or is he the husband of Pa Ọlọkọ's daughter [Atinukẹ Ige, née Ọlọkọ]?"[159] When the Nigerian Federal Court of Appeals decided in favor of the National Party of Nigeria's candidate, Shehu Shagari, over preeminent Yorùbá politician and Unity Party of Nigeria leader Ọbafẹmi Awolọwọ in the contested 1979 Nigerian presidential election result, Bamidele was content that the country had found a legal solution to the impasse between the two national political parties: "I was pleased to read about the decision of the Appeals Court with regards to the result of the presidential election. Now that everything has been settled in the political sphere, I hope all the politicians will be wise enough to work for unity and progress rather than fight each other."[160] At this time of transition to multiparty democracy in Nigeria, Bamidele worried about growing authoritarianism in Sierra Leone, writing in July 1978, "At long last, Sierra Leone has become a one party state last month. God only knows what type of government we shall now have. We sincerely hope it will not be a dictatorship."[161]

During the democratic government of Shehu Shagari from 1979 to 1983, Bamidele followed Nigeria's federal government policies closely and, like many Nigerians, offered unsolicited recommendations for national development. In one instance, he argued that Nigeria's major economic problem lay in its overreliance on the exportation of crude oil since the country's oil boom in the early 1970s. To address this problem, Bamidele called for the diversification of the Nigerian economy:

> Nigeria should no longer depend on her crude oil for her main source of revenue. If she does, she may regret it as Ghana is now regretting it today for depending too much on COCOA in the sixties and seventies as her main source of revenue. It appears that the big industrial powers like the USA, UK, France, Germany want to break down the collective commercial strength of OPEC which dictates the price of crude oil in the world market. I pray that the Nigerian politicians will be wide awake to the stark realities facing them now and unite as ONE nation to solve the problem.[162]

Earlier in 1981, only a year into the Shagari administration, when the Nigerian federal government announced a well-publicized "green revolution," Bamidele applauded this national agrarian policy: "I read in the newspaper *West Africa* about President Shehu Shagari's visit to the UK last month and learnt about the big five-year development plan called the 'Green Revolution.' It is indeed a laudable plan which will make Nigeria one of the nations in the world to be reckoned with."[163] Furthermore, advocating for an agrarian revolution that would reverse Nigeria's endemic poverty, Bamidele criticized the growing gap between Nigeria's political class and its masses of poor people:

> It is my opinion that if the wealth of Nigeria is evenly spread or distributed and workers are well paid for a good day's job well done, and if at the same time large scale and mechanized farming is well established, thereby producing enough food for all and cash crops (cocoa, etc.) then Nigeria will be the greatest country

> in Africa. But if only the politicians and the business tycoons want to eat the nation's cake (wealth) and are not prepared to share it with others like the workers and the farmers, then I am afraid they are looking for trouble.[164]

In March 1982 Bamidele informed his uncle of a steel policy initiative undertaken by the Shagari administration that he had learned about from his voracious consumption of news on Nigerian politics. He was convinced that Nigeria's economic development must have a sustained industrial policy and agrarian reform. "It is interesting to read that Nigeria is now producing steel at Aladja in Bendel State. This is a big step taken in the industrial history of the country. It is possible that Sierra Leone will be selling its iron ore to Nigeria instead of sending it to Europe or Japan," Bamidele noted on an aspect of Nigeria's industrial policy. With regard to agrarian policy, "We read so much in the papers about big agricultural projects costing millions of dollars in different federal states and yet one hears of so much money spent on importing food into the country for consumption. The same thing happens here."[165] Bamidele also commented on the Shagari administration's controversial expulsion of thousands of immigrants from various African countries, especially Ghanaians in the early 1980s: "The expulsion of illegal immigrants from Nigeria in January 1983 has not come as a surprise to many of us here who read the newspapers."[166]

When writing about Sierra Leone, Bamidele focused his comments on the effects of the country's precarious economy on the conditions of his family, while in the case of Nigeria he was concerned about the country's precipitous decline since the attainment of independence in 1960. "I earnestly pray that God may send help to save Nigeria from calamity," he wrote in 1967. "We who are outside Nigeria and only hear news about events there, shudder at what is happening and express fear for the future. May God protect you all from all dangers, Amen."[167]

Bamidele's and Rotimi's insightful articulation of Nigerian, Sierra Leonean, and broader African political and economic conditions reflected the perspective of astute analysts in many African countries during decolonization and immediately after independence. Their engagements with political and economic developments in Nigeria and Sierra Leone in their many letters were farsighted in scope and insightful in analytical thought. The ideas expressed in these letters were reflected against the backdrop of the remarkable success of Bamidele's children during the first three decades of Sierra Leonean and Nigerian independence from the 1960s to the 1990s.

As the political and economic crisis in Nigeria and Sierra Leone deepened in the 1980s and 1990s, Bamidele's engagement of these issues intensified. Bamidele worried about the long-term implications of the wave of religious violence in northern and central Nigeria in the 1980s for Nigeria's political stability: "Some of us are happy to learn that the unpleasant incidents in Kano where many innocent people were killed because of their religious belief have been checked before they spread to others parts of the country. Conflicts caused by religious beliefs are more dangerous than those caused by political differences."[168] As the religious violence in predominantly Muslim northern Nigeria increased in the early 1980s, Bamidele's reports of the news from the Sierra Leonean national news agency and the BBC grew more ominous: "We were shocked when we heard over the radio some time ago about the violent incidents which took place in Maiduguri and Kaduna because of religious differences among Muslim sects. It was even reported that in Kano some Muslim students burnt down some Christian churches. This is indeed very serious. If the Federal Government and all the religious leaders in Nigeria, especially the Muslim and Christian leaders, do not take appropriate action to put a stop to such things as burning churches by Muslims, I am afraid Nigeria is heading for a big, big trouble."[169]

Nigeria experienced another political setback with the fall of its second civil-democratic government following the military coup on New Year's Eve of 1983, which ushered in the military regime of Major General Muhammadu Buhari. In his letters, Bamidele expressed frustration about Nigeria's recurring political crisis. For the time being, he was willing to put his faith in the new military regime's insistence on discipline in Nigerian society, following the widespread political corruption of the ousted politicians. "We have been following with keen interest the news about Nigeria both in the papers and on the air since the coup of December 1983," he told Abiọdun. "We pray sincerely that God will give the military government wisdom, humility, and courage to lead the country through the mess and morass, I mean financial of course, which the civilian government left the once wealthy and prosperous country. I really don't know whether our African politicians, especially the Nigerian politicians, don't learn from other people's mistakes. Or is it that they care less for their fellow brothers and sisters? May the Lord have mercy on them for their sins."[170]

Several months later, Bamidele expressed more concern about the damaging impact of corruption in Nigerian society and applauded the military regime's "war on corruption": "One thing I observe the military is trying to eradicate in Nigerian society during their tenure in office, and that is corruption in high places. Corruption is a cankerworm in many African countries. I wish they will succeed in wiping out corruption in Nigeria."[171] Later in the year, Bamidele was even more specific about his analysis of the scale of corruption not only in Nigeria but also in Sierra Leone and other African countries. Drawing from his Ibadan CMS values, Bamidele endorsed the federal military government's anticorruption campaign:

> The Nigerian Government has or rather is trying to introduce the campaign on "War against indiscipline." The military is really trying to correct the causes of corruption which is rampant in Nigeria and other parts of Africa including Sierra Leone. This in my opinion can best be done from the home and schools. If the individual homes (the parents) work together with the churches, the schools, and the mosques to train and discipline their children according to religious ethics, Nigeria will be well disciplined and produce good and honest citizens that many countries in the world will envy.[172]

In June 1985 Abiọdun's "cousin" and onetime mentor during the colonial years, S. A. Ọlọkọ, died (see chapter 3). Bamidele, who knew him as a boy growing up in Ibadan, expressed heartfelt condolences: "I am indeed sorry to learn from you about the death of Pa Ọlọkọ. How old was he? He must have reached 90 years or over no doubt. May his soul Rest In perfect Peace. I have written to his daughter Justice Atinukẹ IGE through your address to express my sympathy and that of my family to her mother and all the members of their family."[173]

Amid reports of recurring political instability and economic crisis in Nigeria and Sierra Leone in the early 1980s, Bamidele, as always, found time for levity, this time in a transcontinental Vaughan family story he obtained from the airwaves: "I heard over the wireless on the BBC network Africa Programme which is broadcast every day at 5: 15 am some time ago this month about the family or families of the VAUGHANS in America are trying to form a sort of union or association whereby they could contact the VAUGHANS in Nigeria and communicate with them. They even invited any direct descendant of the Vaughans in Nigeria to contact the Union in the USA."[174]

With deepening economic crisis in many African countries by the mid-1980s, neoliberal economic reforms in the form of structural adjustment policies were imposed on African states by the World Bank and the International Monetary Fund with the support of Western industrial nations. This led to massive cuts in essential social services such as health care and education and drastic devaluation of local currencies and high inflation, resulting in severe economic shocks in many African countries.[175] Similar to those of his earlier reports on political developments in Nigeria and Sierra Leone in the two decades after independence in the 1960s and 1970s, Bamidele's depth of analysis and scope of intellectual engagement with these political and economic developments were insightful and thought-provoking.

Following the first wave of the implementation of structural adjustment policies in Sierra Leone and Nigeria in the mid-1980s, Bamidele reported his assessment to his uncle. His insightful perspective on this particular economic crisis is worth quoting in full:

> We thank God Almighty for life spared us. But economically our country [Sierra Leone] is in troubled waters. On the suggestion of the International Monetary Fund (IMF), from whom the Sierra Leone government wants to raise some loans for development purposes, the Government has devalued the currency of the country. Consequently, prices of consumer goods like food, clothing, etc. have risen sharply without commensurate increase in salaries. . . . Mismanagement of the country's financial resources has very often caused the downfall of many African governments. I have been following with keen interest the doctors' strike in Nigeria. I am really sorry their action has made many people die, although they have a good case. How can a doctor perform his duty without drugs and medicine, especially in university teaching hospitals?[176]

A special letter from Bamidele written on May 25, 1987, interrupted his stream of reportage on Nigerian and Sierra Leonean political and economic crises. This was Bamidele's report on the celebration of one of the most important events in modern African history: the bicentenary anniversary of the founding of Freetown, capital of Sierra Leone, as a resettlement colony for free Black people across the Atlantic world. In his inimitable professorial fashion, Bamidele not only called the celebration to Abiọdun's attention but also seized the opportunity to lecture him on its historical significance: "Early last month we celebrated the bicentenary anniversary of the founding of the city of Freetown. In other words, in May 1787 (200 years ago) the first sets of freed settlers from Nova Scotia and America and England arrived in Freetown to inhabit the land. The Duke and Duchess of Kent and other dignitaries from all over the world attended the celebration which lasted four weeks." He concluded this letter by acknowledging the death of the great Yorùbá—and Nigerian—political leader earlier in the year: "We were sorry to hear about the demise of the great Nigerian leader, Chief Ọbafẹmi Awolowo. He was one of the few incorruptible Nigerian leaders who work hard for the betterment of the country he loved so much."[177]

The early 1990s witnessed the end of the Freetown files, consisting of the correspondence of three generations that lasted slightly less than four decades. These last letters remain decidedly political, revealing Bamidele's moral engagement with Nigerian and Sierra Leonean politics and society. As always, Bamidele's discussions of postcolonial African politics not only were intellectually sophisticated and far-reaching but also reflected the moral anguish among political commentators in many African countries who held up hope for progress in their countries after independence in the early 1960s. However, as the crisis of the postcolonial African nation-state intensified in the 1990s with the consolidation of statism, neopatrimonialism, and neoliberalism, Bamidele's analysis of the news on political developments in Nigeria and Sierra Leone grew more ominous.

With regard to Nigerian politics and society, the story line that animated Bamidele was yet another attempted military transition to democracy, this time the failed transition to civil-democratic government under another northern Muslim general, Ibrahim Babangida.[178] When Babangida announced his regime's transition to a liberal democratic government in 1990, Bamidele, in keeping with his style, took the time to tell Abiọdun that he got the information from one of his favorite sources of African and global news, the radio: "I heard over the radio about how General Ibrahim Babangida is preparing Nigeria for the handing over of government [to civilians] in 1992. To be candid Uncle, I don't blame the soldiers too much. It is the politicians and their supporters that should be blamed [for recurring military interventions in Nigerian politics]."[179]

Following a convoluted transition program to democracy by the military regime in which the Yorùbá politician Moshood Abiọla, the Social Democratic Party candidate, won the presidential election in July 1993, Bamidele wrote triumphantly, "In my last letter I predicted that Chief Bashorun MKO Abiọla would win the presidential elections. My prediction has become true. I pray that God will make it possible for him to be enthroned as president of Nigeria by August 23, 1993, never mind what the military might say."[180] When General Babangida suppressed the election results, Bamidele wrote: "The ship of state in Nigeria is still sailing on an unsteady sea. It appears the captain of the ship has still not got control of the steering wheel hence there seems to be confusion in the Government circle to salvage the country from perennial military rule to truly democratic rule."[181]

During this moment of military-imposed transition to civil-democratic government in Nigeria, Sierra Leone experienced a dramatic political development of its own, largely through the spillover of a civil war in neighboring Liberia, a country with a similar history. Liberia was a colony established by free Black men and women from the United States in the early nineteenth century.[182] At the onset of the Liberian Civil War, Bamidele reported on the initial effects of the war on Sierra Leone's fragile state institutions, vulnerable social structure, and meager resources: "I have no doubt you have heard over the BBC world service news about the civil war being waged or fought in neighboring Liberia.

Thousands of citizens of that country have consequently fled their homes and villages to seek refuge in Sierra Leone in 1990. We have problems here as to how to feed, house and provide clothing for these people. Fortunately, the Sierra Leone Government is being helped by UNHCR (the United Nations High Commission for Refugees)."[183] As the Liberian Civil War intensified the following year, with serious implications for Sierra Leone's stability and territorial integrity, Bamidele, in an apparent reply to Abiọdun, updated his uncle on the devastating impact of the war: "Many thanks for your concern over the predicament in Sierra Leone due to the invasion by Liberian troops into parts of southern and eastern provinces of Sierra Leone. Many lives have been lost and thousands of our people have fled to neighboring Republic of Guinea as refugees. We who live in Freetown (Western area) and in the Northern Province are so far lucky because the war has not reached our area, but we are suffering the effects of the war all the same."[184]

The final letter in the files Abiọdun Vaughan labeled Freetown was far from optimistic about Nigeria's political future, curtailing the hope that Bamidele held for the country of his upbringing immediately after independence in the early 1960s. Aside from the Nigerian-Biafran War from 1967 to 1970, this was the most ominous episode in Nigerian political history: General Babangida annulled the presidential election won decisively by Moshood Abiọla on June 4, 1993. Bamidele predicted a dire future: "We in Sierra Leone are praying for you all in Nigeria especially for Chief Moshood Abiọla that God will make you conquer the evil machinations and duplicity of these 'khaki' boys [military rulers] who want to dominate, suppress, and oppress you the populace because they have control of the machine guns and tanks." But he ended with an expression of faith: "If you people in the Western and Southern regions together with the Middle Belt work to make REAL DEMOCRACY to prevail in Nigeria, God will make your resolution come to reality."[185] With this panoramic political discourse, Bamidele and his son Rotimi offered a far-reaching and comprehensive overview of Nigerian and Sierra Leonean political history in the first three decades of the countries' independence from Britain from the early 1960s to the early 1990s.

Following a prolonged illness, Bamidele Theo Brainerd died in 2005 at age eighty-nine. An active member of St. George's Cathedral (Anglican) Church, Freetown, he was buried at the Ascension Town Cemetery, Freetown. His wife, Viola, was buried next to him when she died in 2015.

~

Drawing on about 192 letters, this chapter analyzes the correspondence between Abiọdun Vaughan—retired from the Department of Agriculture, working as a manager at the Cooperative Union Bank and at West African Breweries, and later becoming a businessman in Ibadan—and his nephew Bamidele Theo Brainerd, based in Freetown, Sierra Leone, as well as Bamidele's family, on matters pertaining to family obligations and general issues of family wellbeing spanning thirty-eight years, from 1956 to 1994. These intergenerational letters underscore the resilience of Yorùbá kinship ties, revealing family obligations based on the values of *alájọbí* in a transnational landscape between Nigeria and Sierra Leone. Alongside intimate family matters—such as care for Bamidele's aging mother, the celebration of her life following her death, and the evolution of Bamidele's family from the 1950s to the 1990s—the letters analyzed in this chapter also contain fascinating dialogues on the complicated political developments in Nigeria and Sierra Leone in the first three decades after the attainment of independence in the 1960s. Despite the geographical distance between Nigeria and Sierra Leone, the medium of letter writing sustained dynamic Yorùbá kinship ties shaped by deep personal trust between Abiọdun and Bamidele for almost four decades.[186]

These strong kinship ties between Abiọdun and Bamidele were drawn from a shared past that was solidified through the lives of the next generation of the Vaughan family in Freetown, Ibadan, and beyond. In the intergenerational and transnational dialogues that ensued, essential *values of care* proliferated through the medium of letter writing. While the dominant issues discussed in these letters revealed familial obligations that sometimes required support for Bamidele's family in Freetown, they were predicated on a reciprocal moral order not always evident in a straightforward reading of the letters. For instance, when the letters of Abiọdun's natal family are analyzed together, especially the Vaughan matriarchs' letters, Abiọdun's care for his ailing older sister Dorcas Ọlayinka (Bamidele's mother) articulated this value of care within the ethos of a tightknit Ibadan CMS community embedded in the Yorùbá kinship system of *alájọbí*.

As the major letter writer in this chapter, Bamidele, residing in Freetown with his family, was linked to Nigeria through memory of his upbringing in Ibadan, deep moral obligations to his mother, Dorcas Olayinka, and firm solidarity with his uncle Abiọdun. Connecting these important issues to the dynamic conditions of his family in Freetown and Ibadan, Bamidele diligently constructed scripts for and pathways to a home he longed for but to which he could not return. Nevertheless, the relationships that evolved from intersecting and multilayered dialogues were consolidated not only through the intergenerational and transnational correspondence between Bamidele, his children, and their uncle Abiọdun but also among various members of the Vaughan natal family and their in-laws, close friends, and compatriots.

Conclusion

THROUGH CAREFUL textual and contextual analysis of the extensive letters Abiọdun Vaughan compiled from 1926 to 1994, I have constructed stories that reveal how the everyday lives of my father and his natal family were interwoven with those of their wider Ibadan CMS socioreligious kinship network of in-laws, close friends, and compatriots. Based on the medium of letter writing, this kinship network crisscrossed four generations of the Vaughan family, traversing local, regional, national, and transnational spaces in a rapidly changing colonial and postcolonial Yorùbá society.

Following Akinṣọla Akiwọwọ's conceptualization of *alájọbí-alájọgbé* Yorùbá kinship relations, my analysis traces tapestries of interpersonal, familial, and generational relations among a small group of men and women with strong roots in Ibadan's CMS community, starting with the consolidation of colonial rule in southern Nigeria in the late 1920s. In Abiọdun Vaughan's correspondence with his older brother Samuel Ariyibi, the moral order that initially defined the brothers' relationship transcends conventional relations between two brothers, even by the normative standards of Yorùbá society of the time. Twenty years Abiọdun's senior and already assuming some paternal responsibilities for a much younger brother, Samuel Ariyibi wrote letters that were authoritative in tone, assuming a role akin to a surrogate father teaching a son the ways of the modern world with discipline and authority. While drawing on Yorùbá values in an evolving colonial world, Samuel Ariyibi also sought to assert patriarchal control over the Vaughan natal family, ultimately alienating older family members, especially his mother, Mariam Vaughan, sister Dorcas Olayinka Brainerd, and younger brother Abiọdun.

As a natural extension of the brothers' correspondence, the letters from the older women in Abiọdun's family, notably, his mother, Mariam, and sisters Dorcas Ọlayinka and Jadesọla Juliana, ground the Vaughan family in their natal house in Gbenla, an indispensable physical and emotional space for this evolving Ibadan CMS family. As custodians of the Vaughan natal family, these matriarchs nurtured the structure on which Abiọdun's obligations and social aspirations were firmly knitted, not only those of his natal family but also those of their small but formidable socioreligious network, centered in the CMS community at St. Peter's Church on Aremo Hill. With Abiọdun sustaining a career as a civil servant in branches of the colonial Department of Agriculture in far-flung northern and southern Nigeria, the letters of these dynamic women were a critical medium for the moral essence of the Vaughan natal family—reflected through the notion of *alájọbí*—at a time of dramatic social change in colonial Yorùbá society from the 1930s to the 1950s.

Through the medium of letter writing, Abiọdun's natal family was in turn loosely connected to a wider socioreligious network with strong affiliations to CMS mission stations at Aremọ, Kudeti, and Ogunpa. This critical node of *alájọgbé* was emphatically expressed through the longtime correspondence between Abiọdun Vaughan and S. A. Ọlọkọ, a fellow Ọmọ Aremọ and Ibadan CMS stalwart, as well as through Abiọdun's correspondence with other members of their wider Ibadan socioreligious network from the late 1920s to the late 1950s. Sustained by the integration of Yorùbá traditional values, kinship ties, and Western training acquired from CMS socioreligious institutions, the correspondence between Abiọdun and these men consistently reflected a strong commitment to social mobility, professional advancement, elite consolidation, and civic virtue. With membership in two vibrant mutual aid groups extensively documented in the S. A. Ọlọkọ files—the Ibadan Brotherhood Fund Association and the Ibadan Cooperative Savings Society—these Ibadan Christian-educated men reflected Yorùbá enlightenment values of *ọ̀làjú* and the civic virtue of *ìlọsíwájú* that proliferated in Yorùbá cities by the waning years of colonial rule.[1]

My analysis of this emergent Yorùbá modern social world, encapsulated in the values of Ibadan's CMS community, is further exemplified in the files that contained Abiọdun's correspondence with his second wife, Adukẹ Vaughan, from 1943 to 1961 alongside the letters he exchanged with his mother-in-law, Rachel Ayọdele Akinloye, in the 1940s and his brother-in-law Adisa Akinloye, a law student at the London School of Economics from 1946 to 1950. Analyzed in the framework of an evolving Yorùbá family life, the letters in these files reflect mutually reinforcing moral obligations between Abiọdun and Adukẹ and with Abiọdun's in-laws. This contingent moral order was expressed in four major issues that dominated the letters in the files Abiọdun labeled Gladys Adukẹ Vaughan: the courtship of Abiọdun and Adukẹ from 1943 to 1944, the tragic loss of Abiọdun and Adukẹ's three infant children from 1945 to 1949, Adukẹ's residence in London from 1958 to 1961, and Adisa Akinloye's time as a law student in London immediately after World War II. In her letters, Adukẹ insisted on personal progress, professional advancement, and social uplift, asserting her position as a wife, mother, and professional woman. Discussed in the context of the Yorùbá kinship system, Ibadan CMS enlightenment values, and dramatic social changes in the latter decades of colonial rule, the stories teased out from the letters in these files complicate African studies' gender discourse. Nevertheless, these letters reveal remarkable fortitude by Adukẹ, a woman with deep roots in Ibadan's CMS Aremo community. This woman was my mother, and she—and my grandmother Rachel Ayodele Akinloye—shared fragments of these stories with me and my siblings twenty to thirty years after they occurred in presentist narrations steeped in Yorùbá Anglican virtue.[2]

It is instructive that the stories teased out of the letters compiled by Abiọdun came to an end with Abiọdun's correspondences with post-Ibadan CMS Vaughan natal family members—two succeeding generations spearheaded by the compelling letters of Abiọdun's nephew Bamidele Brainerd and several of his children—from Freetown, Sierra Leone, in the first three decades of Nigerian independence. Despite geographical, linguistic, customary, and generational barriers, the bonds of *alájọbí* were asserted in a moral order that reinforced the reciprocity of familial obligations and wellbeing spanning thirty-eight years of letter writing. The strong *alájọbí* values expressed in these letters were conceived in the vortex of a socioreligious experience that integrated Yorùbá CMS Anglican values, Yorùbá traditions, and West African cosmology. These intergenerational and transnational letters are multivalent and multilayered, not only revealing prevailing Yorùbá kinship ties, modern professional training, and Ibadan CMS elite values but also providing vivid insight into the precarious politics of state-building in postcolonial Nigeria and Sierra Leone.

The dominant story lines that shape the contours of this book critically reflect major themes in Africanist scholarship since the decolonization process after World War II: mission Christianity, Western education, social mobility, modern development, civic values, elite formation, and gender relations in colonial and postcolonial Nigerian contexts. The extensive letters compiled by my father—and the book I have created from them—have allowed me to interrogate these themes in novel, interpersonal, and everyday contexts through the lens of one Yorùbá family, their close relatives, and their compatriots against the backdrop of the evolution of modern Nigerian history.[3]

Incubated in dynamic Yorùbá communities in the last quarter of the nineteenth century, this small but vibrant Ibadan CMS nucleus drew its moral authority from the Yorùbá kinship system of *àjọbí-àjọgbé* relations. With the consolidation of British colonial rule in the Yorùbá region by the early twentieth century, Abiọdun Vaughan's family integrated a complicated kinship network that included in-laws, relatives, and close friends, as well as compatriots in civic and professional institutions. This mutually reinforcing familial and kinship system reconciled endogenous and exogenous forces that critically engaged the human agency of the letter writers, revealing how Yorùbá values and Western training acquired from CMS socioreligious institutions were imbricated under colonial rule.

It is significant that the letters discussed in this book underscore the quotidian concerns of Yorùbá men and women whose social world was firmly anchored to an evolving colonial society at the turn of the twentieth century. Given the significance of an emergent Christian-educated class (typified by the older generation of letter writers in this book) in the transformation of major Yorùbá ancestral hometowns such as Ìbàdàn, Abẹ́òkúta, Ìjẹ̀bú-Òde, Iléṣà, Ògbómọ̀ṣọ́, Òṣogbo, Ọ̀yọ́, and Ilé-Ifẹ̀, by the early years of colonial rule at the beginning of the twentieth century, the social world of the major protagonists in this book, analyzed through the medium of letter writing, complicates John Peel's contention that members of the Yorùbá Protestant clergy, mostly of Saro origin as Yorùbá returnees from Sierra Leone, were the architects of Yorùbá modernity starting in the second half of the nineteenth century.[4] In many Yorùbá cities, especially in Atlantic Nigeria, thousands of men and women like those in this book who were functioning not only in the modern professionals as clerks, administrators, health officers, teachers, and nurses but also as cultural innovators such as writers and artists consolidated the foundation of what became modern Yorùbá society in the first half of the twentieth century. Spanning seven decades and traversing Nigerian, West African, and Atlantic histories, this book, as a microhistory of Yorùbá family life, kinship ties, and social mobility, has uncovered new primary research materials to analyze the everyday lives and social world of Yorùbá local actors in the making of modern Nigerian society.

Abiọdun Vaughan was not unique among his contemporaries in the way he compiled primary documents over many decades that constituted critical moments in Nigerian colonial and postcolonial history. This practice of curating documents was common among Western-educated men and women of Abiọdun Vaughan's social experience and training in Atlantic West Africa by the turn of the twentieth century, when Britain imposed its colonial rule on the Nigerian region. With roots in Atlantic Nigeria during the last quarter of the nineteenth century, meticulous recordkeeping was essential practice by many of the men and women from Abiọdun Vaughan's social orientation by the early decades of colonial rule at the turn of the twentieth century. Despite the prevalence of this practice, it is unfortunate that primary documents from a group of men and women actively engaged in the foundation of modern Nigeria have been conspicuously absent in the construction of Nigerian history. In the specific case of the Christian-educated Ibadan men who featured in this book, I am aware that men such as S. A. Ọlọkọ, J. A. Ayọrinde, G. O. Ogunṣọla, and E. O. Alayande, like their compatriot Abiọdun Vaughan, compiled thousands of documents throughout their adult lives.[5] With the exception of J. A. Ayọrinde, who donated primary documents to the University of Ife (later Obafemi Awolowo University) in the late 1970s, it is likely that the thousands of documents compiled by the three other men—Ọlọkọ, Ogunsola, and Alayande—in their adult lives were not preserved after their deaths.[6] The absence of primary documents from men and women such as S. A. Ọlọkọ, G. O. Ogunsola, E. O. Alayande, Adisa Akinloye, and their Ibadan compatriots—as well as thousands of others from this critical generation in Nigerian history—has created a major gap in the written archive of modern Nigeria.

Since this extensive recordkeeping was an important aspect of the social world of Western-educated Yorùbá Christian men such as Abiọdun Vaughan at a critical juncture in Nigerian colonial history, we might ask, What drove this practice of self-curating and archiving by Abiọdun and his compatriots? Naturally, sustaining this pattern of letter writing and the preservation of documents over many decades required a high level of discipline and commitment.[7] The identity and self-image of *akòwé* (clerk, writer, learned person) was bound up with the record of one's epistolary fecundity and productivity.[8] In this context, archiving, along with the idea of possessing and populating a personal library with documents, was an essential element of the self-fashioning of Abiọdun and his compatriots as *alákòwé* (a literate person, a writer).[9] Ironically, this self-fashioning of *akòwé* and the massive archives these men accumulated are marginal in the story of modern Nigeria.

Despite the dramatically different context of the contemporary global age, parallels abound from the major issues that predominated in the world of the letter writers in this book and the issues confronting many Nigerians in the neoliberal global world. In their fidelity to kinship values, civic orientation, and collective social action, Nigerian citizens in a fragmented neoliberal world, similar to the Ibadan CMS men and women whose letters I analyze in this book, have consistently utilized new modes of communication, financial institutions, and technological instruments to sustain mutually beneficial relationships with family members, relatives, close friends, and compatriots in Nigeria and around the world. For example, financial remittances to advance the wellbeing of family members and sustain crumbling civic institutions are ubiquitous among millions of Nigerians in a contemporary neoliberal world. Consequently, similar to the letter writers in this book, twenty-first-century Nigerian social actors—along local, regional, national, and transnational pathways—use new media, technologies, and remittances to sustain familial, kinship, hometown, ethnonational, religious, and civic structures amid the dramatic transformations of the global age.[10]

Given the unconventional nature of this work in Africanist scholarship, I feel compelled as a progeny of many of the letter writers to end this conclusion with a personal reflection of what analyzing these letters has meant to me as a scholar. Since I grew up with fragments of some of the stories discussed in the letters, writing this book has been an extraordinary exploration of the many layers of family stories of which I only have limited background knowledge.[11] The process involved in critically reading the letters, uncovering family stories, and researching the issues that culminated in this book has provided me with the gift of a lifetime: the unique opportunity to look back in time and knit together multilayered, overlapping, and intersecting stories of my forebears and their descendants, close friends, and compatriots from the late nineteenth century to the end of the twentieth century—the complicated moment that defined modern Yorùbá society against the backdrop of the history of Nigeria.

To end this conclusion, it is instructive to note that the issues discussed by these letter writers eschewed the metanarrative of an essentialized "African" world shoehorned into the strictures of modern Nigerian history.[12] Firmly located in their Ibadan CMS ethos and legitimated by old-age Yorùbá kinship values, the daily lives of these men and women, through the medium of letter writing, effortlessly traversed dynamic local, national, and transnational spaces in rapidly changing twentieth-century Nigerian colonial and postcolonial contexts. My analysis of the letters in this book reveals how the moment of Ìgbà Òyìnbó (the white man's era) is embedded in the structures of Yorùbá society to articulate dialectical tensions between tradition and modernity, local and global, national and transnational, grounded on the moral authority of a dynamic Yorùbá kinship system. While the unfolding drama of Nigerian colonial and postcolonial history provides an important context in which these letter writers were compelled to order their lives, these men and women, through the medium of letter writing, nevertheless demonstrated considerable imagination and dynamism in the construction of their own social world.

Notes

Introduction

1. For a detailed discussion of the protracted Yorùbá Wars in the nineteenth century, which defined the essence of modern Yorùbá society, see Samuel Johnson, *The History of the Yorubas: From the Earliest Times to the Beginning of the British Protectorate* (Lagos: Church Missionary Society, 1921).

2. For detailed discussions of the foundational impact of Protestant missions in the transformation of modern Nigeria, starting in the second half of the nineteenth century, see J. F. Ade Ajayi, *Christian Missions in Nigeria, 1841–1891* (London: Longman, 1966); E. A. Ayandele, *The Missionary Impact on Modern Nigeria, 1842–1914* (London: Longman, 1967).

3. St. Peter's Church, Aremọ (called Church Aremọ by generations of its dedicated members), one of the most influential CMS Anglican churches in Nigeria, the cornerstone of the mission station in the Aremọ area of the city of Ibadan, became the Cathedral Church of St. Peter's in 2005, 140 years after its establishment in 1865.

4. Established in 1899 as a model farm for the cultivation of rubber trees and other agricultural raw materials, the plantation became an experiment station in 1905, largely for research on the cultivation of cotton for Britain's textile industry at the turn of the twentieth century under the leadership of the British high commissioner, Sir Ralph Moor, after whom the original experiment station was named as Moor Plantation. In 1910 Moor Plantation became the headquarters of the colonial Department of Agriculture, with satellite branches in major cities throughout colonial southern and northern Nigeria, such as Lagos, Enugu, Zaria, Benin, and Jos by the 1920s.

5. See, for example, Isaac Schapera, *Married Life in an African Tribe* (London: Faber & Faber, 1941); Christopher Fyfe, ed., *Our Children Free and Happy: Letters from Black Settlers in Africa in the 1790s* (Edinburgh: Edinburgh University Press, 1991); Karin Barber, ed., *Africa's Hidden Histories: Everyday Literacy and the Making of Self* (Bloomington: Indiana University Press, 2006); Sean Hawkins, *Writing and Colonialism in Northern Ghana: The Encounter between the LoDagaa and the World of Paper* (Toronto: University of Toronto Press, 2002); Benjamin Lawrence, Emily Lynn Osborn, and Richard L. Roberts, eds., *Intermediaries, Interpreters, and Clerks: African Employees in the Making of Colonial Africa* (Madison: University of Wisconsin Press,

2006); Bernth Lindfors, *Recovering Letters, Discovering Numbers: Literary and Statistical Studies* (Trenton, NJ: Africa World Press, 2004); Ghazala Begum Esoop, "Trusting the Private into the Public Sphere: North African Women's Writing Identities in Epistolary Form," *Journal of Literary Studies* 32, no. 1 (2016): 105–13; Terence Ranger, *Are We Not Men: The Samkange Family and African Politics in Zimbabwe*, 1920–64 (London: James Currey, 1995); Nancy Rose Hunt, "Letter-Writing, Nursing Men, and Bicycles in the Belgian Congo: Notes towards the Identity of a Colonial Category," in *Paths to the Past: African Historical Essays in Honor of Jan Vansina*, ed. Robert W. Harms, Joseph C. Miller, David S. Newbury, and Michele D. Wagner (Atlanta, GA: African Studies Association, 1994), 187–210.

6. See Bọlanle Awẹ, "The Rise of Ibadan as a Yoruba Power in the Nineteenth Century" (PhD diss., University of Oxford, 1963). For a comprehensive study of the Yorùbá Wars in the nineteenth century, see J. F. Ade Ajayi and Robert Smith, *Yoruba Warfare in the Nineteenth Century* (Cambridge: Cambridge University Press, 1964).

7. For a critical analysis of the dialectical interactions between internal and external forces in the history and politics of modern African states and society, see Jean-François Bayart, *The State in Africa: The Politics of the Belly* (London: Longman, 1993), 31.

8. Akinṣọla Akiwọwọ, "Ajobi and Ajogbe: Variations on the Theme of Sociation," Inaugural Lecture Series 46, University of Ife, Nigeria, 1980, 13–14. For an insightful discussion of Akiwọwọ's analysis of Yoruba kinship values, see also M. W. Payne, "Akiwowo, Orature, and Divination: Approaches to the Construction of an Emic Sociological Paradigm of Society," *Sociological Analysis* 53, no. 1 (1992): 175–87.

9. Akiwọwọ, *Ajobi and Ajogbe*, 23–24.

10. By 1893, when the British imposed their colonial rule on Ibadan, the city had three CMS churches, St. David's, Kudẹti (1854), St. Peter's, Aremọ (1865), and St. James, Ògùnpa (1865), as well as elementary schools in Kudẹti and Ogunpa, and it would later have a school at Aremọ. When the English missionary Reverend Harding arrived in Ibadan to lead the mission in 1889, Ibadan, a city whose inhabitants were predominantly Muslims and adherents of indigenous Yoruba religion and the most populous in the Yoruba region of what soon became southwestern Nigeria, had four hundred CMS members—the main Christian group in the city—under the care of six CMS agents. Three additional missions were established in the late nineteenth century: Yemetu in 1894, Inalende in 1897, and Mapo in 1899. See *A Short History of St. Peter's Church, Aremo, Ibadan, 1852–1985* (Ibadan: Bolayele Commercial Press, 1987); Bọlanle Awẹ, *From Mission Station to a Cathedral: St. James the Great. Oke Bola, Ibadan, 1860–2010* (Ibadan: John Archers, 2018). See also George Jenkins, "Groups in Ibadan," 1965, George D. Jenkins Papers, Hoover Institution Archives, Stanford University Library, Stanford, California; A. B. Akinyele, *Iwe Itan Ibadan* (History of Ibadan) (London: James Townsend & Sons, Ltd., 1946). See also, Jacob Kehinde Olupona, *In My Father's Parsonage: The Story of an Anglican Family in Yoruba-Speaking Nigeria* (Ibadan: University Press, 2012).

11. For a South African case study on epistolary networks and Christian mission stations, see Cyrius Vukile Khumalo, "Epistolary Networks and the Politics of Cultural Production in KwaZulu-Natal, 1860–1910" (PhD diss., University of Michigan, 2004).

12. In this context, I reflect on C. Wright Mills's concept of "sociological imagination," in which he posits that the "imaginative thoughts" of individuals—that is, their

individual social actions—can profoundly shape outcomes within the social and historical contexts in which individuals are compelled to operate and live. For detailed analysis, see C. Wright Mills, *The Sociological Imagination* (Oxford: Oxford University Press, 1959).

13. Mills, *The Sociological Imagination*, 6.

14. I. A. Akinjogbin, *Dahomey and Its Neighbours, 1708–1818* (Cambridge: Cambridge University Press, 1967). For an authoritative analysis of traditional Yoruba society, see Rowland Abiodun, *Yoruba Art and Language: Seeking the African in African Art* (Cambridge: Cambridge University Press, 2014).

15. J. D. Y. Peel, *Religious Encounter and the Making of the Yoruba* (Bloomington: Indiana University Press, 2000).

16. See, for example, in a broader African context, David Chidester, "African Christian Communities," in *The Oxford Handbook of Global Religions*, ed. Mark Juergensmeyer (New York: Oxford University Press, 2006), 350. In Ibadan, the hometown of the letter writers, the first CMS mission was established by a Basel-trained CMS Swiss German missionary, the Reverend David Hinderer, and his English wife, Anna, along with their Egba-Yorùbá assistant, Daniel Olubi. They arrived in the city from CMS stronghold Abeokuta, about forty miles to the south, in May 1853. Immediately after their arrival, David and Anna Hinderer and Yorùbá CMS missionaries established elementary schools for the children of Christian converts, first in Kudeti and subsequently in two other mission stations at Aremo and Ogunpa. Since Western education in Ibadan was under the exclusive control of Christian missions—especially CMS—Christian converts and their children, though largely from humble backgrounds, soon emerged as the new educated elite in the city. The letter writers in this book, both male and female, reflect the perspectives of this critical social class in a rapidly changing Yorùbá society in modern southern Nigeria. See Kemi Morgan, *History of Ibadan* (Ibadan: Caxton Press, n.d.).

17. On literacy in modern Africa, see, for example, Hawkins, *Writing and Colonialism*; and Barber, *Africa's Hidden Histories*.

18. See, for example, Obafemi Awolowo, *The Autobiography of Chief Obafemi Awolowo* (Cambridge: Cambridge University Press, 1960); J. D. Y. Peel, *Ijesha and Nigerians: The Incorporation of a Yoruba Kingdom, 1890s–1970s* (Cambridge: Cambridge University Press, 1983); Richard Sklar, *Nigerian Political Parties: Power in an Emergent African Nation* (Princeton, NJ: Princeton University Press, 1963); M. A. Ajasin, *Memoirs and Memories* (Lagos: Ajasin Foundation, 2003); Gavin P. Williams, "The Political Sociology of Western Nigeria, 1939–1965," BPhil thesis, University of Oxford, 1967.

19. Liz Stanley, "The Epistolarium: On Theorizing Letters and Correspondences," *Auto/Biography* 12 (2004): 202. See also Stanley, *The Racialising Process: Whites Writing Whiteness in Letters, South Africa, 1770–1970* (Edinburgh: X Press, 2017). See also Harry Akussah, "A Calendar of the Kwame Nkrumah Papers in the Documentation Centre of the Institute of African Studies, University of Ghana, 1935–1948," *History in Africa* 21 (1994): 389–402. For an analysis of how "real life letters" shape narrative research, see Maria Tamboukou, "Interfaces in Narrative Research: Letters as Technologies of the Self and as Traces of Social Forces," *Qualitative Research* 11, no. 5 (2011): 625–41.

20. For an authoritative book on neo-Victorian Christian marriages and Yorùbá marriage practices in colonial Lagos, see Kristin Mann, *Marrying Well: Marriages, Status,*

and Social Change among the Educated Elite in Colonial Lagos (Cambridge: Cambridge University Press, 1985).

21. Sara Berry, *Fathers Work for Their Sons: Accumulation, Mobility, and Class Formation in an Extended Yorùbá Community* (Berkeley: University of California Press, 1985).

22. See Oyeronke Oyewumi, *The Invention of Women: Making an African Sense of Western Gender Discourses* (Minneapolis: University of Minnesota Press, 1997); Niara Sudarkasa, "The 'Status of Women' in Indigenous African Society," *Feminist Studies* 12, no. 1 (1986): 91–103.

23. Ọlọkọ was at the center of this exciting dialogue. He exemplified the leadership qualities and temperament that reflected the mission of the three mutual aid and civic groups. For his notable professional and civic work, Ọlọkọ—and another senior member of this Ibadan socioreligious network, G. O. Ogunṣọla, senior schoolmaster at Baptist Boys High School, Abẹokuta—were awarded MBEs (member of the British Empire) by the British Crown in 1950. A few years later, J. A. Ayorinde, another active member of the network and classmate of Abiọdun Vaughan at Ibadan Grammar School, was awarded an MBE. Ayorinde, who rose to a senior traditional chieftaincy title in Ibadan later on in his life, was also awarded an honorary doctorate in humanities for exceptional work as a local historian by the University of Ife (later Obafemi Awolowo University) during Nigeria's second decade of independence in the 1970s. Another active member of the Ibadan CMS network, E. O. Alayande, who became the principal of the CMS Ibadan Grammar School from the late 1940s to the 1960s, was awarded an MBE in the late 1950s.

24. See, for example, Peel, *Ijesha and Nigerians.*

25. Abiọdun's marriage to his first wife, Dorcas Bọlaji Ajibose-Vaughan, ended in 1943.

26. Adukẹ lost her first three infant children in succession from 1945 to 1949. This led to some discussions of the Yorùbá belief of *àbíkú,* a cosmological phenomenon in which certain spirit children are said to occupy the liminal space of spirit and temporal worlds by some of the letter writers. For the case of the Igbo people of southeastern Nigeria and the phenomenon of *ogbanje,* see the African literary classic by Chinua Achebe, *Things Fall Apart* (London: Penguin, 1994).

Chapter 1. The Brothers' Letters

1. The Vaughan family local history records that Akintọla obtained a few years of formal education at a CMS training school while he was in Freetown to retrieve his younger brother, Adeguyi, who had been liberated by British squadrons from a slave ship destined for the Americas off the West African coast about the late 1870s during the Yorùbá Wars. On his return to the Atlantic Nigerian region, Adegbuyi, who was educated at Fourah Bay College, became a schoolteacher in Lagos and later served as the private secretary of Captain Robert L. Bower, first British Resident in Ibadan between 1893 and 1897. It is claimed that the brothers adopted the name of their American benefactor, one Reverend Vaughan, during their stay in Freetown in the late 1870s. This information is recorded in a typed document of Vaughan family history contained in a file in Abiọdun Vaughan's possession.

2. Interview, Lamide Bakare, née Vaughan, Ibadan, June 2021. Lamide Bakare, Abiọdun's first child and Mariam's granddaughter, told me that Mariam taught her to

read the Bible in Yorùbá written in the Latin alphabet before attending elementary school in the mid-1940s.

3. There were only about ten secondary schools in colonial Nigeria by the late 1920s when Abiọdun Vaughan completed his education at Ibadan Grammar School. For information about Ibadan Grammar School, see *Ibadan Grammar School, Fiftieth Anniversary Souvenir Handbook, 1913–1963* (George D. Jenkins Papers, Hoover Institution Archives, Stanford University Library).

4. For landmark anthropological and sociological analyses of case studies on elite formation, especially the impact of Western education on the formation of elites in colonial and early postcolonial African societies, see Peter C. Lloyd, ed., *The New Elites in Tropical Africa* (London: Oxford University Press, 1966); Edwin Ardener, "The Notion of the Elite," *African Affairs* 66, no. 262 (1967): 64–66.

5. For a historical overview of the Nigerian colonial railway system, see John Stocker, *Nigerian Railway Jubilee, 1901–1951: An Illustrated and Descriptive History of the Nigerian Railway* (Lagos: Railway Printer, 1951).

6. For a detailed study, see Adedoyin Teriba, "Afro-Brazilian Architecture in Southwest Nigeria, 1890s–1940s" (PhD diss., Princeton University, 2017).

7. Relatives who informed me about this, notably, Lamide Bakare, née Vaughan, also told me that Dorcas Ọlayinka Brainerd, a sister seven years Samuel Ariyibi's junior and thirteen years Abiọdun's senior, joined in supporting Abiọdun at this time.

8. Interview, Lamide Bakare, June 2021. I also observed these developments in the letters written by other major letter writers, notably, Abiọdun Vaughan's mother and sisters. For a good study on the complexities of Western education and social mobility in colonial Ibadan based on source materials from personal documents, see Ruth Watson, "What Is Our Intelligence, Our School Going, and Our Reading of Books without Getting Money: Akinpelu Obisesan and His Diary," in *Africa's Hidden Histories: Everyday Literacy and the Making of Self, ed. Karin Barber* (Bloomington: Indiana University Press, 2006): 52–77.

9. Interview, Lamide Bakare, June 2021.

10. S. A. Vaughan, T.T. School, Port Harcourt, Eastern Nigeria, June 17, 1929. For a landmark sociological analysis of the central role of Western education in the emergence of a modern Yoruba elite in colonial southern Nigeria, see Barbara B. Lloyd, "Education and Family Life in the Development of Class Identification among the Yoruba," in P. Lloyd, *The New Elites*, 163–183.

11. S. A. Vaughan, T.T. School, Port Harcourt, Eastern Nigeria, July 17, 1929.

12. S. A. Vaughan, T.T. School, Port Harcourt, Eastern Nigeria, August 11, 1930.

13. S. A. Vaughan, T.T. School, Port Harcourt, Eastern Nigeria, May 23, 1929.

14. S. A. Vaughan, T.T. School, Port Harcourt, Eastern Nigeria, July 26, 1929.

15. S. A. Vaughan, T.T. School, Port Harcourt, Eastern Nigeria, March 5, 1931.

16. S. A. Vaughan, T.T. School, Port Harcourt, Eastern Nigeria, January 14, 1931.

17. S. A. Vaughan, T.T. School, Port Harcourt, Eastern Nigeria, July 28, 1931.

18. S. A. Vaughan, T.T. School, Port Harcourt, Eastern Nigeria, August 5, 1931.

19. S. A. Vaughan, T.T. School, Port Harcourt, Eastern Nigeria, August 26, 1931.

20. S. A. Vaughan, T.T. School, Port Harcourt, Eastern Nigeria, August 26, 1931.

21. S. A. Vaughan, Port Harcourt, Eastern Nigeria, July 7, 1929.

22. S. A. Vaughan, Port Harcourt, Eastern Nigeria, August 8, 1929.

23. S. A. Vaughan, Port Harcourt, Eastern Nigeria, July 31, 1930.
24. S. A. Vaughan, Port Harcourt, Eastern Nigeria, December 12, 1930.
25. S. A. Vaughan, Port Harcourt, Eastern Nigeria, September 10, 1931.
26. S. A. Vaughan, Port Harcourt, Eastern Nigeria, October 15, 1931.
27. S. A. Vaughan, Port Harcourt, Eastern Nigeria, October 23, 1931.
28. S. A. Vaughan, Port Harcourt, Eastern Nigeria, November 7, 1931.
29. S. A. Vaughan, Port Harcourt, Eastern Nigeria, November 11, 1931.
30. S. A. Vaughan, Port Harcourt, Eastern Nigeria, December 10, 1931.
31. S. A. Vaughan, Port Harcourt, Eastern Nigeria, December 10, 1931.
32. S. A. Vaughan, Port Harcourt, Eastern Nigeria, December 21, 1931.
33. S. A. Vaughan, Port Harcourt, Eastern Nigeria, January 17, 1932.
34. S. A. Vaughan, Aba Station, Eastern Nigeria, February 27, 1932.
35. S. A. Vaughan, Port Harcourt, Eastern Nigeria, April 1932.
36. S. A. Vaughan, Port Harcourt, Eastern Nigeria, April 1932.
37. S. A. Vaughan, Port Harcourt, Eastern Nigeria, April 11, 1932.
38. S. A. Vaughan, Port Harcourt, Eastern Nigeria, April 11, 1932.
39. S. A. Vaughan, Jos Station, Northern Nigeria, May 9, 1932.
40. S. A. Vaughan, Jos Station, Northern Nigeria, May 20, 1932.
41. S. A. Vaughan, Jos Station, Northern Nigeria, July 1, 1932.
42. S. A. Vaughan, Port Harcourt, Eastern Nigeria, August 12, 1932.
43. S. A. Vaughan, Port Harcourt, Eastern Nigeria, July 14, 1931.
44. S. A. Vaughan, Port Harcourt, Eastern Nigeria, August 20, 1931.
45. Abiọdun Alfred Vaughan, Ibadan, December 3, 1931.
46. Abiọdun Alfred Vaughan, Agricultural Department, Moor Plantation, Ibadan, January 1, 1932. For a comprehensive analysis of the administrative transformation of colonial Ibadan in the 1930s and 1940s, see Toyin Falola, *Ibadan: Foundation, Growth, and Change, 1930–1960* (Ibadan: Bookcraft, 2012).
47. Abiọdun Alfred Vaughan, Agricultural Department, Moor Plantation, Ibadan, January 19, 1933.
48. S. A. Vaughan, Port Harcourt, Eastern Nigeria, January 12, 1932.
49. S. A. Vaughan, Port Harcourt, Eastern Nigeria, July 7, 1932.
50. S. A. Vaughan, Port Harcourt, Eastern Nigeria, August 1932.
51. Abiọdun Alfred Vaughan, Agricultural Department, Moor Plantation, Ibadan, September 1932.
52. Interview, Lamide Bakare, June 2021.
53. Abiọdun Alfred Vaughan, Agricultural Department, Ibadan, August 16, 1933.
54. Abiọdun Alfred Vaughan, Agricultural Department, Ibadan, October 20, 1933.
55. Abiọdun Alfred Vaughan, Agricultural Department, Moor Plantation Ibadan, February 6, 1934.
56. Abiọdun Alfred Vaughan, Agricultural Department, Moor Plantation, Ibadan, February 12, 1934.
57. Abiọdun Alfred Vaughan, Agricultural Department, Samaru, Zaria, Northern Nigeria, September 2, 1934.
58. Interview, Abiọdun Pomary, née Vaughan, June 2021. I also recall my mother making a similar statement in the 1970s. My father was not one to go down memory lane on any matter, however lighthearted or memorable. He was genuinely self-

effacing. I cannot recall him ever sharing any information about his talents and accomplishments. He was one of those rare people who took pleasure in listening to the achievements of others. If I had the opportunity to interview him for this book, it would have been challenging to get much information out of him.

59. Abiọdun Alfred Vaughan, Agricultural Department, Samaru, Zaria, Northern Nigeria, August 10, 1935.

60. Abiọdun Alfred Vaughan, Agricultural Department, Samaru, Zaria, Northern Nigeria, November 12, 1935.

61. Abiọdun Alfred Vaughan, Agricultural Department, Samaru, Zaria, Northern Nigeria, November 12, 1935.

62. Abiọdun Alfred Vaughan, Agricultural Department, Samaru, Zaria, Northern Nigeria, September 21, 1935.

63. Abiọdun Alfred Vaughan, Agricultural Department, Samaru, Zaria, Northern Nigeria, October 8, 1935.

64. S. A. Vaughan, Local Goods Shed, Iddo, Lagos, November 5, 1935.

65. Abiọdun Alfred Vaughan, Agricultural Department, Samaru, Zaria, Northern Nigeria, November 28, 1935.

66. Abiọdun Alfred Vaughan, Agricultural Department, Samaru, Zaria, Northern Nigeria, 1934.

67. Abiọdun Alfred Vaughan, Agricultural Department, Samaru, Zaria, Northern Nigeria, November 2, 1934.

68. Abiọdun Alfred Vaughan, Agricultural Department, Samaru, Zaria, Northern Nigeria, December 1934.

69. Abiọdun Alfred Vaughan, Agricultural Department, Samaru, Zaria, Northern Nigeria, December 1934.

70. For an authoritative social history of Western Christian marriage practices in colonial Yoruba society, see Mann, *Marrying Well.*

71. Abiọdun Alfred Vaughan, Agricultural Department, Ibadan, September 8, 1932.

72. Abiọdun Alfred Vaughan, Agricultural Department, Ibadan, August 16, 1933.

73. S. A. Vaughan, Oshogbo, Ọyọ Province, Nigeria, September 6, 1933.

74. Abiọdun Alfred Vaughan, Agricultural Department, Ibadan, October 2, 1933.

75. S. A. Vaughan, Oshogbo, Ọyọ Province, Nigeria, August 31, 1933.

76. Abiọdun Alfred Vaughan, Agricultural Department, Ibadan, December 11, 1933.

77. S. A. Vaughan, Oshogbo, Ọyọ Province, Nigeria, December 15, 1933.

78. S. A. Vaughan, Ibadan, December 20, 1933.

79. Abiọdun Alfred Vaughan, Agricultural Department, Samaru, Zaria, Northern Nigeria, June 13, 1934.

80. Abiọdun Alfred Vaughan, Agricultural Department, Samaru, Zaria, Northern Nigeria, June 13, 1934.

81. S. A. Vaughan, Ibadan, July 6, 1934.

82. Theo Bamidele Brainerd was the son of Samuel Ariyibi and Abiọdun's sister Dorcas Ọlayinka Brainerd. For detailed analysis of Bamidele's letters, see chapter 5, "From Freetown with Love."

83. Abiọdun Alfred Vaughan, Agricultural Department, Samaru, Zaria, Northern Nigeria, January 23, 1935.

84. Abiọdun Alfred Vaughan, Agricultural Department, Samaru, Zaria, Northern Nigeria, February 28, 1935.

85. Abiọdun Alfred Vaughan, Agricultural Department, Samaru, Zaria, Northern Nigeria, May 4, 1935.

86. Abiọdun Alfred Vaughan, Agricultural Department, Samaru, Zaria, Northern Nigeria, April 29, 1935.

87. The tensions that arose in these dynamic kinship relations of *alájọbí* were evident in some of the issues explored in my analysis of the letters of Abiọdun's mother and sisters in chapter 2, "The Matriarchs' Letters."

88. Abiọdun Alfred Vaughan, Agricultural Department, Samaru, Zaria, Northern Nigeria, June 11, 1935.

89. S. A. Vaughan, Yaba Estate, Lagos, June 17, 1935.

90. Abiọdun Vaughan, Agricultural Department, Abẹokuta, March 1937.

91. Abiọdun Vaughan, Agricultural Department, Abẹokuta, March 1937.

92. Abiọdun Alfred Vaughan, Agricultural Department, Abẹokuta, January 18, 1938. A notarized typed document titled "Declaration as to How the Property at N5/441 Gbenla Street, Ibadan, Ọyọ State, Belonging to Pa. Solomon Akintọla Vaughan Was Shared among the Direct Descendants," written by Abiọdun Vaughan, was kept in one of the S. A. Vaughan files. It outlined the history of the land on which the Vaughan natal house was constructed in the late 1930s. The document noted that three modern houses built by Solomon Akintọla Vaughan (Abiọdun's father) by the turn of the twentieth century were demolished by the colonial authorities to make way for the "expansion and dualization of the narrow road" to connect Agodi to the core of the city of Ibadan in the mid-1930s following the death of Solomon Akintọla in 1930. Samuel Ariyibi and Abiọdun later collaborated to construct a new Vaughan natal house on a smaller portion of the preexisting land that had been approved by the colonial authorities in the late 1930s.

93. Abiọdun Alfred Vaughan, Agricultural Department, Abẹokuta, January 18, 1938. See B. Lloyd, "Education and Family Life."

94. Abiọdun Alfred Vaughan, Agricultural Department, Abẹokuta, September 19, 1940.

95. Abiọdun Alfred Vaughan, Agricultural Department, Abẹokuta, October 23, 1940.

96. S. A. Vaughan, Ibadan, October 29, 1940.

97. S. A. Vaughan, Ibadan, October 29, 1940.

98. Abiọdun Alfred Vaughan, Agricultural Department, Abẹokuta, November 1940.

Chapter 2. The Matriarchs' Letters

1. For a landmark sociological study of the structure of traditional Yoruba cities, see Peter C. Lloyd, "The Yoruba Town Today," *Sociological Review* 7, no. 1 (1959): 45–63.

2. These translators were Sunday Awotodu, Iyabo Fagbongbe, and Shade Ojedeji, elementary schoolteachers at Ọmọlẹwa Nursery and Primary School, Ibadan, a private elementary school founded by Gladys Aduke Vaughan in 1962.

3. Oladunjoye (or Ladunjoye), who was constantly referenced in the letters written by his mother, brothers, and sisters, had severe health challenges from which he eventually died in his early forties in 1941. He wrote a few letters to his brother Abiọdun in the 1930s.

4. Mariam O. Vaughan, Gbenla Street, Agodi, Ibadan, July 12, 1934.
5. Mariam O. Vaughan, Gbenla Street, Agodi, Ibadan, August 7, 1934.
6. Mariam O. Vaughan, Gbenla Street, Agodi, Ibadan, April 11, 1934.
7. Mariam O. Vaughan, Gbenla Street, Agodi, Ibadan, October 21, 1934.
8. Mariam O. Vaughan, Gbenla Street, Agodi, Ibadan, November 13, 1934.
9. Mariam O. Vaughan, Gbenla Street, Agodi, Ibadan, February 6, 1935.
10. Mariam O. Vaughan, Gbenla Street, Agodi, Ibadan, March 8, 1935.
11. Ladunjoye Vaughan, Gbenla Street, Agodi, Ibadan, March 8, 1935.
12. Mariam O. Vaughan, Gbenla Street, Agodi, Ibadan, August 28, 1935.
13. Mariam O. Vaughan, Gbenla Street, Agodi, Ibadan, August 28, 1935.
14. Mariam O. Vaughan, Gbenla Street, Agodi, Ibadan, July 25, 1935.
15. Mariam O. Vaughan, Gbenla Street, Agodi, Ibadan, May 5, 1936.
16. Mariam O. Vaughan, Gbenla Street, Agodi, Ibadan, March 17, 1939.
17. Mariam O. Vaughan, Gbenla Street, Agodi, Ibadan, December 4, 1939.
18. Mariam O. Vaughan, Gbenla Street, Agodi, Ibadan, June 20, 1945.
19. Mariam O. Vaughan, Gbenla Street, Agodi, Ibadan, December 14, 1947.
20. Mariam O. Vaughan, Gbenla Street, Agodi, Ibadan, March 31, 1949.
21. Mariam O. Vaughan, Gbenla Street, Agodi, Ibadan, September 9, 1949.
22. Mariam O. Vaughan, Gbenla Street, Agodi, Ibadan, June 7, 1949.
23. Mariam O. Vaughan, Gbenla Street, Agodi, Ibadan, May 19, 1949.
24. Mariam O. Vaughan, Gbenla Street, Agodi, Ibadan, June 13, 1949.
25. Mariam O. Vaughan, Gbenla Street, Agodi, Ibadan, July 14, 1949.
26. Mariam O. Vaughan, Gbenla Street, Agodi, Ibadan, October 29, 1949.
27. Mariam O. Vaughan, Agodi Post Office, Ibadan, November 5, 1949.
28. Mariam O. Vaughan, Gbenla Street, Agodi, November 16, 1947.
29. Mariam O. Vaughan, Gbenla Street, Agodi, Ibadan, September 24, 1948.
30. Mariam O. Vaughan, Gbenla Street, Agodi, Ibadan, September 29, 1948.
31. Mariam O. Vaughan, Gbenla Street, Agodi, Ibadan, September 2, 1948.
32. Mariam O. Vaughan, Gbenla Street, Agodi, Ibadan, November 6, 1931.
33. Mariam O. Vaughan, Gbenla Street, Agodi, Ibadan, March 19, 1934.
34. Mariam O. Vaughan, Gbenla Street, Agodi, Ibadan, July 23, 1934.
35. Mariam O. Vaughan, Gbenla Street, Agodi, Ibadan, September 3, 1934.
36. What is referred to in modern Yoruba marriages (shaped by CMS Anglicanism) as "introduction" by this time in colonial Yoruba society is an engagement ceremony where key figures in the families of the bride-to-be and the groom-to-be are formally introduced. This aspect of modern Yoruba marriage practice derived its origin from Yoruba norms and customary ways.
37. Mariam O. Vaughan, Gbenla Street, Agodi, Ibadan, November 5, 1934.
38. Mariam O. Vaughan, Gbenla Street, Agodi, Ibadan, November 22, 1934.
39. Mariam O. Vaughan, Gbenla Street, Agodi, Ibadan, January 7, 1935.
40. Mariam O. Vaughan, Gbenla Street, Agodi, Ibadan, April 27, 1935.
41. Mariam O. Vaughan, Gbenla Street, Agodi, Ibadan, November 24, 1948.
42. Mariam O. Vaughan, Gbenla Street, Agodi, Ibadan, February 23, 1949.
43. Mariam O. Vaughan, Gbenla Street, Agodi, Ibadan, March 31, 1949.
44. Mariam O. Vaughan, c/o Mr. S. Salau, Post Office, Agodi, Ibadan, April 20, 1949.

45. Mariam O. Vaughan, Gbenla Street, Agodi, Ibadan, May 19, 1949.

46. As noted earlier in this chapter, Ladunjoye, the other brother, was ill at home in Ibadan from the mid-1930s to 1941, when he died in his early forties.

47. Interview, Lamide Bakare, June 2021.

48. Jadesọla Ọdẹbunmi, Ile-Ifẹ, June 6, 1934.

49. Jadesọla Ọdẹbunmi, Alafara Street, Ibadan, November 12, 1934.

50. Jadesọla Ọdẹbunmi, Alafara Street, Ibadan, November 4, 1934.

51. Jadesọla Ọdẹbunmi, Alafara Street, Ibadan, January 31, 1935. J. A. Ayọrinde was Abiọdun's close friend, classmate at Ibadan Grammar School, and colleague at the Department of Agriculture.

52. Jadesọla Ọdẹbunmi, Ile-Ifẹ.

53. Jadesọla Ọdẹbunmi, Alafara Street, Ibadan, May 2, 1935.

54. Jadesọla Ọdẹbunmi, Alafara Street, Ibadan, April 2, 1935.

55. Although polygamy was an aspect of Yoruba custom, Christian missions—and certainly Yoruba CMS Anglicans—discouraged it. However, the idea of taking another "wife" after the formal Christian and state-sanctioned marriage was not uncommon among this earlier generation of Yoruba Christian men.

56. Jadesọla Ọdẹbunmi, Alafara Street, Ibadan, June 13, 1935.

57. Jadesọla Ọdẹbunmi, Alafara Street, Ibadan, November 6, 1940.

58. Jadesọla Ọdẹbunmi, Alafara Street, Ibadan, April 23, 1947.

59. Jadesọla Ọdẹbunmi, Alafara Street, Ibadan, September 27, 1949.

60. Jadesọla Ọdẹbunmi, Alafara Street, Ibadan, July 11, 1952.

61. Jadesọla Ọdẹbunmi, Isale Agbede, Lagos, October 16, 1947.

62. Jadesọla Ọdẹbunmi, Alafara Street, Ibadan, March 3, 1949.

63. Jadesọla Ọdẹbunmi, Alafara Street, Ibadan, January 1950.

64. In Yorùbá cosmology, *àbíkú* is expressed through infants who are said to occupy the liminal space of spirit and temporal worlds. For these infants to find their place in a temporal world, special care and rituals drawn from age-old Yorùbá beliefs may be required to reassure and pacify them. In the case of the Igbo of southeastern Nigeria, see the phenomenon of *ogbanje* in the African classic novel by Chinua Achebe, *Things Fall Apart*. See also Chidi T. Maduka, "African Religious Beliefs in Literary Imagination: Oganje and Abiku in Chinua Achebe, J. P. Clark, and Wole Soyinka," *Journal of Commonwealth Literature*, March 1, 1987.

65. Jadesọla Ọdẹbunmi, Alafara Street, Ibadan, February 23, 1949.

66. Since Abiọdun had one child, Lamide, at this time, Jadesọla was referring to Abiọdun's nieces and nephews as his children.

67. Jadesọla Ọdẹbunmi, Alafara Street, Ibadan, March 9, 1949.

68. Jadesọla Ọdẹbunmi, Alafara Street, Ibadan, March 9, 1949.

69. Jadesọla Ọdẹbunmi, Alafara Street, Ibadan, August 22, 1949.

70. Jadesọla Ọdẹbunmi, Alafara Street, Ibadan, November 10, 1949.

71. Jadesọla Ọdẹbunmi, Alafara Street, Ibadan, September 27, 1949.

72. Jadesọla Ọdẹbunmi, Alafara Street, Ibadan, February 24, 1948.

73. Jadesọla Ọdẹbunmi, Alafara Street, Ibadan, August 1, 1951.

74. Jadesọla Ọdẹbunmi, Alafara Street, Ibadan, April 30, 1938.

75. Jadesọla Ọdẹbunmi, Alafara Street, Ibadan, January 29, 1949.

76. Interview, Lamide Bakare, June 2021.

77. Stocker, *Nigerian Railway Jubilee.*
78. Dorcas Ọlayinka Brainerd, Ekotẹdo, Ibadan, April 6, 1934.
79. Dorcas Ọlayinka Brainerd, Ibadan, September 2, 1935.
80. Dorcas Ọlayinka Brainerd, Ibadan, October 25, 1935.
81. Dorcas Ọlayinka Brainerd, Ibadan, May 10, 1935. Several letters from Dorcas Olayinka Brainerd to her younger brother Abiodun underscore the importance of an elite secondary school education—alongside high academic achievement—for her son, Bamidele, at Igbobi College, Lagos. On the central role of Western education and elite formation during colonial rule and the early years of independence in Yoruba society, see B. Lloyd, "Education and Family Life."
82. Dorcas Ọlayinka Brainerd, Ibadan, November 5, 1936.
83. Dorcas Ọlayinka Brainerd, Gbenla Street, Ibadan, September 8, 1940.
84. Dorcas Ọlayinka Brainerd, 26 Elegbeta Street, Lagos, August 9, 1947.
85. Dorcas Ọlayinka Brainerd, Ibadan, December 28, 1934.
86. Dorcas Ọlayinka Brainerd, Ibadan, February 4, 1935.
87. Dorcas Ọlayinka Brainerd, Ibadan, February 6, 1935.
88. Dorcas Ọlayinka Brainerd, Gbenla Street, Agodi, Ibadan, October 2, 1935.
89. Dorcas Ọlayinka Brainerd, via Jebba, April 25, 1941.
90. Dorcas Ọlayinka Brainerd, Ibadan, July 1934.
91. Dorcas Ọlayinka Brainerd, Ibadan, October 29, 1934.
92. Dorcas Ọlayinka Brainerd, Ibadan, October 25, 1935.
93. Dorcas Ọlayinka Brainerd, Ibadan, January 1, 1935.
94. Dorcas Ọlayinka Brainerd, 3 Breadfruit Street, Lagos, July 10, 1937.
95. Dorcas Ọlayinka Brainerd, Ibadan, September 15, 1938.
96. Dorcas Ọlayinka Brainerd, 26 Elegbeta Street, Lagos, May 18, 1945.
97. Dorcas Ọlayinka Brainerd, Ekotẹdo, Ibadan, July 1934.
98. Dorcas Ọlayinka Brainerd, Ekotẹdo Street, Ibadan, August 22, 1934.
99. Dorcas Ọlayinka Brainerd, Ibadan, November 5, 1934.
100. Dorcas Ọlayinka Brainerd, Ekotẹdo, Ibadan, June 5, 1935.
101. Dorcas Ọlayinka Brainerd, 37 Breadfruit Street, Lagos, 1947.
102. Dorcas Ọlayinka Brainerd, 37 Breadfruit Street, Lagos, July 10, 1937.
103. Dorcas Ọlayinka Brainerd, 26, Elegbeta Street, Lagos, May 4, 1947. For background information on the construction of the Vaughan natal house, see "Declaration as to How the Property."
104. Dorcas Ọlayinka Brainerd, 26 Elegbeta Street, Lagos, November 2, 1947.
105. Dorcas Bọlaji Vaughan, Gbenla Street, Agodi, Ibadan, September 19, 1937.
106. Dorcas Bọlaji Vaughan, Gbenla Street, Agodi, Ibadan, September 1937.
107. This was confirmed in an interview with Lamide Bakare (Dorcas's daughter) in June 2021.
108. Abiọdun Alfred Vaughan, Agriculture Department, Abẹokuta, September 13, 1938.
109. Dorcas Bọlaji Vaughan, Ibara Omiọla, Abẹokuta, September 1938.
110. Dorcas Bọlaji Vaughan, Gbenla Street, Agodi, Ibadan, September 30, 1938.
111. Abiọdun Alfred Vaughan, Agricultural Department, Abẹokuta, September 27, 1938. For a literary and sociocultural discussion on beads, gender, and Yoruba traditional practices, see G. O. Ajibade, *Finding Female Voice: A Socio-cultural Appraisal of Yoruba Nuptial Poetry* (Cologne: Rudiger Koppe Verlag, 2009).

112. Abiọdun Alfred Vaughan, Agricultural Department, Abẹokuta, October 1, 1938.
113. Dorcas Bọlaji Vaughan, Gbenla Street, Agodi, Ibadan, October 9, 1938.
114. Dorcas Bọlaji Vaughan, Gbenla Street, Agodi, Ibadan, October 12, 1938, October 22, 1938.
115. Abiọdun Alfred Vaughan, Agricultural Department, Abẹokuta, November 4, 1938.
116. Abiọdun Alfred Vaughan, Agricultural Department, Abẹokuta, November 14, 1938.
117. Dorcas Bọlaji Vaughan, Gbenla Street, Agodi, Ibadan, November 16, 1938.
118. Dorcas Bọlaji Vaughan, Gbenla Street, Agodi, Ibadan, November 29, 1938.
119. Abiọdun Alfred Vaughan, Agricultural Department, Abẹokuta, December 2, 1938.
120. The absence of letters from Dorcas Vaughan from January 1939 to January 1943 in the Vaughan Family files can be attributed in part to the fact that Abiọdun had a one-year assignment in the headquarters of the Department of Agriculture in Ibadan from 1939 to 1940 when Dorcas resided in Ibadan. This still does not explain the absence of letters from 1941 to 1943, when they divorced, except if Dorcas returned to Abeokuta with Abiọdun when the latter resumed work in the Abeokuta branch of the Department of Agriculture.
121. Dorcas Bọlaji Vaughan, Ishaga, Abẹokuta, February 23, 1943.
122. Dorcas Bọlaji Vaughan, Pala Village, March 17, 1943.
123. Dorcas Bọlaji Vaughan, Karo Division, April 6, 1943.
124. Dorcas Bọlaji Vaughan, Isala Ishaga, Ibara, Abẹokuta, August 7, 1944.
125. Ladunjoye Vaughan, Gbenla Street, Agodi, January 7, 1935.
126. Ladunjoye Vaughan, Gbenla Street, Agodi, August 4, 1935.
127. Kehinde Vaughan, Gbenla Street, Agodi, Ibadan, August 8, 1934.
128. Ẹbun, Gbenla Street, Agodi, Ibadan.
129. Adeoti Vaughan, Gbenla Street, Agodi, Ibadan, January 31, 1938.
130. Adenikẹ, Agbeni Street, Ibadan, April 28, 1943.
131. Adukẹ Ige, Gbenla Street, Agodi, Ibadan, February 28, 1949.
132. Akinola Vaughan, Gbenla Street, Agodi, Ibadan, February 28, 1949.
133. Olamide Vaughan, Gbenla Street, Agodi, Ibadan, December 14, 1947.

Chapter 3. Ibadan CMS Men

1. See Robin Law, *The Ọyọ Empire, c. 1600–c. 1836: A West African Imperialism in the Era of the Atlantic Slave Trade* (Oxford: Clarendon Press, 1977).
2. Interview, Lamide Bakare, Ibadan, Nigeria, June 2021; interview, Abiọdun Pomary, Ibadan, Nigeria, June 2021.
3. Interview, Lamide Bakare, Ibadan, June 2021; interview, Abiọdun Pomary, Ibadan, June 2021.
4. For a discussion of the Ibadan Progressive Union, see Kenneth Post and George Jenkins, *The Price of Liberty: Personality and Power in Colonial Nigeria* (Cambridge: Cambridge University Press, 1973).
5. Awẹ, "The Rise of Ibadan"; George D. Jenkins, "Ibadan Politics" (PhD diss., Northwestern University, 1965).
6. For a brilliant memoir of this class of men in the CMS stronghold of Abẹokuta in colonial Yorùbá society, see Wole Soyinka, *Isara: A Voyage around "Essay"* (New York: Random House, 1989).

7. After about two decades as a civil servant in the colonial Department of Agriculture, with its headquarters in Moor Plantation, Ibadan, Abiọdun was promoted to senior clerk in 1952, one of the most senior positions an African could attain in the Department of Agriculture before the imposition of decolonization in the early 1950s. S. A. Ọlọkọ rose to the position of acting accountant in the Department of Agriculture in 1950, another senior administrative position. A third group in which many of these men were members, the Ibadan Progressive Union—with Ọlọkọ as cofounder—was referenced in some of the letters in the files. The correspondence among the officials of this prominent civic organization that dominated Ibadan civic and political life was handled more directed by Ọlọkọ and other senior officials of the organization during the colonial era, especially in the 1930s and 1940s. For detailed analysis, see Post and Jenkins, *Price of Liberty*.

8. Although these men operated under the dominant socioreligious orbit of Ibadan CMS, some of them were members of other Protestant denominations, notably, Wesleyan Methodist and Baptist. For example, G. O. Ogunṣọla was a prominent member of Araromi Baptist Church, Ibadan, in the 1950s and 1960s. Telephone interview, Bimpe Lawson (daughter of G. O. Ogunṣọla), Amherst, MA, February 2022.

9. See Sklar, *Nigerian Political Parties*.

10. A copy of the full text of this document is filed under the Ibadan Brotherhood Fund Association section of the S. A. Ọlọkọ files.

11. Signed January 27, 1940, by J. A. Ọjẹrinọla, secretary, IBFA; Abẹokuta Center: G. O. Ogunṣọla, A. A. Vaughan, H. A. Ọjẹrinọla, E. A. Ajani, G. A. Adelu; Ilesha Center: S. A. Fajẹmbọla, S. A. Latinwo; Ibadan Center: G. O. Ṣijuwolu, S. A. Babalọla, E. A. Ogunṣọla; Ondo: E. O. Alayande. Many of the Ibadan CMS men who became members of the Ibadan Brotherhood Fund Association and the Ibadan Cooperative Savings Society were also members of the following civic and mutual aid groups in the city from the 1930s to the 1960s: Ibadan Old Grammarians Society, Ibadan Progressive Union (including its study circle), Union Club, Western Circle, St. Peter's Church, Aremo, Mutual Improvement Society.

12. November 27, 1942.

13. May 3, 1942.

14. E. A. Ajani, Provincial Office, Abẹokuta, March 1, 1941.

15. G. O. Ogunṣọla, Baptist Boys High School, Abẹokuta, Western Nigeria, February 8, 1942.

16. G. O. Ogunṣọla, Baptist Boys High School, Abẹokuta, Western Nigeria, May 8, 1943.

17. G. O. Ogunṣọla, Provincial Office, Ijẹbu-Ode, November 27, 1942.

18. A. A. Akinrinade, BATC Ltd., Ogbomosho, June 2, 1941.

19. A. A. Akinrinade, BATC Ltd., Ogbomosho, December 30, 1942.

20. For a detailed analysis of the distinguished career of E. O. Alayande as a prominent Nigerian educationist, see E. O. Adeoti, *Alayande as Educationist, 1948–1983: A Study of Alayande's Contribution to Education and Social Change* (Ibadan: Heinemann, 1997).

21. E. O. Alayande, Ondo Boys High School, Ondo, April 8, 1941.

22. E. A. Bọlaji, Abẹokuta, February 22, 1943.

23. Latidoye Ayọọla, Agricultural Department, Abẹokuta, July 8, 1941.

24. Olu Osikalu, Agricultural Department, Abẹokuta, December 15, 1942.
25. Olu Osikalu, Agricultural Department, Abẹokuta, March 27, 1943.
26. Olu Osikalu, Agricultural Department, Ibadan, June 23, 1941.
27. Abiọdun Alfred Vaughan, Department of Agriculture, Abẹokuta, July 31, 1941.
28. Josiah O. Keleko, Department of Agriculture, Ibadan, April 11, 1935.
29. S. A. Ọlọkọ, Agricultural Department, Moor Plantation, Ibadan, November 20, 1939.
30. S. A. Ọlọkọ, Agricultural Department, Moor Plantation, Ibadan, May 1940.
31. Abiọdun Alfred Vaughan, Agricultural Department, Abeokuta, September 21, 1940.
32. Abiọdun Alfred Vaughan, Samaru, Zaria, Northern Nigeria, May 31, 1934.
33. S. Alabi, Agricultural Department, Moor Plantation, Ibadan, August 23, 1937.
34. Agricultural Department, Ibadan, January 23, 1943.
35. S. A. Ọlọkọ, Agricultural Department, Moor Plantation, Ibadan, April 26, 1949.
36. S. A. Ọlọkọ, Agricultural Department, Moor Plantation, Ibadan, April 26, 1949.
37. S. A. Ọlọkọ, Agricultural Department, Moor Plantation, Ibadan, November 27, 1949.
38. S. A. Ọlọkọ, Department of Agriculture, Ibadan, June 12, 1952.
39. E. A. Akintola, Baptist School, PO Box 82, Ibadan, 1934.
40. Josiah O. Keleko, Agricultural Department, Ibadan, May 22, 1934.
41. A. Akinrinade, Ago-Are, BAIC, June 28, 1946.
42. Olu S. Osikalu, Agricultural Department, Abẹokuta, Western Nigeria, April 12, 1941.
43. Olu S. Osikalu, Agricultural Department, Abẹokuta, Western Nigeria, December 15, 1942.
44. G. O. Ogunṣọla, Baptist Boys High School, Abẹokuta, Western Nigeria, November 20, 1942.
45. J. A. Ọjẹrinọla, Ibadan, May 13, 1943.
46. J. A. Ọjẹrinọla, Ibadan, December 17, 1940.
47. S. A. Ọlọkọ, Agricultural Department, Moor Plantation, Ibadan, April 6, 1934. For information about Ibadan Grammar School, see *Ibadan Grammar School, Fiftieth Anniversary*.
48. Abiọdun Alfred Vaughan, Agricultural Department, Abẹokuta, April 5, 1938.
49. S. A. Ọlọkọ, Agricultural Department, Moor Plantation, Ibadan, December 12, 1934.
50. S. A. Ọlọkọ, Agricultural Department, Moor Plantation, Ibadan, March 5, 1934.
51. S. A. Ọlọkọ, Agricultural Department, Moor Plantation, Ibadan, December 28, 1934.
52. E. O. Alayande, P. O. Box 25, Ondo, February 24, 1943.
53. A. M. O. Afinne, Agricultural Department, Bida, Northern Nigeria, May 24, 1943.
54. G. O. Ogunṣọla, Baptist Boys High School, Abẹokuta, Western Nigeria, March 15, 1943.
55. G. O. Ogunṣọla, Baptist Boys High School, Abẹokuta, Western Nigeria, March 29, 1943. Government College is the second colonial government (Southern Provinces)

secondary school for boys in the Yorùbá region founded in 1929 by the colonial authorities after King's College, Lagos (national government), founded in 1909.

56. A. A. Akinrinade, BAT C, Ogbomosho, March 30, 1943.
57. Okunola Idowu, 4 Griffith Street, Ebute-Metta, Lagos, April 3, 1943.
58. S. A. Ọlọkọ, Agricultural Department, Moor Plantation, Ibadan, August 13, 1938.
59. S. A. Ọlọkọ, Agricultural Department, Moor Plantation, Ibadan, October 4, 1940.
60. S. A. Ọlọkọ, Agricultural Department, Moor Plantation, Ibadan, April 1935.
61. S. A. Ọlọkọ, Agricultural Department, Moor Plantation, Ibadan, July 9, 1934.
62. S. A. Ọlọkọ, Agricultural Department, Moor Plantation, Ibadan, May 17, 1935.
63. Abiọdun Alfred Vaughan, Samaru, Zaria, Northern Nigeria, May 17, 1935.
64. S. A. Ọlọkọ, Agricultural Department, Moor Plantation, Ibadan, July 15, 1935.
65. Ekotedo, Ibadan, c/o Mr. S. A. Ọlọkọ, July 29, 1944.
66. E. O. Alayande, Ondo Boys High School, Ondo, 1943.
67. S. A. Ọlọkọ, Agricultural Department, Moor Plantation, Ibadan, April 26, 1949.
68. S. A. Ọlọkọ, Agricultural Department, Moor Plantation, Ibadan, May 26, 1949.
69. S. A. Ọlọkọ, Agricultural Department, Moor Plantation, Ibadan, January 15, 1948.
70. S. A. Ọlọkọ, Agricultural Department, Moor Plantation, Ibadan, January 15, 1948.
71. E. A. Ajani, Meko, Western Nigeria, April 18, 1941.
72. E. A. Ajani, Meko, Western Nigeria, November 24, 1950.
73. A. A. Akinrinade, BATC, Ogbomosho, Western Nigeria, March 24, 1943.
74. S. A. Ọlatundun, Messrs J. A. O. Ibana, Abẹokuta, March 13, 1941.
75. S. A. Ọlọkọ, Agricultural Department, Moor Plantation, Ibadan, December 13, 1940.
76. S. A. Ọlọkọ, Agricultural Department, Moor Plantation, Ibadan, January 14, 1940.
77. S. A. Ọlọkọ, Agricultural Department, Moor Plantation, Ibadan, August 23, 1937.
78. S. A. Ọlọkọ, Agricultural Department, Moor Plantation, Ibadan, August 3, 1938.
79. S. A. Ọlọkọ, Agricultural Department, Moor Plantation, Ibadan, August 3, 1938.
80. S. A. Ọlọkọ, Agricultural Department, Moor Plantation, Ibadan, October 22, 1940.
81. S. A. Ọlọkọ, Agricultural Department, Moor Plantation, Ibadan, June 10, 1934.
82. S. A. Ọlọkọ, Agricultural Department, Moor Plantation, Ibadan, 1934.
83. S. A. Ọlọkọ, Agricultural Department, Moor Plantation, Ibadan, March 8, 1935.
84. S. A. Ọlọkọ, Agricultural Department, Moor Plantation, Ibadan, December 23, 1934.
85. S. A. Ọlọkọ, Agricultural Department, Moor Plantation, Ibadan, April 15, 1935.
86. S. A. Ọlọkọ, Agricultural Department, Moor Plantation, Ibadan, July 9, 1934.
87. S. A. Ọlọkọ, Agricultural Department, Moor Plantation, Ibadan, November 18, 1935.
88. S. A. Ọlọkọ, Agricultural Department, Moor Plantation, Ibadan, October 23, 1949, January 15, 1948, March 23, 1948.

89. S. A. Ọlọkọ, Agricultural Department, Moor Plantation, Ibadan, January 23, 1948.

90. S. A. Ọlọkọ, Agricultural Department, Moor Plantation, Ibadan, January 23, 1948.

91. S. A. Ọlọkọ, Agricultural Department, Moor Plantation, Ibadan, November 4, 1948.

92. S. A. Ọlọkọ, Agricultural Department, Moor Plantation, Ibadan, February 25, 1949.

93. S. A. Ọlọkọ, Agricultural Department, Moor Plantation, Ibadan, March 23, 1949.

94. Ibidun Ọlọkọ, c/o S. A. Ọlọkọ, Agricultural Department, Moor Plantation, Ibadan, March 4, 1949.

95. S. A. Ọlọkọ, Agricultural Department, Moor Plantation, Ibadan, July 28, 1949.

96. S. A. Ọlọkọ, Agricultural Department, Moor Plantation, Ibadan, July 23, 1934.

97. S. A. Ọlọkọ, Agricultural Department, Moor Plantation, Ibadan, July 9, 1934.

98. S. A. Ọlọkọ, Agricultural Department, Moor Plantation, Ibadan, July 23, 1934.

99. S. A. Ọlọkọ, Agricultural Department, Moor Plantation, Ibadan, March 17, 1935, March 8, 1935, July 23, 1935.

100. E. A. Bọlaji, Ola Oluwa Chamber, Labiran Street, Ibadan, June 5, 1934.

101. E. A. Bọlaji, Ola Oluwa Chamber, Labiran Street, Ibadan, June 20, 1934.

102. E. A Bọlaji, Ola Oluwa Chamber, Labiran Street, Ibadan, October 1934.

103. E. A. Bọlaji, Ola Oluwa Chamber, Labiran Street, Ibadan, March 16, 1934. A parlor marriage denotes a modern Western-oriented marriage.

104. E. A. Bọlaji, Ola Oluwa Chamber, Labiran Street, Ibadan, March 28, 1934.

105. Abiọdun Alfred Vaughan, Agricultural Department, Samaru, Zaria, September 1, 1934.

106. S. A. Ọlọkọ, Agricultural Department, Moor Plantation, Ibadan, August 30, 1937.

107. E. A. Ajani, Meko, Western Nigeria, October 18, 1947.

108. E. A. Ajani, Meko, Western Nigeria, November 24, 1950.

109. E. A. Ajani, Meko, Western Nigeria, July 27, 1949.

110. G. O. Ogunṣọla, Abẹokuta, Western Nigeria, April 6, 1941.

111. G. O. Ogunṣọla, Abẹokuta, Western Nigeria, April 20, 1941.

112. G. Amosun, Agricultural Department, Ibadan.

113. G. Obasa, Otta Town, Northern Nigeria, June 8, 1941.

114. D. O. Ilori, Ibadan, May 9, 1941.

115. J. A. Ọjẹrinọla, Provincial Office, Abẹokuta, Western Nigeria, April 23, 1941.

116. J. O. Morakinyo, Agricultural Department, Ibadan, April 26, 1941; Ogunkunle, Agricultural Department, Ibadan, April; E. Bọlaji, Ola Oluwa Chamber, Labiran Street, Ibadan, March 16, 1934.

117. Moses Gbenro, Mapo Police Office, Ibadan, July 3, 1934.

118. Moses Gbenro, Mapo Police Office, Ibadan, November 2, 1934.

119. Abiọdun Alfred Vaughan, Agricultural Department, Abẹokuta, October 23, 1939.

120. E. A. Bọlaji, Ola Oluwa Chamber, Ibadan, Labiran Street, PO Box 168, Ibadan, May 14, 1934.

121. J. A. Ọjẹrinọla, Gbenla Street, Ibadan, September 28, 1939.

122. E. A. Akinpẹlu, Education Office, Lagos, January, 25, 1939. Akinpẹlu was a clerk in the Education Office in Lagos.

123. As discussed above, the exception was the extensive correspondence over professional advancement by these men as junior civil servants in the colonial Department of Agriculture, especially on matters pertaining to promotion and transfers under the mentorship of S. A. Ọlọkọ.

124. Abiọdun Alfred Vaughan, Agricultural Department, Samaru, Zaria, Northern Nigeria, March 20, 1934.

125. Abiọdun Alfred Vaughan, Agricultural Department, Abẹokuta, Western Nigeria, September 17, 1938.

126. Abiọdun Alfred Vaughan, Agricultural Department, Abẹokuta, Western Nigeria, July 25, 1940.

127. Abiọdun Alfred Vaughan, Agricultural Department, Abẹokuta, Western Nigeria, July 25, 1940.

128. G. O. Ogunṣọla, Baptist Boys High School, Abẹokuta, Western Nigeria, April 11, 1943.

129. E. Fabunmi, Agricultural Department, Ibadan, July 23, 1934. On the critical analysis of the policy on the status of Ibadan Division in Ọyọ Province under H. L. Ward-Price, Resident of Ọyọ Province, see J. A. Atanda, *The New Oyo Empire: Indirect Rule and Change in Western Nigeria, 1894–1934* (London: Longman, 1973). See also Olufemi Vaughan, *Nigerian Chiefs: Traditional Power in Modern Politics, 1890s–1990s* (Rochester, NY: University of Rochester Press, 2000).

130. S. A. Ọlọkọ, Agricultural Department, Ibadan, March 19, 1934, March 23, 1934.

131. S. A. Ọlọkọ, Agricultural Department, Moor Plantation, Ibadan, February 25, 1948.

132. S. A. Ọlọkọ, Agricultural Department, Moor Plantation, Ibadan, January 12, 1952. Ọlọkọ's daughter Atinuke Ige, née Ọlọkọ, later studied law in England and went on to become a distinguished Nigerian jurist, retiring as justice of the Nigerian Federal Court of Appeals in the early 2000s.

133. D. J. Ogungbe, Agricultural Department, Moor Plantation, Ibadan, September 21, 1940.

134. For detailed discussion of the Ibadan Progressive Union, see Jenkins, "Ibadan Politics."

135. S. A. Ọlọkọ, Agricultural Department, Moor Plantation, Ibadan, September 30, 1952.

136. S. A. Ọlọkọ, "Inaugural Conference of the Egbe Omo Oduduwa, 1949." For an insightful analysis of the significance of the Ẹgbẹ́ Ọmọ Odùduwà in Nigerian political history during the decolonization process in the late 1940s and 1950s, see Sklar, *Nigerian Political Parties*. See also S. O. Arifalo, *Egbe Omo Oduduwa: A Study of Ethnic and Cultural Nationalism, 1945–1965* (Akure, Nigeria: Stebak Books, 2001).

137. For a good study of the transformation of a Yorùbá city during this period, see B. A. Agiri, "The Development of Local Government in Ogbomosho, 1850–1950" (MA thesis, University of Ibadan, 1966).

138. For an authoritative study of the political biography of Obafemi Awolowo during the colonial period, see Insa Nolte, *Obafemi Awolowo and the Making of Remo: The*

Local Politics of a Nigerian Nationalist (Edinburgh: Edinburgh University Press, 2009); Wale Adebanwi, *Yoruba Elites and Ethnic Politics in Nigeria: Obafemi Awolowo and Corporate Agency* (Cambridge: Cambridge University Press, 2014).

139. S. A. Ọlọkọ, "Inaugural Conference of the Egbe Omo Oduduwa, 1949."

140. See, for example, N. D. Oyerinde, *Iwe Itan Ogbomosho* [A history of Ogbomosho] (Jos, 1934); Kemi Morgan, *Akinyele's Outline History of Ibadan* (Ibadan: Caxton, n.d.); J. D. Y. Peel, "Olaju: A Yoruba Concept of Development," *Journal of Development Studies* 14, no. 2 (1978): 139–65; Peel, *Ijesha and Nigerians.*

141. In Ileṣa, a Yorùbá city about fifty-eight miles northeast of Ibadan, for instance, a group of Christian elites and produce buyers founded the Egbe Atunluse (Ijesha Improvement Society) to mobilize local opinion for the modernization of their city. The members of the group lobbied for the establishment of a community secondary school, the Ileṣa Grammar School, a CMS-oriented school, in 1934 and agitated for administrative reform, which led to the reconstitution of Ilesha as the capital of the northeastern province. See Peel, *Ijesha and Nigerians.*

142. It is notable that Ọlọkọ was awarded an MBE in 1951; a senior member of the network, G. O. Ogunṣọla, senior schoolmaster at Baptist Boys High School, Abẹokuta, was awarded an MBE the same year; J. A. Ayọrinde, active member of the network and schoolmate of Abiọdun Vaughan at Ibadan Grammar School who later became a renowned local historian, was awarded an MBE a few years later; and E. O. Alayande, another active member of Ibadan CMS men's network, was awarded an MBE in the 1950s.

143. To a lesser extent, G. O. Ogunṣọla, the senior schoolmaster at Baptist Boys High School, Abẹokuta, also provided leadership for many of the men in this socioreligious network.

Chapter 4. The Gladys Adukẹ Vaughan Files

1. Abiọdun Vaughan's marriage to his first wife, Dorcas Bolaji Ajibose-Vaughan, ended in 1943.

2. "Ibadan Grammar School, Golden Jubilee," George D. Jenkins Papers, Hoover Institution, Stanford University, Stanford, California. This information about my maternal great-grandfather was recounted by older relatives, especially my maternal grandmother, Rachel Ayọdele Akinloye.

3. Akanbi's mother, Omolewa, an illustrious Muslim trader, enrolled her son in Aremọ's CMS primary school in the early 1900s. Interview, Abiọdun Pomary, Ibadan, June 2021.

4. With growing influence among the traditional chiefs in Ibadan's two ruling chieftaincy lines, the Baálẹ̀ (later Olubadan) and Balogun lines, Islam had established itself as an influential world religion in Ibadan by the late nineteenth century. Christianity, despite its growing influence because of the monopoly of the CMS over Western education, was the religion of a very small minority in Ibadan at the turn of the twentieth century when the British were beginning to consolidate their colonial rule in the city. See Toyin Falola, *Politics and Economy in Ibadan* (Lagos: Modelor, 1989). Ọyọ-Yorùbá people, largely from communities with strong cultural affinity to the Old Ọyọ Empire (largely contemporary Ọyọ and Osun Yorùbá subgroups), had firmly estab-

lished their military dominance over other Yorùbá subgroups such as the Egba, Egbado, and Ijesa in the emergent garrison city state of Ibadan by the 1850s. Akanbi Akinloye's grandfather Egunjemi was a prominent figure among these influential Ọyọ-oriented lineages in the mid-nineteenth century.

5. Adukẹ sometimes addressed Abiọdun as "Dear uncle" in her salutations, an indication of their thirteen-year age difference and their fictive kinship as CMS Ọmọ Aremọ.

6. At the time of Adukẹ's departure for London, her five children's ages ranged from eight years old to ten months: Abiọdun, eight; Ibironkẹ, six; Oluwọle, four; Subusọla, two; and Olufẹmi (myself), ten months.

7. Abiọdun Alfred Vaughan, Agricultural Department, Abeokuta, June 1943.

8. Abiọdun Alfred Vaughan, Ibadan, July 26, 1943.

9. Abiọdun Alfred Vaughan, As Known, September 15, 1943.

10. Abiọdun Alfred Vaughan, Ibadan, 1943.

11. Gladys Adukẹ Akinloye, Oba Ademola School, Afin Ake, Abeokuta, December 19, 1943.

12. Gladys Adukẹ Akinloye, Aremọ, Ibadan, January 20, 1944.

13. Gladys Adukẹ Akinloye, Oba Ademola School, Afin Ake, Abeokuta, February 15, 1944.

14. Gladys Adukẹ Akinloye, Oba Ademola School, Afin Ake, Abeokuta, February 15, 1944.

15. See the analysis later in this chapter of Adisa Akinloye's letters as a law student at the London School of Economics from 1946 to 1950.

16. Adisa M. Akinloye, Zaria, Northern Nigeria, March 7, 1944.

17. Abiọdun Alfred Vaughan, Agricultural Department, Ibadan, March 13, 1944.

18. Abiọdun Alfred Vaughan, Agricultural Department, Ibadan, March 13, 1944.

19. Gladys Adukẹ Akinloye, Oba Ademola School, Afin Ake, Abeokuta, March 1944.

20. It is instructive to note that Rachel Ayọdele's intervention into these pressing health issues extended beyond that of a concerned mother. She was a trained nurse and midwife who worked at a missionary hospital in Abeokuta, Southern Provinces, and at a colonial government welfare center in Abuja, Northern Provinces, in the 1940s. This professional training undoubtedly influenced the advice she provided.

21. Rachel Ayọdele Akinloye, as usual, May 17, 1945.

22. Adukẹ's eldest daughter, Abiọdun, had a daughter named Tiwalolu thirty-four years later. Since grandparents play important roles in naming their grandchildren in many Yorùbá families, the relatively uncommon Christianized Yorùbá name Tiwalolu (ours is for the Almighty God) can hardly be a coincidence. While there was no longer any direct and open reference to the tragic loss of the infant born in 1945, the naming of Adukẹ's granddaughter Tiwalolu suggests that she might have been named after Adukẹ's infant daughter who died thirty-four years earlier.

23. Rachel Ayọdele Akinloye, Welfare Center, Abuja, Northern Nigeria, July 8, 1946.

24. Rachel Ayọdele Akinloye, as usual, July 14, 1946.

25. Rachel Ayọdele Akinloye, as usual, October 28, 1946.

26. Rachel Ayọdele Akinloye, Welfare Center, Abuja, Northern Nigeria, November 11, 1946.

27. Rachel Ayọdele Akinloye, Welfare Centre, c/o the District Office, Olaiya via Minna, November 30, 1946. For an insightful study of spirit forces and spiritual warfare in the African Christian charismatic movement, see Nimi Wariboko, *Nigerian Pentecostalism* (Rochester, NY: University of Rochester Press, 2014).

28. Rachel Ayọdele Akinloye, Welfare Centre, c/o the District Office, Olaiya via Minna, November 4, 1948.

29. Rachel Ayọdele Akinloye, Welfare Centre, c/o the District Office, Olaiya via Minna, February 23, 1948.

30. Rachel Ayọdele Akinloye, Welfare Centre, c/o the District Office, Olaiya via Minna, February 23, 1948.

31. Rachel Ayọdele Akinloye, Welfare Centre, c/o the District Office, Abuja via Minna, March 20, 1949.

32. Rachel Ayọdele Akinloye, Welfare Centre, c/o the District Office, Abuja via Minna, September 8, 1949.

33. Rachel Ayọdele Akinloye, Welfare Centre, c/o the District Office, Abuja via Minna, November 14, 1949.

34. Rachel Ayọdele Akinloye, Welfare Centre, c/o the District Office, Abuja via Minna, September 9, 1950.

35. Rachel Ayọdele Akinloye, Aremọ, Ibadan, May 26, 1949.

36. Rachel Ayọdele Akinloye, Aremọ, Ibadan, October 24, 1949.

37. Rachel Ayọdele Akinloye, Aremọ, Ibadan, December 29, 1949.

38. Rachel Ayodele Akinloye, 56 Kano Street, Ebute-Meta, Lagos, August 12, 1951.

39. Adisa Akinloye was Rachel Ayọdele's stepson, while Ọlayinka Odumosu was her biological son from a previous marriage. Because Adisa and Olayinka were about the same age, Rachel Ayọdele, raised both boys, and another brother, Supo Akinloye, alongside her daughter Aduke for a while, while married to Akanbi Akinloye.

40. Ọlayinka Odumosu, London, November 10, 1947.

41. Duro is a nickname for the full name Durojaiye, which, in Yorùbá cosmology, is a plea to the infant to stay and enjoy the wonderful things this world has to offer. A first name such as this one reflects Yorùbá belief in *abiku*. For a glimpse into this belief among the Igbo, another major southern Nigerian ethnic group, see Achebe, *Things Fall Apart*. See also Debo Kotun, *Abiku: A Novel of Heart-Stopping Suspense* (Pasadena, CA: Nepotist Books, 1998). On the significance of names in Yoruba Abiku belief, see Abiodun, *Yoruba Art and Language*, 270.

42. Gladys Adukẹ Vaughan, as usual, Ibadan, October 31, 1948. Bisi Alalade was Abiọdun's niece and Jadesola Ọdẹbunmi's daughter.

43. Gladys Adukẹ Vaughan, Ibadan, September 29, 1948.

44. Gladys Adukẹ Vaughan, Ibadan, October 3, 1948.

45. Gladys Adukẹ Vaughan, Ilesha, September 4, 1949.

46. Gladys Adukẹ Vaughan, Ilesha, October 16, 1949.

47. Gladys Adukẹ Vaughan, Ilesha, October 16, 1949.

48. Gladys Adukẹ Vaughan, Ilesha, September 17, 1949.

49. Gladys Adukẹ Vaughan, c/o Mr. J. C. Priddy, Ilesha, October 23, 1949.

50. Gladys Adukẹ Vaughan, c/o Mr. J. C. Priddy, Ilesha, November 20, 1949.

51. Gladys Adukẹ Vaughan, c/o Mr. J. C. Priddy, Ilesha, September 26, 1949.

52. Gladys Adukẹ Vaughan, c/o Mr. J. C. Priddy, Marketing & Export Department, Ilesha, October 6, 1949.

53. Gladys Adukẹ Vaughan, c/o Mr. J. C. Priddy, Marketing & Export Department, Ilesha, November 27, 1949.

54. Gladys Adukẹ Vaughan, c/o J. C. Priddy, Marketing & Export Department, Ilesha, December 5, 1949.

55. Gladys Adukẹ Vaughan, c/o Mr. J. C. Priddy, Marketing & Export Department, Ilesha, December 14, 1949.

56. J. C. Priddy, Ilesha, December 27, 1949.

57. Gladys Adukẹ Vaughan, as usual, January 30, 1950.

58. Gladys Adukẹ Vaughan, Ibadan, January 10, 1950.

59. Gladys Adukẹ Vaughan, Ibadan, March 30, 1950.

60. Gladys Adukẹ Vaughan, Ibadan, June 8, 1952.

61. Gladys Adukẹ Vaughan, Ibadan, March 30, 1952.

62. See Oyewumi, *The Invention of Women*; Sudarkasa, "The 'Status of Women.'"

63. See the Commission on Higher Education in West Africa (Eliot Report on Higher Education in British West Africa), 1943, Nigerian National Archive, Ibadan, Nigeria.

64. Abiọdun filed the letters of Adisa and his wife, Nkpa—as well as letters from Rachel Ayọdele Akinloye, Adukẹ's mother, and Ọlayinka Odumosu, her other brother—in the Gladys Adukẹ Vaughan files.

65. See the discussion of the letter above.

66. Adisa Akinloye, Zaria, Northern Nigeria, July 15, 1946.

67. Adisa wrote Abiọdun and Aduke about fifty-six letters during his four-year sojourn in London.

68. On the importance of cocoa, the main cash crop in colonial southwestern Nigeria, in the economy of colonial Nigeria, see Sara Berry's groundbreaking book, *Cocoa, Custom and Socio-economic Change in Rural Western Nigeria* (Oxford: Clarendon Press, 1975).

69. For example, in August 1948, two years into his legal studies, Adisa shared his success in a milestone examination with Abiọdun and Adukẹ. Adisa M. A. Akinloye, London School of Economics, August 18, 1948.

70. Adisa A. Akinloye, Colonial Centre, 36 Tavistock Square, London, December 18, 1946.

71. Adisa A. Akinloye, London School of Economics, June 26, 1947.

72. Adisa A. Akinloye, London School of Economics, November 1948.

73. Adisa A. Akinloye, Colonial Centre, 36 Tavistock Square, London, February 23, 1947.

74. Adisa Akinloye, London School of Economics, May 20, 1947.

75. Adisa A. Akinloye, London School of Economics, January 26, 1948.

76. Adisa A. Akinloye, London School of Economics, January 26, 1948.

77. Adisa A. Akinloye, London School of Economics, January 26, 1948.

78. Adisa A. Akinloye, London School of Economics, January 26, 1948.

79. Adisa A. Akinloye, London School of Economics, February 21, 1948.

80. Adisa A. Akinloye, London School of Economics, June 22, 1948.

81. Adisa Akinloye, London School of Economics, June 30, 1948.
82. Adisa Akinloye, London School of Economics.
83. Adisa Akinloye, 7 Westmoreland Place, London, January 16, 1950. Adukẹ is also known as Yetunde (the mother has returned, indicating the reincarnation of a recently departed direct woman ancestor, especially a grandmother). Yoruba children are often given several names by parents and grandparents, and it is not unusual for close relatives to call younger family members by names that are not commonly in use to show intimacy within the natal family.
84. Adisa Akinloye, London School of Economics, November 28, 1947.
85. Adisa A. Akinloye, London School of Economics, February 21, 1948.
86. Adisa A. Akinloye, London School of Economics, February 21, 1948.
87. U. E. Akinloye, c/o Adisa Akinloye, London School of Economics, March 20, 1948.
88. Adisa M. A. Akinloye, London School of Economics, August 18, 1948.
89. Adisa Akinloye, London School of Economics, January 13, 1949.
90. For an authoritative monograph on the political career of the legendary Adegoke Adelabu in Ibadan during decolonization, see Post and Jenkins, *Price of Liberty*.
91. For an insightful analysis of Nigeria politics during this turbulent period of transition from colonial rule to independence, see Kenneth Post and Michael Vickers, *Structure and Conflict in Nigeria, 1960–1967* (London: Heinemann, 1973).
92. For a critical analysis of this party's role in Nigerian politics during the Second Republic, see Richard Joseph, *Democracy and Prebendal Politics in Nigeria* (Cambridge: Cambridge University Press, 1987).
93. See Akinyele Omoyajowo, *The Anglican Church in Nigeria, 1842–1992* (Lagos: Macmillan, 1994).
94. Omoyajowo, *The Anglican Church*.
95. G. A. Vaughan, c/o Oke, 70 Hemberton Road, London, December 9, 1958.
96. Akin Fatimehin, *Humble and Remarkable: The Biography of Chief S. L. Durosaro, Osi-Olubadan of Ibadan* (Ibadan: Ark Communications, 1998).
97. G. A. Vaughan, 65 Brackenbury Road, Hammersmith, London, December 20, 1958.
98. G. A. Vaughan, 65 Brackenbury Road, Hammersmith, London, December 26, 1958.
99. Abiọdun Alfred Vaughan, NW 6/106, Ayọrinde Street, Race Course, Ibadan, February 1959.
100. Abiọdun Alfred Vaughan, NW 6/106, Ayọrinde Street, Race Course, Ibadan, October 23, 1959.
101. Gladys Adukẹ Vaughan, London, February 1959.
102. Gladys Adukẹ Vaughan, London, November 1959.
103. Gladys Adukẹ Vaughan, London, January 22, 1959.
104. Gladys Adukẹ Vaughan, London, April 5, 1959.
105. Gladys Adukẹ Vaughan, London, September 28, 1959.
106. Gladys Adukẹ Vaughan, London, January 1960.
107. Gladys Adukẹ Vaughan, London, January 1961.
108. Gladys Adukẹ Vaughan, London, 1960.
109. Gladys Adukẹ Vaughan, London, June 1960.

110. Abiọdun Alfred Vaughan, NW 6/106, Ayọrinde Street, Race Course, Ibadan, September 1959.

111. Gladys Adukẹ Vaughan, London, January 1959; Abiọdun Alfred Vaughan, Ayọrinde Street, Race Course, Ibadan, January 1959.

112. Gladys Adukẹ Vaughan, London, January 1959.

113. Gladys Adukẹ Vaughan, Bournemouth, England, April 5, 1959.

114. Abiọdun Alfred Vaughan, NW 6/106, Ayọrinde Street, Race Course, Ibadan, August 26, 1959.

115. Abiọdun Alfred Vaughan, NW 6/106, Ayọrinde Street, Race Course, Ibadan, October 1959.

116. Abiọdun Alfred Vaughan, NW 6/106, Ayọrinde Street, Race Course, Ibadan, October 28, 1959.

117. Abiọdun Alfred Vaughan, NW 6/106, Ayọrinde Street, Race Course, Ibadan, October 28, 1959.

118. Gladys Adukẹ Vaughan, 12 Southerland Grove, London.

119. Abiọdun Alfred Vaughan, NW 6/106, Ayọrinde Street, Race Course, Ibadan, December 1959.

120. Gladys Adukẹ Vaughan, London, February 17, 1960.

121. Gladys Adukẹ Vaughan, London, January 1960.

122. Gladys Adukẹ Vaughan, Tudor Lodge, 90 Wimbledon Park Side, London, January 1961.

123. Abiọdun Alfred Vaughan, NW 6/106, Ayọrinde Street, Race Course, Ibadan, March 1960.

124. Abiọdun Alfred Vaughan, NW 6/106, Ayọrinde Street, Race Course, Ibadan, February 1961.

125. Abiọdun Alfred Vaughan, NW 6/106, Ayọrinde Street, Race Course, Ibadan, February 1961.

126. Gladys Adukẹ Vaughan, Tudor Lodge, 90 Wimbledon Park Side, London, January 22, 1959.

127. Gladys Adukẹ Vaughan, Tudor Lodge, 90 Wimbledon Park Side, London, February 1959.

128. Gladys Adukẹ Vaughan, Tudor Lodge, 90 Wimbledon Park Side, London, April 1959.

129. Gladys Adukẹ Vaughan, Tudor Lodge, 90 Wimbledon Park Side, London, October 10, 1959.

130. Gladys Adukẹ Vaughan, Tudor Lodge, 90 Wimbledon Park Side, London, January 24, 1960.

131. Gladys Adukẹ Vaughan, Tudor Lodge, 90 Wimbledon Park Side, London, November 18, 1960.

132. Gladys Adukẹ Vaughan, Tudor Lodge, 90 Wimbledon Park Side, London, August 1960.

133. Gladys Adukẹ Vaughan, Tudor Lodge, 90 Wimbledon Park Side, London, April 1961.

134. This perspective was described to me by the distinguished Nigerian historian and Ọmọ Aremọ Professor Bọlanle Awẹ, née Fajembola, who wrote her groundbreaking doctoral dissertation, "The Rise of Ibadan as a Military Power in the Nineteenth

Century," at Somerville College, University of Oxford, under the supervision of the foremost historian of British colonial administration in Africa, Margery Perham, during this time. Interview, Professor Bọlanle Awẹ, Ibadan, June 2021.

135. For example, Atinukẹ Ọlọkọ, daughter of S. A. Ọlọkọ, granddaughter of Samson Ọkẹowo (also referred to as Oke), and first cousin of Adukẹ, married Bọla Ige, an old Ibadan Grammar School student, graduate of University College, Ibadan, and law student at University College, London, in the late 1950s. Ige later became governor of Ọyọ State and Nigeria's minister of justice. For her part, Atinuke Ige, became a judge in the Nigerian appeals court. Ṣọla Ọkẹowo, another granddaughter of Samson Ọkẹowo and first cousin of Adukẹ, married Richard Oṣunolale Akinjide, Ọmọ Aremọ, graduate of Oduduwa College, Ile-Ife, and law student in London in the late 1950s. Akinjide became Nigeria's minister of justice. Bayo Ọkẹowo, grandson of Samson Ọkẹowo, first cousin of Adukẹ, Ọmọ Aremọ, Abeokuta Grammar School alumnus, and engineering student, was married to Vieda Ọkẹowo in London in the mid-1950s. Ikepo Ọkẹowo, brother of Bayọ and Sola Okẹowo, married Ayo Adesina, an engineering student in London, in the late 1950s. Mojisọla Ọdẹbunmi, daughter of Abiọdun's older sister Jadesola Ọdẹbunmi, married Ọlaniyi Ọladeji, Ibadan CMS Ọmọ Ogunpa, graduate of Government College, Ibadan, and engineering student at Queen Mary College, University of London, in 1959. Bisi Ọdẹbunmi, another daughter of Jadesọla Ọdẹbunmi, married Duro Alalade, Ọmọ Aremọ, in the late 1940s and studied in Manchester in the late 1940s and early 1950s, while his brother, an old Ibadan Grammar School student, was a law student in London in the late 1950s. Funmi Ogunṣọla, daughter of G. O. Ogunṣọla, a student in England in the late 1950s, was married to Emiọla Adeṣina, Ọmọ Aremọ and graduate of Government College and University College, Ibadan. Bolanle Fajembola, Ọmọ Aremọ, doctoral student in history at Oxford University, and daughter of Ibadan CMS man S. A. Fajembola, married a graduate of Government College, Olumuyiwa Awe, a doctoral student in biology at Cambridge University in the late 1950s and early 1960s. Bolanle Awe, née Fajembola, became a commissioner for education in the defunct Western State and distinguished scholar. Finally, Lamide Vaughan, Abiọdun Vaughan's eldest daughter, married Lokun Bakare, Ọmọ Aremọ, old Ibadan Grammar School student, and engineering student in London, in the early 1960s.

136. Gladys Adukẹ Vaughan, London, May 31, 1959.

137. Gladys Adukẹ Vaughan, London, May 1, 1959.

138. Abiọdun Alfred Vaughan, NW 6/106, Ayọrinde Street, Race Course, Ibadan, May 9, 1959.

139. Headmaster, Sabo Memorial School, Ibadan, June 1959.

140. Gladys Adukẹ Vaughan, London, August 1959.

141. Gladys Adukẹ Vaughan, London, September 20, 1959.

142. Gladys Adukẹ Vaughan, London, September 8, 1960.

143. Abiọdun Alfred Vaughan, London, May 4, 1960.

144. Abiọdun Alfred Vaughan, NW 6/106, Ayọrinde Street, Race Course, Ibadan, July 1, 1959.

145. Gladys Adukẹ Vaughan, 65 Brackenbury Road, London, August 23, 1959.

146. Gladys Adukẹ Vaughan, 65 Brackenbury Road, London, September 1959.

147. Gladys Adukẹ Vaughan, Tudor Lodge, 90 Wimbledon Park Side, London, March 16, 1961.

148. Abiọdun Alfred Vaughan, NW 6/106, Ayọrinde Street, Ibadan, December 1959.

149. Gladys Adukẹ Vaughan, London, July 1961.

150. Gladys Adukẹ Vaughan, Tudor Lodge, 90 Wimbledon Park Side, London.

151. Gladys Adukẹ Vaughan, London, September 6, 1961.

152. Abiọdun Alfred Vaughan, NW 6/106, Ayọrinde Street, Race Course, Ibadan, September 28, 1961.

153. Gladys Adukẹ Vaughan, Tudor Lodge, 90 Wimbledon Park Side, London, May 16, 1961.

154. For an authoritative analysis of this historic moment in Nigeria's political transformation, see James Coleman, *Nigeria: Background to Nationalism* (Berkeley: University of California Press, 1958). See also Arthur Creech Jones, *Despatch from the Secretary of State for the Colonies to the Governors of African Territories*, February 25, 1947 (London: HMSO, 1947); *Development in the Western Region, 1955–1960* (Ibadan: Government Printer, 1960).

155. Abiọdun Alfred Vaughan, NW 6/106, Ayọrinde Street, Race Course, Ibadan, February 1959.

156. Abiọdun Alfred Vaughan, NW 6/106, Ayọrinde Street, Race Course, Ibadan, April 1960.

157. R. O. Ọdẹlusi, 9 Maude Road, London, November 1, 1961.

158. Gladys Adukẹ Vaughan, London, October 1961. This letter provides a notable reference to the important matter of family planning at a time when this subject was hardly discussed in the Nigerian public, even in more "progressive" southern Nigeria, with its strong Western social orientation, in comparison to the conservative Muslim North, where public discussions of such issues were an anathema. The Gladys Adukẹ Vaughan files did not include a carbon copy reply of Abiọdun to Adukẹ on this matter.

159. Gladys Adukẹ Vaughan, November 1, 1961.

160. The exception was Bamidele Theo Brainerd in Freetown, Sierra Leone, discussed in the next chapter.

161. For more on *àbíkú*, see Achebe, *Things Fall Apart*.

162. Based on a similar nexus between Yorùbá CMS and traditional Yorùbá beliefs, Nigerian Nobel Prize winner in literature Wole Soyinka's classic childhood autobiography, *Ake*, is a useful reminder of the complexities of the interconnections between Yorùbá Anglicanism and traditional religious beliefs during this time in Nigerian colonial history. A contemporary of Ibadan's emerging generation of CMS men and women in the 1950s and 1960s listed above, such as Atinuke Ige, Bola Ige, Richard Akinjide, Bolanle Awe, Emiola Adesina, and Olaniyi Oladeji, Wole Soyinka was raised in a strong Yorùbá CMS Anglican family in CMS stronghold Abeokuta in the 1940s.

163. For other examples, see Jordanna Bailkin, *The Afterlife of Empire* (Berkeley: University of California Press, 2012).

Chapter 5. From Freetown with Love

1. The Black Nova Scotians were the descendants of enslaved Black Americans who had fought on the side of the British during the American War of Independence.

2. See Johnson U. J. Asiegbu, *Slavery and the Politics of Liberation, 1787–1891: A Study of Liberated African Emigration and the British Anti-slavery Policy* (New York: Africana Publishing Corporation, 1969). See also Fyfe, *Our Children Free and Happy.*

3. Interview, Mojisọla Ọladeji, Ibadan, July 2019; interview, Lamide Bakare, Ibadan, July 2019; Stocker, *Nigerian Railway Jubilee.*

4. Interview, Lamide Bakare, Ibadan, July 2019.

5. The connection of the Vaughan family to Freetown, Sierra Leone, predates Dorcas Ọlayinka's marriage to John Brainerd. There is a family history that claims that the Vaughan name was added to Akintọla, Abiọdun's grandfather's name, after his older son arrived in Freetown to recover his younger brother Adegbuyi from a training school in that city, having being liberated by British squadrons from a slave ship probably destined for Brazil or Cuba off the coast of West Africa around the late 1870s. It is claimed that the brothers adopted the surname Vaughan from their American benefactor, one Reverend Vaughan. A document probably typed in the 1940s that narrates this version of the origins of the Vaughan family name is included in the files compiled by Abiọdun Vaughan.

6. Theo Bamidele Brainerd, 68 Fort Street, Freetown, Sierra Leone, November 19, 1958.

7. Theo Bamidele Brainerd, 47 Liverpool Street, Freetown, Sierra Leone, April 21, 1969.

8. Theo Bamidele Brainerd, 47 Liverpool Street, Freetown, Sierra Leone, September 21, 1969.

9. Theo Bamidele Brainerd, 68 Fort Street, Freetown, Sierra Leone, December 31, 1958.

10. Theo Bamidele Brainerd, 68 Fort Street, Freetown, Sierra Leone, May 13, 1960.

11. For an insightful book on African foodways, culture, and migration, see James McCann, *Stirring the Pot: A History of African Cuisine* (Athens: Ohio University Press, 2009).

12. Theo Bamidele Brainerd, 68 Fort Street, Freetown, Sierra Leone, September 1, 1963.

13. Theo Bamidele Brainerd, 68 Fort Street, Freetown, Sierra Leone, September 22, 1963.

14. Interview, Lamide Bakare, Ibadan, July 2021.

15. Abiọdun Vaughan, Cooperative Union of Western Nigeria, Private Mail Bag 5101, Ibadan, October 10, 1962.

16. John P. Brainerd, Lower Sarma, Sumbuya, Sierra Leone, November 16, 1962.

17. Theo Bamidele Brainerd, 47 Liverpool Street, Freetown, Sierra Leone, May 23, 1968.

18. Theo Bamidele Brainerd, 47 Liverpool Street, Freetown, Sierra Leone, February 17, 1969.

19. Theo Bamidele Brainerd, 47 Liverpool Street, Freetown, Sierra Leone, July 7, 1971.

20. Theo Bamidele Brainerd, 47 Liverpool Street, Freetown, Sierra Leone, October 25, 1967.

21. Theo Bamidele Brainerd, 47 Liverpool Street, Freetown, Sierra Leone, April 6, 1972.

22. Theo Bamidele Brainerd, 47 Liverpool Street, Freetown, Sierra Leone, June 6, 1972.

23. Theo Bamidele Brainerd, 47 Liverpool Street, Freetown, Sierra Leone, August 6, 1967.

24. Theo Bamidele Brainerd, 47 Liverpool Street, Freetown, Sierra Leone, September 1, 1967.

25. Fọlakẹ Brainerd, 48 Liverpool Street, Freetown, Sierra Leone, n.d.

26. Ọlaolu Brainerd, 47 Liverpool Street, Freetown, Sierra Leone, July 8, 1973.

27. Abiọdun Vaughan, NW 6/106, Ayọrinde Street, Race Course, Ibadan, n.d.

28. Viola Brainerd, 47 Liverpool Street, Freetown, Sierra Leone, August 2, 1973.

29. Viola Brainerd, 47 Liverpool Street, Freetown, Sierra Leone, August 2, 1973. It is not entirely clear whether the "guests" that Viola referenced in her letter are the spirits of the departed, living relatives, and friends, or something in between—a combination of all.

30. Theo Bamidele Brainerd, 47 Liverpool Street, Freetown, Sierra Leone, July 16, 1973.

31. Rotimi Brainerd, 47 Liverpool Street, Freetown, Sierra Leone, July 21, 1973.

32. Theo Bamidele Brainerd, 47 Liverpool Street, Freetown, Sierra Leone, July 25, 1973.

33. Theo Bamidele Brainerd, 47 Liverpool Street, Freetown, Sierra Leone, n.d.

34. Viola Brainerd, 47 Liverpool Street, Freetown, Sierra Leone, August 2, 1973.

35. Theo Bamidele Brainerd, 47 Liverpool Street, Freetown, Sierra Leone, August 24, 1973.

36. Fọlakẹ Brainerd, 47 Liverpool Street, Freetown, Sierra Leone, July 15, 1973.

37. Ọlaolu Brainerd, 47 Liverpool Street, Freetown, Sierra Leone, July 8, 1973.

38. Bal Front, Jos, Nigeria, July 7, 1973.

39. Rotimi Brainerd, 47 Liverpool Street, Freetown, Sierra Leone, August 24, 1973.

40. Rotimi Brainerd, 47 Liverpool Street, Freetown, Sierra Leone, March 17, 1974.

41. Rotimi Brainerd, 47 Liverpool Street, Freetown, Sierra Leone, April 20, 1974.

42. Rotimi Brainerd, 47 Liverpool Street, Freetown, Sierra Leone, July 6, 1974.

43. Theo Bamidele Brainerd, 47 Liverpool Street, Freetown, Sierra Leone, June 10, 1974.

44. Theo Bamidele Brainerd, 47 Liverpool Street, Freetown, Sierra Leone, May 22, 1974.

45. Theo Bamidele Brainerd, 47 Liverpool Street, Freetown, Sierra Leone, June 10, 1974.

46. Theo Bamidele Brainerd, 47 Liverpool Street, Freetown, Sierra Leone, July 15, 1974.

47. Theo Bamidele Brainerd, 47 Liverpool Street, Freetown, Sierra Leone, July 15, 1974.

48. Theo Bamidele Brainerd, 47 Liverpool Street, Freetown, Sierra Leone, May 22, 1974.

49. Theo Bamidele Brainerd, 47 Liverpool Street, Freetown, Sierra Leone, October 9, 1975.

50. Theo Bamidele Brainerd, 47 Liverpool Street, Freetown, Sierra Leone, October 13, 1987.

51. Folake Brainerd, 47 Liverpool Street, Freetown, Sierra Leone, October 17, 1987.

52. Theo Bamidele Brainerd, 47 Liverpool Street, Freetown, Sierra Leone, August 29, 1988.

53. Theo Bamidele Brainerd, 47 Liverpool Street, Freetown, Sierra Leone, March 26, 1992.

54. Theo Bamidele Brainerd, 47 Liverpool Street, Freetown, Sierra Leone, August 25, 1975.

55. Theo Bamidele Brainerd, 47 Liverpool Street, Freetown, Sierra Leone, October 9, 1975.

56. Theo Bamidele Brainerd, 47 Liverpool Street, Freetown, Sierra Leone, May 25, 1976.

57. Theo Bamidele Brainerd, 47 Liverpool Street, Freetown, Sierra Leone, August 24, 1973.

58. Theo Bamidele Brainerd, 47 Liverpool Street, Freetown, Sierra Leone, June 16, 1980.

59. Theo Bamidele Brainerd, 47 Liverpool Street, Freetown, Sierra Leone, April 21, 1969.

60. Theo Bamidele Brainerd, 47 Liverpool Street, Freetown, Sierra Leone, February 11, 1970.

61. Theo Bamidele Brainerd, 47 Liverpool Street, Freetown, Sierra Leone, August 24, 1970.

62. Theo Bamidele Brainerd, 47 Liverpool Street, Freetown, Sierra Leone, October 24, 1973.

63. Theo Bamidele Brainerd, 47 Liverpool Street, Freetown, Sierra Leone, November 28, 1973.

64. Rotimi Brainerd, 47 Liverpool Street, Freetown, Sierra Leone, December 11, 1973. See also Rotimi Brainerd, 47 Liverpool Street, Freetown, Sierra Leone, November 11, 1973.

65. Theo Bamidele Brainerd, 47 Liverpool Street, Freetown, Sierra Leone, January 15, 1968.

66. Theo Bamidele Brainerd, 47 Liverpool Street, Freetown, Sierra Leone, November 10, 1971.

67. Theo Bamidele Brainerd, 47 Liverpool Street, Freetown, Sierra Leone, January 28, 1974.

68. Theo Bamidele Brainerd, 68 Fort Street, Freetown, Sierra Leone, August 8, 1963.

69. Theo Bamidele Brainerd, 68 Fort Street, Freetown, Sierra Leone, August 24, 1964.

70. Theo Bamidele Brainerd, 47 Liverpool Street, Freetown, Sierra Leone, October 23, 1966.

71. Theo Bamidele Brainerd, 47 Liverpool Street, Freetown, Sierra Leone, August 15, 1966.

72. Fọlakẹ Brainerd, 47 Liverpool Street, Freetown, Sierra Leone, September 20, 1966.

73. Fọlakẹ Brainerd, 47 Liverpool Street, Freetown, Sierra Leone, August 30, 1970.

74. Fọlakẹ Brainerd, 47 Liverpool Street, Freetown, Sierra Leone, January 15, 1968. See also Fọlakẹ Brainerd, 47 Liverpool Street, Freetown, Sierra Leone, August 30, 1970.

75. Fọlakẹ had graduated from the University of Sierra Leone in 1970. At the time, the University of Sierra Leone's BA degree was conferred by Durham University in England. Theo Bamidele Brainerd, 47 Liverpool Street, Freetown, Sierra Leone, August 24, 1970.

76. Theo Bamidele Brainerd, 47 Liverpool Street, Freetown, Sierra Leone, August 24, 1970. Rotimi Theophilus Brainerd was an alumnus of one of Sierra Leone's foremost secondary schools, the Prince of Wales Secondary School, and the University of Sierra Leone. He received a PhD in marine resource economics from the University of Rhode Island in 1986 and rose to the position of deputy director of the Southeast Fisheries Center of the US National Oceanic and Atmospheric Administration. He died in Fort Myers, Florida, age seventy-one, in January 2021. His letters to his granduncle Abiọdun will feature prominently later in this chapter.

77. Theo Bamidele Brainerd, 47 Liverpool Street, Freetown, Sierra Leone, October 19, 1970.

78. Theo Bamidele Brainerd, 47 Liverpool Street, Freetown, Sierra Leone, August 24, 1973.

79. Theo Bamidele Brainerd, 47 Liverpool Street, Freetown, Sierra Leone, July 7, 1971.

80. Theo Bamidele Brainerd, 47 Liverpool Street, Freetown, Sierra Leone, June 6, 1972.

81. Rotimi Theo Brainerd, 47 Liverpool Street, Freetown, Sierra Leone, October 11, 1973.

82. Rotimi Theo Brainerd, 47 Liverpool Street, Freetown, Sierra Leone, November 11, 1973.

83. Rotimi Theo Brainerd, 47 Liverpool Street, Freetown, Sierra Leone, December 11, 1973.

84. Rotimi Theo Brainerd, 47 Liverpool Street, Freetown, Sierra Leone, March 17, 1974, April 20, 1974.

85. Rotimi Theo Brainerd, 47 Liverpool Street, Freetown, Sierra Leone, May 26, 1974.

86. Theo Bamidele Brainerd, 47 Liverpool Street, Freetown, Sierra Leone, October 24, 1973.

87. Theo Bamidele Brainerd, 47 Liverpool Street, Freetown, Sierra Leone, January 28, 1974.

88. Theo Bamidele Brainerd, 47 Liverpool Street, Freetown, Sierra Leone, March 11, 1974.

89. Theo Bamidele Brainerd, 47 Liverpool Street, Freetown, Sierra Leone, May 22, 1974.

90. Theo Bamidele Brainerd, 47 Liverpool Street, Freetown, Sierra Leone, July 15, 1974.

91. Rotimi Brainerd, 47 Liverpool Street, Freetown, Sierra Leone, July 6, 1974.

92. Theo Bamidele Brainerd, 47 Liverpool Street, Freetown, Sierra Leone, September 24, 1974.

93. Rotimi Theo Brainerd, 47 Liverpool Street, Freetown, Sierra Leone, October 5, 1974.

94. Rotimi Theo Brainerd, 47 Liverpool Street, Freetown, Sierra Leone, November 22, 1974.

95. Theo Bamidele Brainerd, 47 Liverpool Street, Freetown, Sierra Leone, May 22, 1975.
96. Fọlakẹ Brainerd, Durham, England, August 30, 1972.
97. Rotimi Theo Brainerd, 47 Liverpool Street, Freetown, Sierra Leone, January 24, 1975.
98. Theo Bamidele Brainerd, 47 Liverpool Street, Freetown, Sierra Leone, February 10, 1975.
99. Theo Bamidele Brainerd, 47 Liverpool Street, Freetown, Sierra Leone, October 24, 1972.
100. Fọlakẹ Brainerd, Durham, England, February 10, 1973.
101. Abiọdun Vaughan, NW 6/106, Ayọrinde Street, Race Course, Ibadan, n.d.
102. Theo Bamidele Brainerd, 47 Liverpool Street, Freetown, Sierra Leone, May 5, 1976.
103. Theo Bamidele Brainerd, 47 Liverpool Street, Freetown, Sierra Leone, August 13, 1976.
104. Theo Bamidele Brainerd, 47 Liverpool Street, Freetown, Sierra Leone, October 10, 1976.
105. Theo Bamidele Brainerd, 47 Liverpool Street, Freetown, Sierra Leone, June 16, 1975.
106. Rotimi Brainerd, 47 Liverpool Street, Freetown, Sierra Leone, July 4, 1975.
107. Theo Bamidele Brainerd, 47 Liverpool Street, Freetown, Sierra Leone, August 13, 1976.
108. Theo Bamidele Brainerd, 47 Liverpool Street, Freetown, Sierra Leone, May 25, 1976.
109. Theo Bamidele Brainerd, 47 Liverpool Street, Freetown, Sierra Leone, August 13, 1976.
110. Theo Bamidele Brainerd, 47 Liverpool Street, Freetown, Sierra Leone, July 31, 1978.
111. Theo Bamidele Brainerd, 47 Liverpool Street, Freetown, Sierra Leone, August 20, 1979.
112. Theo Bamidele Brainerd, 47 Liverpool Street, Freetown, Sierra Leone, September 20, 1979.
113. Theo Bamidele Brainerd, 47 Liverpool Street, Freetown, Sierra Leone, August 28, 1983.
114. Theo Bamidele Brainerd, 47 Liverpool Street, Freetown, Sierra Leone, November 24, 1983.
115. Theo Bamidele Brainerd, 47 Liverpool Street, Freetown, Sierra Leone, July 5, 1984.
116. Theo Bamidele Brainerd, 47 Liverpool Street, Freetown, Sierra Leone, December 14, 1984.
117. Theo Bamidele Brainerd, 47 Liverpool Street, Freetown, Sierra Leone, November 27, 1986.
118. Theo Bamidele Brainerd, 47 Liverpool Street, Freetown, Sierra Leone, March 29, 1988.
119. Theo Bamidele Brainerd, 47 Liverpool Street, Freetown, Sierra Leone, September 29, 1988.

120. Theo Bamidele Brainerd, 47 Liverpool Street, Freetown, Sierra Leone, August 15, 1987.

121. Theo Bamidele Brainerd, 47 Liverpool Street, Freetown, Sierra Leone, June 13, 1989.

122. Theo Bamidele Brainerd, 47 Liverpool Street, Freetown, Sierra Leone, October 9, 1992. Gbemi Brainerd also obtained a master's degree in business administration from the University of Ibadan. Zoom interviews, Gbemi Brainerd, June and July 2022.

123. See Humphrey J. Fisher, "Elections and Coups in Sierra Leone, 1967," *Journal of Modern African Studies* 7, no. 1 (1969): 611–36.

124. Theo Bamidele Brainerd, 47 Liverpool Street, Freetown, Sierra Leone, September 1, 1967. The scholarship on the Nigerian Civil War is extensive. See Chinua Achebe, *There Was a Country* (London: Penguin, 2013); and A. H. M. Kirk-Greene, *Crisis and Conflict in Nigeria: A Documentary Sourcebook, 1966–1971* (London: Oxford University Press, 1971). See also Billy Dudley, *Instability and Political Order: Politics and Crisis in Nigeria* (Ibadan: University of Ibadan Press, 1973).

125. Theo Bamidele Brainerd, 47 Liverpool Street, Freetown, Sierra Leone, September 25, 1967. See also his letters of September 1, 1967, November 7, 1967, August 28, 1967, October 26, 1967, and November 19, 1967.

126. Theo Bamidele Brainerd, 47 Liverpool Street, Freetown, Sierra Leone, February 11, 1970.

127. Theo Bamidele Brainerd, 47 Liverpool Street, Freetown, Sierra Leone, April 21, 1969. I was informed by Gbemi Brainerd, Bamidele's youngest child, that her father was a stand-out sportsman at Igbobi College. Telephone interview, Gbemi Brainerd, June 29, 2022.

128. Theo Bamidele Brainerd, 47 Liverpool Street, Freetown, Sierra Leone, January 15, 1960. On the Nigerian independence constitution, see *Nigerian Independence Constitution* (Ibadan: Government Printer, 1960). See also Theo Bamidele Brainerd, 47 Liverpool Street, Freetown, Sierra Leone, April 4, 1967.

129. Theo Bamidele Brainerd, 47 Liverpool Street, Freetown, Sierra Leone, November 19, 1974.

130. Theo Bamidele Brainerd, 47 Liverpool Street, Freetown, Sierra Leone, April 10, 1974. See Keith Panter-Brick, ed., *Soldiers and Oil: The Political Transformation of Nigeria* (London: Frank Cass, 1978).

131. Theo Bamidele Brainerd, 47 Liverpool Street, Freetown, Sierra Leone, April 10, 1974.

132. Theo Bamidele Brainerd, 47 Liverpool Street, Freetown, Sierra Leone, October 2, 1975.

133. Rotimi Brainerd, 47 Liverpool Street, Freetown, Sierra Leone, January 24, 1975.

134. Theo Bamidele Brainerd, 47 Liverpool Street, Freetown, Sierra Leone, October 24, 1973.

135. Rotimi Brainerd, 47 Liverpool Street, Freetown, Sierra Leone, November 11, 1973.

136. Rotimi Brainerd, 47 Liverpool Street, Freetown, Sierra Leone, December 11, 1973.

137. Rotimi Brainerd, 47 Liverpool Street, Freetown, Sierra Leone, March 17, 1974.

138. Rotimi Brainerd, 47 Liverpool Street, Freetown, Sierra Leone, May 26, 1974.

139. Rotimi Brainerd, 47 Liverpool Street, Freetown, Sierra Leone, July 6, 1974.
140. Theo Bamidele Brainerd, 47 Liverpool Street, Freetown, Sierra Leone, November 28, 1973.
141. Theo Bamidele Brainerd, 47 Liverpool Street, Freetown, Sierra Leone, February 20, 1974.
142. Rotimi Brainerd, 47 Liverpool Street, Freetown, Sierra Leone, March 11, 1974.
143. Theo Bamidele Brainerd, 47 Liverpool Street, Freetown, Sierra Leone, February 10, 1975.
144. See Post and Vickers, *Structure and Conflict.*
145. Theo Bamidele Brainerd, 47 Liverpool Street, Freetown, Sierra Leone, August 25, 1975.
146. Theo Bamidele Brainerd, 47 Liverpool Street, Freetown, Sierra Leone, August 25, 1975.
147. Theo Bamidele Brainerd, 47 Liverpool Street, Freetown, Sierra Leone, October 9, 1975.
148. Theo Bamidele Brainerd, 47 Liverpool Street, Freetown, Sierra Leone, October 9, 1975.
149. Theo Bamidele Brainerd, 47 Liverpool Street, Freetown, Sierra Leone, October 9, 1975.
150. Rotimi Brainerd, 47 Liverpool Street, Freetown, Sierra Leone, July 4, 1975.
151. Rotimi Brainerd, 47 Liverpool Street, Freetown, Sierra Leone, November 12, 1974.
152. Theo Bamidele Brainerd, 47 Liverpool Street, Freetown, Sierra Leone, June 16, 1978.
153. Theo Bamidele Brainerd, 47 Liverpool Street, Freetown, Sierra Leone, June 16, 1975.
154. Theo Bamidele Brainerd, 47 Liverpool Street, Freetown, Sierra Leone, October 20, 1976.
155. Theo Bamidele Brainerd, 47 Liverpool Street, Freetown, Sierra Leone, May 25, 1976.
156. Theo Bamidele Brainerd, 47 Liverpool Street, Freetown, Sierra Leone, August 13, 1976. For comprehensive discussion of the federal military government's transition program to civil-democratic government in the late 1970s, see *Report of the Constitution Drafting Committee Containing the Draft Constitution*, vols. 1 and 2 (Lagos: Federal Ministry of Information, 1976).
157. Theo Bamidele Brainerd, 47 Liverpool Street, Freetown, Sierra Leone, October 19, 1977.
158. Theo Bamidele Brainerd, 47 Liverpool Street, Freetown, Sierra Leone, June 13, 1978. See *Constitution of the Federal Republic of Nigeria* (Lagos: Federal Government Printer, 1979).
159. Theo Bamidele Brainerd, 47 Liverpool Street, Freetown, Sierra Leone, August 20, 1979.
160. Theo Bamidele Brainerd, 47 Liverpool Street, Freetown, Sierra Leone, October 15, 1979.
161. Theo Bamidele Brainerd, 47 Liverpool Street, Freetown, Sierra Leone, July 31, 1978.

162. Theo Bamidele Brainerd, 47 Liverpool Street, Freetown, Sierra Leone, February 2, 1983.
163. Theo Bamidele Brainerd, 47 Liverpool Street, Freetown, Sierra Leone, April 9, 1981.
164. Theo Bamidele Brainerd, 47 Liverpool Street, Freetown, Sierra Leone, May 29, 1981.
165. Theo Bamidele Brainerd, 47 Liverpool Street, Freetown, Sierra Leone, March 4, 1982.
166. Theo Bamidele Brainerd, 47 Liverpool Street, Freetown, Sierra Leone, March 14, 1983.
167. Theo Bamidele Brainerd, 47 Liverpool Street, Freetown, Sierra Leone, October 16, 1967.
168. Theo Bamidele Brainerd, 47 Liverpool Street, Freetown, Sierra Leone, January 12, 1981. For detailed analysis of these waves of religious violence in the 1980s, see Olufemi Vaughan, *Religion and the Making of Nigeria* (Durham, NC: Duke University Press, 2016). See especially chapter 4.
169. Theo Bamidele Brainerd, 47 Liverpool Street, Freetown, Sierra Leone, December 13, 1982.
170. Theo Bamidele Brainerd, 47 Liverpool Street, Freetown, Sierra Leone, March 10, 1984.
171. Theo Bamidele Brainerd, 47 Liverpool Street, Freetown, Sierra Leone, June 4, 1984.
172. Theo Bamidele Brainerd, 47 Liverpool Street, Freetown, Sierra Leone, December 14, 1984.
173. Theo Bamidele Brainerd, 47 Liverpool Street, Freetown, Sierra Leone, June 21, 1985.
174. Theo Bamidele Brainerd, 47 Liverpool Street, Freetown, Sierra Leone, August 19, 1980.
175. For good analyses, see Julius Ihonvbere, *Nigeria: The Politics of Adjustment and Democracy* (New Brunswick, NJ: Transaction Press, 1994); Adebayo Olukoshi, ed., *The Politics of Structural Adjustment in Nigeria* (London: James Currey, 1993).
176. Theo Bamidele Brainerd, 47 Liverpool Street, Freetown, Sierra Leone, March 21, 1985.
177. Theo Bamidele Brainerd, 47 Liverpool Street, Freetown, Sierra Leone, June 25, 1987.
178. For detailed discussion of the failed transition to democracy under Babangida, see Paul Beckett and Crawford Young, eds., *Dilemmas of Democracy in Nigeria* (Rochester, NY: University of Rochester Press, 1997).
179. Theo Bamidele Brainerd, 47 Liverpool Street, Freetown, Sierra Leone, September 11, 1990. For the political reforms proposed by the federal military authorities in the early 1990s, see *Constitution of the Federal Republic of Nigeria* (Lagos: Federal Government Printer, May 1989).
180. Theo Bamidele Brainerd, 47 Liverpool Street, Freetown, Sierra Leone, July 20, 1993.
181. Theo Bamidele Brainerd, 47 Liverpool Street, Freetown, Sierra Leone, February 16, 1994.

182. For a good analysis of the history of Liberia, see Claude Andrew Clegg, *The Price of Liberty: African Americans and the Making of Liberia* (Chapel Hill: University of North Carolina Press, 2004).

183. Theo Bamidele Brainerd, 47 Liverpool Street, Freetown, Sierra Leone, July 2, 1990.

184. Theo Bamidele Brainerd, 47 Liverpool Street, Freetown, Sierra Leone, August 17, 1991.

185. Theo Bamidele Brainerd, 47 Liverpool Street, Freetown, Sierra Leone, August 23, 1994.

186. "Alájọbí á gbè ẹ́ o" (Your kinship through your bloodline will affirm you) is a special greeting that I recall my maternal grandmother, Rachel Ayodele Akinloye, express repeatedly in greetings when a blood relative lent support to or affirmed another relative.

Conclusion

1. See J. D. Y. Peel, *Ijeshas and Nigerians: The Incorporation of a Yoruba Kingdom, 1890s–1970s* (Cambridge: Cambridge University Press, 1983).

2. Of all the issues in the files of letters analyzed in this book, the only ones about which I had a superficial knowledge while I was growing up in Ibadan in the late 1960s and 1970s were those discussed in the Gladys Aduke Vaughan files. In telling these stories, my mother and maternal grandmother underscored the resilience of their religious faith as embodied in their Aremo CMS tradition. As I analyzed the letters that described these events as they were happening in "real time," I could not help but have a deep appreciation for the courage and resilience of these women, especially Adukẹ Vaughan, as a young wife, mother, and professional woman.

3. This book addresses well-known Africanist themes in novel and innovative ways by engaging these issues in words that explain the everyday existence of West Africans through the medium of letter writing.

4. Peel, *Religious Encounter*.

5. In the course of my interviews with the grown children of these men from 2020 to 2022, I inquired about their fathers' countless papers. All the children confirmed that they grew up knowing that their fathers kept thousands of documents; unfortunately, the children cannot account for these papers since their fathers' deaths many years ago. Indeed, the youngest child of Bamidele Theo Brainerd told me that thousands of family documents were burned after the death of her mother, Viola Brainerd, in 2015. (Viola Brainerd outlived her husband, Bamidele Theo Brainerd, who died in 2005.)

6. By the completion of this manuscript in the summer of 2022, I had consulted archivists at several university and college libraries, including Amherst College, where I teach, in order to explore a reliable location for the documents analyzed in this book.

7. For an insightful case of South Africa, see Keith Breckenridge, "Reasons for Writing: African Working-Class Letter-Writing in Early-Twentieth-Century South Africa," in *Africa's Hidden Histories: Everyday Literacy and the Making of Self*, ed. Karin Barber (Bloomington: Indiana University Press, 2006): 143–54.

8. For the seminal work on literacy, print culture, and modernity, see Benedict Anderson, *Imagined Communities* (London: Verso, 1996).

9. For detailed analysis, see Barber, *Africa's Hidden Histories.*

10. The social, civic, and economic transactions revealed in the intense dialogues sustained in these letters reflect some of the same kinship and familial values that shaped the local, national, and transnational interactions in many African contexts in the midst of the protracted nation-state crisis in the global era. See Mojúbàolú Olúfúnké Okome and Olufemi Vaughan, eds., *West African Migrations: Transnational and Global Pathways in a New Century* (New York: Palgrave Macmillan, 2012).

11. I was a toddler in the years when my mother, Gladys Adukẹ Vaughan, was a mature student in London, discussed in chapter 4. Given my position as one of the younger members of the families of the key letter writers, I knew these men and women many years after their letter-writing experience from the late 1920s to the 1960s. The letter writing that coincided with my adult life, from the Freetown files in chapter 5, happened in faraway Freetown, Sierra Leone. I have only a vague recollection of meeting Folake Brainerd, daughter of Bamidele Theo Brainerd, during one of her visits to Ibadan in the early 1970s. I had a brief telephone conversation with her brother, Rotimi Brainerd, in 2019, two years before his death in 2021, and extensive interactions with Bamidele's youngest child, Gbemi Brainerd, in the summer of 2022. Gbemi reminded me during one of our conversations that she lived with my mother, Gladys Aduke Vaughan, in Ibadan while Gbemi was a graduate student at the University of Ibadan in the 1990s. During that time, I lived in New York, teaching at Stony Brook University (SUNY). In July 2022 I had an extensive discussion with Folake, Olaolu, Olufemi, and Gbemi Brainerd in a Zoom meeting.

12. For critical analyses, see Bill Freund, *The Making of Contemporary Africa: The Development of African Society since 1800* (Bloomington: Indiana University Press, 1983); V. Y. Mudimbe, *The Invention of Africa: Gnosis, Philosophy, and the Order of Knowledge* (Bloomington: Indiana University Press, 1988); and Kwame Anthony Appiah, *In My Father's House: Africa in the Philosophy of Culture* (New York: Oxford University Press, 1993).

Bibliography

Primary Sources

Letters

264 letters written by Samuel Ariyibi and Abiọdun Alfred Vaughan. The letters in chapter 1 were written from 1928 to 1941 (S. A. Vaughan files).

297 letters written by Mariam O. Vaughan, Dorcas Olayinka Brainerd, Jadesola Juliana Odebunmi, Dorcas Bolaji Ajibose-Vaughan, and Abiọdun Alfred Vaughan. Some letters were also written by Oladunjoye Vaughan and some of the grandchildren of Mariam O. Vaughan. The letters in chapter 2 were written from 1931 to 1958 (Vaughan Family files).

324 letters written by S. A. Ọlọkọ, Abiọdun Vaughan, and friends and associates from the Ibadan Brotherhood Fund Association and the Ibadan Cooperative Savings Society, including G. O. Ogunsola and E. O. Alayande. The letters in chapter 3 were written from 1931 to 1962 (S. A. Ọlọkọ files).

285 letters and documents written by Gladys Aduke Vaughan, Rachel Ayodele Akinloye, Adisa Meredith Augustus Akinloye, Ọlayinka Odumosu, and Abiọdun Alfred Vaughan. The letters in chapter 4 were written from 1943 to 1961 (Gladys Aduke Vaughan files).

195 letters written by Theo Bamidele Brainerd, Viola Brainerd, Folake Brainerd, Rotimi Brainerd, Olaolu Brainerd, and Abiọdun Alfred Vaughan. The letters in chapter 5 were written from 1956 to 1994 (Freetown files).

Archives

Bodleian Library, University of Oxford.

Church Missionary Society Archives, Birmingham, England.

Jenkins, George D. Papers. Hoover Institution Archives, Stanford University Library, Stanford, California.

Nigerian National Archives, Ibadan.

Unpublished Documents

"Awolowo on Egbe Omo Oduduwa." Document in S. A. Ọlọkọ file.

"Declaration as to How the Property at N5/441 Gbenla Street, Ibadan, Oyo State, Belonging to Pa. Solomon Akintọla Vaughan Was Shared among the Direct Descendants." S. A. Vaughan files.

Ọlọkọ, S. A. "Inaugural Conference of the Egbe Omo Oduduwa, 1949." Ibadan Brotherhood Fund Association section, S. A. Ọlọkọ files.

Published Civic Pamphlets

Ibadan Grammar School, Enrollment Rolls, 1913–63. George D. Jenkins Papers.

Ibadan Grammar School, Fiftieth Anniversary Souvenir Handbook, 1913–1963. George D. Jenkins Papers.

Ibadan Old Grammarians Society, Rules and Regulations, 1930. George D. Jenkins Papers.

IPU (Ibadan Progressive Union) Study Circle, Rules and Regulations, 1934. George D. Jenkins Papers.

IPU Study Circle, Rules and Regulations, 1954. George D. Jenkins Papers.

St. Peter's Church, Aremo, Mutual Improvement Society, Programme and Activities. George D. Jenkins Papers.

Union Club Ibadan, Rules and Regulations. George D. Jenkins Papers.

Published Government Documents

Bourdillon, Bernard H. "*Memorandum on the Future of Political Development in Nigeria.*" Lagos: Government Printer, 1939.

Constitution of the Federal Republic of Nigeria. Lagos: Federal Government Printer, 1979.

Constitution of the Federal Republic of Nigeria. Lagos: Federal Government Printer, May 1989.

Creech Jones, Arthur. *Despatch from the Secretary of State for the Colonies to the Governors of African Territories*, February 25, 1947. London: HMSO, 1947.

Development in the Western Region, 1955–1960. Ibadan: Government Printer, 1960.

Nigerian Independence Constitution. Ibadan: Government Printer, 1960.

Report of the Commission on Higher Education in West Africa (Eliot Report on Higher Education in British West Africa), London, Colonial Office. 1945.

Report of the Constitution Drafting Committee Containing the Draft Constitution, Volumes 1 and 2. Lagos: Federal Ministry of Information, 1976.

Interviews

Adefope, née Vaughan, Ibironkẹ, born 1952. Daughter of Abiọdun Vaughan and Gladys Aduke Vaughan; granddaughter of Mariam Vaughan; granddaughter of Rachel Ayodele Akinloye.

Adegbola, née Ige, Funso, born 1960. Granddaughter of S. A. Ọlọkọ, leader of the Ibadan Brotherhood Fund Association and the Ibadan Cooperative Savings Society, leader of the Ibadan Progressive Union, and active member of Ibadan's CMS community.

Awe, née Fajembola, Bolanle, born 1933. Daughter of S. A. Fajembola, active member of the Ibadan Brotherhood Fund Association and Ibadan's CMS community.

Bakare, née Vaughan, Lamide, born 1938. Daughter of Abiọdun Vaughan and Dorcas Bolaji Ajibose-Vaughan; granddaughter of Mariam Vaughan.

Brainerd, Gbemi, born 1963. Daughter of Bamidele Theo Brainerd; granddaughter of Dorcas Olayinka; great-granddaughter of Mariam O. Vaughan; grandniece of Abiọdun Alfred Vaughan.

Brainerd, Olufemi, born 1955. Son of Bamidele Theo Brainerd; grandson of Dorcas Olayinka Brainerd; great-grandson of Mariam Vaughan; grandnephew of Abiọdun Alfred Vaughan.

Idowu, née Odumosu, Lawunmi, born 1947. Daughter of Ọlayinka Odumosu; niece of Gladys Aduke Vaughan; granddaughter of Rachel Ayodele Akinloye.

Lawson, née Ogunsola, Bimpe, born 1942. Daughter of G. O. Ogunsola, active member of the Ibadan Brotherhood Fund Association and the Ibadan Cooperative Savings Society.

Oladeji, née Odebunmi, Mojisola, born 1930. Daughter of Jadesola Juliana Odebunmi; niece of Abiọdun Vaughan; granddaughter of Mariam Vaughan.

Pomary, née Vaughan, Abiọdun, born 1949. Daughter of Abiọdun Vaughan and Gladys Aduke Vaughan; granddaughter of Mariam Vaughan; granddaughter of Rachel Ayodele Akinloye.

Thomas, née Brainerd, Folake, born 1947. Daughter of Bamidele Theo Brainerd; granddaughter of Dorcas Olayinka Brainerd; great-granddaughter of Mariam Vaughan; grandniece of Abiọdun Alfred Vaughan.

Thomas, née Brainerd, Olaolu, born 1952. Daughter of Bamidele Theo Brainerd; granddaughter of Dorcas Olayinka Brainerd; great-granddaughter of Mariam Vaughan; grandniece of Abiọdun Alfred Vaughan.

Secondary Sources

Abiodun, Rowland. *Yoruba Art and Language: Seeking the African in African Art*. Cambridge: Cambridge University Press, 2014.

Achebe, Chinua. *There Was a Country*. London: Penguin, 2013.

Achebe, Chinua. *Things Fall Apart*. London: Penguin, 1994.

Adebanwi, Wale. *Yoruba Elites and Ethnic Politics in Nigeria: Obafemi Awolowo and Corporate Agency*. Cambridge: Cambridge University Press, 2014.

Adeoti, E. O. *Alayande as Educationist, 1948–1983: A Study of Alayande's Contribution to Education and Social Change*. Ibadan: Heinemann, 1997.

Adesina, Emiola. *Destined? Ordained? Autobiography of Chief Emiola Adesina OOON, JP*. Ibadan: Daybis Limited, n.d.

Agiri, B. A. "The Development of Local Government in Ogbomosho, 1850–1950." MA thesis, University of Ibadan, 1966.

Ajasin, M. A. *Memoirs and Memories*. Lagos: Ajasin Foundation, 2003.

Ajayi, J. F. Ade. *Christian Missions in Nigeria, 1841–1891*. London: Longman, 1965.

Ajayi, J. F. Ade and Robert Smith. *Yoruba Warfare in the Nineteenth Century*. Cambridge: Cambridge University Press, 1964.

Ajibade, G. O. *Finding Female Voice: A Socio-cultural Appraisal of Yoruba Nuptial Poetry*. Cologne: Rudiger Koppe Verlag, 2009.

Akinjogbin, I. A. *Dahomey and Its Neighbours, 1708–1818*. Cambridge: Cambridge University Press, 1967.

Akinyele, I. B. *Iwe Itan Ibadan*. London: James Townsend & Sons, Ltd., 1946.

Akiwọwọ, Akinṣọla. "Ajobi and Ajogbe: Variations on the Theme of Sociation." Inaugural Lecture Series 46, University of Ife, Nigeria, 1980.

Akussah, Harry. "A Calendar of the Kwame Nkrumah Papers in the Documentation Centre of the Institute of African Studies, University of Ghana, 1935–1948." *History in Africa* 21 (1994): 389–402.

Anderson, Benedict. *Imagined Communities*. London: Verso, 1996.

Appiah, Kwame Anthony. *In My Father's House: Africa in the Philosophy of Culture*. New York: Oxford University Press, 1993.

Ardener, Edwin. "The Notion of the Elite." *African Affairs* 66, no. 262 (1967): 64–66.

Arifalo, S. O. *Egbe Omo Oduduwa: A Study of Ethnic and Cultural Nationalism, 1945–1965*. Akure, Nigeria: Stebak Books, 2001.

Asiegbu, Johnson U. J. *Slavery and the Politics of Liberation, 1787–1891: A Study of Liberated African Emigration and the British Anti-slavery Policy*. New York: Africana Publishing Corporation, 1969.

Atanda, J. A. *The New Oyo Empire: Indirect Rule and Change in Western Nigeria, 1894–1934*. London: Longman, 1973.

Awẹ, Bọlanle. *From Mission Station to a Cathedral: St. James the Great, Oke Bola, Ibadan, 1860–2010*. Ibadan: John Archer, 2018.

Awẹ, Bọlanle. "The Rise of Ibadan as a Yoruba Power in the Nineteenth Century." PhD diss., University of Oxford, 1963.

Awolowo, Obafemi. *The Autobiography of Chief Obafemi Awolowo*. Cambridge: Cambridge University Press, 1960.

Ayandele, E. A. *The Missionary Impact on Modern Nigeria, 1842–1914: A Political and Social Analysis*. London: Longman, 1966.

Bailkin, Jordanna. *The Afterlife of Empire*. Berkeley: University of California Press, 2012.

Barber, Karin, ed. *Africa's Hidden Histories: Everyday Literacy and the Making of Self*. Bloomington: Indiana University Press, 2006.

Bayart, Jean-François. *The State in Africa: The Politics of the Belly*. London: Longman, 1989.

Beckett, Paul, and Crawford Young, eds. *Dilemmas of Democracy in Nigeria*. Rochester, NY: University of Rochester Press, 1997.

Berry, Sara. *Cocoa, Custom, and Socio-economic Change in Rural Western Nigeria*. Oxford: Clarendon Press, 1975.

Berry, Sara. *Fathers Work for Their Sons: Accumulation, Mobility, and Class Formation in an Extended Yorùbá Community*. Berkeley: University of California Press, 1985.

Breckenridge, Keith. "Reasons for Writing: African Working-Class Letter-Writing in Early-Twentieth-Century South Africa." In *Africa's Hidden Histories: Everyday Literacy and the Making of Self*, edited by Karin Barber, 143–54. Bloomington: Indiana University Press, 2006.

Chidester, David. "African Christian Communities." In *The Oxford Handbook of Global Religions*, edited by Mark Juergensmeyer, 349–56. New York: Oxford University Press, 2006.

Clegg, Claude Andrew. *The Price of Liberty: African Americans and the Making of Liberia*. Chapel Hill: University of North Carolina Press, 2004.

Coleman, James. *Nigeria: Background to Nationalism*. Berkeley: University of California Press, 1958.

Dudley, Billy. *Instability and Political Order: Politics and Crisis in Nigeria*. Ibadan: University of Ibadan Press, 1973.

Esoop, Ghazala Begum. "Trusting the Private into the Public Sphere: North African Women's Writing Identities in Epistolary Form." *Journal of Literary Studies* 32, no. 1 (2016): 105–13.

Falola, Toyin. *Ibadan: Foundation, Growth, and Change, 1930–1960*. Ibadan: Bookcraft, 2012.

Falola, Toyin. *Politics and Economy in Ibadan*. Lagos: Modelor, 1989.

Fatimehin, Akin. *Humble and Remarkable: The Biography of Chief S. L. Durosaro, Osi-Olubadan of Ibadan*. Ibadan: Ark Communications, 1998.

Fisher, Humphrey J. "Elections and Coups in Sierra Leone, 1967." *Journal of Modern African Studies* 7, no. 1 (1969): 611–36.

Freund, Bill. *The Making of Contemporary Africa: The Development of African Society since 1800*. Bloomington: Indiana University Press, 1983.

Fyfe, Christopher, ed. *Our Children Free and Happy: Letters from Black Settlers in Africa in the 1790s*. Edinburgh: Edinburgh University Press, 1991.

Hawkins, Sean. *Writing and Colonialism in Northern Ghana: The Encounter between the LoDagaa and the World of Paper*. Toronto: University of Toronto Press, 2002.

Hunt, Rose, Nancy. "Letter-Writing, Nursing Men, and Bicycles in the Belgian Congo: Notes towards the Identity of a Colonial Category." In *Paths to the Past: African Historical Essays in Honor of Jan Vansina*, edited by Robert W. Harms, Joseph C. Miller, David S. Newbury, and Michele D. Wagner, 187–210. Atlanta, GA: African Studies Association, 1994.

Ihonvbere, Julius. *Nigeria: The Politics of Adjustment and Democracy*. New Brunswick, NJ: Transaction Press, 1994.

Jenkins, George. "Ibadan Politics." PhD diss., Northwestern University, 1965.

Jenkins, George. "Groups in Ibadan." 1965. George D. Jenkins Papers. Hoover Institution Archives, Stanford University Library.

Johnson, Samuel. *The History of the Yorubas: From the Earliest Times to the Beginning of the British Protectorate*. Lagos: Church Missionary Society, 1921.

Joseph, Richard. *Democracy and Prebendal Politics in Nigeria*. Cambridge: Cambridge University Press, 1987.

Khumalo, Cyrus Vukile. "Epistolary Networks and the Politics of Cultural Production in KwaZulu-Natal, 1860–1910." PhD diss., University of Michigan, 2004.

Kirk-Greene, A. H. M. *Crisis and Conflict in Nigeria: A Documentary Source Book, 1966–1969*. London: Oxford University Press, 1971.

Kotun, Debo. *Abiku: A Novel of Heart-Stopping Suspense*. Pasadena, CA: Nepotist Books, 1998.

Law, Robin. *The Ọyọ Empire, c. 1600–c. 1836: A West African Imperialism in the Era of the Atlantic Slave Trade*. Oxford: Clarendon Press, 1977.

Lawrence, Benjamin, Emily Lynn Osborn, and Richard L. Roberts, eds. *Intermediaries, Interpreters, and Clerks: African Employees in the Making of Colonial Africa*. Madison: University of Wisconsin Press, 2006.

Lindfors, Bernth. *Recovering Letters, Discovering Numbers: Literary and Statistical Studies*. Trenton, NJ: Africa World Press, 2004.

Lloyd, Barbara B. "Education and Family Life in the Development of Class Identification among the Yoruba." In *The New Elites in Tropical Africa*, edited by Peter C. Lloyd, 163–83. London: Oxford University Press, 1966.

Lloyd, Peter C., ed. *The New Elites in Tropical Africa*. London: Oxford University Press, 1966.

Lloyd, Peter C. "The Yoruba Town Today." *Sociological Review* 7, no. 1 (1959): 45–63.

Maduka, Chidi T. "African Religious Beliefs in Literary Imagination: Oganje and Abiku in Chinua Achebe, J. P. Clark and Wole Soyinka." *Journal of Commonwealth Literature*, 22, no. 1 (1987): 17–30.

Mann, Kristin. *Marrying Well: Marriage, Status, and Social Change among the Educated Elite in Colonial Lagos*. Cambridge: Cambridge University Press, 1985.

McCann, James. *Stirring the Pot: A History of African Cuisine*. Athens: Ohio University Press, 2009.

Mills, C. Wright. *The Sociological Imagination*. Oxford: Oxford University Press, 1959.

Morgan, Kemi. *Akinyele's Outline History of Ibadan*. Ibadan: Caxton, n.d.

Mudimbe, V. Y. *The Invention of Africa: Gnosis, Philosophy, and the Order of Knowledge*. Bloomington: Indiana University Press, 1988.

Nkrumah, Kwame. *The Conakry Years, His Life and Letters*. Compiled by June Milne. New York: Zed Press, 1990.

Nolte, Insa. *Obafemi Awolowo and the Making of Remo: The Local Politics of a Nigerian Nationalist*. Edinburgh: Edinburgh University Press, 2009.

Okome, Mojúbàolú Olúfúnké, and Olufemi Vaughan, eds. *West African Migrations: Transnational and Global Pathways in a New Century*. New York: Palgrave Macmillan, 2012.

Olukoshi, Adebayo, ed. *The Politics of Structural Adjustment in Nigeria*. London: James Currey, 1993.

Olupona, Jacob Kehinde. *In My Father's Parsonage: The Story of an Anglican Family in Yoruba-Speaking Nigeria*. Ibadan: University Press, 2012.

Omoyajowo, Akinyele. *The Anglican Church in Nigeria, 1842–1992*. Lagos: Macmillan, 1994.

Oyerinde, N. D. *Iwe Itan Ogbomosho* [A history of Ogbomosho]. Jos, 1934.

Oyewumi, Oyeronke. *The Invention of Women: Making an African Sense of Western Gender Discourses*. Minneapolis: University of Minnesota Press, 1997.

Panter-Brick, S. K., ed. *Soldiers and Oil: The Political Transformation of Nigeria*. London: Frank Cass, 1978.

Payne, M. W. "Akiwowo, Orature and Divination: Approaches to the Construction of an Emic Sociological Paradigm of Society." *Sociological Analysis* 53, no. 1 (1992): 175–87.

Peel, J. D. Y. *Ijeshas and Nigerians: The Incorporation of a Yoruba Kingdom, 1890s–1970s*. Cambridge: Cambridge University Press, 1983.

Peel, J. D. Y. "Olaju: A Yoruba Concept of Development." *Journal of Development Studies* 14, no. 2 (1978): 139–65.

Peel, J. D. Y. *Religious Encounter and the Making of the Yoruba*. Bloomington: Indiana University Press, 2000.

Post, Kenneth, and George Jenkins. *The Price of Liberty: Personality and Politics in Colonial Nigeria*. Cambridge: Cambridge University Press, 1973.

Post, Kenneth, and Michael Vickers. *Structure and Conflict in Nigeria, 1960–1967*. London: Heinemann, 1973.

Ranger, Terence. *Are We Not Men: The Samkange Family and African Politics in Zimbabwe, 1920–1964*. London: James Currey, 1995.

Schapera, Isaac. *Married Life in an African Tribe*. London: Faber & Faber, 1941.

Sklar, Richard. *Nigerian Political Parties: Power in an Emergent African Nation*. Princeton, NJ: Princeton University Press, 1963.

Soyinka, Wole. *Ake: The Years of Childhood*. New York: Vintage, 1989.

Soyinka, Wole. *Isara: A Voyage around "Essay."* New York: Random House, 1989.

St. Peter's Church, Aremo, Ibadan—later Cathedral Church of St. Peter's, Ibadan (see this church publication: *A Short History of St. Peter's Church, Aremo, Ibadan, 1852–1985* (Ibadan: Bolayele Commercial Press, 1987).

Stanley, Liz. "The Epistolarium: On Theorizing Letters and Correspondences." *Auto/Biography* 12 (2004): 201–35.

Stanley, Liz. *The Racialising Process: Whites Writing Whiteness in Letters, South Africa, 1770–1970*. Edinburgh: X Press, 2017.

Stocker, John. *Nigerian Railway Jubilee, 1901–1951: An Illustrated and Descriptive History of the Nigerian Railway*. Lagos: Railway Printer, 1951.

Sudarkasa, Niara. "The 'Status of Women' in Indigenous African Society." *Feminist Studies* 12, no. 1 (1986): 91–103.

Tamboukou, Maria. "Interfaces in Narrative Research: Letters as Technologies of the Self and as Traces of Social Forces." *Qualitative Research* 11, no. 5 (2011): 625–41.

Teriba, Adedoyin. "Afro-Brazilian Architecture in Southwest Nigeria, 1890s–1940s." PhD diss., Princeton University, 2017.

Vassen, Robert D. *Letters from Robben Island: A Selection of Ahmed Kathrada's Prison Correspondence, 1964–1989*. Lansing: Michigan State University Press, 1999.

Vaughan, Olufemi. *Nigerian Chiefs: Traditional Power in Modern Politics, 1890s–1990s*. Rochester, NY: University of Rochester Press, 2000.

Vaughan, Olufemi. *Religion and the Making of Nigeria*. Durham, NC: Duke University Press, 2016.

Wariboko, Nimi. *Nigerian Pentecostalism*. Rochester, NY: University of Rochester Press, 2014.

Watson, Ruth. "What Is Our Intelligence, Our School Going, and Our Reading of Books without Getting Money: Akinpelu Obisesan and His Diary." In *Africa's Hidden Histories: Everyday Literacy and the Making of Self*, edited by Karin Barber, 52–77. Bloomington: Indiana University Press, 2006.

Williams, Gavin P. "The Political Sociology of Western Nigeria, 1939–1965." BPhil thesis, University of Oxford, 1967.

Index

Africa and the Diaspora: History, Politics, Culture

Edited by Neil Kodesh and James H. Sweet

Postcolonial Paris: Fictions of Intimacy in the City of Light
Laila Amine

Spirit, Structure, and Flesh: Gendered Experiences in African Instituted Churches among the Yoruba of Nigeria
Deidre Helen Crumbley

Farming and Famine: Landscape Vulnerability in Northeast Ethiopia, 1889–1991
Donald Crummey; edited by James C. McCann

A Hill among a Thousand: Transformations and Ruptures in Rural Rwanda
Danielle de Lame; translated by Helen Arnold

Spirit Children: Illness, Poverty, and Infanticide in Northern Ghana
Aaron R. Denham

Defeat Is the Only Bad News: Rwanda under Musinga, 1896–1931
Alison Liebhafsky Des Forges; edited by David Newbury

Entrepreneurial Goals: Development and Africapitalism in Ghanaian Soccer Academies
Itamar Dubinsky

Education as Politics: Colonial Schooling and Political Debate in Senegal, 1850s–1914
Kelly M. Duke Bryant

Power in Colonial Africa: Conflict and Discourse in Lesotho, 1870–1960
Elizabeth A. Eldredge

Nachituti's Gift: Economy, Society, and Environment in Central Africa
David M. Gordon

Cubans in Angola: South-South Cooperation and Transfer of Knowledge, 1976–1991
Christine Hatzky

Whose Agency: The Politics and Practice of Kenya's HIV-Prevention NGOs
Megan Hershey

Health in a Fragile State: Science, Sorcery, and Spirit in the Lower Congo
John M. Janzen

Intermediaries, Interpreters, and Clerks: African Employees in the Making of Colonial Africa
Edited by Benjamin N. Lawrance, Emily Lynn Osborn, and Richard L. Roberts

Naming Colonialism: History and Collective Memory in the Congo, 1870–1960
Osumaka Likaka

Early African Entertainments Abroad: From the Hottentot Venus to Africa's First Olympians
Bernth Lindfors

Religious Entanglements: Central African Pentecostalism, the Creation of Cultural Knowledge, and the Making of the Luba Katanga
David Maxwell

Violence in Rural South Africa, 1880–1963
Sean Redding

Mau Mau's Children: The Making of Kenya's Postcolonial Elite
David P. Sandgren

The Names of the Python: Belonging in East Africa, 900 to 1930
David L. Schoenbrun

Senegal Abroad: Linguistic Borders, Racial Formations, and Diasporic Imaginaries
Maya Angela Smith

Whispering Truth to Power: Everyday Resistance to Reconciliation in Postgenocide Rwanda
Susan Thomson

Antecedents to Modern Rwanda: The Nyiginya Kingdom
Jan Vansina

Being Colonized: The Kuba Experience in Rural Congo, 1880–1960
Jan Vansina

Letters, Kinship, and Social Mobility in Nigeria
Olufemi Vaughan

Kongo in the Age of Empire, 1860–1913: The Breakdown of a Moral Order
Jelmer Vos

The Postcolonial State in Africa: Fifty Years of Independence, 1960–2010
Crawford Young